REAL WORLD
MACRO

THIRTY-FIRST EDITION

EDITED BY JOHN MILLER, ZOE SHERMAN, BRYAN SNYDER, CHRIS STURR,

AND THE *DOLLARS & SENSE* COLLECTIVE

REAL WORLD MACRO, THIRTY-FIRST EDITION

ISBN: 978-1-939402-12-7

Published by:
Economic Affairs Bureau, Inc. d/b/a *Dollars & Sense*
One Milk Street, Boston, MA 02109
617-447-2177; dollars@dollarsandsense.org.
For order information, contact Economic Affairs Bureau or visit: www.dollarsandsense.org.

Real World Macro is edited by the *Dollars & Sense* Collective, which also publishes *Dollars & Sense* magazine and the classroom books *Microeconomics: Individual Choice in Communities, Real World Micro, Current Economic Issues, Real World Globalization, The Economic Crisis Reader, America Beyond Capitalism, Labor and the Global Economy, Real World Latin America, Real World Labor, Real World Banking and Finance, The Wealth Inequality Reader, The Economics of the Environment, Introduction to Political Economy, Unlevel Playing Fields: Understanding Wage Inequality and Discrimination, Striking a Balance: Work, Family, Life,* and *Grassroots Journalism*.

The 2013 *Dollars & Sense* Collective:
Betsy Aron, Arpita Banerjee, Nancy Banks, Ellen Frank, John Miller, Kevin O'Connell, Larry Peterson, Linda Pinkow, Paul Piwko, Smriti Rao, Alejandro Reuss, Dan Schneider, Bryan Snyder, Chris Sturr, and Jeanne Winner.

Co-editors of this volume: John Miller, Zoe Sherman, Bryan Snyder, and Chris Sturr
Design and layout: Alejandro Reuss

Printed in U.S.A.

CONTENTS

CHAPTER 8 • INTERNATIONAL TRADE AND FINANCE

CHAPTER 9 • RESISTANCE AND ALTERNATIVES

THE TWO ECONOMIES

It sometimes seems that the United States has not one, but two economies. The first economy exists in economics textbooks and in the minds of many elected officials. It is an economy in which no one is unemployed for long, families are rewarded with an ever-improving standard of living, and anyone who works hard can live the American Dream. In this economy, people are free and roughly equal, and each individual carefully looks after him- or herself, making voluntary choices to advance his or her own economic interests. Government has some limited roles in this world, but it is increasingly marginal, since the macroeconomy is a self-regulating system of wealth generation.

The second economy is described in the writings of progressives, environmentalists, union supporters, and consumer advocates—as well as honest business writers who recognize that the real world does not always conform to textbook models. This second economy features vast disparities of income, wealth, and power. It is an economy where economic instability and downward mobility are facts of life. Jobs disappear, workers suffer long spells of unemployment, and new jobs seldom afford the same standard of living as those lost. And, periodically, market economies unravel, much like today. As for the government, it sometimes adopts policies that ameliorate the abuses of capitalism, and other times does just the opposite, but it is always an active and essential participant in economic life.

If you are reading this introduction, you are probably a student in an introductory college course in macroeconomics. Your textbook will introduce you to the first economy, the harmonious world of self-regulating stability. *Real World Macro* will introduce you to the second.

Why "Real World" Macro?

A standard economics textbook is full of powerful concepts. It is also, by its nature, a limited window on the economy. What is taught in most introductory macroeconomics courses today is a relatively narrow set of concepts. Inspired by classical economic theory, most textbooks depict an inherently stable economy in little need of government intervention. Fifty years ago, textbooks were very different. Keynesian economic theory, which holds that government action can and must stabilize modern monetized economies, occupied a central place in introductory textbooks. Even Marxist economics, with its piercing analysis of class structure and instability

1

in capitalism, appeared regularly on the pages of those textbooks. The contraction of economics education has turned some introductory courses into little more than celebrations of today's economy as "the best of all possible worlds."

Real World Macro, designed as a supplement to standard macroeconomics textbooks, is dedicated to widening the scope of economic inquiry. Its articles confront mainstream theory with a more complex reality—providing vivid, real-world illustrations of economic concepts. And where most texts uncritically present the key assumptions and propositions of traditional macroeconomic theory, *Real World Macro* asks provocative questions: What are alternative propositions about how the economy operates and who it serves? What difference do such propositions make? What might actually constitute the best of all possible macroeconomic worlds?

For instance, *Real World Macro* questions the conventional wisdom that economic growth "lifts all boats," or benefits all of us. While mainstream textbooks readily allow that economic growth has not benefited us all to the same degree, we go further and ask: Who benefits from economic growth and how much? Who has been left behind by the economic growth of the last two decades? The answers are quite disturbing. Today, economic growth, when it occurs, benefits far fewer of us than it did just a few decades ago. Economic growth during the last business-cycle expansion did more to boost profits and less to lift wages than during any economic upswing since World War II. This pattern has continued during the slow recovery following the Great Recession. Spreading the benefits of economic growth more widely, through public policies intended to improve the lot of most people in the work-a-day world, would not only make our economy more equitable, but would also start to resolve today's economic crisis.

Today's economy is emerging from what is widely recognized to be the worst crisis since the Great Depression. But you might not know that the day-to-day operation of the market economy—unregulated financial markets, the increasing concentration of power in the hands of business, and burgeoning inequality— caused the accumulation of debt that set the stage for the crisis and fueled the speculative excesses that ultimately pulled the trigger. Explaining how and why that happened and what to do about it is every responsible economist's job.

Today, unemployment remains stubbornly high and the unemployed go longer and longer without jobs. Government needs to step in to ensure full employment. Similarly, with the financial system having been shaken to the core, the government needs to properly regulate financial markets and institutions. Those two steps would go a long way toward improving the lot of those who have fallen on hard times and would reduce the likelihood of future crises. Finally, genuine and sustained full employment, with unemployment rates as low as 2%, would lead to "a major reduction in the incidence of poverty, homelessness, sickness, and crime," as William Vickery, the Nobel Prize-winning economist, once argued. We think that policies like these, and the alternative perspectives that lie behind them, are worth debating—and that requires hearing a range of views.

What's in This Book

Real World Macro is organized to follow the outline of a standard economics text. Each chapter leads off with a brief introduction, including study questions for the chapter, and then provides several short articles from *Dollars & Sense* magazine that illustrate the chapter's key concepts. Here is a quick walk through the contents.

Chapter 1, Perspectives on Macroeconomic Theory, introduces alterna tives to classical inspired macroeconomic theory. The chapter explains in everyday language the roots of the economic crisis—the extreme inequality, elite power, and unregulated financial markets of today's economy. It looks at what's wrong with neoliberal policies that would turn the operation of the domestic and international economy over to unregulated markets. Finally, the chapter moves beyond Keynesianism, to develop environmentalist, feminist, and Marxist perspectives on the macroeconomy.

Chapter 2, Measuring Economic Performance, takes a critical look at the standard measures of economic activity, including GDP, recession dating, and the unemployment rate. What do those measures actually tell us about the quality of life in today's economy, and what crucial aspects of economic life do they leave uncounted? This chapter also looks at how the current crisis and feeble recovery have left so many in dire straits, and whether the official numbers adequately reflect this reality.

Chapter 3, Wealth, Inequality, and Poverty, examines these three outcomes of economic activity and growth. *Dollars & Sense* authors show who is accumulating wealth and who isn't, both in the United States and worldwide. They examine the reasons for increasing inequality in the United States over the last several decades and argue that inequality is not a prerequisite for economic growth, but rather a major contributor to today's economic crisis.

Chapter 4, Savings and Investment, peers inside the pump house of economic growth and comes up with some probing questions. What factors affect the pace of investment? What role did financial deregulation and exotic new financial instruments play in the economic crisis? Who owns stocks and who doesn't? And what alternative public policies can promote stable investment and functional housing and financial markets?

Chapter 5, Fiscal Policy, Deficits, and Austerity, assesses current government spending and tax policy. The chapter's authors examine the insufficient and halting fiscal stimulus in the face of the Great Recession and argue that more needs to be done. Current deficit and debt levels, they argue, do not constitute a crisis and should not be an impediment to government action. Meanwhile, they look at current tax policy, explaining the realities of taxes on both rich and poor and their relation to investment and growth.

Chapter 6, Monetary Policy, Banking, and Financial Markets, explains the basics of money and monetary policy. It looks at how money is created and how the Federal Reserve (aka "the Fed") conducts monetary policy. It details the Fed's efforts to bail out financial institutions brought down in the crisis and explains how those institutions have become yet larger and more powerful. It examines Fed attempts at stimulating lending during the crisis and why these have had limited effect. And it looks at the sources of financial instability that detonated the crisis in the first place.

Chapter 7, Unemployment and Inflation, looks at the relationships between these two macroeconomic variables and addresses the causes of high unemployment today. It begins with a discussion of the "tradeoff" between unemployment and inflation and a critique of the "natural rate of unemployment." It considers alternate views of the causes of mass unemployment during the Great Recession and weak recovery. And it examines the impacts of unemployment on different groups in society.

Chapter 8, International Trade and Finance, assesses the prevailing neoliberal policy prescriptions for the global economy. The articles criticize globalization based on "free trade" and financial liberalization, looking closely at its effects on economic growth and development, as well as inequality and poverty. They consider the changing place of the United States in the global economy, including the role of the dollar and the growth of "offshore outsourcing," and the impacts on U.S. businesses and households.

Chapter 9, Resistance and Alternatives, returns to many of the issues covered in the course of the previous eight chapters, but with a special focus on challenges to prevailing economic policies and institutions. Among the issues addressed are employment, the environment, health care, labor relations, international capital flows, and economic crisis and austerity. ❑

Chapter 1

PERSPECTIVES ON MACROECONOMIC THEORY

INTRODUCTION

Years ago, political economist Bob Sutcliffe developed a sure-fire economic indicator that he called the Marx/Keynes ratio—the ratio of references to Karl Marx to references to John Maynard Keynes in Paul Samuelson's *Economics*, the bestselling introductory economics textbook during the decades following World War II. During a recession or period of sluggish economic growth, the Marx/Keynes ratio would climb, as social commentators and even economists fretted over the future of capitalism. During economic booms, however, Marx's predictions of the collapse of capitalism disappeared from the pages of Samuelson's textbook, while the paeans to Keynesian demand-management policies multiplied.

Today, Sutcliffe's ratio wouldn't work very well. Marx has been pushed off the pages of most introductory macroeconomics textbooks altogether, and even Keynes has been left with only a minor role. Mainstream textbooks now favor "New Classical" economics, which depicts the private economy as inherently stable and self-regulating, and dismisses Keynesian demand-management policies as ineffectual or counterproductive. Our authors disagree. In this chapter, they critically assess the classical-inspired mainstream models and reintroduce the dissident schools of thought that have been purged from economics textbooks in recent decades. And they offer a serious look at the forces that brought on the economic crisis and what to do about them.

Arthur MacEwan locates the root causes of the current crisis in the growing economic and social power of the wealthy, free-market ideology, and rising inequality. He argues that addressing these factors through expanded social programs, stronger unions, and market regulation are all crucial steps to making the economy more egalitarian, and will go a long way toward resolving capitalism's current problems (Article 1.1).

In "Keynes, Wage and Price 'Stickiness,' and Deflation," (article 1.2) Alejandro Reuss turns to the writings of John Maynard Keynes and arguments about whether declining money wages are the cure for unemployment. He outlines Keynes' classic arguments—against conservative economists who believed that wage declines were part of the economy's "self-correction" during a depression—that wage declines could actually worsen depression conditions.

Next, economist Robert Pollin (Article 1.3) tackles the underpinnings of neo-liberal policy prescriptions for the global economy. As he sees it, unfettered global-ization will be unable to resolve three basic problems: an ever-larger "reserve army of the unemployed" that reduces the bargaining power of workers in all countries (the "Marx problem"); the inherent instability and volatility of investment and financial markets (the "Keynes problem"); and the erosion of the protections of the welfare state (the "Polanyi problem").

Environmentalist Jonathan Rowe offers a green perspective on the economy. He is critical of economists' worship of economic growth, and argues that relying on mea-sures (like GDP) that count environmental destruction, worsening health, and ruin-ous overconsumption as contributions to economic growth has misled economists, policymakers, and the public about the goals we should be pursuing (Article 1.4).

Economist Randy Albelda explains poverty and gender from a feminist per-spective. Feminist economists have illuminated the ways in which having and car-ing for children alters the economic status of women—including those who are not mothers but are still relegated to poorly paid care-giving jobs. Feminist econ-omists, argues Albelda, provide the best understanding of the obstacles low-income families face and the options that might improve their position in today's economy (Article 1.5).

Economist Alejandro Reuss contributes a primer on Marxist economics. Marx rejected the idea of a self-equilibrating economy, and argued that capitalism was inher-ently dynamic and unstable. Reuss describes some of Marx's key ideas, including the nature of capitalist exploitation, and what Marx saw as two ingredients of an eventual crisis of capitalism: overproduction and the falling rate of profit (Article 1.6).

Discussion Questions

1. (Article 1.1) In MacEwan's analysis, how did inequality, power, and ideology lead to the recent economic crisis? How might addressing these causes allevi-ate the crisis?

2. (Article 1.2) What arguments drawn from Keynes's *General Theory* does Reuss use to make the case that lower money wages will not cure unemployment?

3. (Article 1.3) Summarize the Marx, Keynes, and Polanyi problems. Why does Pollin think that neoliberal globalization policies will be unable to resolve them?

4. (Article 1.4) Why is Rowe convinced that more economic growth and a rising GDP are not necessarily desirable? How would he change the ground rules of the econo-my to produce more genuine economic growth?

5. (Article 1.5) How does feminist economics' focus on gender challenge other theories of poverty? How are feminist theories of poverty different from Keynesian, Marx-ist, Institutionalist, and neoclassical views?

6. (Article 1.6) What roles do a "falling rate of profit," a "reserve army of the unemployed," and "overproduction" play in Marx's theory of capitalist crisis? Do you think today's macroeconomy displays any of those tendencies?

Article 1.1

INEQUALITY, POWER, AND IDEOLOGY
Understanding the Causes of the Current Economic Crisis

BY ARTHUR MacEWAN
March/April 2009; revised November 2012

I t is hard to solve a problem without an understanding of what caused it. For example, in medicine, until we gained an understanding of the way bacteria and viruses cause various infectious diseases, it was virtually impossible to develop effective cures. Of course, dealing with many diseases is complicated by the fact that germs, genes, diet, and the environment establish a nexus of causes.

The same is true in economics. Without an understanding of the causes of the current crisis, we are unlikely to develop a solution; certainly we are not going to get a solution that has a lasting impact. And determining the causes is complicated because several intertwined factors have been involved.

The current economic crisis was brought about by a nexus of factors that involved: a growing concentration of political and social power in the hands of the wealthy; the ascendance of a perverse leave-it-to-the-market ideology which was an instrument of that power; and rising income inequality, which both resulted from and enhanced that power. These various factors formed a vicious circle, reinforcing one another and together shaping the economic conditions that led us to the present situation. Several other factors were also involved—the growing role of credit, the puffing up of the housing bubble, and the increasing deregulation of financial markets have been very important. However, these are best understood as transmitters of our economic problems, arising from the nexus that formed the vicious circle.

What does this tell us about a solution? Economic stimulus, repair of the housing market, and new regulation are all well and good, but they do not deal with the underlying causes of the crisis. Instead, progressive groups need to work to shift each of the factors I have noted—power, ideology, and income distribution—in the other direction. In doing so, we can create a *virtuous* circle, with each change reinforcing the other changes. If successful, we not only establish a more stable economy, but we lay the foundation for a more democratic, equitable, and sustainable economic order.

A crisis by its very nature creates opportunities for change. One good place to begin change and intervene in this "circle"—and transform it from vicious to virtuous —is through pushing for the expansion and reform of social programs, programs that directly serve social needs of the great majority of the population (for example: single-payer health care, education programs, and environmental protection and repair). By establishing changes in social programs, we will have impacts on income distribution and ideology, and, perhaps most important, we set in motion *a power shift* that improves our position for preserving the changes. While I emphasize social programs as a means to initiate social and economic change, there are other ways to intervene in the circle. Efforts to re-strengthen unions would be especially important; and there are other options as well.

Causes of the Crisis: A Long Time Coming

Sometime around the early 1970s, there were some dramatic changes in the U.S. economy. The 25 years following World War II had been an era of relatively stable economic growth; the benefits of growth had been widely shared, with wages rising along with productivity gains, and income distribution became slightly less unequal (a good deal less unequal as compared to the pre-Great Depression era). There were severe economic problems in the United States, not the least of which were the continued exclusion of African Americans, large gender inequalities, and the woeful inadequacy of social welfare programs. Nonetheless, relatively stable growth, rising wages, and then the advent of the civil rights movement and the War on Poverty gave some important, positive social and economic character to the era—especially in hindsight!

In part, this comparatively favorable experience for the United States had depended on the very dominant position that U.S. firms held in the world economy, a position in which they were relatively unchallenged by international competition. The firms and their owners were not the only beneficiaries of this situation. With less competitive pressure on them from foreign companies, many U.S. firms accepted unionization and did not find it worthwhile to focus on keeping wages down and obstructing the implementation of social supports for the low-income population. Also, having had the recent experience of the Great Depression, many wealthy people and business executives were probably not so averse to a substantial role for government in regulating the economy.

A Power Grab

By about 1970, the situation was changing. Firms in Europe and Japan had long recovered from World War II, OPEC was taking shape, and weaknesses were emerging in the U.S. economy. The weaknesses were in part a consequence of heavy spending for the Vietnam War combined with the government's reluctance to tax for the war because of its unpopularity. The pressures on U.S. firms arising from these changes had two sets of consequences: slower growth and greater instability; and concerted efforts—a power grab, if you will—by firms and the wealthy to shift the costs of economic deterioration onto U.S. workers and the low-income population.

These "concerted efforts" took many forms: greater resistance to unions and unionization, battles to reduce taxes, stronger opposition to social welfare programs, and, above all, a push to reduce or eliminate government regulation of economic activity through a powerful political campaign to gain control of the various branches and levels of government. The 1980s, with Reagan and Bush Sr. in the White House, were the years in which all these efforts were solidified. Unions were greatly weakened, a phenomenon both demonstrated and exacerbated by Reagan's firing of the air traffic controllers in response to their strike in 1981. The tax cuts of the period were also important markers of the change. But the change had begun earlier; the 1978 passage of the tax-cutting Proposition 13 in California was perhaps the first major success of the movement. And the changes continued well after the 1980s, with welfare reform and deregulation of finance during the Clinton era, to say nothing of the tax cuts and other actions during Bush Jr.

Ideology Shift

The changes that began in the 1970s, however, were not simply these sorts of concrete alterations in the structure of power affecting the economy and, especially, government's role in the economy. There was a major shift in ideology, the dominant set of ideas that organize an understanding of our social relations and both guide and rationalize policy decisions.

Following the Great Depression and World War II, there was a wide acceptance of the idea that government had a major role to play in economic life. Less than in many other countries but nonetheless to a substantial degree, at all levels of society, it was generally believed that there should be a substantial government safety net and that government should both regulate the economy in various ways and, through fiscal as well as monetary policy, should maintain aggregate demand. This large economic role for government came to be called Keynesianism, after the British economist John Maynard Keynes, who had set out the arguments for an active fiscal policy in time of economic weakness. In the early 1970s, as economic troubles developed, even Richard Nixon declared: "I am now a Keynesian in economics."

The election of Ronald Reagan, however, marked a sharp change in ideology, at least at the top. Actions of the government were blamed for all economic ills: government spending, Keynesianism, was alleged to be the cause of the inflation of the 1970s; government regulation was supposedly crippling industry; high taxes were, it was argued, undermining incentives for workers to work and for businesses to invest; social welfare spending was blamed for making people dependent on the government and was charged with fraud and corruption (the "welfare queens"); and so on and so on.

On economic matters, Reagan championed supply-side economics, the principal idea of which was that tax cuts yield an increase in government revenue because the cuts lead to more rapid economic growth through encouraging more work and more investment. Thus, so the argument went, tax cuts would reduce the government deficit. Reagan, with the cooperation of Democrats, got the tax cuts—and, as the loss of revenue combined with a large increase in military spending, the federal budget deficit grew by leaps and bounds, almost doubling as a share of GDP over the course of the 1980s. It was all summed up in the idea of keeping the government out of the economy; let the free market work its magic.

Growing Inequality

The shifts of power and ideology were very much bound up with a major redistribution upwards of income and wealth. The weakening of unions, the increasing access of firms to low-wage foreign (and immigrant) labor, the refusal of government to maintain the buying power of the minimum wage, favorable tax treatment of the wealthy and their corporations, deregulation in a wide range of industries and lack of enforcement of existing regulation (e.g., the authorities turning a blind eye to off-shore tax shelters) all contributed to these shifts.

Many economists, however, explain the rising income inequality as a result of technological change that favored more highly skilled workers; and changing technology has probably been a factor. Yet the most dramatic aspect of the rising inequality has been the rapidly rising share of income obtained by those at the very top (see figures below), who get their incomes from the ownership and control of business, not from their skilled labor. For these people the role of new technologies was most important through its impact on providing more options (e.g., international options) for the managers of firms, more thorough means to control labor, and more effective ways—in the absence of regulation—to manipulate finance. All of these gains that might be associated with new technology were also gains brought by the way the government handled, or didn't handle (failed to regulate), economic affairs.

Several sets of data demonstrate the sharp changes in the distribution of income that have taken place in the last several decades. Most striking is the changing position of the very highest income segment of the population. In the mid-1920s, the share of all pre-tax income going to the top 1% of households peaked at 23.9%. This elite group's share of income fell dramatically during the Great Depression and World War II to about 12% at the end of the war and then slowly fell further during the next thirty years, reaching a low of 8.9% in the mid-1970s. Since then, the top 1% has regained its exalted position of the earlier era, with 21.8% of income in 2005. Since 1993, more than one-half of all income gains have accrued to this highest 1% of the population.

Figures 1 and 2 show the gains (or losses) of various groups in the 1947 to 1979 period and in the 1979 to 2005 period. The difference is dramatic. For example, in the earlier era, the bottom 20% saw its income in real (inflation-adjusted) terms rise by 116%, and real income of the top 5% grew by only 86%. But in the latter era, the bottom 20% saw a 1% decline in its income, while the top 5% obtained a 81% increase. Figure 3 on the next page shows what happened to the incomes of the different groups after 2005.

The Emergence of Crisis

These changes, especially these dramatic shifts in the distribution of income, set the stage for the increasingly large reliance on credit, especially consumer and mortgage credit, that played a major role in the emergence of the current economic crisis. Other factors were involved, but rising inequality was especially important in effecting the increase in both the demand and supply of credit.

Credit Expansion

On the demand side, rising inequality translated into a growing gap between the incomes of most members of society and their needs. For the 2000 to 2007 period, average weekly earnings in the private sector were 12% below their average for the 1970s (in inflation-adjusted terms). From 1980 to 2005 the share of income going to the bottom 60% of families fell from 35% to 29%. Under these circumstances, more and more people relied more and more heavily on credit to meet their needs—everything from food to fuel, from education to entertainment, and especially housing.

While the increasing reliance of consumers on credit has been going on for a long time, it has been especially marked in recent decades. Consumer debt as a share of after-tax personal income averaged 20% in the 1990s, and then jumped up to an average of 25% in the first seven years of the new millennium. But the debt expansion was most marked in housing, where mortgage debt as a percent of after-tax personal income rose from 89% to 94% over the 1990s, and then ballooned to 140% by 2006 as housing prices skyrocketed.

On the supply side, especially in the last few years, the government seems to have relied on making credit readily available as a means to bolster aggregate demand and maintain at least a modicum of economic growth. During the 1990s, the federal funds interest rate averaged 5.1%, but fell to an average of 3.4% in the 2000 to 2007 period—and averaged only 1.4% in 2002 to 2004 period. (The federal funds interest rate is the rate that banks charge one another for overnight loans and is a rate directly affected by the Federal Reserve.) Corresponding to the low interest rates, the money supply grew twice as fast in the new millennium as it had in the 1990s.

The increasing reliance of U.S. consumers on credit has often been presented as a moral weakness, as an infatuation with consumerism, and as a failure to look beyond the present. Whatever moral judgments one may make, however, the expansion of the credit economy has been a response to real economic forces—inequality and government policies, in particular.

The Failure to Regulate

The credit expansion by itself, however, did not precipitate the current crisis. Deregulation—or, more generally, the failure to regulate—is also an important part of the story. The government's role in regulation of financial markets has been a central feature in the development of this crisis, but the situation in financial markets has been part of a more general process—affecting airlines and trucking, telecommunications, food processing, broadcasting, and of course international trade and investment. The process has been driven by a combination of power (of large firms and wealthy individuals) and ideology (leave it to the market, get the government out).

The failure to regulate financial markets that transformed the credit expansion into a financial crisis shows up well in three examples:

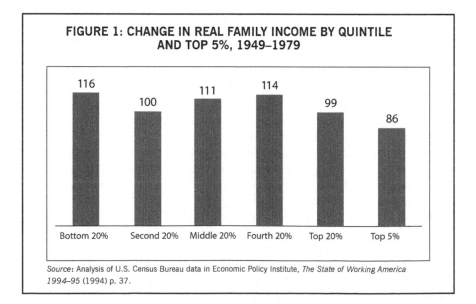

FIGURE 1: CHANGE IN REAL FAMILY INCOME BY QUINTILE AND TOP 5%, 1949–1979

Bottom 20%	Second 20%	Middle 20%	Fourth 20%	Top 20%	Top 5%
116	100	111	114	99	86

Source: Analysis of U.S. Census Bureau data in Economic Policy Institute, *The State of Working America 1994–95* (1994) p. 37.

The 1999 repeal of the Glass-Steagall Act. Glass-Steagall had been enacted in the midst of the Great Depression, as a response to the financial implosion following the stock market crash of 1929. Among other things, it required that different kinds of financial firms—commercial banks, investment banks, insurance companies—be separate. This separation both limited the spread of financial problems and reduced conflicts of interest that could arise were the different functions of these firms combined into a single firm. As perhaps the most important legislation regulating the financial sector, the repeal of Glass-Steagall was not only a substantive change but was an important symbol of the whole process of deregulation.

The failure to regulate mortgage lending. Existing laws and regulations require lending institutions to follow prudent practices in making loans, assuring that borrowers have the capacity to be able to pay back the loans. And of course fraud—lying about the provisions of loans—is prohibited. Yet in an atmosphere where regulation was "out," regulators were simply not doing their jobs. The consequences are illustrated in a December 28, 2008, *New York Times* story on the failed Washington Mutual Bank. The article describes a supervisor at a mortgage processing center as having been "accustomed to seeing baby sitters claiming salaries worthy of college presidents, and schoolteachers with incomes rivaling stockbrokers'. He rarely questioned them. A real estate frenzy was under way and WaMu, as his bank was known, was all about saying yes."

One may wonder why banks—or other lending institutions, mortgage firms, in particular—would make loans to people who were unlikely to be able to pay them back. The reason is that the lending institutions quickly combined such loans into packages (i.e., a security made up of several borrowers' obligations to pay) and sold them to other investors in a practice called "securitization."

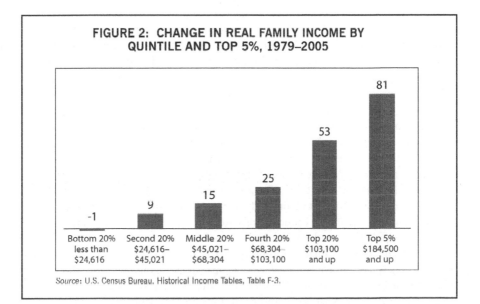

FIGURE 2: CHANGE IN REAL FAMILY INCOME BY QUINTILE AND TOP 5%, 1979–2005

Source: U.S. Census Bureau, Historical Income Tables, Table F-3.

Credit-default swaps. Perhaps the most egregious failure to regulate in recent years has been the emergence of credit-default swaps, which are connected to securitization. Because they were made up of obligations by a diverse set of borrowers, the packages of loans were supposedly low-risk investments. Yet those who purchased them still sought insurance against default. Insurance sellers, however, are regulated—required, for example, to keep a certain amount of capital on hand to cover possible claims. So the sellers of these insurance policies on packages of loans called the policies "credit-default swaps" and thus were allowed to avoid regulation. Further, these credit-default swaps, these insurance policies, themselves were bought and sold again and again in unregulated markets in a continuing process of speculation.

The credit-default swaps are a form of derivative, a financial asset the value of which is derived from some other asset—in this case the value of packages of mortgages on which they were the insurance policies. When the housing bubble began to collapse and people started to default on their mortgages, the value of credit-default swaps plummeted and their future value was impossible to determine. No one would buy them, and several banks that had speculated in these derivatives were left holding huge amounts of these "toxic assets."

Bubble and Bust

The combination of easy credit and the failure to regulate together fueled the housing bubble. People could buy expensive houses but make relatively low monthly payments. Without effective regulation of mortgage lending, they could get the loans even when they were unlikely to be able to make payments over the long run. Moreover, as these pressures pushed up housing prices, many people bought houses simply to resell them quickly at a higher price, in a process called "flipping." And such speculation pushed the prices up further. Between 2000 and 2006, housing prices rose by 90% (as consumer prices generally rose by only 17%).

While the housing boom was in full swing, both successful housing speculators and lots of people involved in the shenanigans of credit markets made a lot of money. However, as the housing bubble burst—as all bubbles do—things fell apart. The packages of loans lost value, and the insurance policies on them, the credit-default swaps, lost value. These then became "toxic" assets for those who held them, assets not only with reduced value but with unknown value. Not only did large financial firms—for example, Lehman Brothers and AIG—have billions of dollars in losses, but no one knew the worth of their remaining assets. The assets were called "toxic" because they poisoned the operations of the financial system. Under these circumstances, financial institutions stopped lending to one another—that is, the credit markets "froze up." The financial crisis was here.

The financial crisis, not surprisingly, very quickly shifted to a general economic crisis. Firms in the "real" economy rely heavily on a well-functioning financial system to supply them with the funds they need for their regular operations—loans to car buyers, loans to finance inventory, loans for construction of new facilities, loans for new equipment, and, of course, mortgage loans. Without those loans (or with the loans much more difficult to obtain), there has been a general cut-back in economic activity, what is becoming a serious and probably prolonged recession.

What Is to Be Done?

So here we are. The shifts in power, ideology, and income distribution have placed us in a rather nasty situation. There are some steps that will be taken that have a reasonable probability of yielding short-run improvement. In particular, a large increase in government spending—deficit spending—will probably reduce the depth and shorten the length of the recession. And the actions of the Federal Reserve and Treasury to inject funds into the financial system are likely, along with the deficit spending, to "un-freeze" credit markets (the mismanagement and, it seems, outright corruption of the bailout notwithstanding). Also, there is likely to be some re-regulation of the financial industry. These steps, however, at best will restore things to where they were before the crisis. They do not treat the underlying causes of the crisis—the vicious circle of power, ideology, and inequality.

Opportunity for Change

Fortunately, the crisis itself has weakened some aspects of this circle. The cry of "leave it to the market" is still heard, but is now more a basis for derision than a guide to policy. The ideology and, to a degree, the power behind the ideology, have been severely weakened as the role of "keeping the government out" has shown to be a major cause of the financial mess and our current hardships. There is now widespread support among the general populace and some support in Washington for greater regulation of the financial industry.

Whether or not the coming period will see this support translated into effective policy is of course an open question. Also an open question is how much the turn away from "leaving it to the market" can be extended to other sectors of the economy. With regard to the environment, there is already general acceptance of the principle that the government (indeed, many governments) must take an active role in regulating economic activity. Similar principles need to be recognized with regard to health care, education, housing, child care, and other support programs for low-income families.

The discrediting of "keep the government out" ideology provides an opening to develop new programs in these areas and to expand old programs. Furthermore, as the federal government revs up its "stimulus" program in the coming months, opportunities will exist for expanding support for these sorts of programs. This support is important, first of all, because these programs serve real, pressing needs—needs that have long existed and are becoming acute and more extensive in the current crisis.

Breaking the Circle

Support for these social programs, however, may also serve to break into the vicious power-ideology-inequality circle and begin transforming it into a virtuous circle. Social programs are inherently equalizing in two ways: they provide their benefits to low-income people and they provide some options for those people in their efforts to demand better work and higher pay. Also, the further these programs develop, the more they establish the legitimacy of a larger role for social control of—government involvement in—the economy; they tend to bring about an ideological shift. By affecting a positive distributional shift and by shifting ideology, the emergence of stronger social programs can have a wider impact on power. In other words, efforts to promote social programs are one place to start, an entry point to shift the vicious circle to a virtuous circle.

There are other entry points. Perhaps the most obvious ones are actions to strengthen the role of unions. It will be helpful to establish a more union-friendly Department of Labor and National Labor Relations Board. Raising the minimum wage—ideally indexing it to inflation—would also be highly desirable. While conditions have changed since the heyday of unions in the middle of the 20th century, and we cannot expect to restore the conditions of that era, a greater role for unions would seem essential in righting the structural conditions at the foundation of the current crisis.

Shifting Class Power

None of this is assured, of course. Simply starting social programs will not necessarily mean that they have the wider impacts that I am suggesting are possible. No one should think that by setting up some new programs and strengthening some existing ones we will be on a smooth road to economic and social change. Likewise, rebuilding the strength of unions will involve extensive struggle and will not be accomplished by a few legislative or executive actions.

Also, all efforts to involve the government in economic activity—whether in finance or environmental affairs, in health care or education, in work support or job training programs—will be met with the worn-out claims that government involvement generates bureaucracy, stifles initiative, and places an excessive burden on private firms and individuals. We are already hearing warnings that in dealing with the financial crisis the government must avoid "over-regulation." Likewise, efforts to strengthen unions will suffer the traditional attacks, as unions are portrayed as corrupt and their members privileged. The response to the auto firms' troubles demonstrated the attack, as conservatives blamed the United Auto Workers for the industry's woes and demanded extensive concessions by the union.

Certainly not all regulation is good regulation. Aside from excessive bureaucratic controls, there is the phenomenon by which regulating agencies are often captives of the industries that they are supposed to regulate. And there are corrupt unions. These are real issues, but they should not be allowed to derail change.

The current economic crisis emerged in large part as a shift in the balance of class power in the United States, a shift that began in the early 1970s and continued into the new millennium. Perhaps the present moment offers an opportunity to shift things back in the other direction. Recognition of the complex nexus of causes of the current economic crisis provides some guidance where people might start. Rebuilding and extending social programs, strengthening unions, and other actions that contribute to a more egalitarian power shift will not solve all the problems of U.S. capitalism. They can, however, begin to move us in the right direction.

Afterword, November 2012

When this article was written in early 2009, the U.S. economy was in a severe recession, which came to be called the Great Recession. The economic downturn—defined in terms of a drop-off in total output, or gross domestic product

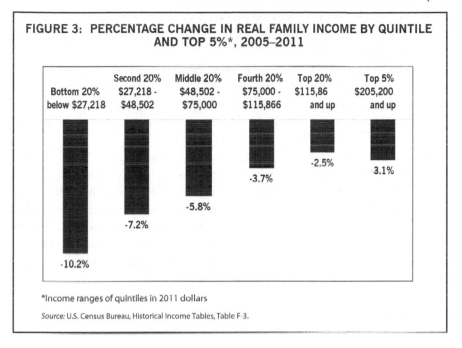

FIGURE 3: PERCENTAGE CHANGE IN REAL FAMILY INCOME BY QUINTILE AND TOP 5%*, 2005–2011

*Income ranges of quintiles in 2011 dollars

Source: U.S. Census Bureau, Historical Income Tables, Table F-3.

(GDP)—had begun at the end of 2007. Although the recession came to a formal end by June 2009, when GDP started to grow again, economic conditions continued to be very poor. With slow economic growth, unemployment remained high, falling below 8% only in late 2012, and many people simply gave up looking for work and were not even counted among the unemployed.

Several factors contribute to an explanation of the weak recovery from the Great Recession. When economic downturns are brought about by financial crises, they tend to be more lasting because the machinery of the credit system and the confidence of lenders have been so severely damaged. Also, while the Great Recession developed in the United States, it spread to much of the rest of the world. Conditions in Europe, especially, have hampered full recovery in the United States.

The continuing economic malaise, however, also has its bases in the political conditions of Washington, in the weakness of the federal government's response to the Great Recession. While it is possible to debate the extent to which the weak response has been the responsibility of the recalcitrant role of Republicans in Congress versus the limited actions of President Obama, there is no doubt regarding the several aspects of that weak response:

- The fiscal stimulus implemented at the beginning of 2009, the American Recovery and Reinvestment Act (ARRA), was too small. This action did stem the decline of the economy, probably preventing things from getting much worse. But given the severity of the downturn, the ARRA was insufficient to reestablish growth that would have moved the United States strongly back toward full employment.

- Programs to relieve the dreadful damage done to millions of homeowners have been minimal, leaving families in dire straits and leaving the housing market in the doldrums.
- The Wall Street Reform and Consumer Protection Act, the Dodd-Frank bill, was enacted in 2010. Yet it was a weak bill, failing to deal with the most serious problems in the financial sector—for example, leaving several banks "too big to fail." Also, many of its provisions were sufficiently vague to allow the Wall Street firms to use their influence to blunt its impact.
- The huge bailout of the financial sector, the Troubled Asset Relief Program (TARP) and other actions of the Federal Reserve, probably did make an important contribution to preventing an even worse financial crisis. But TARP was a tremendous boon to the bankers who had been instrumental actors in bringing about the crisis. There were other actions that could have been taken. Moreover, the continuing weak response of the economy to the Fed's continued efforts to stimulate economic growth demonstrated the insufficiency of monetary policy to deal with a severe economic downturn.

Even if the government's actions had been more forceful, the underlying causes of the crisis remain unaddressed—economic inequality, power, and ideology remain largely as they were as the crisis emerged. Figure 3 shows that from 2005 through 2011, all groups have seen their incomes decline. However, with those at the bottom suffering the most severe decline, income inequality has increased. Also, there is no indication that the power of the elite has been curtailed. Indeed, with the evisceration of campaign finance regulations (the Citizens United Supreme Court decision in particular), money and power are increasingly tied firmly together.

What of ideology? The outcome of the 2012 election suggests that a majority of the electorate rejects the leave-it-to-the-market ideology that has supported inequality and the concentration of political power and that led into the crisis. Whatever the limits of the Obama administration, it portrayed itself with rhetoric of social responsibility and promised some regulation of markets. Regardless of the limited extent to which reality in the subsequent years will match this rhetoric, the actions of a majority of the electorate suggest that there are some possibilities for positive change. Moreover, when the Occupy Wall Street (OWS) movement appeared in late 2011, it forced a discussion of basic issues of inequality, power, and ideology onto the public agenda. Whatever happens to OWS, it is likely that these issues will continue to be well recognized.

The sorts of changes advocated in this article, changes that would affect the underlying causes of the economic crisis, continue to be necessary. They also continue to be possible. ❏

An elaboration of the points in this afterword is contained in a book that grew out of the original article: Economic Collapse and Economic Change: Getting to the Roots of the Crisis, *by Arthur MacEwan and John A. Miller, M.E. Sharpe Publisher, 2011.*

Article 1.2

KEYNES, WAGE AND PRICE "STICKINESS," AND DEFLATION

BY ALEJANDRO REUSS

August 2009

Most people are accustomed to worrying about inflation, which has been a durable fact of life in the United States for half a century. The overall price level in the U.S. economy (a sort of average of prices across the economy), as measured by the Consumer Price Index, has increased every calendar year since 1957. Or, rather, had increased every year since 1957, until 2008. Last year, as the U.S. economy went into its most severe recession since the Great Depression, the CPI declined by 0.2%. For the first time in decades, there is reason in the United States to worry about the dangers of deflation.

Deflation: What's Not to Like?

Lower prices may sound appealing, but deflation can make a bad recession worse. Deflation can bring down overall demand. If individuals and firms expect prices to decline, they may postpone purchases. Why buy today, if the price will be lower tomorrow? Declining prices and wages can exacerbate firms' negative expectations about future sales and profits, discouraging current investment. If a firm does not think it will be able to sell future output at a sufficient profit, it will not make purchases of new plant and equipment now. Deflation can also make the cost of borrowing higher, and increase the burden of past debt. This can ruin debtors and bankrupt firms, as each dollar owed becomes harder to come by as prices drop. Over the three years with the sharpest drop in output and employment during the Great Depression, 1930-1933, the Consumer Price Index dropped by over 25%. More broadly, a study by economists Michael Bruno and William Easterly of over 100 countries from the 1960s to 1990s showed that rates of deflation between 0% and 20% were associated with lower rates of economic growth than low to moderate rates of inflation (up to 30%) were.

Such concerns about deflation run sharply counter to the "mainstream" or neoclassical view of recessions. Neoclassical economists argue that the economy is "self-correcting," and that if it dips into recession it will quickly return itself to "full employment" without any need for deliberate government action. One of their main arguments for this view is that prices—including wages (the price of labor) and interest rates (the price of money)—are flexible. If there is excess supply of labor (unemployment), workers will reduce their wage demands, causing employers to want to hire more labor and workers to offer less labor for sale, until the surplus is eliminated. Likewise, if there is excess saving, the interest rate will decline, causing people to save less and borrow more, until that surplus is eliminated. In this view, a recovery (from a period of low employment and output) involves a decrease in the price level. Deflation, in other words, is the cure for what ails us.

What Is Price "Stickiness"?

One response to the neoclassical argument is that, in fact, prices are not perfectly flexible (they exhibit "stickiness"). For this reason, the economy is not self-correcting, at least not in the short run. Wages and prices may be "too high" (and, therefore, result in suppliers offering larger quantities for sale than demanders are able and willing to buy), but not come down quickly and eliminate the market surplus. This view has been widely attributed to John Maynard Keynes, and is, in fact, a key argument in what is known as "New Keynesian" economic theory. But this was not Keynes' argument.

Keynes expressed, in numerous passages in *The General Theory*, the view that wages were "sticky" in terms of money. He noted, for example, that workers and unions tended to fight tooth-and-nail against any attempts by employers to reduce money wages (the actual sum of money workers receive, as opposed to the real purchasing power of these wages, taking account of changes in the cost of living), even by a little bit, in a way they did not fight for increases in wages every time there was a small rise in the cost of living eroding their "real wages." Keynes argued emphatically, however, against the idea that the stickiness of money wages was the cause of unemployment, or that full flexibility of money wages (in particular, a decline in money wages) was likely to be a cure for depressions.

Is Wage Flexibility the Solution?

Keynes was careful to describe many different possible effects of declining money wages, some pointing towards increased consumption or investment (and therefore an increase in total output and incomes), and some pointing in the opposite direction. He pointed out two fundamental errors in the conventional view that lower money wages would necessarily result in increased employment. First, he noted that, while one worker could gain employment (at the expense of someone else) by accepting a lower wage, this did not automatically mean that lower money wages across the board would cause overall employment to increase. Second, he argued that, while decreased money wages would result in increased employment if total ("aggregate") demand were unchanged, there was no reason to believe that would be the case.

Keynes made at least four major arguments that declining money wages were not the cure for unemployment (and depressions) that classical economists thought.

1. Workers do not decide their level of real wages, and so cannot reduce these to a level that will ensure full employment. Keynes pointed out that particular workers (or groups of workers) and employers bargained not over real wages, but money wages. Real wages depended not only on these money-wage bargains but also on the overall price level. The price level, in turn, depended on money-wage bargains made between many different groups of workers and employers across the economy as a whole. Keynes argued that, if workers in general were to accept lower money wages, the overall price level could not possibly remain unchanged. The price level, instead, would decline by a similar proportion, so real wages might not change very much at all. In that case, employers would not have an incentive to hire more workers, and overall employment would change very little.

2. Reductions in workers' money wages may result in decreased consumption, and therefore can result in lower incomes and output. Keynes argued that declines in money wages change the distribution of income—increasing the incomes of owners of other factors of production (capitalists and landowners) at the expense of workers, and those of rentiers (owners of money capital) at the expense of entrepreneurs (owners of businesses). These changes in distribution could result in a decrease in the "marginal propensity to consume" (the amount spent on consumption out of each additional dollar of income). Declining money wages (and the resulting decline in the price level) would tend to redistribute income from lower-income individuals (who tend to consume a very large proportion of their incomes) to higher-income individuals (who tend to consume lower proportions of their incomes, and to save higher proportions).

3. Declining wages can create incentives for employers to postpone purchases of durable equipment. Keynes argued that the effects of the reduction in money wages on the incentive for capitalists to invest (purchase durable equipment) depended on the expectations of future changes in money wages. If money wages declined, but capitalists expected them to go up in the immediate future (that is, money wages were thought to have "bottomed out"), Keynes argued, the effect on investment would be positive, since the cost of producing durable equipment now would be lower than in the future. However, if the decline in money wages made capitalists expect continued future declines, the effect on investment would be negative. Durable equipment purchased in the current period would, in Keynes' words, have to "compete … with the output from equipment produced [in the future] … at a lower labor cost." Owners of the more expensive equipment would have to cut their prices and accept lower profits to match the prices that owners of the less expensive equipment would be willing to accept (having the advantage of lower costs). This would produce an incentive to put off purchases of such equipment into the future.

4. A decline in the price level creates increased real burdens for debtors. When the price level goes down, the purchasing power of the currency increases. We would say, "A dollar becomes more valuable." Since most debts take the form of a specific sum of money owed, and the real purchasing power of this sum increases as the price level decreases, the real purchasing power that the debtor has to hand over also increase. Looked at another way, across-the-board deflation means that the debtor cannot charge as much for whatever she sells, but the amount of money she has to pay to the creditor does not change. Therefore, she now has to sell more units (of whatever it is she sells) to pay back the debt. Debt service will swallow up an increasing proportion of her gross income. "If the fall of wages and prices goes far … those entrepreneurs who are heavily indebted," Keynes argues, "may soon reach the point of insolvency." That is, deflation can result in an epidemic of bankruptcies.

Keynes' arguments on the effects of declining wages and prices during a recession were part of his case, contrary to the mainstream economics of his time (and ours), that capitalist economies were not inherently "self-correcting." Depression conditions, Keynes argued, would not necessarily set off a chain of events pulling the economy back to its "full employment" level of output. Declining money wages and prices could, in fact, lead to a downward spiral deeper into recession. Capitalist economies could get stuck in a low-output, high-unemployment condition. Keynes believed that government action was necessary to guarantee a return to and maintenance of full employment. For this reason, he argued that the complacent attitude of conventional economists toward economic crises—that, eventually, the problem would solve itself—was not of much use. "Economists set them too easy, too useless a task," he wrote, "if in tempestuous seasons they can only tell us that when the storm is over the ocean is flat again." ❑

Resources: John Maynard Keynes, *The General Theory of Employment, Interest, and Money* (New York: Harcourt, Inc., 1964); John Maynard Keynes, *A Tract on Monetary Reform* (London: MacMillan, 1923); Consumer Price Index, All Urban Consumers (CPI-U), Economagic; Michael Bruno and William Easterly, "Inflation Crises and Long-Run Growth," Policy Research Working Paper, World Bank, September 1995.

Article 1.3

WHAT'S WRONG WITH NEOLIBERALISM?
The Marx, Keynes, and Polanyi Problems

BY ROBERT POLLIN
May/June 2004

During the years of the Clinton administration, the term "Washington Consensus" began circulating to designate the common policy positions of the U.S. administration along with the International Monetary Fund (IMF) and World Bank. These positions, implemented in the United States and abroad, included free trade, a smaller government share of the economy, and the deregulation of financial markets. This policy approach has also become widely known as *neoliberalism*, a term which draws upon the classical meaning of the word *liberalism*.

Classical liberalism is the political philosophy that embraces the virtues of free-market capitalism and the corresponding minimal role for government interventions, especially as regards measures to promote economic equality within capitalist societies. Thus, a classical liberal would favor minimal levels of government spending and taxation, and minimal levels of government regulation over the economy, including financial and labor markets. According to the classical liberal view, businesses should be free to operate as they wish, and to succeed or fail as such in a competitive marketplace. Meanwhile, consumers rather than government should be responsible for deciding which businesses produce goods and services that are of sufficient quality as well as reasonably priced. Businesses that provide overexpensive or low-quality products will then be out-competed in the marketplace regardless of the regulatory standards established by governments. Similarly, if businesses offer workers a wage below what the worker is worth, then a competitor firm will offer this worker a higher wage. The firm unwilling to offer fair wages would not survive over time in the competitive marketplace.

This same reasoning also carries over to the international level. Classical liberals favor free trade between countries rather than countries operating with tariffs or other barriers to the free flow of goods and services between countries. They argue that restrictions on the free movement of products and money between countries only protects uncompetitive firms from market competition, and thus holds back the economic development of countries that choose to erect such barriers.

Neoliberalism and the Washington Consensus are contemporary variants of this longstanding political and economic philosophy. The major difference between classical liberalism as a philosophy and contemporary neoliberalism as a set of policy measures is with implementation. Washington Consensus policy makers are committed to free-market policies when they support the interests of big business, as, for example, with lowering regulations at the workplace. But these same policy makers become far less insistent on free-market principles when invoking such principles might damage big business interests. Federal Reserve and IMF interventions to bail out wealthy asset holders during the frequent global financial crises in the 1990s are obvious violations of free-market precepts.

Broadly speaking, the effects of neoliberalism in the less developed countries over the 1990s reflected the experience of the Clinton years in the United States. A high proportion of less developed countries were successful, just in the manner of the United States under Clinton, in reducing inflation and government budget deficits, and creating a more welcoming climate for foreign trade, multinational corporations, and financial market investors. At the same time, most of Latin America, Africa, and Asia—with China being the one major exception—experienced deepening problems of poverty and inequality in the 1990s, along with slower growth and frequent financial market crises, which in turn produced still more poverty and inequality.

If free-market capitalism is a powerful mechanism for creating wealth, why does a neoliberal policy approach, whether pursued by Clinton, Bush, or the IMF, produce severe difficulties in terms of inequality and financial instability, which in turn diminish the market mechanism's ability to even promote economic growth? It will be helpful to consider this in terms of three fundamental problems that result from a free-market system, which I term "the Marx Problem," "the Keynes problem," and "the Polanyi problem." Let us take these up in turn.

The Marx Problem

Does someone in your family have a job and, if so, how much does it pay? For the majority of the world's population, how one answers these two questions determines, more than anything else, what one's standard of living will be. But how is it decided whether a person has a job and what their pay will be? Getting down to the most immediate level of decision-making, this occurs through various types of bargaining in labor markets between workers and employers. Karl Marx argued that, in a free-market economy generally, workers have less power than employers in this bargaining process because workers cannot fall back on other means of staying alive if they fail to get hired into a job. Capitalists gain higher profits through having this relatively stronger bargaining position. But Marx also stressed that workers' bargaining power diminishes further when unemployment and underemployment are high, since that means that employed workers can be more readily replaced by what Marx called "the reserve army" of the unemployed outside the office, mine, or factory gates.

Neoliberalism has brought increasing integration of the world's labor markets through reducing barriers to international trade and investment by multinationals. For workers in high-wage countries such as the United States, this effectively means that the reserve army of workers willing to accept jobs at lower pay than U.S. workers expands to include workers in less developed countries. It isn't the case that businesses will always move to less developed countries or that domestically produced goods will necessarily be supplanted by imports from low-wage countries. The point is that U.S. workers face an increased *credible* threat that they can be supplanted. If everything else were to remain the same in the U.S. labor market, this would then mean that global integration would erode the bargaining power of U.S. workers and thus tend to bring lower wages.

But even if this is true for workers in the United States and other rich countries, shouldn't it also mean that workers in poor countries have greater job opportunities and better bargaining positions? In fact, there are areas where workers in poor countries are gaining enhanced job opportunities through international trade and multinational investments. But these gains are generally quite limited. This is because a long-term transition out of agriculture in poor countries continues to expand the reserve army of unemployed and underemployed workers in these countries as well. Moreover, when neoliberal governments in poor countries reduce their support for agriculture—through cuts in both tariffs on imported food products and subsidies for domestic farmers—this makes it more difficult for poor farmers to compete with multinational agribusiness firms. This is especially so when the rich countries maintain or increase their own agricultural supports, as has been done in the United States under Bush. In addition, much of the growth in the recently developed export-oriented manufacturing sectors of poor countries has failed to significantly increase jobs even in this sector. This is because the new export-oriented production sites frequently do not represent net additions to the country's total supply of manufacturing firms. They rather replace older firms that were focused on supplying goods to domestic markets. The net result is that the number of people looking for jobs in the developing countries grows faster than the employers seeking new workers. Here again, workers' bargaining power diminishes.

This does not mean that global integration of labor markets must necessarily bring weakened bargaining power and lower wages for workers. But it does mean that unless some non-market forces in the economy, such as government regulations or effective labor unions, are able to counteract these market processes, workers will indeed continue to experience weakened bargaining strength and eroding living standards.

The Keynes Problem

In a free-market economy, investment spending by businesses is the main driving force that produces economic growth, innovation, and jobs. But as John Maynard Keynes stressed, private investment decisions are also unavoidably risky ventures. Businesses have to put up money without knowing whether they will produce any profits in the future. As such, investment spending by business is likely to fluctuate far more than, say, decisions by households as to how much they will spend per week on groceries.

But investment fluctuations will also affect overall spending in the economy, including that of households. When investment spending declines, this means that businesses will hire fewer workers. Unemployment rises as a result, and this in turn will lead to cuts in household spending. Declines in business investment spending can therefore set off a vicious cycle: the investment decline leads to employment declines, then to cuts in household spending and corresponding increases in household financial problems, which then brings still more cuts in business investment and financial difficulties for the business sector. This is how capitalist economies produce mass unemployment, financial crises, and recessions.

Keynes also described a second major source of instability associated with private investment activity. Precisely because private investments are highly risky propositions, financial markets have evolved to make this risk more manageable for any given investor. Through financial markets, investors can sell off their investments if they need or want to, converting their office buildings, factories, and stock of machinery into cash much more readily than they could if they always had to find buyers on their own. But Keynes warned that when financial markets convert long-term assets into short-term commitments for investors, this also fosters a speculative mentality in the markets. What becomes central for investors is not whether a company's products will produce profits over a long term, but rather whether the short-term financial market investors *think* a company's fortunes will be strong enough in the present and immediate future to drive the stock price up. Or, to be more precise, what really matters for a speculative investor is not what they think about a given company's prospects per se, but rather what they think *other investors are thinking*, since that will be what determines where the stock price goes in the short term.

Because of this, the financial markets are highly susceptible to rumors, fads, and all sorts of deceptive accounting practices, since all of these can help drive the stock price up in the present, regardless of what they accomplish in the longer term. Thus, if U.S. stock traders are convinced that Alan Greenspan is a *maestro*, and if there is news that he is about to intervene with some kind of policy shift, then the rumor of Greenspan's policy shift can itself drive prices up, as the more nimble speculators try to keep one step ahead of the herd of Greenspan-philes.

Still, as with the Marx problem, it does not follow that the inherent instability of private investment and speculation in financial markets are uncontrollable, leading inevitably to persistent problems of mass unemployment and recession. But these social pathologies will become increasingly common through a neoliberal policy approach committed to minimizing government interventions to stabilize investment.

The Polanyi Problem

Karl Polanyi wrote his classic book *The Great Transformation* in the context of the 1930s depression, World War II, and the developing worldwide competition with Communist governments. He was also reflecting on the 1920s, dominated, as with our current epoch, by a free-market ethos. Polanyi wrote of the 1920s that "economic liberalism made a supreme bid to restore the self-regulation of the system by eliminating all interventionist policies which interfered with the freedom of markets."

Considering all of these experiences, Polanyi argued that for market economies to function with some modicum of fairness, they must be embedded in social norms and institutions that effectively promote broadly accepted notions of the common good. Otherwise, acquisitiveness and competition—the two driving forces of market economies—achieve overwhelming dominance as cultural forces, rendering life under capitalism a Hobbesian "war of all against all." This same idea is also central for Adam Smith. Smith showed how the invisible hand of self-interest and competition will yield higher levels of individual effort that increases the wealth of nations, but that it will also produce the corruption of our moral sentiments unless the market is itself governed at a fundamental level by norms of solidarity.

In the post-World War II period, various social democratic movements within the advanced capitalist economies adapted the Polanyi perspective. They argued in favor of government interventions to achieve three basic ends: stabilizing overall demand in the economy at a level that will provide for full employment; creating a financial market environment that is stable and conducive to the effective allocation of investment funds; and distributing equitably the rewards from high employment and a stable investment process. There were two basic means of achieving equitable distribution: relatively rapid wage growth, promoted by labor laws that were supportive of unions, minimum wage standards, and similar interventions in labor markets; and welfare state policies, including progressive taxation and redistributive programs such as Social Security. The political ascendancy of these ideas was the basis for a dramatic increase in the role of government in the post-World War II capitalist economies. As one indicator of this, total government expenditures in the United States rose from 8% of GDP in 1913, to 21% in 1950, then to 38% by 1992. The International Monetary Fund and World Bank were also formed in the mid-1940s to advance such policy ideas throughout the world—that is, to implement policies virtually the opposite of those they presently favor. John Maynard Keynes himself was a leading intellectual force contributing to the initial design of the International Monetary Fund and World Bank.

From Social Democracy to Neoliberalism

But the implementation of a social democratic capitalism, guided by a commitment to full employment and the welfare state, did also face serious and persistent difficulties, and we need to recognize them as part of a consideration of the Marx, Keynes, and Polanyi problems. In particular, many sectors of business opposed efforts to sustain full employment because, following the logic of the Marx problem, full employment provides greater bargaining power for workers in labor markets, even if it also increases the economy's total production of goods and services. Greater worker bargaining power can also create inflationary pressures because businesses will try to absorb their higher wage costs by raising prices. In addition, market-inhibiting financial regulations limit the capacity of financial market players to diversify their risk and speculate.

Corporations in the United States and Western Europe were experiencing some combination of these problems associated with social democratic capitalism. In particular, they were faced with rising labor costs associated with low unemployment rates, which then led to either inflation, when corporations had the ability to pass on their higher labor costs to consumers, or to a squeeze on profits, when competitive pressures prevented corporations from raising their prices in response to the rising labor costs. These pressures were compounded by the two oil price "shocks" initiated by the Oil Producing Exporting Countries (OPEC)—an initial fourfold increase in the world price of oil in 1973, then a second four-fold price spike in 1979.

These were the conditions that by the end of the 1970s led to the decline of social democratic approaches to policymaking and the ascendancy of neoliberalism. The two leading signposts of this historic transition were the election in 1979 of Margaret Thatcher as Prime Minister of the United Kingdom and in 1980 of Ronald Reagan as the President of the United States. Indeed, it was at this point that Mrs. Thatcher made her famous pronouncement that "there is no alternative" to neoliberalism.

This brings us to the contemporary era of smaller government, fiscal stringency and deregulation, i.e., to neoliberalism under Clinton, Bush, and throughout the less-developed world. The issue is not a simple juxtaposition between either regulating or deregulating markets. Rather it is that markets have become deregulated to support the interests of business and financial markets, even as these same groups still benefit greatly from many forms of government support, including investment subsidies, tax concessions, and rescue operations when financial crises get out of hand. At the same time, the deregulation of markets that favors business and finance is correspondingly the most powerful regulatory mechanism limiting the demands of workers, in that deregulation has been congruent with the worldwide expansion of the reserve army of labor and the declining capacity of national governments to implement full-employment and macroeconomic policies. In other words, deregulation has exacerbated both the Marx and Keynes problems.

Given the ways in which neoliberalism worsens the Marx, Keynes, and Polanyi problems, we should not be surprised by the wreckage that it has wrought since the late 1970s, when it became the ascendant policy model. Over the past generation, with neoliberals in the saddle almost everywhere in the world, the results have been straightforward: worsening inequality and poverty, along with slower economic growth and far more unstable financial markets. While Margaret Thatcher famously declared that "there is no alternative" to neoliberalism, there are in fact alternatives. The experience over the past generation demonstrates how important it is to develop them in the most workable and coherent ways possible. ❑

Article 1.4

THE GROWTH CONSENSUS UNRAVELS

BY JONATHAN ROWE
July/August 1999

Economics has been called the dismal science, but beneath its gray exterior is a system of belief worthy of Pollyanna. Yes, economists manage to see a dark cloud in every silver lining. Downturn follows uptick, and inflation rears its ugly head. But there's a story within that story—a gauzy romance, a lyric ode to Stuff. It's built into the language. A thing produced is called a "good," for example, no questions asked. The word is more than just a term of art. It suggests the automatic benediction which economics bestows upon commodities of any kind.

By the same token, an activity for sale is called a "service." In conventional economics there are no "dis-services," no actions that might be better left undone. The bank that gouges you with ATM fees, the lawyer who runs up the bill—such things are "services" so long as someone pays. If a friend or neighbor fixes your plumbing for free, it's not a "service" and so it doesn't count.

The sum total of these products and activities is called the Gross Domestic Product, or GDP. If the GDP is greater this year than last, then the result is called "growth." There is no bad GDP and no bad growth; economics does not even have a word for such a thing. It does have a word for less growth. In such a case, economists say growth is "sluggish" and the economy is in "recession." No matter what is growing—more payments to doctors because of worsening health, more toxic cleanup—so long as there is more of it, then the economic mind declares it good.

This purports to be "objective science." In reality it is a rhetorical construct with the value judgments built in, and this rhetoric has been the basis of economic debate in the United States for the last half century at least. True, people have disagreed over how best to promote a rising GDP. Liberals generally wanted to use government more, conservatives less. But regarding the beneficence of a rising GDP, there has been little debate at all.

If anything, the Left traditionally has believed in growth with even greater fervor than the Right. It was John Maynard Keynes, after all, who devised the growth-boosting mechanisms of macroeconomic policy to combat the Depression of the 1930s; it was Keynesians who embraced these strategies after the War and turned the GDP into a totem. There's no point in seeking a bigger pie to redistribute to the poor, if you don't believe the expanding pie is desirable in the first place.

Today, however, the growth consensus is starting to unravel across the political spectrum and in ways that are both obvious and subtle. The issue is no longer just the impact of growth upon the environment—the toxic impacts of industry and the like. It now goes deeper, to what growth actually consists of and what it means in people's lives. The things economists call "goods" and "services" increasingly don't strike people as such. There is a growing disconnect between the way people experience growth and the way the policy establishment talks about it, and this gap is becoming an unspoken subtext to much of American political life.

The group most commonly associated with an antigrowth stance is environmentalists, of course. To be sure, one faction, the environmental economists, is trying to put green new wine into the old bottles of economic thought. If we would just make people pay the "true" cost of, say, the gasoline they burn, through the tax system for example, then the market would do the rest. We'd have benign, lesspolluting growth, they say, perhaps even more than now. But the core of the environmental movement remains deeply suspicious of the growth ethos, and probably would be even if the environmental impacts somehow could be lessened.

In the middle are suburbanites who applaud growth in the abstract, but oppose the particular manifestations they see around them—the traffic, sprawl and crowded schools. On the Right, meanwhile, an anti-growth politics is arising practically unnoticed. When social conservatives denounce gambling, pornography, or sex and violence in the media, they are talking about specific instances of the growth that their political leaders rhapsodize on other days.

Environmentalists have been like social conservatives in one key respect. They have been moralistic regarding growth, often scolding people for enjoying themselves at the expense of future generations and the earth. Their concern is valid, up to a point—the consumer culture does promote the time horizon of a five year old. But politically it is not the most promising line of attack, and conceptually it concedes too much ground. To moralize about consumption as they do is to accept the conventional premise that it really is something chosen—an enjoyable form of self-indulgence that has unfortunate consequences for the earth.

That's "consumption" in the common parlance—the sport utility vehicle loading up at Wal-Mart, the stuff piling up in the basement and garage. But increasingly that's not what people actually experience, nor is it what the term really means. In economics, consumption means everything people spend money on, pleasurable or not. Wal-Mart is just one dimension of a much larger and increasingly unpleasant whole. The lawyers' fees for the house settlement or divorce; the repair work on the car after it was rear-ended; the cancer treatments for the uncle who was a three-pack-a-day smoker; the stress medications and weight loss regimens—all these and more are "consumption." They all go into the GDP.

Cancer treatments and lawyer's fees are not what come to mind when environmentalists lament the nation's excess consumption, or for that matter when economists applaud America's "consumers" for keeping the world economy afloat. Yet increasingly such things are what consumption actually consists of in the economy today. More and more, it consists not of pleasurable things that people choose, but rather of things that most people would gladly do without.

Much consumption today is addictive, for example. Millions of Americans are engaged in a grim daily struggle with themselves to do less of it. They want to eat less, drink less, smoke less, gamble less, talk less on the telephone—do less buying, period. Yet economic reasoning declares as growth and progress that which people themselves regard as a tyrannical affliction.

Economists resist this reality of a divided self, because it would complicate their models beyond repair. They cling instead to an 18th century model of human psychology—the "rational" and self-interested man—which assumes those complexities away. As David McClelland, the Harvard psychologist, once put it, economists "haven't even discovered Freud, let alone Abraham Maslow." (They also haven't discovered the Apostle Paul, who lamented that "the good that I would I do not, but the evil that I would not, that I do.")

Then too there's the mounting expenditure that sellers foist upon people through machination and deceit. People don't choose to pay for the corrupt campaign finance system or for bloated executive pay packages. The cost of these is hidden in the prices that we pay at the store. The *Washington Post* recently reported that Microsoft hired Ralph Reed, former head of the Christian Coalition, and Grover Norquist, a right-wing polemicist, as lobbyists in Washington. When I bought this computer with Windows 95, Bill Gates never asked me whether I wanted to help support a bunch of Beltway operators like these.

This is compulsory consumption, not choice, and the economy is rife with it today. People don't choose to pay some $40 billion a year in telemarketing fraud. They don't choose to pay 32% more for prescription drugs than do people in Canada. ("Free trade" means that corporations are free to buy their labor and materials in other countries, but ordinary Americans aren't equally free to do their shopping there.) For that matter, people don't choose to spend $25 and up for inkjet printer cartridges. The manufacturers design the printers to make money on the cartridges because, as the Wall Street Journal put it, that's "where the big profit margins are."

Yet another category of consumption that most people would gladly do without arises from the need to deal with the offshoots and implications of growth. Bottled water has become a multibillion dollar business in the United States because people don't trust what comes from the tap. There's a growing market for sound insulation and double-pane windows because the economy produces so much noise. A wide array of physical and social stresses arise from the activities that get lumped into the euphemistic term "growth."

The economy in such cases doesn't solve problems so much as create new problems that require more expenditure to solve. Food is supposed to sustain people, for example. But today the dis-economies of eating sustain the GDP instead. The food industry spends some $21 billion a year on advertising to entice people to eat food they don't need. Not coincidentally there's now a $32 billion diet and weight loss industry to help people take off the pounds that inevitably result. When that doesn't work, which is often, there is always the vacuum pump or knife. There were some 110,000 liposuctions in the United States last year; at five pounds each that's some 275 tons of flab up the tube.

It is a grueling cycle of indulgence and repentance, binge and purge. Yet each stage of this miserable experience, viewed through the pollyanic lens of economics, becomes growth and therefore good. The problem here goes far beyond the old critique of how the consumer culture cultivates feelings of inadequacy, lack and need so people will buy and buy again. Now this culture actually makes life worse, in order to sell solutions that purport to make it better.

Traffic shows this syndrome in a finely developed form. First we build sprawling suburbs so people need a car to go almost anywhere. The resulting long commutes are daily torture but help build up the GDP. Americans spend some $5 billion a year in gasoline alone while they sit in traffic and go nowhere. As the price of gas increases this growth sector will expand.

Commerce deplores a vacuum, and the exasperating hours in the car have spawned a booming subeconomy of relaxation tapes, cell phones, even special bibs. Billboards have 1-800 numbers so commuters can shop while they stew. Talk radio thrives on traffic-bound commuters, which accounts for some of the contentious, get-out-of-my-face tone. The traffic also helps sustain a $130 billion a year car wreck industry; and if Gates succeeds in getting computers into cars, that sector should get a major boost.

The health implications also are good for growth. Los Angeles, which has the worst traffic in the nation, also leads—if that's the word—in hospital admissions due to respiratory ailments. The resulting medical bills go into the GDP. And while Americans sit in traffic they aren't walking or getting exercise. More likely they are entertaining themselves orally with a glazed donut or a Big Mac, which helps explain why the portion of middle-aged Americans who are clinically obese has doubled since the 1960s.

C. Everett Koop, the former Surgeon General, estimates that some 70% of the nation's medical expenses are lifestyle induced. Yet the same lifestyle that promotes disease also produces a rising GDP. (Keynes observed that traditional virtues like thrift are bad for growth; now it appears that health is bad for growth too.) We literally are growing ourselves sick, and this puts a grim new twist on the economic doctrine of "complementary goods," which describes the way new products tend to spawn a host of others. The automobile gave rise to car wash franchises, drive-in restaurants, fuzz busters, tire dumps, and so forth. Television produced an antenna industry, VCRs, soap magazines, ad infinitum. The texts present this phenomenon as the wondrous perpetual motion machine of the market— goods beget more goods. But now the machine is producing complementary ills and collateral damages instead.

Suggestive of this new dynamic is a pesticide plant in Richmond, California, which is owned by a transnational corporation that also makes the breast cancer drug tamoxifen. Many researchers believe that pesticides, and the toxins created in the production of them, play a role in breast cancer. "It's a pretty good deal," a local physician told the East Bay Express, a Bay Area weekly. "First you cause the cancer, then you profit from curing it." Both the alleged cause and cure make the GDP go up, and this syndrome has become a central dynamic of growth in the U.S. today.

Mainstream economists would argue that this is all beside the point. If people didn't have to spend money on such things as commuting or medical costs, they'd simply spend it on something else, they say. Growth would be the same or even greater, so the actual content of growth should be of little concern to those who promote it. That view holds sway in the nation's policy councils; as a result we try continually to grow our way out of problems, when increasingly we are growing our way in.

To the extent conventional economics has raised an eyebrow at growth, it has done so mainly through the concept of "externalities." These are negative side effects suffered by those not party to a transaction between a buyer and a seller. Man buys car, car pollutes air, others suffer that "externality." As the language implies, anything outside the original transaction is deemed secondary, a subordinate reality, and therefore easily overlooked. More, the effects upon buyer and seller—the "internalities" one might say—are assumed to be good.

Today however that mental schema is collapsing. Externalities are starting to overwhelm internalities. A single jet ski can cause more misery for the people who reside by a lake, than it gives pleasure to the person riding it.

More importantly, and as just discussed, internalities themselves are coming into question, and with them the assumption of choice, which is the moral linchpin of market thought.

If people choose what they buy, as market theory posits, then—externalities aside—the sum total of all their buying must be the greatest good of all. That's the ideology behind the GDP. But if people don't always choose, then the model starts to fall apart, which is what is happening today. The practical implications are obvious. If growth consists increasingly of problems rather than solutions, then scolding people for consuming too much is barking up the wrong tree. It is possible to talk instead about ridding our lives of what we don't want as well as forsaking what we do want—or think we want.

Politically this is a more promising path. But to where? The economy may be turning into a kind of round robin of difficulty and affliction, but we are all tied to the game. The sickness industry employs a lot of people, as do ad agencies and trash haulers. The fastest-growing occupations in the country include debt collectors and prison guards. What would we do without our problems and dysfunctions?

The problem is especially acute for those at the bottom of the income scale who have not shared much in the apparent prosperity. For them, a bigger piece of a bad pie might be better than none.

This is the economic conundrum of our age. No one has more than pieces of an answer, but it helps to see that much growth today is really an optical illusion created by accounting tricks. The official tally ignores totally the cost side of the growth ledger—the toll of traffic upon our time and health for example. In fact, it actually counts such costs as growth and gain. By the same token, the official tally ignores the economic contributions of the natural environment and the social structure; so that the more the economy destroys these, and puts commoditized substitutes in their places, the more the experts say the economy has "grown." Pollute the lakes and oceans so that people have to join private swim clubs and the economy grows. Erode the social infrastructure of community so people have to buy services from the market instead of getting help from their neighbors, and it grows some more. The real economy—the one that sustains us—has diminished. All that has grown is the need to buy commoditized substitutes for things we used to have for free.

So one might rephrase the question thus: how do we achieve real growth, as opposed to the statistical illusion that passes for growth today? Four decades ago, John Kenneth Galbraith argued in *The Affluent Society* that conventional economic reasoning is rapidly becoming obsolete. An economics based upon scarcity simply doesn't work in an economy of hyper-abundance, he said. If it takes a $200 billion (today) advertising industry to maintain what economists quaintly call "demand," then perhaps that demand isn't as urgent as conventional theory posits. Perhaps it's not even demand in any sane meaning of the word.

Galbraith argued that genuine economy called for shifting some resources from consumption that needs to be prodded, to needs which are indisputably great: schools, parks, older people, the inner cities and the like. For this he was skewered as a proto-socialist. Yet today the case is even stronger, as advertisers worm into virtually every waking moment in a desperate effort to keep the growth machine on track.

Galbraith was arguing for a larger public sector. But that brings dysfunctions of its own, such as bureaucracy; and it depends upon an enlarging private sector as a fiscal base to begin with. Today we need to go further, and establish new ground rules for the economy, so that it produces more genuine growth on its own. We also need to find ways to revive the nonmarket economy of informal community exchange, so that people do not need money to meet every single life need.

In the first category, environmental fiscal policy can help. While the corporate world has flogged workers to be more productive, resources such as petroleum have been in effect loafing on the job. If we used these more efficiently the result could be jobs and growth, even in conventional terms, with less environmental pollution. If we used land more efficiently—that is, reduced urban sprawl—the social and environmental gains would be great.

Another ground rule is the corporate charter laws. We need to restore these to their original purpose: to keep large business organizations within the compass of the common good. But such shifts can do only so much. More efficient cars might simply encourage more traffic, for example. Cheap renewable power for electronic devices could encourage more noise. In other words, the answer won't just be a more efficient version of what we do now. Sooner or later we'll need different ways of thinking about work and growth and how we allocate the means of life.

This is where the social economy comes in, the informal exchange between neighbors and friends. There are some promising trends. One is the return to the traditional village model in housing. Structure does affect content. When houses are close together, and people can walk to stores and work, it encourages the spontaneous social interaction that nurtures real community. New local currencies, such as Time Dollars, provide a kind of lattice work upon which informal nonmarket exchange can take root and grow.

Changes like these are off the grid of economics as conventionally defined. It took centuries for the market to emerge from the stagnation of feudalism. The next organizing principle, whatever it is, most likely will emerge slowly as well. This much we can say with certainty. As the market hurtles towards multiple implosions, social and environmental as well as financial, it is just possible that the economics profession is going to have to do what it constantly lectures the rest of us to do: adjust to new realities and show a willingness to change. ❑

Article 1.5

UNDER THE MARGINS
Feminist economists look at gender and poverty.

BY RANDY ALBELDA
September/October 2002

For all the hype about welfare-to-work, most former welfare recipients are still living in poverty. It is true that, since the advent of 1990s-style "welfare reform," families no longer on welfare are earning more, on average, than those still on welfare. But more often than not, the jobs that former welfare mothers find don't provide employer-sponsored health insurance, vacation time, sick leave, or wages sufficient to support their families. In fact, the percentage of families who are "desperately" poor (with incomes at or below 50% of the official poverty line) has gone up since the mid-1990s, and so has the percentage of former welfare recipients who report hardships such as difficulty feeding their families or paying bills. And remember: All of this occurred during a so-called economic boom.

So why does the emphasis on work (and now marriage) continue to dominate the welfare debate? In large part, this is because the poverty "story" of the last 20 years—created and perpetuated by conservative ideologues and politicians—blames poor people for their own poverty. Women supposedly have too many children without husbands, poor black urban dwellers exhibit pathological behaviors, and liberal welfare policies—by expanding government spending and providing an attractive alternative to jobs and marriage—have made matters worse.

At least one group of theorists—feminist economists—says it isn't so. It is women's particular economic role in capitalism—as caregiver—that shapes their relationship to the labor market, men, and the state. Feminist economists have shown how having and caring for children affects the economic status of women—including women who are not mothers but are still relegated to poorly paid care-giving jobs. While their voices are largely ignored in research and policy circles, feminist economists' analyses provide the best understanding of the obstacles low-income families face and the range of policy options that might work.

Women and Poverty

Almost everywhere, women are the majority of poor adults. Recently, a group of so ciologists from several U.S. universities looked at poverty in eight industrialized nations. Using a relative poverty measure (half of median family income), they found that, in the 1990s, women's poverty rates exceeded men's in all countries but Sweden. Further, they found that single-mother poverty rates—even in countries with deep social welfare systems—are exceptionally high. (See Figure 1.)

In the United States in 2000, women comprised just over half of the adult population but constituted 61% of all poor adults. (The U.S. poverty income threshold is based on an absolute dollar figure determined in the 1960s and since indexed for inflation.) Toss in children, and the data are even grimmer; 16.2% of all children were poor, while over one-third of all single-mother families were poor. Together, women and children comprised 76% of the poor in the United States, far surpassing their 62% representation in the population as a whole.

Since the late 1950s (when the data were first collected), single-mother families in the United States have never constituted more than 13% of all families; however, they form just under half of all poor families. Figure 2 depicts the proportion of all families—and all poor families—that are single-mother families. The steepest increase occurred in the late 1960s on the heels of the War on Poverty, as poverty rates for everyone were falling.

Economic Theory and Poverty

From Adam Smith onward, most economists have understood poverty by looking at labor markets, labor-market inequality, and economic growth. According to this approach, it is underemployment or the lack of employment—and the resulting lack of income—that causes poverty. A brief summary of the dominant economic theories in the last half of the 20th century illustrates the point.

Keynesian economic theory argues that the lack of demand in the economy as a whole leads to unemployment. When investors and consumers can't jumpstart the economy, we need fiscal or monetary economic stimuli to induce demand. It was this wisdom that has guided economists to promote economic growth as a way to

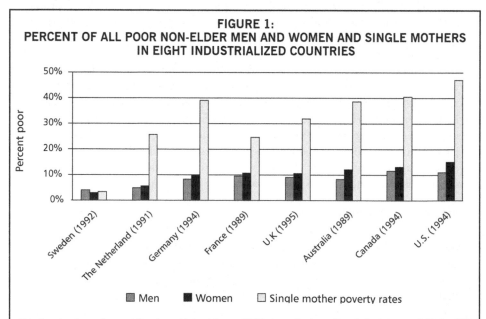

FIGURE 1:
PERCENT OF ALL POOR NON-ELDER MEN AND WOMEN AND SINGLE MOTHERS IN EIGHT INDUSTRIALIZED COUNTRIES

Note: Poverty rates are the proportion of non-elderly adults ages 25-54 whose after-tax and transfer family incomes fall below 50% of the median family income.

Source: Table 1, in Karen Christopher et al., "Gender Inequality in Poverty in Affluent Nations: The Role of Single Motherhood and the State," in Karen Vleminckx and Timothy Smeeding, eds., *Child Well-Being, Child Poverty and Child Policy in Modern Nations* (London: Policy Press, 2001).

reduce poverty, arguing that "a rising tide lifts all boats"—as, for example, during the Kennedy and Johnson administrations.

Marxian theorists say that, under capitalism, unemployment cannot be totally eliminated because it is a necessary component of capitalist production that serves to "discipline" workers. Unless we make radical changes to the economic system, there will always be families that are without employment and therefore poor.

Like Marxian economists, *institutional* economists also believe that economic outcomes aren't simply the result of pure market forces; cultural, social, and political forces also come into play. In the 1970s, economists Peter Doeringer and Michael Piore identified distinct labor-market segments. Younger workers, workers of color, and women tend to end up in what they call the "secondary labor market"—characterized by low wages, few promotional opportunities, and easy-to-acquire skills—more than other workers. These workers are particularly vulnerable to unemployment and hence more likely to be poor. The way to relieve poverty is to help these workers move into better jobs, or to create policies that make their jobs better.

These understandings of poverty offer little or no gender analysis—presumably what ails men is equally applicable to women. Analyses of insufficient (aggregate) demand, unemployment, and labor-market inequality rarely mention women or discuss how and why gender matters—unless feminist scholars provide them.

Neoclassical (mainstream) economists also argue that poverty is caused by lack of employment and low wages—but they consider workers responsible for their own

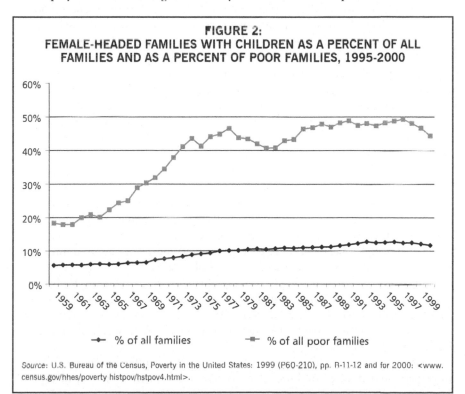

FIGURE 2:
FEMALE-HEADED FAMILIES WITH CHILDREN AS A PERCENT OF ALL FAMILIES AND AS A PERCENT OF POOR FAMILIES, 1995-2000

—◆— % of all families   —■— % of all poor families

Source: U.S. Bureau of the Census, Poverty in the United States: 1999 (P60-210), pp. B-11-12 and for 2000: <www.census.gov/hhes/poverty histpov/hstpov4.html>.

wage levels. Workers who choose not to pursue education, training, or on-the-job experience will participate in the labor force less often than more highly trained and skilled workers, be less productive, and receive lower wages. Unlike the political economy theorists just discussed, many non-feminist economists—the most well known being Nobel Prize winner Gary Becker—have tackled the topic of women's lower wages. But they consistently conclude that women's lack of employment, or employment at low wages, results from rational individual choice. Only policies that boost incentives for individuals to invest in themselves (like tax credits for education) will alleviate poverty.

Gender Matters

It is true that one reason women are poor is that they are not in the labor force or are underemployed. But while employment is an important underpinning to understanding poverty, it is not the same for women as for men.

Most economists who study labor markets assume that workers in capitalist economies are "unencumbered"—that they don't have significant constraints on their time outside of paid work. Encumbered workers are treated as a "special case"—worthy of examination, but understood and analyzed as an exception rather than the rule.

Since the beginnings of capitalism, however, female workers have almost always been "encumbered." And women's role as caregivers—their main encumbrance—has shaped their participation in the economy, as feminist historians and economic historians have shown. Historically, women's economic opportunities have been severely constricted, with race, age, and marital status sending important market "signals" about where women could or should be employed. For example, until the 1960s, many professional and some clerical jobs had "marriage bars," i.e., employers refused to hire married women on the assumption that they did not need the salaries these jobs paid, and would not stick around once they had children. Similarly, before anti-discrimination laws were enacted, many workers of color could not get jobs as managers in many professions, or even as sales clerks if the business catered to a white clientele.

For more than a century, this labor market "ordering" has given rise to employment, income, and wage policies that reinforce and reproduce women's political and economic dependence on men (and non-whites' inferior status in relation to whites). These policies assume that the standard family is a heterosexual married couple with a lone male breadwinner employed in industrial production. For example, in order to collect unemployment insurance benefits, workers must work a minimum number of hours and receive a minimum amount of earnings. Because many women work part-time and earn low wages, they are much less likely to qualify for benefits than men. Similarly, Social Security benefits are based on previous earnings over a sustained period of employment. Women who have spent most of their adult lives as caregivers are thus ineligible for benefits on their own, and must rely on their husbands' contributions instead.

Men's and women's employment patterns are very different. Women's labor force participation rates are lower than men's, and women's employment experiences in economic downturns often differ from men's. Women's job options and choices are also highly influenced by care-giving responsibilities; mothers are more likely than fathers to trade higher-paying jobs for jobs that are closer to childcare, have more flexible schedules, or require fewer hours.

In addition to shaping women's paid labor-market activities, care work has been economically, socially, and politically undervalued, as feminist economists point out. This is true both when that work is done in the home for free and when others do it for low pay. Among the few jobs immigrant women and women of color can almost always find are low-paying care-work jobs, and they are disproportionately represented in those jobs. For example, in 2001, women were 47% of all workers but 97% of child care workers, 93% of registered nurses, 90% of health aides, and 72% of social workers. Black workers comprised 11% of the workforce but were 33% of health aides, 23% of licensed practical nurses, and 20% of cleaning service workers. This type of occupational "stereotyping" reinforces the care-giving roles that women and people of color fill, and the low pay (relative to jobs with similar skill requirements) reinforces women's dependence on men and racial inequality. Economist Nancy Folbre, in her 2001 book *The Invisible Heart: Economics and Family Values*, calls this the "care penalty."

It is because of their low-paid and unpaid care work, then, that women are particularly economically vulnerable and much more likely to be poor than are men. The role of care giving—as distinct from other factors like employment, economic growth, and labor-market inequality—helps to explain not only women's employment patterns but also women's poverty. So theories of poverty that rely on analyses of employment that assume all people are men—or that women are a special case of men—are not only incomplete, they are wrong.

Feminist Analyses of Poverty

It is no coincidence that, when there has been a viable women's movement—in the early part of the 20th century and in the late 1960s—feminists and women researchers have paid particular attention to poor women.

Documenting Poor Families: Early Efforts

In the early 20th century, there was a good deal of concern about how women fit into the capitalist economy. Social scientists living in or near poor communities—often in settlement houses established by women reformers—conducted surveys of women workers, mostly through government-sponsored research. Many of the surveys found that the biggest problems faced by two-parent families were a lack of employment and insufficient wages. Researchers readily recognized that families headed by women were constrained by women's role as caregiver and women's low wages. Instead of advocating more employment for women, they promoted relatively meager levels of public assistance.

In the 1910s and 1920s, women reformers were key players not only in doing research but also in creating policies directed toward poor women and children. These women imposed white middle-class values about child-rearing, hygiene, and education; their construction of "deservingness" replicated and reinforced the ways in which women and men, immigrants and non-immigrants, were supposed to act. At the same time, they successfully implemented income supplement programs for single-mother families at the state level, and they were instrumental in incorporating AFDC (Aid to Families with Dependent Children) into the Social Security Act of 1935. Feminist poverty researchers and reformers did not emerge again until the late 1960s.

Sisterhood May Be Powerful, But Motherhood Is Not: Recent Efforts

The women's movement of the late 1960s and 1970s laid some important foundations for understanding women's poverty, even though its main economic strategies were aimed at improving the wages of women who were employed. Feminists fought for affirmative action, which was most successful in creating opportunities for college-educated women. Today, women hold 46% of executive and professional jobs—exactly their representation in all jobs—and comprise just under 30% of all doctors and lawyers. Feminists also organized for comparable worth, which was intended to lift wages for low-income women by recognizing and rewarding the skill level and effort needed to perform low-paying women's jobs (including care-giving ones).

At the same time, feminist scholars called attention to women's "double day" (now called "work/family conflict") and theorized about the role of care work and reproduction in capitalist economies. From the outset, feminist analysts understood that "housework" was work and a vital component of capitalist production. This intellectual work paralleled "wages for housework" campaigns that were launched in Italy, Canada, Great Britain, and the United States.

Using these tools to reinterpret poverty was not hard. Among the first to apply a feminist analysis to women's poverty was sociologist Diana Pearce, in an 1978 article entitled "The Feminization of Poverty: Women, Work, and Welfare." Pearce called attention to the fact that women were disproportionately represented among the poor. Her phrase—"the feminization of poverty"—became very popular in feminist circles as well as in the mainstream press.

Economist Nancy Folbre followed up with a theoretical framework directly linking women's care work as mothers to their poverty. In her 1985 article, "The Pauperization of Motherhood: Patriarchy and Social Policy in the U.S.," she argued that, when the costs of raising children are shifted onto women, women (and children) become dependent on men. Then, when fathers abandon their families, women and children are consigned to poverty. Folbre also argues that public policies around divorce, child support, unemployment insurance, and welfare reinforce this relationship. For example, welfare policies—even before the 1990s reforms—never provided enough income for women to support their families without working "under the table" or getting unreported income, paying a big price for not being married.

Single mothers especially bear the burden of these policies in the form of incredibly high poverty rates. But, Folbre points out, the benefits of care labor—healthy, productive children who become tax-paying adults—are enjoyed by all of society, not merely the mothers who provided the care. If society recognized the value of women's care work and compensated them for it, then fewer women would be poor.

Current Trends

Currently, some feminist scholars are addressing the ways that gender influences government allocation of income supports (like pensions, unemployment insurance, and welfare) and non-cash assistance (e.g., education and child care). Sociologist Ann Orloff and political scientists Diane Sainsbury and Jane Lewis argue that state welfare policies (construed broadly) embody deeply gendered notions of citizenship and need. Much of this work is theoretical and does not explicitly address poverty. However, it helps to explain the lack of policies that would correct women's poverty.

Other researchers are focusing on how people's capacity—access to health and education, living conditions, how they are treated in a society—affects their potential to generate income and causes poverty. Building on the work of economist Amartya Sen, feminist economists in the United States have shown that it is unreasonable and unlikely to expect single mothers to "work" their way out of poverty—because women earn lower wages than men, because they have care-giving responsibilities, and because the additional costs associated with caring for children restrict their capacity to be employed even while family needs remain high. For example, Barbara Bergmann and Trudi Renwick developed budgets for low-income families in the 1990s. Chris Tilly and I have demonstrated that the income needs of single-mother families far exceed their earnings possibilities—even with full-time employment. This work refutes the claims of liberals who supported welfare reform in the naïve belief that welfare recipients could easily substitute earnings for public assistance.

Finally, feminist economists are documenting how low-income women—especially single-mother families in which the same adult is both caregiver and breadwinner—relate to the labor market, fathers, and the state. Using longitudinal data, feminist social scientists Roberta Spalter-Roth and Heidi Hartmann found that many poor single-mother families either combine government assistance with wages (under or above the table) or cycle between the two. This research is confirmed and extended by feminist sociologists like Kathryn Edin and Laura Lein, who, through extensive interviews with poor single mothers, documented the particular ways and times that poorly paying jobs as well as men and their incomes drift in and out of women's lives. These studies make it clear that women's employment is not family-sustaining, and that, to survive, single-mother families need a sane combination of earnings, child support, *and* government assistance. In contrast to the narrowly focused, incentive-based literature that characterizes poor women's behavior as pathological, these approaches demonstrate that poor women's lives are dynamic yet fragile, and that the decisions they make are creative, adaptive, and almost always child-centered.

Who Cares?

Despite their efforts, feminist scholars have not had much impact on the poverty literature—at least not in economics—nor have they influenced policies intended to alleviate poverty. Much (though not all) poverty research is grant-funded, and it tends to focus narrowly on evaluating the individual impact of welfare reform, mostly by looking at welfare "leavers." These factors discourage the use of feminist analysis, since most funding goes either to conservative think tanks with a specific ideological aversion to feminism or to "liberal" think tanks that have made their fortunes in mainstream analysis fitted to their main consumer—the federal government.

Further, these conventional studies often preclude the larger political economy approach taken by feminists. Welfare reform is a mechanism of social control over poor single women—especially women of color—that is part of a larger conservative agenda to justify if not exacerbate economic inequality, assure a large pool of low-wage labor, and silence important political movements. Feminist analysis suggests the need for policies that would not only reduce poverty but also change women's (and people of color's) relationship to the labor market, (white) men, and the state, thus loosening the grip of economic dependence. This isn't in line with the right-wing agenda at all.

However, feminist economic analysis has been very useful to activists who are trying to help poor women. For example, in the mid-1990s, Wider Opportunity for Women (WOW), a feminist group based in Washington, D.C., started conducting family economic self-sufficiency standard projects. Currently, WOW operates projects in 40 states and D.C. The studies demonstrate how much income a single-mother family needs to survive, and are being used as organizing tools in the states.

During the mid-1990s welfare reform debates and in later discussions about reauthorization of Temporary Assistance for Needy Families (TANF), feminist scholars—connected informally through the "Women's Committee of 100"—have argued that raising children is work and that responsible legislation should recognize unpaid work as work. The Committee has called for a caregiver's allowance. And while Congress has not embraced these ideas, a TANF reauthorization bill sponsored by Representative Patsy Mink (D-Hawaii) in the spring of 2002 garnered support from close to 90 members of the House.

Feminist economists argue that the role of economists is to understand how societies do or do not provide for people's needs. Through their research and skills, they provide the tools for activists to argue that women's employment status and care-giving responsibilities place many at the bottom of the economic pecking order. At the same time, feminist economists are connecting their work directly to social movements, lending their expertise—and their own voices—to living wage campaigns, efforts to improve compensation for child care workers and home health aides, and efforts to eliminate poverty, not welfare. ❑

Resources: Kathryn Edin and Laura Lein, *Making Ends Meet: How Single Mothers Survive Welfare and Low Wage Work* (Russell Sage Foundation, 1997); Nancy Folbre, "The Pauperization of Motherhood: Patriarchy and Social Policy in the U.S.," *Review of Radical Political Economics*, vol. 16, no. 4 (1984): 72-88; Nancy Folbre, *The Invisible Heart: Economics and Family Values* (New York: The New Press, 2001); Jane Lewis, "Gender and the Development of Welfare Regimes," *Journal of European Social Policy* 3 (1992): 159-73; Alice O'Connor, *Poverty Knowledge: Social Science, Social Policy, and the Poor in Twentieth Century U.S. History* (Princeton, N.J.: Princeton University Press, 2001); Ann Orloff, "Gender and the Social Rights of Citizenship: The

Comparative Analysis of Gender Relations and Welfare States," *American Sociological Review* 58 (1993): 303-28; Diana Pearce, "The Feminization of Poverty; Women, Work, and Welfare," *Urban and Social Change Review* (February 1978); Trudi Renwick and Barbara Bergmann, "A Budget-based Definition of Poverty with an Application to Single-parent Families," *Journal of Human Resources* 28, no. 1 (1993): 1-24; Diane Sainsbury, *Gender, Equality, and Welfare States* (Cambridge: Cambridge University Press, 1996); Amartya K. Sen, *Development as Freedom* (New York: Alfred A. Knopf, 1999); Roberta SpalterRoth et al., *Welfare That Works: The Working Lives of AFDC Recipients* (Washington, D.C.: Institute for Women's Policy Research, 1995); Chris Tilly and Randy Albelda, "Family Structure and Family Earnings: The Determinants of Earnings Differences among Family Types," *Industrial Relations* 33, no. 2 (1994): 151-167; U.S. Census, *Current Population Surveys* <www.census. gov/hhes/income/histinc/histpovtb.html>; Bureau of Labor Statistics, *Employment and Earnings*, Table 11 *<www.bls.gov/cps/home.htm#charemp.§§>*

Article 1.6

OPENING PANDORA'S BOX
The Basics of Marxist Economics

BY ALEJANDRO REUSS
February 2000

In most universities, what is taught as "economics" is a particular brand of orthodox economic theory. The hallmark of this school is a belief in the optimal efficiency (and, it goes without saying, the equity) of "free markets."

The orthodox macroeconomists—who had denied the possibility of general economic slumps—were thrown for a loop by the Great Depression of the 1930s, and by the challenge to their system of thought by John Maynard Keynes and others. Even so, the orthodox system retains at its heart a view of capitalist society in which individuals, each roughly equal to all others, undertake mutually beneficial transactions tending to a socially optimal equilibrium. There is no power and no conflict. The model is a perfectly bloodless abstraction, without all the clash and clamor of real life.

Karl Marx and the Critique of Capitalist Society

One way to pry open and criticize the orthodox model of economics is by returning to the idiosyncrasies of the real world. That's the approach of most of the articles in this book, which describe real-world phenomena that the orthodox model ignores or excludes. These efforts may explain particular facts better than the orthodoxy, while not necessarily offering an alternative general system of analysis. They punch holes in the orthodox lines but, ultimately, leave the orthodox model in possession of the field.

This suggests the need for a different conceptual system that can supplant orthodox economics as a whole. Starting in the 1850s and continuing until his death in 1883, the German philosopher and revolutionary Karl Marx dedicated himself to developing a conceptual system for explaining the workings of capitalism. The system which Marx developed and which bears his name emerged from his criticism of the classical political economy developed by Adam Smith and David Ricardo. While Marx admired Smith and Ricardo, and borrowed many of their concepts, he approached economics (or "political economy") from a very different standpoint. He had developed a powerful criticism of capitalist society before undertaking his study of the economy. This criticism was inspired by French socialist ideas and focused on the oppression of the working class. Marx argued that wage workers—those working for a paycheck—were "free" only in the sense that they were not beholden to a single lord or master, as serfs had been under feudalism. But they did not own property, nor were they craftspeople working for themselves, so they were compelled to sell themselves for a wage to one capitalist or another. Having surrendered their freedom to the employer's authority, they were forced to work in the way the employer told them while the latter pocketed the profit produced by their labor.

Marx believed, however, that by creating this oppressed and exploited class of workers, capitalism was creating the seeds of its own destruction. Conflict between the workers and the owners was an essential part of capitalism. But in Marx's view of history, the workers could eventually overthrow the capitalist class, just as the capitalist class, or "bourgeoisie," had grown strong under feudalism, only to supplant the feudal aristocracy. The workers, however, would not simply substitute a new form of private property and class exploitation, as the bourgeoisie had done. Rather, they would bring about the organization of production on a cooperative basis, and an end to the domination of one class over another.

This line of thinking was strongly influenced by the ideas of the day in German philosophy, which held that any new order grows in the womb of the old, and eventually bursts forth to replace it. Marx believed that the creation of the working class, or "proletariat," in the heart of capitalism was one of the system's main contradictions. Marx studied capitalist economics in order to explain the conditions under which it would be possible for the proletariat to overthrow capitalism and create a classless society. The orthodox view depicts capitalism as tending towards equilibrium (without dynamism or crises), serving everyone's best interests, and lasting forever. Marx saw capitalism as crisis-ridden, full of conflict, operating to the advantage of some and detriment of others, and far from eternal.

Class and Exploitation

Marx studied history closely. Looking at economic systems historically, he saw capitalism as only the latest in a succession of societies based on exploitation. When people are only able to produce the bare minimum needed to live, he wrote, there is no room for a class of people to take a portion of society's production without contributing to it. But as soon as productivity exceeds this subsistence level, it becomes possible for a class of people who do not contribute to production to live by appropriating the surplus for themselves. These are the masters in slave societies, the lords in feudal societies, and the property owners in capitalist society.

Marx believed that the owners of businesses and property—the capitalists—take part of the wealth produced by the workers, but that this appropriation is hidden by the appearance of an equal exchange, or "a fair day's work for a fair day's pay."

Those who live from the ownership of property—businesses, stocks, land, etc—were then a small minority and now are less than 5% of the population in countries like the United States. (Marx wrote before the rise of massive corporations and bureaucracies, and did not classify managers and administrators who don't own their own businesses as part of the bourgeoisie.) The exploited class, meanwhile, is the vast majority who live by earning a wage or salary— not just "blue collar" or industrial workers but other workers as well.

Marx's view of how exploitation happened in capitalist society depended on an idea, which he borrowed from Smith and Ricardo, called the labor theory of value. The premise of this theory, which is neither easily proved nor easily rejected, is that labor alone creates the value which is embodied in commodities and which creates profit for owners who sell the goods. The workers do not receive the full value created by their labor and so they are exploited.

Students are likely to hear in economics classes that profits are a reward for the "abstinence" or "risk" of a businessperson—implying that profits are their just deserts. Marx would argue that profits are a reward obtained through the exercise of power—the power owners have over those who own little but their ability to work and so must sell this ability for a wage. That power, and the tribute it allows owners of capital to extract from workers, is no more legitimate in Marx's analysis than the power of a slaveowner over a slave. A slaveowner may exhibit thrift and take risks, after all, but is the wealth of the slaveowner the just reward for these virtues, or a pure and simple theft from the slave?

As Joan Robinson, an important 20th-century critic and admirer of Marx, argues, "What is important is that owning capital is not a productive activity. The academic economists, by treating capital as productive, used to insinuate the suggestion that capitalists deserve well by society and are fully justified in drawing income from their property."

The Falling Rate of Profit

Marx believed that his theory had major implications for the crises that engulf capitalist economies. In Marx's system, the raw materials and machinery used in the manufacture of a product do not create the extra value that allows the business owner to profit from its production. That additional value is created by labor alone.

Marx recognized that owners could directly extract more value out of workers in three ways: cutting their wages, lengthening their working day, or increasing the intensity of their labor. This need not be done by a direct assault on the workers. Capitalists can achieve the same goal by employing more easily exploited groups or by moving their operations where labor is not as powerful. Both of these trends can be seen in capitalism today, and can be understood as part of capital's intrinsic thirst for more value and increased exploitation.

With the mechanization of large-scale production under capitalism, machines and other inanimate elements of production form a larger and larger share of the inputs to production. Marx believed this would result in a long-term trend of the rate of profit to fall, as the enriching contribution of human labor declined (relative to the inert contribution of these other inputs). This, he believed, would make capitalism increasingly vulnerable to economic crises.

This chain of reasoning, of course, depends on the labor theory of value (seeing workers as the source of the surplus value created in the production process) and can be avoided by rejecting this theory outright. Orthodox economics has not only rejected the labor theory of value, but abandoned the issue of "value" altogether. After lying fallow for many years, value analysis was revived during the 1960s by a number of unorthodox economists including the Italian economist Piero Sraffa. Marx did not get the last word on the subject.

Unemployment, Part I: The "Reserve Army of the Unemployed"

Marx is often raked over the coals for arguing that workers, under capitalism, were destined to be ground into ever-more-desperate poverty. That living standards improved in rich capitalist countries is offered as proof that his system is fatally flawed. While Marx was not optimistic about the prospect of workers raising their standard of living very far under capitalism, he was critical of proponents of the "iron law of wages," such as Malthus, who held that any increase in wages above the minimum necessary for survival would simply provoke population growth and a decline in wages back to subsistence level.

Marx emphasized that political and historical factors influencing the relative power of the major social classes, rather than simple demographics, determined the distribution of income.

One economic factor to which Marx attributed great importance in the class struggle was the size of the "reserve army of the unemployed." Marx identified unemployment as the major factor pushing wages down—the larger the "reserve" of unemployed workers clamoring for jobs, the greater the downward pressure on wages. This was an influence, Marx believed, that the workers would never be able to fully escape under capitalism. If the workers' bargaining power rose enough to raise wages and eat into profits, he argued, capitalists would merely substitute labor-saving technology for living labor, recreating the "reserve army" and reasserting the downward pressure on wages.

Though this has not, perhaps, retarded long-term wage growth to the degree that Marx expected, his basic analysis was visionary at a time when the Malthusian (population) theory of wages was the prevailing view. Anyone reading the business press these days—which is constantly worrying that workers might gain some bargaining power in a "tight" (low unemployment) labor market, and that their wage demands will provoke inflation—will recognize its basic insight.

Unemployment, Part II: The Crisis of Overproduction

Marx never developed one definitive version of his theory of economic crises (recessions) under capitalism. Nonetheless, his thinking on this issue is some of his most visionary. Marx was the first major economic thinker to break with the orthodoxy of "Say's Law." Named after the French philosopher Jean-Baptiste Say, this theory held that each industry generated income equal to the output it created. In other words, "supply creates its own demand." Say's conclusion, in which he was followed by Smith, Ricardo, and orthodox economists up through the Great Depression, was that while a particular industry such as the car industry could overproduce, no generalized overproduction was possible. In this respect, orthodox economics flew in the face of all the evidence. In his analysis of overproduction, Marx focused on what he considered the basic contradiction of capitalism—and, in microcosm, of the commodity itself—the contradiction between "use value" and "exchange value." The idea is that a commodity both satisfies a specific need (it has "use value") and can be exchanged for other articles (it has "exchange value"). This distinction was not invented by Marx; it can be found in the work of Smith. Unlike Smith, however, Marx emphasized the way exchange value—what something is worth in the market—overwhelms the use value of a commodity. Unless a commodity can be sold, the portion of society's useful labor embodied in it is wasted (and the product is useless to those in need). Vast real needs remain unsatisfied for the majority of people, doubly so when—during crises of overproduction—vast quantities of goods remain unsold because there is not enough "effective demand."

It is during these crises that capitalism's unlimited drive to develop society's productive capacity clashes most sharply with the constraints it places on the real incomes of the majority to buy the goods they need. Marx developed this notion of a demand crisis over 75 years before the so-called "Keynesian revolution" in economic thought (whose key insights were actually developed before Keynes by the Polish economist Michal Kalecki on the foundations of Marx's analysis).

Marx expected that these crises of overproduction and demand would worsen as capitalism developed, and that the crises would slow the development of society's productive capacities (what Marx called the "forces of production"). Ultimately, he believed, these crises would be capitalism's undoing. He also pointed to them as evidence of the basic depravity of capitalism. "In these crises," Marx writes in the *Communist Manifesto*,

> there breaks out an epidemic that, in all earlier epochs would have seemed an absurdity, the epidemic of overproduction. Society suddenly finds itself put back into a state of momentary barbarism; it appears as if a famine, a universal war of devastation had cut off the supply of every means of subsistence; industry and commerce seem to be destroyed; and why? Because there is too much civilization, too much means of subsistence, too much industry, too much commerce ...
>
> And how does the bourgeoisie get over these crises? On the one hand by destruction of productive resources; on the other hand, by the conquest of new markets, and by the more thorough exploitation of old ones.

This kind of crisis came so close to bringing down capitalism during the Great Depression that preventing them became a central aim of government policy. While government intervention has managed to smooth out the business cycle, especially in the wealthiest countries, capitalism has hardly become crisis-free.

While the reigning complacency about a new, crisis-free capitalism is much easier to sustain here than in, say, East Asia, capitalism clearly has not yet run up against any absolute barrier to its development. In fact, Marx's discussions (in the *Communist Manifesto* and elsewhere) of capitalism's irresistible expansive impulse— capital breaking down all barriers, expanding into every crevice, always "thirsting for surplus value" and new fields of exploitation—seem as apt today as they did 150 years ago.

Marx as Prophet

Marx got a great deal about capitalism just right—its incessant, shark-like forward movement; its internal chaos, bursting forth periodically in crisis; its concentration of economic power in ever fewer hands. Judged on these core insights, the Marxist system can easily stand toe-to-toe with the orthodox model. Which comes closer to reality? The capitalism that incessantly bursts forth over new horizons, or the one that constantly gravitates towards comfortable equilibrium? The one where crisis is impossible, or the one that lurches from boom to bust to boom again? The one where perfect competition reigns, or the one where a handful of giants tower over every industry?

In all these respects, Marx's system captures the thundering dynamics of capitalism much better than the orthodox system does. As aesthetically appealing as the clockwork harmony of the orthodox model may be, this is precisely its failing. Capitalism is anything but harmonious.

There was also a lot that Marx, like any other complex thinker, predicted incorrectly, or did not foresee. In this respect, he was not a prophet. His work should be read critically, and not, as it has been by some, as divine revelation. Marx, rather, was the prophet of a radical approach to reality. In an age when the "free market" rides high, and its apologists claim smugly that "there is no alternative," Joan Robinson's praise of Marx is apt: "[T]he nightmare quality of Marx's thought gives it … an air of greater reality than the gentle complacency of the orthodox academics. Yet he, at the same time, is more encouraging than they, for he releases hope as well as terror from Pandora's box, while they preach only the gloomy doctrine that all is for the best in the best of all *possible* worlds." ❏

Sources: Joan Robinson, *An Essay on Marxian Economics* (Macmillan, 1952); "Manifesto of the Community Party," and "Crisis Theory (from Theories of Surplus Value)," in Robert C. Tucker, ed., *The Marx-Engels Reader* (W.W. Norton, 1978); Roman Rosdolsky, *The Making of Marx's 'Capital'* (Pluto Press, 1989); Ernest Mandel, "Karl Heinrich Marx"; Luigi L. Pasinetti, "Joan Violet Robinson"; and John Eatwell and Carlo Panico, "Piero Sraffa"; in John Eatwell, Murray Milgate, and Peter Newman, eds., *The New Palgrave: A Dictionary of Economics* (Macmillan, 1987).

Chapter 2

MEASURING ECONOMIC PERFORMANCE

INTRODUCTION

Most macroeconomics textbooks begin with a snapshot of today's economy as seen through the standard measures of economic performance. This chapter provides a different view of today's economy, one far more critical of current economic policy and performance, one that asks what the standard measures of economic performance really tell us and what they might be missing.

In "Recovery Delayed is Recovery Denied," economist John Miller explains how the National Bureau of Economic Research identifies the waves of business activity that constitute the business cycle. Miller traces the course of the business cycle in recent years, from a feeble expansion, which did little to improve the standard of living of most people, to the Great Recession, which left millions of people in dire straits. He asks when the disastrous downturn will end in the real world, not just in economists' record books (Article 2.1).

Miller's next article shows how the official unemployment rate understates the extent of unemployment. Correcting the official rate for underemployed workers and discouraged job-seekers, the unemployment rate is still over 12% (Article 2.2).

In "Unemployment is Down, So What's the Problem?" (Article 2.3) economist Alejandro Reuss unpacks the arithmetic of the "headline" unemployment rate to reveal that the falling unemployment rate of the last few years is not in fact the result of improving employment prospects, but declining labor force participation. A decline in the labor force participation rate does not have to be a bad thing by definition, but Reuss's assessment of the possible explanations leads to the conclusion that it is the grim condition of the labor market that is keeping so many people from participating.

Real GDP, or Gross Domestic Product adjusted for inflation, is the standard measure of the value of economic output. Increases in real GDP define economic growth and, for economists, rising real GDP per capita shows that a nation's standard of living is improving. But our authors are not convinced. Alejandro Reuss summarizes the main critiques of GDP, focusing on income distribution, non-market production, and environmental quality (Article 2.4). Lena Graber and John Miller focus on what GDP excludes: work in the home that is essential to economic well-being. They report that counting home-based work—from cleaning to child-care—would add substantially to the GDPs of industrialized economies and even more to those of developing economies (Article 2.5).

The next article focuses on a way to measure the performance of the economy by considering the economy a means of achieving social goals rather than treating economic activity as an end in itself. Alejandro Reuss (Article 2.6) describes the ins and outs of the Human Development Index (HDI), the United Nations Development Programme's alternative measure of economic well-being, and compares its ranking of countries to that produced by GDP per capita.

Discussion Questions

1. (Article 2.1) How does the National Bureau of Economic Research determine when a recession has begun and when it is over? Under what conditions would you declare the "Great Recession" of recent years to be over?

2. (Article 2.2) What are the shortcomings of the official (U-3) unemployment rate? Using the data in the table, calculate the more comprehensive U-6 unemployment rate for February 2014. Be sure to show each step of the conversion from the U-3 unemployment rate to the U-6 rate.

3. (Article 2.3) Reuss explains the official definitions of three groups: the employed, the unemployed, and those not in the labor force. Only the first two groups are considered in the calculation of the unemployment rate. The unemployment rate has been dropping recently (which means by definition that the employment rate has been rising), so what *is* the problem that Reuss identifies? *Why* is it a problem?

4. (Article 2.4) How is GDP measured, and what does it represent? What are the three main criticisms of GDP described by Reuss? Do you find them convincing?

5. (Article 2.5) Wages for housework might sound outlandish, but there are several economic justifications for valuing work in the home. What are they? In your opinion, should this work be paid? If so, by whom?

6. (Article 2.5) Suppose we decided that home-based work should be included in macroeconomic measures. How should it be counted?

7. (Articles 2.6) How does the HDI differ from GDP per capita? What shortcomings of GDP as a measure of well-being does the HDI attempt to overcome? How successfully do you think the HDI does overcome these shortcomings?

Article 2.1

RECOVERY DENIED
Growth and Prosperity Continue to Go Their Separate Ways

BY JOHN MILLER
May/June 2014

> The big story continues to be the rapid, healthy growth that hasn't returned since the Great Recession. ...
>
> According to Congress's Joint Economic Committee, average growth over the 19 quarters of this recovery has been 2.2%. ... The average for all post-1960 recoveries is 4.1%. ... The average for the Reagan expansion was 4.9%. ...
>
> These are huge differences in foregone prosperity. ...
>
> The main White House growth plan is to have government borrow more money to spend more on the transfer payments that didn't stimulate the economy the last time. ...
>
> Americans will be receptive to an agenda to lift the middle class with growth, not redistribution.
>
> —"The Growth Deficit," *Wall Street Journal*, May 1, 2014.

A "growth deficit" surely has been one of the hallmarks of the U.S. economy since the end of the Great Recession. But the *Wall Street Journal* editors must not be paying attention if they think that doubling down on the pro-rich, free-market policies initiated during the Reagan administration is going to restore of "forgone prosperity" for most people.

It's not just a growth deficit that has plagued the U.S. economy, but also an equality deficit. The economic growth there has been during "this not so great recovery," as the editors call it, has gone overwhelming to the very richest and has done less to improve the economic well-being of the rest than during any economic recovery in the last sixty years.

This is not just a matter of a single recovery delayed. Economic growth and prosperity for most people parted company some three decades ago. Chanting the *Journal* editors' mantra of "growth not redistribution" will only drive them further apart, resigning all but the super-rich to an economic slump that persists even during economic recoveries.

Recovery Delayed

This recovery has surely been delayed. According to National Bureau of Economic Research (NBER), the nation's arbiter of the business cycle, the Great Recession ended back in June 2009. (See box on business-cycle dating, p. 54.) By the official scorecard, the current recovery will hit the five-year mark this June, making it longer than the average recovery (58 months). But the economy has grown at about half of the pace of the average recovery since 1960, as the editors report, and is the slowest of all recoveries since 1950.

Some of that dismal growth record should be attributed to the severity of the Great Recession, the worst economic crisis since the 1930s. Typically, recoveries from financial crises have been protracted. That this recovery seems to conform to the historical pattern, however, is cold comfort for those waiting for the economic suffering of the Great Recession to subside.

To undo the economic suffering inflicted during a recession, a recovery must first create enough jobs to replace those lost in the downturn. That is admittedly a large undertaking this time around. Still, no recovery has taken longer to replace the jobs lost in the previous recession. By this June, more than six years since the onset of the recession, the recovery will finally get back to the pre-recession level of employment. That's longer than the four years the "jobless" recovery took to replace

---

A Date with a Business Cycle

Let's look more closely at what economists mean when they declare that a recession is over and a recovery is underway. This will help show why that announcement is unlikely to mean that happy days are here again for most people, especially those looking for work.

The National Bureau of Economic Research (NBER) tracks the ebb and flow of economic activity over a business cycle—from the low point ("trough") of a recession to high point ("peak") of an expansion, and back again. In the first phase of the cycle, the expansion, the economy grows. In the second, it contracts. The NBER has identified nine complete business cycles in the U.S. economy since World War II.

The NBER's business-cycle-dating committee, a group of seven economists, has no rigid rules for determining the start or end of a business cycle. The members study a broad array of macroeconomic indicators, including Gross Domestic Product (GDP), industrial production, employment, real income, trade, several interest rates, and personal income, as well as several composite indices, including the index of coincident indicators, which measures employment, income, output, and sales. In short, they eyeball the data.

Economists traditionally define a recession as two consecutive quarters of negative real growth, or declining output, as measured by GDP. But applying even this shorthand definition is not easy. In December 2008, for instance, the economy had not yet suffered two consecutive quarters of negative economic growth. Nonetheless, mounting monthly job losses convinced the NBER to declare that a recession had begun a whole year earlier, in December 2007. The economy had lost jobs every month from December 2007 on— already the longest period of uninterrupted job-loss since the Great Depression.

Determining when a recession finishes and an expansion begins isn't any simpler. Economists generally date the expansion back to when the economy begins to grow again,recouping the output lost during the recession.In September 2010, the NBER declared that the Great Recession had ended—reached its trough—back in June 2009,. But even itsannouncement cautioned that "economic activity is typicaly below normal in the early stages of the expansion, and it sometimes remains so well into the expansion."

That has surely been the case this time. Economic growth returned to the U.S. economy beginning in the third quarter of 2009. But job losses continued until March 2010,.

the jobs lost in in the much milder 2000 recession, and much longer than the then-record three years it took to replace the jobs lost in the 1991 recession.

But replacing the jobs lost in the recession is not enough to close the jobs gap. Each month, approximately 125,000 people enter the labor force in search of work. These new entrants must be able to find jobs before unemployment returns to pre-recession levels. The Hamilton Project, a policy group dedicated to restoring broad-based economic growth, calculates that if the economy were to add 208,000 jobs a month, matching the best year of job creation in the 2000s, it would still take until August 2018 to close the jobs gap.

And that says nothing of the quality of the jobs created. A study conducted by the National Employment Law Project (NELP) compared the distribution of

And nearly five years later the recovery has yet to replace the jobs lost during the Great Recession, the official "headline" unemployment rate remains elevated, and millions more have dropped out of the labor force altogether or are working part-time even though they want full-time jobs.

Economic expansions are supposed to improve our life-chances, not just swell the economy. That has not happened in this economic recovery, even some five years after the NBER declaredthat the crisis was officially over.

Sources: "Determination of the December 2007 Peak in Economic Activity," National Bureau of Economic Research, Dec. 11, 2008, www.nber.org/cycles/dec2008.html; and, "The June 2009 trough was announced Speptember 20,2010," http://www.nber.org/cycles/sept2010.html.

U.S. BUSINESS CYCLES, 1949-2014

Trough	Peak	Trough	Expansion (months)	Contraction (months)	Full Cycle (months)
Oct 1949	July 1953	Aug 1954	45	13	58
Aug 1954	July 1957	Apr 1958	35	9	44
Apr 1958	May 1960	Feb 1961	25	9	34
Feb 1961	Nov 1969	Nov 1970	105	12	117
Nov 1970	Dec 1973	Mar 1975	37	16	53
Mar 1975	Jan 1980	July 1980	57	6	63
July 1980	July 1981	Nov 1982	12	16	28
Nov 1982	July 1990	Mar 1991	93	8	101
Mar 1991	Mar 2001	Nov 2001	120	8	128
Nov 2001	Dec 2007	June 2009	73	18	91
June 2009	NA	NA	60*	NA	NA

Source: Economic Cycle Research Institute, National Bureau of Economic Research.

* Through June 2014

the jobs lost during the Great Recession to those created during the recovery (as of 2012). They looked at three equal-sized groups of occupations: low-wage jobs (paying median hourly wages from $7.69 to $13.83), mid-wage jobs ($13.84 to $21.13), and high-wage jobs ($21.14 to $54.55). Their results were striking. While three-fifths (60%) of the jobs lost in the Great Recession were in mid-wage occupations, just over one-fifth (22%) created during the recovery were in these occupations. The exact opposite held for low-wage jobs. These accounted for more than one-fifth (21%) of the jobs lost, but nearly three-fifths (58%) of the jobs created, with the biggest job gains in retail sales and food preparation.

No wonder inflation-adjusted hourly pay, for all but the top 10% of wage workers, were lower in 2013 than in 2009 (at the beginning of the recession). The median real household income in June 2013, meanwhile, was an alarming 4.4% lower, as reported by the Sentier Research Group.

Recovery Enjoyed

For the best off, the last five years have surely not been times of forgone prosperity. Just how well have they done during the recovery? By the end of 2013, corporate profits had risen so far that *WSJ* reporter Justin Lahart fretted about the "The Next Problem: Too Much Profit." What is driving profits to new record highs? "The tight lid companies have put on costs," answers Lahart. "They've been slow to hire and slow to raise wages."

It's clear that record profits have come at the expense of wages (and jobs), judging from the profit share of Gross Domestic Product (GDP). Corporate profits now stand at 11.1% of GDP, the highest share since 1948. Meanwhile, employee compensation (wages and benefits) has fallen to its lowest share.

Stock market investors have also done quite well. Stock values have surpassed their pre-recession peaks. But this is of little help for most households. Less than one-half of households own any stock, even indirectly through retirement accounts.

This tale of two recoveries has led to the greatest concentration of economic gains on record. From 2009 to 2012, 95% of income gains went to the richest 1%, those with incomes over $394,000, as economists Emmanuel Saez and Thomas Piketty have documented. That was greater than the 65% share that went to the top 1% during the 2002-2007 recovery prior to the Great Recession or even the 70% share during the 1923-1929 recovery before the Great Depression.

Reagan's Revenge, Recovery Denied

The Reagan recovery might have boasted a high rate of economic growth, as the *Journal* editors note, but that hardly suggests that Reagan's free-market, pro-rich tax policies would restore broad-based economic growth.

One reason the economy grew more quickly during the Reagan recovery is that the 1982 recession did much less damage than the Great Recession. Another is that, in practice, Reagan's economic policies were more Keynesian than Obama's. In the Reagan recovery, real per capita government spending grew twice as quickly (2.6% per year) as during the Obama administration (1.3%). On top of that, state and local government spending, adjusted for inflation and population, increased during the first half of the 1980s—while it declined from 2008 to 2012.

Nonetheless, Reagan's anti-government, "free-market" ideology took hold, saddling the economy with jobless recoveries that benefit almost exclusively the super rich, fail to replace middle-income jobs, and make inequality far worse. In their recent book Getting Back to Full Employment, economists Dean Baker and Jared Bernstein explain that, between the 1950s and 1970s, slack labor markets with high unemployment occurred about one-third of the time. Since Reagan, from 1980 to 2013, slack conditions have prevailed more than twice as often. And that's made a difference for inequality. When Reagan took office, the richest 1% pulled down about 10% of the nation's income, less than one half of 22.5% they get today.

The Reagan legacy includes pro-rich tax cuts that have reduced government revenues and kept government spending in check, union-busting labor relations that have eroded the bargaining power of workers, deregulation that paved the wave for financialization, and "free-trade" policies that have made it easy for companies to threaten offshoring unless workers make concessions. In its most recent *Global Wage Report*, the International Labor Organization found that wages as share of output in developed economies have dropped steadily since 1990. The most important drivers of the decline, in declining order of importance, are financialization, two institutional factors (smaller size of government and declining union density), and globalization.

If those long-term trends don't convince you that the *Journal* editors' preferred policies led to the separation of growth and prosperity, consider this: In the early 2000s, we conducted a full field test of those polices under the George W. Bush administration. The result was an economic recovery that added fewer jobs than even the Obama recovery, left the economy in the throes of the worst economic crisis since the 1930s, and increased the economic chasm between the super-rich and the rest of us.

Trying those same policies again will only be a way to ensure that, for most of us, it will be not just a recovery delayed, but recovery denied. ❑

Sources: Paul Krugman, "Reagan was a Keynesian," New York Times, June 7, 2012; Dean Baker and Jared Bernstein, "Getting Back to Full Employment," Center on Children and Families at Brookings, March 2014; Justin Lahart, "The Next Problem: Too Much Profit," Wall Street Journal, March 27, 2014; "The Low-Wage Recovery and Growing Inequality," National Employment Law Project, August 2012; "Global Wage Report 2013/13," International Labour Organization, 2013; "Evolution of the "Jobs Gap" and Possible Scenarios for Growth," The Hamilton Project at Brookings, May 2, 2014; Heidi Schierholz, "Six Years From Its Beginning, The Great Recession's Shadow Looms Over the Labor Market," Economic Policiy Institute, January 2014.

Article 2.2

THE *REAL* UNEMPLOYMENT RATE STILL IN DOUBLE DIGITS

BY JOHN MILLER
July/August 2009; last updated March 2014

In February 2014, after nearly five years of economic recovery, the official unemployment rate stood at 6.7%, down from its October 2009 peak of 10.1% during the Great Recession. But even at that, the unemployment rate was still well above the 4.4% unemployment rate at the onset of the Great Recession, and higher than the unemployment rate five years into any of the last three economic recoveries. Even the recovery from the 1982 recession, which was the most severe economic slump between the Great Depression of the 1930s and the recent Great Recession, was followed by a faster reduction in unemployment. (See figure 2.)

Some groups of workers faced even higher official unemployment rates. As of February 2014, unemployment rates for black, Hispanic, and teenage workers were 12.0%, 8.7% and 21.4%, respectively. Workers without a high-school diploma confronted a 9.8% unemployment rate. Some 13.1% of construction workers were still unemployed. In Rhode Island, the hardest hit state, unemployment was at 9.3% (in December, 2013). Unemployment rates in four other states were above 8.0% as well.

Other telltale signs suggested that the unemployment picture was yet worse than those official rates indicate. More than one in three of the officially unemployed have gone without work for more than one half a year. The long term unemployed never exceeded one quarter of the unemployed in the sixty years prior to the Great Recession. The proportion of workers employed part time who would prefer to work full-time remained at historically high levels as well. "Those observations," Janet Yellen, the new head of the Federal Reserve Board, told Congress, "underscore the importance of considering more than the unemployment rate when evaluating the condition of the U.S. labor market."

She is right. As bad as they are, the official figures dramatically understate the true extent of unemployment. First, they exclude anyone without a job who is ready to work but has not actively looked for a job in the previous four weeks. The Bureau of Labor Statistics (BLS) classifies such workers as "marginally attached

THE FEBRUARY 2014 UNEMPLOYMENT PICTURE (DATA IN THOUSANDS, NOT SEASONALLY ADJUSTED)	
Civilian Labor Force	155,027
Employed	144,134
Unemployed	10,893
Marginally Attached Workers	2,303
Discouraged workers	755
Reasons other than discouragement	1,548
Part-time for Economic Reasons	7,397
Slack work or business conditions	4,506
Could only find part-time work	2,598

Sources: Bureau of Labor Statistics, Tables A-1, A-8. A-15, A-16. Data are not seasonally adjusted because seasonally adjusted data for marginally attached workers are not available.

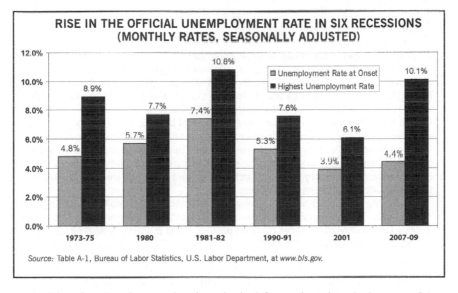

RISE IN THE OFFICIAL UNEMPLOYMENT RATE IN SIX RECESSIONS
(MONTHLY RATES, SEASONALLY ADJUSTED)

Source: Table A-1, Bureau of Labor Statistics, U.S. Labor Department, at www.bls.gov.

to the labor force" so long as they have looked for work within the last year. Marginally attached workers include so-called discouraged workers who have given up looking because repeated job searches were unsuccessful, plus others who have given up for reasons such as school and family responsibilities, ill health, or transportation problems.

Second, the official unemployment rate leaves out part-time workers looking for full-time work: part-time workers are "employed" even if they work as little as one hour a week. The vast majority of people working part-time involuntarily have had their hours cut due to slack or unfavorable business conditions. The rest are working part-time because they could only find part-time work.

To its credit, the BLS has developed alternative unemployment measures that go a long way toward correcting the shortcomings of the official rate. The broadest alternative measure, called U-6, counts as unemployed "marginally attached workers" as well as those employed "part time for economic reasons." And even the business press, including The Wall Street Journal, has taken to reporting this more comprehensive measure of unemployment along with the official unemployment rate.

In February 2014, the broader measure of the unemployment rate was 12.6%, just about double the official, or U-3 rate. While considerably below its peak of 17.4% back in October 2009, the February 2014 adjusted unemployment rate was still higher than any time between 1994, when the BLS introduced the U-6 measure, and the onset of the Great Recession in 2008.

Why is the real unemployment rate so much higher than the official, or U-3, rate? First, since the Great Recession forced part-time work has reached higher levels than anytime since1956. In February 2014, 7.4 million workers were forced to work part time for economic reasons. Forced part-timers are concentrated in wholesale and retail trade, leisure and hospitality, and education and health service; they are nearly equally men and women but disproportinately younger workers (20 to 24 years old) and older workers (over 55 years old). The number of discouraged workers is also quite high today. In February 2014, the BLS counted 2.3 million "marginally

---

Calculating the Real Unemployment Rate

The BLS calculates the official unemployment rate, U-3, as the number of unemployed as a percentage of the civilian labor force. The civilian labor force consists of employed workers plus the officially unemployed, those without jobs who are available to work and have looked for a job in the last 4 weeks. Applying the data found in Table 2 yields an official unemployment rate of 7.0%, or a seasonally adjusted rate of 6.7% for February 2014.

The comprehensive U-6 unemployment rate adjusts the official rate by adding marginally attached workers and workers forced to work part time for economic reasons to the officially unemployed. To find the U-6 rate the BLS takes that higher unemployment count and divides it by the official civilian labor force plus the number of marginally attached workers. (No adjustment is necessary for forced part-time workers since they are already counted in the official labor force as employed workers.)

Accounting for the large number of marginally attached workers and those working part-time for economic reasons raises the count of unemployed from 10.9 million to 20.6 million workers for February 2014. Those numbers push up the U-6 unemployment rate to 13.1% or a seasonally adjusted rate of 12.6%.

---

attached" workers. That figure exceeds the number of marginally attached workers in any month prior the Great Recession going back to 1994, when the agency introduced the measure.

In February 2014, nearly five years into an economic recovery, U.S. labor markets continued to impose devastating costs on society and much of the burden goes unaccounted for by a traditional unemployment rate. Of those who are counted as unemployed by the traditional measure, 37% had gone more 27 weeks without work. The persistence of such high levels of long term unemployment are sure to sever further the connection of those without work to the labor force. After many months of looking for work, some of the long-term unemployed are likely to give up the search, falling into the category of marginally attached and disappearing from the official measure of unemployment. And even more of the victims of the malfunctioning U.S. labor market will go uncounted by the traditional unemployment rate in the month and years ahead. ❏

Sources: U.S. Dept. of Labor, "The Unemployment Rate and Beyond: Alternative Measures of Labor Underutilization," *Issues in Labor Statistics*, June 2008; John E. Bregger and Steven E. Haugen, "BLS introduces new range of alternative unemployment measures," *Monthly Labor Review*, October 1995. "Fed's Yellen Sets Course for Steady Bond-Buy Cuts," by Hilsenrath and McGrane, *Wall Street Journal*, Feb. 11, 2014; and, "Don't Sweat the Rise in the Unemployment Rate," by Izzo, *Wall Street Journal*, March 7, 2014.

Article 2.3

UNEMPLOYMENT IS DOWN, SO WHAT'S THE PROBLEM?

BY ALEJANDRO REUSS
May/June 2013

The "headline" unemployment rate, or U-3 by its Bureau of Labor Statistics (BLS) designation, has declined from a peak of 10.0% in late 2009 to 7.5% now. The unemployment rate—the number of unemployed people as a percentage of the labor force (the employed plus unemployed)—is still abnormally high. Before the onset of the current crisis, it had been this high for only five months (May-September 1992) in the previous 24 years.

The jobs situation now is certainly drastically different from 2008-2010, when unemployment was increasing dramatically—there's no argument about that. At the bleakest point of the recession, in each of two consecutive months (January-February 2009), over half a million more people went from being employed to unemployed than from unemployed to employed. In March 2013, in contrast, over 250,000 more people went from being unemployed to employed than the reverse. But the end of the employment freefall is hardly the same thing as a robust recovery.

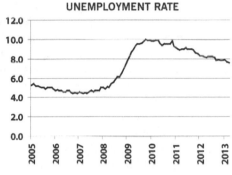

UNEMPLOYMENT RATE

The trend in the employment-to-population ratio—a much less familiar indicator than the headline unemployment rate—tells a different tale. This figure is the number of employed individuals as a percentage of the working-age civilian noninstitutional population. The civilian noninstitutional population excludes military personnel, people in prison, and so on. Working age, meanwhile, is defined as 16 years and over. So there are two big differences between this measure and the unemployment rate. First, the numerator is employment rather than unemployment (so it's looking at the other side of the employment coin). Second, the denominator is not the size of the labor force (the employed plus the unemployed), but the civilian noninstitutional population (which also includes people who are not in the labor force, or NLF). Here, we see not an employment situation that has turned decisively toward recovery, but one that has flatlined for more than three years.

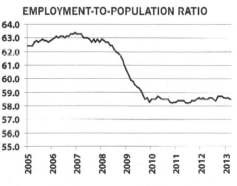

EMPLOYMENT-TO-POPULATION RATIO

Employed, Unemployed, or Neither

How can the unemployment rate have gone steadily down for about three years with hardly a budge to the employment-population ratio? Shouldn't the two move in opposite directions? (They did during the freefall of 2008-2010.) To get a handle on this, we have to look at the way the "headline" unemployment rate is calculated, starting with the official government definition of unemployment. For the BLS to count someone as unemployed, three things have to be true:

1. That person cannot be employed. In this context, being employed means working at all, whether full-time or part-time, "for pay or profit." People who work for wages, work at a business they own, or work even without direct pay at their family business are counted as employed.
2. That person must be actively looking for a job. That means doing things like filling out job applications, visiting an employment office, going to a job interview, etc.
3. That person must be available to start work. This means that someone who is looking for a job, but would not accept a job that required them to start immediately (for example, a student who would not be ready to start until after graduation, some months in the future) is not unemployed for the purposes of calculating U-3.

People who are not employed (meet criterion #1) but are not actively looking for work or are not available to work (do not meet criteria #2 or #3) are classified as not in the labor force. In effect, then, we have defined three distinct groups: employed, unemployed, and not in the labor force. The employed and unemployed, together, constitute the labor force. The working-age population, meanwhile, is divided between those in the labor force and those not in the labor force.

How can we relate the unemployment rate, then, to the employment-to-population ratio? The employment-to-population ratio is equal to the employment rate (employment as a percentage of the labor force) times the labor-force participation rate (the labor force as a percentage of the population). The employment rate and the unemployment rate add up to one. So, if the unemployment rate is going down, the employment rate must be going up. If the employment rate is going up, but the employment-to-population rate is pretty much constant, the labor force participation rate must be going down. So we find the answer to our paradox—a declining unemployment rate with a flatlining employment-to-population ratio—in a plummeting labor force participation rate.

Between the mid 1960s and 1990, the U.S. labor force participation rate (LFPR) increased from just under 60% to about 66-67%, where it hovered until 2008. (The climb was driven by women's labor force participation, which increased fast enough to offset a mild decline in men's labor force participation.) Since the onset of the Great Recession, however, the overall labor force participation rate has dropped by about

LABOR FORCE PARTICIPATION RATE

three percentage points. As economist Brad DeLong puts it, "There has been no closing of the output gap [the difference between actual and 'full employment' output] and no decline in the unemployment rate from putting a greater share of the adult population to work. All of the decline in the output gap and of the decline in the unemployment rate is from the collapse in labor force participation."

OK, Then What?

Higher labor-force participation is not automatically better. People may choose to remain out of the labor force, or to leave the labor force, for reasons that are neither personally nor socially harmful. For example, someone may decide to stay in school (or to return to school after some period in the labor force) and not seek employment "for pay or profit." That decision might enhance their future work opportunities, increase their future labor productivity, and even contribute to the general level of knowledge in society. Increases in the labor force participation rate can reflect positive changes in society (e.g., increased work opportunities for women) or negative (e.g., cuts to retirement benefits). Decreases in the LFPR, by the same token, can happen for good reasons (e.g., increased educational opportunities) or bad (e.g., despair among the unemployed of ever finding a job).

So why has the labor-force participation rate fallen like a stone in the last few years? None of the standard ways to explain away the precipitous decline is convincing:

Skills mismatch. Neoclassical economists have emphasized a supposed mismatch between the skills workers have and those employers are seeking as an explanation of high unemployment since the Great Recession, but it works equally well (that is, equally badly) for people dropping out of the labor force altogether. This view has been roundly refuted by the lack of wage growth (as we would expect if appropriately skilled workers were in short supply), the high prevalence of involuntary part-time employment (these presumably do have the necessary skills yet their employers are not desperate to increase their hours), and other observations.

Demographic changes. As the U.S. population ages, we should expect a decline in the labor force participation rate. (Remember, the definition of the

---

Let's Do the Math!

The employment-to-population ratio (EP) is equal to the number of employed people (E) divided by the size of the working-age civilian noninstitutional population (P).

EP ratio = E/P

The equation remains true if we multiply the right side by (LF/LF), where LF is the size of the labor force, since (LF/LF) = 1. Therefore,

EP ratio = (E/LF) x (LF/P)

LF/P is referred to as the "labor force participation rate." E/LF, meanwhile, is the employment rate.

If the unemployment rate (UE/LF) is 10%, then, the employment rate must be 90%. If the unemployment rate is 5%, the employment rate must be 95%. In other words, the total is always equal to 1.0.

Since: (E/LF) + (UE/LF) = 1

Then: (E/LF) = 1 - (UE/LF)

Therefore,

EP ratio = (1 - (UE/LF)) x (LF/P).

So here we have the relationship between the employment-to-population ratio and the unemployment rate.

If (UE/LF) is declining, then (1 - (UE/LF)) must be increasing. If (1 - (UE/LF)) is increasing, but the EP ratio is constant, this means (LF/P) must be decreasing.

working-age population does not have a maximum age.) As DeLong points out, however, demographic changes account for a decline of less than 0.2 percentage points per year, and so would explain maybe 0.5 points of the decline in the LFPR over the last three years. "One-tenth of our labor-market shift relative to 2007 can be attributable to demography,' he concludes."[N]ine-tenths are the result of the Lesser Depression."

Cultural and political changes. A recent piece by the conservative *New York Times* columnist Ross Douthat, "A World Without Work" (Feb. 23, 2013), suggests that the decline in the LFPR reflects an increasing willingness by those at the bottom of the occupational hierarchy to just drop out of the working world altogether and scratch together a living from "disability payments and food stamps, living with relatives, cobbling together work here and there." This third explanation suffers from the same problem as the second—it's hard to imagine why there would have been such a precipitous change in the span of just a few years. It's not as if the U.S. welfare state has suddenly become more generous. Nor is there evidence of an abrupt cultural change in attitudes toward work.

The best explanation is that the decline is the fallout of a severe recession from which we have far from recovered. There simply are not enough jobs. After long spells of unemployment, many people give up on looking for work ("discouraged workers") and are reclassified as NLF. Others have entered the working-age population—turned 16 years old—or just graduated from high school or college and found few work opportunities. Some older workers retire, leaving the labor force, before they otherwise would have. The declining LFPR, however, is not restricted to younger or older workers. As Heidi Schierholz of the Economic Policy Institute puts it, "[T]he labor force participation rate of the 'prime-age' population, people age 25-54, is also at its lowest point of the downturn ... . It's the lack of job opportunities—the lack of demand for workers—that is keeping these workers from working or seeking work, not other factors."

The decline in the unemployment rate over the last few years has contributed to the complacent view that the worst is over, that most people who made it through without losing their jobs are pretty safe now (at least for the short term), and that no major policy intervention (like further fiscal stimulus) is required to improve the employment situation. It's clear from the employment-to-population and labor-force-participation data how wrong this view is, how inadequate the federal-level fiscal stimulus was, how premature its abandonment was, and how damaging the ongoing state-level austerity has been.

It's clear, in other words, how far down employment and the fates of the unemployed have ranked in the priorities of the ruling elite. ❑

Sources: Bureau of Labor Statistics (BLS), Unemployment rate, Seasonally adjusted, 16 years and over, Series ID: LNS14000000 (bls.gov); BLS, Employment-population ratio, Seasonally adjusted, 16 years and over, Series ID: LNS12300000 (bls.gov); BLS, Civilian labor force participation rate, Seasonally adjusted, 16 years and over, Series ID: LNS11300000 (bls.gov); Brad DeLong, "A Good Employment Report This Month: A Bad Labor Market," Grasping Reality with Both Hands blog (delong.typepad.com), March 8, 2013; Ross Douthat, "A World Without Work," *New York Times*, Feb. 23, 2013 (nytimes.com); Heidi Shierholz, "The unemployment rate is hugely underestimating slack in the labor market," Economic Policy Institute, April 5, 2013. (epi.org).

Article 2.4

GDP AND ITS DISCONTENTS

BY ALEJANDRO REUSS
April 2013

Economists have been thinking for a long time about what it means for a country or its people to be rich or poor. That was one of the main questions Adam Smith, the British philosopher often described as the "father of modern economics," took on in his most famous book *The Wealth of Nations* (1776). At the very outset, Smith made a point of defining the "real wealth" of a country as consisting in the "annual produce of the land and labour of the society." (Note that Smith was using the word "wealth" in a way that is closer to the colloquial meaning of the word than to its current technical meaning in economics. He was actually defining a country's income rather than its wealth.) That definition might seem uncontroversial now. Many economists would certainly respond that *of course* it's the production of goods and services that makes a country wealthy. But Smith had an important axe to grind. He was arguing against the view, widespread in his day, that a country's wealth consisted in the accumulation of gold and silver—an aim that led to a set of policies (especially promoting exports and suppressing imports) known as mercantilism. In his own time, Smith was a maverick.

The kind of approach that Smith advocated, of counting up the total quantities of goods and services produced in a country in a year, is now a central part of macroeconomic measurement. When economists tabulate a country's gross domestic product (GDP), they're trying to measure the "annual produce ... of the society" more or less as Smith proposed. GDP attempts to add up the total value, counted in money units, of the goods and services produced within a country in the course of a year. This approach, while a big advance over the view that a country's wealth consisted primarily of its hoards of precious metals, however, is more problematic and controversial than it might appear at first glance. Economists and other social scientists have, in various ways, criticized the ways that GDP is counted and used as a measure of a country's "wealth" or "development." Here, we'll focus on three key critiques: 1) the distributional critique, 2) the feminist critique, and 3) the environmental critique. The first is really a criticism of the approach of looking at the total (or average) production of goods and services for a society as a whole, and ignoring the distribution of access among its members. The other two argue that GDP is misleading because it fails to count all goods and services (focusing narrowly on those that are easiest to put prices on).

What is GDP Per Capita?

Gross domestic product (GDP) per capita is the standard measure of average income used by mainstream economists, and it has become widely used as a measure of economic well-being. Gross domestic product is a measure of the total value of all the goods and services produced in a country in a year, which we can also think of as the total incomes of all the people in that country. A country's total GDP is a very poor measure of how "rich" or "poor" its people are. A country can have a very high total income, even if the average income is low, just because it has a very high population. China, for example, now has the highest total income of any country in the world, even the United States. Its average income, however, is about one-sixth that of the United States, in terms of real purchasing power (World Bank). China ranks so high in total income because it is the largest country (by population) in the world. By the same token, a country can have a very large average income, but have a low total income, because it has small population. Developed countries have relatively high levels of income per capita. The top twenty countries, by this measure, include thirteen European countries, the United States and two other British offshoots (Australia and Canada), and Japan. Two of the remaining three members of this exclusive list, Qatar and United Arab Emirates, are small, oil-rich countries (World Bank).

This problem, unlike those spotlighted in the three critiques we'll discuss below, is easy to solve. Instead of stopping at total GDP, we can calculate a country's GDP per capita. The phrase "per capita" simply means per person. ("Capita" comes from the Latin word meaning "head," so per capita means "per head.") To get GDP per capita, we just divide a country's GDP by its population. This gives us the average GDP for that country, or a measure of the average income. (Other measures of a country's total income, such as Gross National Product or Gross National Income are similar to GDP, so GNP per capita or GNI per capita are similar to GDP per capita.) Income per capita gives us a better picture of the standards of living in a country than total income.

What's Wrong with GDP Per Capita?

Mainstream economists and policymakers have treated increasing GDP per capita as virtually synonymous with development, so it's important to discuss GDP in more detail. Here, we will focus on three major criticisms of GDP per capita as a measure of well-being or "development":

The Distributional Critique

Average income can be misleading. Average (mean) income is one estimate of the "middle" of the distribution of income in a country. Most people, however, do not get the average income. Most get less than the average, some get more (and a few get much, much more). A relatively small number of people with very high incomes can pull the average up by a great deal, making the average less representative of most people's standard of living.

Figure 1, for example, shows the income distribution for Brazil in 2007. The population has been ranked by income, and then divided into five equal parts (or quintiles). Each bar represents the difference between the average income for one of these quintiles and the average income for the country as a whole. The bar furthest to the left represents the difference between the average income of the lowest-income quintile and the overall average. The next bar represents this difference for the next-lowest-income quintile, and so on, all the way up to the bar at the far right, which represents this difference for the highest-income quintile. (The lowest-income quintile is called the "first" quintile, the next-to-lowest is called the "second" quintile, and so on, up to the highest-income, or "fifth," quintile.) The GDP per capita for Brazil in 2007 was about $9800. Notice that

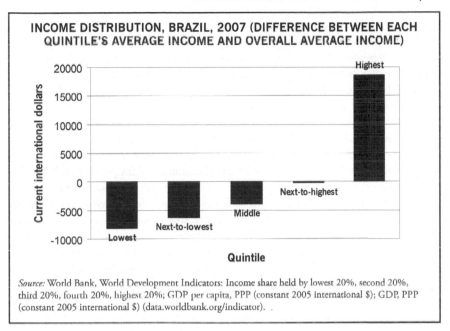

INCOME DISTRIBUTION, BRAZIL, 2007 (DIFFERENCE BETWEEN EACH QUINTILE'S AVERAGE INCOME AND OVERALL AVERAGE INCOME)

Source: World Bank, World Development Indicators: Income share held by lowest 20%, second 20%, third 20%, fourth 20%, highest 20%; GDP per capita, PPP (constant 2005 international $); GDP, PPP (constant 2005 international $) (data.worldbank.org/indicator).

the average income for each of the bottom four quintiles is less than the GDP per capita (or average income) for the society as a whole, as indicated by the bars extending down. The average income for Brazil as a whole is more than six times as much as the average income for the first (lowest-income) quintile, almost three times as much as the average income for the second quintile, and more than one-and-a-half times as much as the average income for the third quintile. Even the average income for the fourth quintile is a little less than the average income for the whole country (so many people in the fourth quintile have incomes below the national average, though some have incomes above it.)

More than two-thirds of Brazil's population, then, have incomes below the country's per capita income—many of them, far below it. The reason GDP per capita for Brazil is so much higher than the incomes of most Brazilians is that the income distribution is so unequal. The average income for the fifth (highest-income) quintile is almost three times the average income for Brazil as a whole.

The Feminist Critique

GDP only counts part of the goods and services produced in a country. Earlier, we said that GDP was "a measure of the total value of goods and services" produced in a country. This is true, but it is a very flawed measure. GDP only includes the value of goods that are produced for sale in markets, ignoring goods and services that people produce for their own consumption, for the consumption of family members, and so on. In developed economies, most individuals or households have money incomes that allow them to buy most of the things they need to live. They also, however, produce goods and services for themselves, family members, and others. For example, people care for and educate their children, cook meals for themselves and other members of their family, clean their own homes, drive themselves and family members to work, school, and errands, and so on. These kinds of goods and services count as part of GDP when someone is paid to do them (for example, when we pay tuition to a school, the bill at a restaurant, the fee to a professional cleaning crew, or the fare to a taxi driver), but not when people do it for themselves, family members, or others free of charge. One could add many other examples, but the first lesson here is that GDP undercounts the total output of goods and services. Since so much of the labor that produces these uncounted goods and services is done by women, feminist economists have been in the forefront of this critique of GDP as a measure of economic development or well-being. (See, Marilyn Waring, *If Women Counted: A New Feminist Economics* (Harper & Row, 1988).)

In some developing economies, the uncounted goods and services may form a larger part of the overall economy than in developed countries. Many people may have small farms and grow their own food. Some people weave their own cloth and make their own clothes. Some people build their own shelters. As economies "develop" economically, they may become more "monetized." This means that people produce fewer goods for their own consumption, for their families, or to trade for other goods (barter), relative to the total amount of goods and services. Instead, they start selling either goods they produce or selling their own labor for money, and buying the things they need. An increase in GDP over time may, in part, reflect an increasing output of goods and services. But it may also reflect, in part, that some goods went uncounted before (because they were not produced for sale in markets) and are now being counted. This means that GDP (or GDP per capita) may exaggerate the growth of economies over time.

The Environmental Critique

GDP does not account for changes in the natural environment. We can think of parts of the natural environment as providing people with valuable "natural services." Until recently, economic measurement has almost completely ignored natural services. Once we start thinking about the environment serieous, it becomes obvious how critical they are for our well-being. A forest, for example, absorbs carbon dioxide from and provides oxygen to the atmosphere, provides flood control, reduces soil erosion, provides habitat for wildlife, offers natural beauty and outdoor recreation, provides some people with sources of food and fuel (especially in lower-income countries), and so on.

If GDP only counts human-produced goods and services, then, it is undercounting the total goods and services. If a forest is cut down for timber, and the wood is sold in a market, this adds to GDP. However, the value of the services the forest provided are not deducted from GDP as conventionally measured, since these are not sold in markets and do not have prices. Cutting down a forest may both add something (harvested wood, which can be used, for example, to build houses or make furniture) and subtract something (natural services) from the well-being of society. There is no way to say, in general, whether what it gained is greater or less than what is lost. However, as long as we think that the services the forest provided were worth *something*, we can say for certain that what GDP measures as being gained is greater than what it is really gained—since GDP only counts what is gained and ignores what is lost.

If Not GDP, then What?

Part of the power of GDP per capita is that it boils everything down to one easy-to-digest number. It is easy to create a table comparing the GDPs of many countries.

(Obviously, it would be harder to compare many countries in more complex ways, including a bunch of descriptive numbers for each.) This is also at the core of the weaknesses of GDP per capita. When we calculate a total or average of anything, we are, in effect, throwing out the information we have about variation between different individuals. This problem is at the heart of the first critique: Calculating total GDP or GDP per capita means excluding information about income distribution. In addition, calculating the total output of goods and services, when a modern economy includes thousands and thousands of different kinds of goods, requires some unit in which we can measure these output of each one. (We can't add together pounds of potatoes and pounds of steel, much less goods and services that can't be measured in pounds at all, like electricity or haircuts.) GDP has accomplished this by measuring everything in terms of monetary units. This leads to the second and third critiques. Monetary measurement has led to a blind spot for goods and services that do not have market prices (household production, environmental services) and are not easy to measure in money terms.

There are three major possibilities. One is to go on calculating GDP per capita, but to do a better job at capturing what GDP misses. For example, some scholars have tried to put a dollar values on non-market production (like subsistence farming or household production) and add these to GDP to get a more accurate estimate.

Another is to come up with an alternative one-number measure to compete with GDP. Two important ones are the genuine progress indicator (GPI) and the human development index (HDI). The GPI incorporates, in addition to market production, measures of both nonmarket production and environmental destruction into a single summary figure (in money terms). It does not address the distributional critique. Calculated by the United Nations Development Programme (UNDP), the HDI combines GDP per capita, average educational attainment, and average life expectancy into a single numerical index. It addresses neither the feminist nor the environmental critique, and it does not explicitly address the distributional critique. However, more equal societies tend to rank better on HDI than on GDP per capita, because they tend to achieve higher average education and life expectancy. (The UNDP also calculates an inequality-adjusted HDI, which explicitly penalizes inequality.)

Finally, a third approach is to abandon the quest for a single summary measurement. Some environmental economists oppose attempts to incorporate environmental changes into GDP or other monetary measures, which requires reducing environmental services to money values. This implies, they argue, that some quantity of produced goods can substitute for any environmental good, which is not true. They propose instead "satellite accounts" that measure environmental changes alongside GDP. Widely used measures of income inequality also exist, and can enhance our picture of an economy. Measurements of median income, access to basic goods (like health and education), economic inequality, nonmarket production, environmental quality, and other factors all should figure, in some way, into our understanding of economic life. We may just have to accept that we need to take into account multiple measures, and that no single-number "bottom line" will do. ❑

Article 2.5

WAGES FOR HOUSEWORK
The Movement and the Numbers

BY LENA GRABER AND JOHN MILLER
July/August 2002

The International Wages for Housework Campaign (WFH), a network of women in Third World and industrialized countries, began organizing in the early 1970s. WFH's demands are ambitious—"for the unwaged work that women do to be recognized as work in official government statistics, and for this work to be paid."

Housewives paid wages? By the government? That may seem outlandish to some, but consider the staggering amount of unpaid work carried out by women. In 1990, the International Labor Organization (ILO) estimated that women do two-thirds of the world's work for 5% of the income. In 1995, the UN Development Programme's (UNDP) Human Development Report announced that women's unpaid and underpaid labor was worth $11 trillion worldwide, and $1.4 trillion in the United States alone. Paying women the wages they "are owed" for unwaged work, as WFN puts it, would go a long way toward undoing these inequities and reducing women's economic dependence on men.

Publicizing information like this, WFH—whose International Women Count Network now includes more than 2,000 non-governmental organizations (NGOs) from the North and South—and other groups have been remarkably successful in persuading governments to count unwaged work. In 1995, the UN Fourth World Conference on Women, held in Beijing, developed a Platform for Action that called on governments to calculate the value of women's unpaid work and include it in conventional measures of national output, such as Gross Domestic Product (GDP).

So far, only Trinidad & Tobago and Spain have passed legislation mandating the new accounting, but other countries—including numerous European countries, Australia, Canada, Japan, and New Zealand in the industrialized world, and Bangladesh, the Dominican Republic, India, Nepal, Tanzania, and Venezuela in the developing world—have undertaken extensive surveys to determine how much time is spent on unpaid household work.

The Value of Housework

Producing credible numbers for the value of women's work in the home is no easy task. Calculating how many hours women spend performing housework—from cleaning to childcare to cooking to shopping—is just the first step. The hours are considerable in both developing and industrialized economies. (See Table 1.)

What value to place on that work, and what would constitute fair remuneration—or wages for housework—is even more difficult to assess. Feminist economists dedicated to making the value of housework visible have taken different approaches to answering the question. One approach, favored by the UN's International Research and Training Institute for the Advancement of Women (INSTRAW), bases the market value of work done at home on the price of market goods and services that are similar to those produced in the home (such as meals served in restaurants or cleaning done by professional firms). These output-based evaluations estimate that counting unpaid household production would add 30-60% to the GDP of industrialized countries, and far more for developing countries. (See Table 2.)

A second approach evaluates the inputs of household production—principally the labor that goes into cooking, cleaning, childcare, and other services performed in the home, overwhelmingly by women. Advocates of this approach use one of three methods. Some base their calculations on what economists call opportunity cost—the wages women might have earned if they had worked a similar number of hours in the market economy. Others ask what it would cost to hire someone to do the work—either a general laborer such as a domestic servant (the generalist-replacement method) or a specialist such as a chef (the specialist-replacement method)—and then assign those wages to household labor. Ann Chadeau, a researcher with the Organization for Economic Cooperation and Development, has found the specialist-replacement method to be "the most plausible and at the same time feasible approach" for valuing unpaid household labor.

These techniques produce quite different results, all of which are substantial in relation to GDP. With that in mind, let's look at how some countries calculated the monetary value of unpaid work.

Unpaid Work in Canada, Great Britain, and Japan

In Canada, a government survey documented the time men and women spent on unpaid work in 1992. Canadian women performed 65% of all unpaid work, shouldering an especially large share of household labor devoted to preparing meals, maintaining clothing, and caring for children. (Men's unpaid hours exceeded women's only for outdoor cleaning.)

TABLE 1:
WOMEN'S TIME SPENT PER DAY PERFORMING HOUSEHOLD LABOR, BY ACTIVITY, IN HOURS:MINUTES

	Childcare Time	Cleaning Time	Food Prep Time	Shopping Time	Water/Fuel Collection	Total Time[a]
Australia (1997[b])	2:27	1:17	1:29	0:58	n.a.	3:39
Japan (1999)	0:24	2:37	n.a.	0:33	n.a.	3:34
Norway (2000)	0:42	1:16	0:49	0:26	0:01	3:56
U.K. (2000)	1:26	1:35	1:08	0:33	n.a.	4:55
Nepal (1996)	1:28	2:00	5:30	0:13	1:10	11:58

Note: Some activities, especially child care, may overlap with other tasks

[a] Totals may include activities other than those listed.

[b] Only some percentage of the population recorded doing these activities. Averages are for that portion of the population. Generally, figures represent a greater number of women than men involved.

Sources: Australia: <www.abs.gov.au/ausstats>; Japan: <www.unescap.org/stat>; Norway: <www.ssb.no/tidsbruk_en>; United Kingdom: <www.statistics.gov.uk/themes/social_finances/TimeUseSurvey>; Nepal: INSTRAW, *Valuation of Household Production and the Satellite Accounts* (Santo Domingo: 1996), 34-35; <www.cbs.nl/isi/iass>.

The value of unpaid labor varied substantially, depending on the method used to estimate its appropriate wage. (See Table 3.) The opportunity-cost method, which uses the average market wage (weighted for the greater proportion of unpaid work done by women), assigned the highest value to unpaid labor, 54.2% of Canadian GDP. The two replacement methods produced lower estimates, because the wages they assigned fell below those of other jobs. The specialist-replacement method, which paired unpaid activities with the average wages of corresponding occupations—such as cooking with junior chefs, and childcare with kindergarten teachers—put the value of Canadian unpaid labor at 43% of GDP. The generalist-replacement method, by assigning the wages of household servants to unpaid labor, produced the lowest estimate of the value of unpaid work: 34% of Canadian GDP. INSTRAW's output-based measure, which matched hours of unpaid labor to a household's average expenditures on the same activities, calculated the value of Canada's unpaid work as 47.4% of GDP.

In Great Britain, where unpaid labor hours are high for an industrialized country (see Table 1), the value of unpaid labor was far greater relative to GDP. The British Office for National Statistics found that, when valued using the opportunity cost method, unpaid work was 112% of Britain's GDP in 1995! With the specialist-replacement method, British unpaid labor was still 56% of GDP—greater than the output of the United Kingdom's entire manufacturing sector for the year.

In Japan—where unpaid labor hours are more limited (see Table 1), paid workers put in longer hours, and women perform over 80% of unpaid work—the value of unpaid labor is significantly smaller relative to GDP. The Japanese Economic

TABLE 2: VALUE OF UNPAID HOUSEHOLD LABOR AS % OF GDP, USING OUTPUT-BASED EVALUATION METHOD

Country	% of GDP
Canada (1992)	47.4%
Finland (1990)	49.1%
Nepal (1991)	170.7%

Source: INSTRAW, *Valuation of Household Production and the Satellite Accounts* (Santo Domingo, 1996), 62, 229.

TABLE 3: VALUE OF UNPAID HOUSEHOLD LABOR IN CANADA AS % OF GDP, 1992

Evaluation Method	% of GDP
Opportunity Cost (before taxes)	54.2 %
Specialist-Replacement	43.0%
Generalist-Replacement	34.0%
Output-Based	47.4%

Source: INSTRAW, *Valuation of Household Production and the Satellite Accounts* (Santo Domingo: 1996), 229.

Planning Agency calculated that counting unpaid work in 1996 would add between 15.2% (generalist-replacement method) and 23% (opportunity-cost method) to GDP. Even at those levels, the value of unpaid labor still equaled at least half of Japanese women's market wages.

Housework Not Bombs

While estimates vary by country and evaluation method, all of these calculations make clear that recognizing the value of unpaid household labor profoundly alters our perception of economic activity and women's contributions to production. "Had household production been included in the system of macro-economic accounts," notes Ann Chadeau, "governments may well have implemented quite different economic and social policies."

For example, according to the UNDP, "The inescapable implication [of recognizing women's unpaid labor] is that the fruits of society's total labor should be shared more equally." For the UNDP, this would mean radically altering property and inheritance rights; access to credit; entitlement to social security benefits, tax incentives, and child care; and terms of divorce settlements.

For WFH advocates, the implications are inescapable as well: women's unpaid labor should be paid—and "the money," WFH insists, "must come first of all from military spending."

Here in the United States, an unneeded and dangerous military buildup begun [in 2002] has already pushed up military spending from 3% to 4% of GDP. Devoting just the additional 1% of GDP gobbled up by the military budget to wages for housework—far from being outlandish—would be an important first step toward fairly remunerating women who perform necessary and life-sustaining household work. ❏

Sources: Ann Chadeau, "What is Households' Non-Market Production Worth?" *OECD Economic Studies* No. 18 (Spring 1992); Economic Planning Unit, Department of National Accounts, Japan, "Monetary Valuation of Unpaid Work in 1996" <unstats.un.org/unsd/methods/timeuse/tusresource_papers/japanunpaid.htm>; INSTRAW, *Measurement and Valuation of Unpaid Contribution: Accounting Through Time and Output* (Santo Domingo: 1995); INSTRAW, *Valuation of Household Production and the Satellite Accounts* (Santo Domingo: 1996); Office of National Statistics, United Kingdom, "A Household Satellite Account for the UK," by Linda Murgatroyd and Henry Neuberger, *Economic Trends* (October 1997) <www.statistics.gov.uk/hhsa/hhsa/Index.html>; Hilkka Pietilä, "The Triangle of the Human Ecology: Household-Cultivation-Industrial Production," *Ecological Economics Journal* 20 (1997); UN Development Programme, Human Development Report (New York: Oxford University Press, 1995).

Article 2.6

MEASURING ECONOMIC DEVELOPMENT
The "Human Development" Approach

BY ALEJANDRO REUSS
April 2012

Some development economists have proposed abandoning GDP per capita, the dominant single-number measure of economic development, in favor of the "human development" approach—which focuses less on changes in average income and more on widespread access to basic goods.

Advocates of this approach to the measurement of development, notably Nobel Prize-winning economist Amartya Sen, aim to focus attention directly on the *ends* (goals) of economic development. Higher incomes, Sen notes, are *means* people use to get the things that they want. The human development approach shifts the focus away from the means and toward ends like a long life, good health, freedom from hunger, the opportunity to get an education, and the ability to take part in community and civic life. Sen has argued that these basic "capabilities" or "freedoms"—the kinds of things almost everyone wants no matter what their goals in life may be—are the highest development priorities and should, therefore, be the primary focus of our development measures.

If a rising average income guaranteed that everyone, or almost everyone, in a society would be better able to reach these goals, we might as well use average income (GDP per capita) to measure development. Increases in GDP per capita, however, do not always deliver longer life, better health, more education, or other basic capabilities to most people In particular, if these income increases go primarily to those who are already better-off (and already enjoy a long life-expectancy, good health, access to education, and so on), they probably will not have much effect on people's access to basic capabilities.

Sen and others have shown that, in "developing" countries, increased average income by itself is not associated with higher life expectancy or better health. In countries where average income was increasing, but public spending on food security, health care, education, and similar programs did not increase along with it, they have found, the increase in average income did not appear to improve access to basic capabilities. If spending on these "public supports" increased, on the other hand, access to basic capabilities tended to improve, whether average income was increasing or not. Sen emphasizes two main lessons based on these observations: 1) A country cannot count on economic growth alone to improve access to basic capabilities. Increased average income appears to deliver "human development" largely by *increasing the wealth a society has available for public supports*, and not in other ways. 2) A country does not have to prioritize economic growth—*does not have to "wait" until it grows richer*—to make basic capabilities like long life, good health, and a decent education available to all.

The Human Development Index (HDI)

The "human development" approach has led to a series of annual reports from the United Nations Development Programme (UNDP) ranking countries according to a "human development index" (HDI). The HDI includes measures of three things: 1) health, measured by average life expectancy, 2) education, measured by average years of schooling and expected years of schooling, and 3) income, measured by GDP per capita. The three categories are then combined, each counting equally, into a single index. The HDI has become the most influential alternative to GDP per capita as a single-number development measure.

Looking at the HDI rankings, many of the results are not surprising. The HDI top 20 is dominated by very high-income countries, including thirteen Western European countries, four "offshoots" of Great Britain (Australia, Canada, New Zealand, and the United States), and two high-income East Asian countries (Japan and South Korea). Most of the next 20 or so are Western or Eastern European, plus a few small oil-rich states in the Middle East. The next 50 or so include most of Latin America and the Caribbean, much of the Middle East, and a good deal of Eastern Europe (including Russia and several former Soviet republics). The next 50 or so are a mix of Latin American, Middle Eastern, South and Southeast Asian, and African countries. The world's poorest continent, Africa, accounts for almost all of the last 30, including the bottom 24.

TABLE 1: HDI RANKS COMPARED TO INCOME-PER-CAPITA RANKS (2010)

Highest HDI ranks compared to income per capita ranks (difference in parentheses)*	Lowest HDI ranks compared to income per capita ranks (difference in parentheses)
New Zealand (+30)	Equatorial Guinea (-78)
Georgia (+26)	Angola (-47)
Tonga (+23)	Kuwait (-42)
Tajikistan (+22)	Botswana (-38)
Madagascar (+22)	South Africa (-37)
Togo (+22)	Qatar (-36)
Fiji (+22)	Brunei (-30)
Ireland (+20)	Gabon (-29)
Iceland (+20)	United Arab Emirates (-28)
Ukraine (+20)	Turkey (-26)

* The numbers in parentheses represent a country's GDP-per-capita rank minus its HDI rank. Remember that in a ranking system, a "higher" (better) rank is indicated by a lower number. If a country is ranked, say, 50th in GDP per capita and 20th in HDI, its number would be 50 – 20 = +30. The positive number indicates that the country had a "higher" HDI rank than GDP per capita rank. If a country is ranked, say, 10th in GDP per capita and 35th in HDI, its number would be 10 – 35 = -25. The negative number indicates that the country had a "lower" HDI rank than GDP per capita rank.

Source: United Nations Development Programme, Indices, Getting and using data, 2010 Report—Table 1. Human Development Index and Its components (hdr.undp.org/en/statistics/data/).

It is not surprising that higher GDP per capita is associated with a higher HDI score. After all, GDP per capita counts for one third of the HDI score itself. The relationship between the two, however, is not perfect. Some countries have a higher HDI rank than GDP per capita rank. These countries are "over-performing," getting more human development from their incomes, compared to other countries. Meanwhile, some countries have a lower HDI rank than GDP per capita rank. These countries are "under-performing," not getting as much human development from their incomes, compared to other countries. The list of top "over-performing" countries includes three very high-income countries that had still higher HDI ranks (Iceland, Ireland, and New Zealand), three former Soviet republics (Georgia, Tajikistan, and Ukraine), two small South Pacific island nations (Fiji, Togo), and two African countries (Madagascar, Tonga). The list of top "under-performing" countries includes four small oil-rich countries (Brunei, Kuwait, Qatar, and United Arab Emirates) and five African countries (Angola, Botswana, Equatorial Guinea, Gabon, and South Africa).

The UNDP also calculates an inequality-adjusted HDI. Note that, for all the measures included in the HDI, there is inequality within countries. The inequality-adjusted HDI is calculated so that, the greater the inequality for any measure included in the HDI (for health, education, or income), the lower the country's score. Since all countries have some inequality, the inequality-adjusted HDI for any country is always lower than the regular HDI. However, the scores for countries with greater inequality drop more than for those with less inequality. That pushes some countries up in the rankings, when inequality is penalized, and others down. Among the thirteen countries moving up the most, five are

TABLE 2: INEQUALITY-ADJUSTED HDI RANKS
COMPARED TO UNADJUSTED HDI RANKS

Highest inequality-adjusted HDI ranks compared to unadjusted HDI ranks (difference in parentheses)	Lowest inequality-adjusted HDI ranks compared to unadjusted HDI ranks (difference in parentheses)
Uzbekistan (+17)	Peru (-26)
Mongolia (+16)	Panama (-20)
Moldova (+16)	Colombia (-18)
Kyrgystan (+15)	South Korea (-18)
Maldives (+14)	Bolivia (-17)
Ukraine (+14)	Belize (-16)
Philippines (+11)	Brazil (-15)
Sri Lanka (+11)	Namibia (-15)
Tanzania, Viet Nam, Indonesia,Jamaica, Belarus (+9)	El Salvador (-14)
	Turkmenistan (-12)

Source: United Nations Development Programme, 2010 Report, Table 3: Inequality-adjusted Human Development Index (hdr. undp.org/en/media/HDR_2010_EN_Table3_reprint.pdf).

former Soviet republics. Among the ten moving down the most, seven are Latin American countries. The United States narrowly misses the list of those moving down the most, with its rank dropping by nine places when inequality is taken into account.

GDP Per Capita and HDI

The relationship between income per capita and the HDI is shown in the "scatterplot" graph below. (Instead of GDP per capita, the graph uses a closely related measure called Gross National Income (GNI) per capita.) Each point represents a country, with its income per capita represented on the horizontal scale and its HDI score represented on the vertical scale. The further to the right a point is, the higher the country's per capita income. The higher up a point is, the higher the country's HDI score. As we can see, the cloud of points forms a curve, rising up as income per capita increases from a very low level, and then flattening out. This means that a change in GDP per capita from a very low level to a moderate level of around $8000

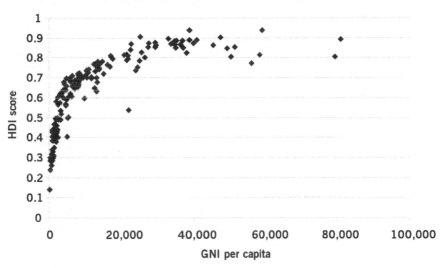

RELATIONSHIP BETWEEN HDI AND INCOME PER CAPITA (2010)

Source: United Nations Development Programme, Indices, 2010 Report - Table 1 Human Development Index and its components (hdr.undp.org/en/statistics/data/).

per year is associated with large gains in human development. Above that, we see, the curve flattens out dramatically. A change in income per capita from this moderate level to a high level of around $25,000 is associated with smaller gains in human development. Further increases in income per capita are associated with little or no gain in human development.

This relationship suggests two major conclusions, both related to greater economic equality.

First, achieving greater equality in incomes between countries, including by redistributing income from high-income countries to low-income countries, could result in increased human development. Over the highest per capita income range, from about $25,000 on up, increases in income are not associated with higher human development. Decreases in income above this threshold, by the same token, need not mean lower human development. On the other hand, over the lowest income range, below $8000, increases in income are associated with dramatic gains in HDI (largely due to increased public supports). Therefore, the redistribution of incomes from high-income countries to low-income countries could increase human development in the latter a great deal, while not diminishing human development in the former by very much (if at all)—resulting in a net gain in human development.

Second, high-income countries might make greater gains in HDI, as their incomes continued to increase, if a larger share of income went to low-income people or to public supports. Part of the reason that the relationship between per capita income and HDI flattens out at high income levels may be that there are inherent limits to variables like life expectancy (perhaps 90-100 years) or educational attainment (perhaps 20 years). These "saturation" levels, however, have clearly not been reached by all individuals, even in very high-income countries. In the United States, as of 2008, the infant mortality rate for African-Americans was more than double that for whites. The life expectancy at birth for white females was more than three years greater than that of African-American females; for white males, more than five years greater than for African-American males. As of 2010, over 40% of individuals over 25 years old have no education above high school. Over 60% have no degree from a two- or four-year college. It is little wonder that higher income would not bring about greatly increased human development, considering that, over the last 30 years, many public supports have faced sustained attack and most income growth has gone to people already at the top. ❑

Sources: Amartya Sen, *Development as Freedom* (New York: Oxford University Press, 1999); United Nations Development Programme, Indices, Getting and using data, *2010 Report*, Table 1 Human Development Index and its components (hdr.undp.org/en/statistics/data/); United Nations Development Programme, *2010 Report*, Table 3: Inequality-adjusted Human Development Index (hdr.undp.org/en/media/HDR_2010_EN_Table3_reprint.pdf); U.S. Census Bureau, The 2012 Statistical Abstract, Births, Deaths, Marriages, & Divorces: Life Expectancy, Table 107. Expectation of Life and Expected Deaths by Race, Sex, and Age: 2008; Educational Attainment, Population 25 Years and Over, U.S. Census Bureau, Selected Social Characteristics in the United States, 2010 American Community Survey, 1-Year Estimates.

Chapter 3

WEALTH, INEQUALITY, AND POVERTY

INTRODUCTION

Wealth and inequality are both end products of today's patterns of economic growth. But while all macroeconomics textbooks investigate wealth accumulation, most give less attention to wealth disparities. The authors in this chapter fill in the gap by looking at who makes out, and who doesn't, in the accumulation of wealth.

Economist Chris Tilly debunks the myth that today's inequality is inevitable or (as many mainstream economists would have it) actually desirable (Article 3.1). He argues that rampant inequality is not necessary for economic growth, showing that among both developing and industrial economies and across individual countries' distinct regions, there is no correlation between higher inequality and faster economic growth. He argues that greater equality actually supports economic growth by bolstering spending, promoting agricultural and industrial productivity, and reducing social conflict.

What is more, the blow of increased inequality of economic outcomes has not been softened by equality of opportunity (Article 3.2). As economist Paul Krugman reports, it is not just left-wing critics who argue that social mobility is on the wane, but the business press as well. The number of people who go from rags to riches (the so-called "Horatio Alger" story)—while always so small as to be near-mythical—has decreased since 1980 as inequality has increased.

And as economist Arthur MacEwan points out, the income share of the richest 1% rose when the share of workers who were union members fell. To MacEwan it seems clear that restoring union size and strength would go a long way toward reducing inequality (Article 3.3).

In the next article, "Black-White Income Differences: What's Happened?" (Article 3.4), MacEwan observes that the income gap between African Americans and whites has hardly budged since 1970. This seeming lack of change, moreover, masks an increase in income inequality among African Americans—with a small number of success stories at the top hiding a worsening of the fortunes of low-income African Americans.

Alejandro Reuss reflects on the attention drawn to economic inequality by the Occupy Wall Street movement and it's language describing society as divided between the 1% (the richest members of society) and the 99% (everyone else). Reuss argues that we should go one step further, recognizing a sharp divide based on how people derive their incomes—from work or from property— and the resulting conflict (or "class struggle") between these two groups (Article 3.5).

What has happened to world income inequality is another matter of intense debate. Many analysts claim that globally, incomes have converged, leading to a sharp reduction in world inequality in the second half of the twentieth century. Many others report that the gaps between the poorest and the richest people and between countries have continued to widen over the last two decades. In a *Dollars & Sense* interview, economist Bob Sutcliffe reports that the best recent scholarship "casts doubt on the idea that world inequality has sharply and unambiguously declined or increased during the epoch of neoliberalism" (Article 3.6). Meanwhile, Robin Broad and John Cavanagh report on shifts in the global composition of the super-wealthy, as more people from the Asia-Pacific region, Brazil, Russia, India, and China move into the ranks of the billionaires (Article 3.7).

Lastly, John Miller lays out the reasons that inequality causes slow economic growth (entering into debate with those who claim that the recent increase in inequality is the result—rather than the cause—of slow growth) (Article 3.8).

Discussion Questions

1. (General) The authors in this chapter believe that income and wealth distribution is as important as income and wealth creation, and consider greater economic equality an important macroeconomic goal. What are some arguments for and against this position? Where do you come down in the debate?

2. (General) "A rising tide lifts all boats," proclaimed John F. Kennedy as he lobbied for pro-business tax cuts in the early 1960s. Have recent periods of economic growth (or "booms") lifted all boats? How have stockholders fared versus wage earners? How has the distribution of income and wealth by income group and by race changed?

3. (Article 3.1) Why do conservatives argue that inequality is good for economic growth? What counterarguments does Tilly use to challenge this traditional view of the "tradeoff" between inequality and growth? What evidence convinces Tilly that equality is good for economic growth? Does that evidence convince you?

4. (Article 3.2) What evidence does Krugman present to argue that social mobility is declining? Would greater inequality of outcomes be acceptable or desirable if there were greater social mobility—if people were not "stuck" in the income group where they started out? Why or why not?

5. (Article 3.3) MacEwan shows that union strength and economic inequality are negatively associated (when one is high, the other is low). What possible explanations does MacEwan offer? Is there good reason to believe that higher unionization was the cause of greater equality in the past, and the decline of unions explains increased inequality in recent years?

6. (Article 3.4) MacEwan notes some spectacular African American "success stories" and, more broadly, an increase in opportunities for African American professionals. Nonetheless, the black-white income gap has hardly budged. Why not? What factors does he blame for worsening the fortunes of many African Americans?

7. (Article 3.5) How does Reuss define "class" in this article? How does the shifting balance of power between classes, in his view, help explain the increase in inequality in recent years? Why does he argue that the economic classes he describes are in a struggle "whether they like it or not"?

8. (Article 3.6) If world inequality has neither declined nor increased sharply during the epoch of neoliberalism, as Sutcliffe argues, what does this suggest about the convergence hypothesis—the idea that per-capita income in countries with similar institutional structures will converge to the higher level?

9. (Article 3.7) Broad and Cavanagh write that the "deregulatory climate of these past two decades sped the rise of the super-rich" around the globe. What is the connection between deregulation and the accumulation or concentration of wealth?

10. (Article 3.8) How does Miller explain the link between inequality and slow growth? How have changes in tax policy affected the distribution of income?

Article 3.1

GEESE, GOLDEN EGGS, AND TRAPS

Why inequality is bad for the economy.

BY CHRIS TILLY
July/August 2004

Whenever progressives propose ways to redistribute wealth from the rich to those with low and moderate incomes, conservative politicians and economists accuse them of trying to kill the goose that lays the golden egg. The advocates of unfettered capitalism proclaim that inequality is good for the economy because it promotes economic growth. Unequal incomes, they say, provide the incentives necessary to guide productive economic decisions by businesses and individuals. Try to reduce inequality, and you'll sap growth. Furthermore, the conservatives argue, growth actually promotes equality by boosting the have-nots more than the haves. So instead of fiddling with who gets how much, the best way to help those at the bottom is to pump up growth.

But these conservative prescriptions are absolutely, dangerously wrong. Instead of the goose-killer, equality turns out to be the goose. Inequality stifles growth; equality gooses it up. Moreover, economic expansion does not necessarily promote equality—instead, it is the types of jobs and the rules of the economic game that matter most.

Inequality: Goose or Goose-Killer?

The conservative argument may be wrong, but it's straightforward. Inequality is good for the economy, conservatives say, because it provides the right incentives for innovation and economic growth. First of all, people will only have the motivation to work hard, innovate, and invest wisely if the economic system rewards them for good economic choices and penalizes bad ones. Robin Hood-style policies that collect from the wealthy and help those who are worse off violate this principle. They reduce the payoff to smart decisions and lessen the sting of dumb ones. The result: people and companies are bound to make less efficient decisions. "We must allow [individuals] to fail, as well as succeed, and we must replace the nanny state with a regime of self-reliance and self-respect," writes conservative lawyer Stephen Kinsella in *The Freeman: Ideas on Liberty* (not clear how the free woman fits in). To prove their point, conservatives point to the former state socialist countries, whose economies had become stagnant and inefficient by the time they fell at the end of the 1980s.

If you don't buy this incentive story, there's always the well-worn trickle-down theory. To grow, the economy needs productive investments: new offices, factories, computers, and machines. To finance such investments takes a pool of savings. The rich save a larger fraction of their incomes than those less well-off. So to spur growth, give more to the well-heeled (or at least take less away from them in the form of taxes), and give less to the down-and-out. The rich will save their money and then invest it, promoting growth that's good for everyone.

Unfortunately for trickle-down, the brilliant economist John Maynard Keynes debunked the theory in his *General Theory of Employment, Interest, and Money* in 1936. Keynes, whose precepts guided liberal U.S. economic policy from the 1940s through the 1970s, agreed that investments must be financed out of savings. But he showed that most often it's changes in investment that drive savings, rather than the other way around. When businesses are optimistic about the future and invest in building and retooling, the economy booms, all of us make more money, and we put some of it in banks, 401(k)s, stocks, and so on. That is, saving grows to match investment. When companies are glum, the process runs in reverse, and savings shrink to equal investment. This leads to the "paradox of thrift": if people try to save too much, businesses will see less consumer spending, will invest less, and total savings will end up diminishing rather than growing as the economy spirals downward. A number of Keynes's followers added the next logical step: shifting money from the high-saving rich to the high-spending rest of us, and not the other way around, will spur investment and growth.

Of the two conservative arguments in favor of inequality, the incentive argument is a little weightier. Keynes himself agreed that people needed financial consequences to steer their actions, but questioned whether the differences in payoffs needed to be so huge. Certainly state socialist countries' attempts to replace material incentives with moral exhortation have often fallen short. In 1970, the Cuban government launched the Gran Zafra (Great Harvest), an attempt to reap 10 million tons of sugar cane with (strongly encouraged) volunteer labor. Originally inspired by Che Guevara's ideal of the New Socialist Man (not clear how the New Socialist Woman fit in), the effort ended with Fidel Castro tearfully apologizing to the Cuban people in a nationally broadcast speech for letting wishful thinking guide economic policy.

But before conceding this point to the conservatives, let's look at the evidence about the connection between equality and growth. Economists William Easterly of New York University and Gary Fields of Cornell University have recently summarized this evidence:

- Countries, and regions within countries, with more equal incomes grow faster. (These growth figures do not include environmental destruction or improvement. If they knocked off points for environmental destruction and added points for environmental improvement, the correlation between equality and growth would be even stronger, since desperation drives poor people to adopt environmentally destructive practices such as rapid deforestation.)
- Countries with more equally distributed land grow faster.
- Somewhat disturbingly, more ethnically homogeneous countries and regions grow faster—presumably because there are fewer ethnically based inequalities.
- In addition, more worker rights are associated with higher rates of economic growth, according to Josh Bivens and Christian Weller, economists at two Washington think tanks, the Economic Policy Institute and the Center for American Progress.

These patterns recommend a second look at the incentive question. In fact, more equality can actually strengthen incentives and opportunities to produce.

Equality as the Goose

Equality can boost growth in several ways. Perhaps the simplest is that study after study has shown that farmland is more productive when cultivated in small plots. So organizations promoting more equal distribution of land, like Brazil's Landless Workers' Movement, are not just helping the landless poor—they're contributing to agricultural productivity!

Another reason for the link between equality and growth is what Easterly calls "match effects," which have been highlighted in research by Stanford's Paul Roemer and others in recent years. One example of a match effect is the fact that well-educated people are most productive when working with others who have lots of schooling. Likewise, people working with computers are more productive when many others have computers (so that, for example, e-mail communication is widespread, and know-how about computer repair and software is easy to come by). In very unequal societies, highly educated, computer-using elites are surrounded by majorities with little education and no computer access, dragging down their productivity. This decreases young people's incentive to get more education and businesses' incentive to invest in computers, since the payoff will be smaller.

Match effects can even matter at the level of a metropolitan area. Urban economist Larry Ledebur looked at income and employment growth in 85 U.S. cities and their neighboring suburbs. He found that where the income gap between those in the suburbs and those in the city was largest, income and job growth was slower for everyone.

"Pressure effects" also help explain why equality sparks growth. Policies that close off the low-road strategy of exploiting poor and working people create pressure effects, driving economic elites to search for investment opportunities that pay off by boosting productivity rather than squeezing the have-nots harder. For example, where workers have more rights, they will place greater demands on businesses. Business owners will respond by trying to increase productivity, both to remain profitable even after paying higher wages, and to find ways to produce with fewer workers. The CIO union drives in U.S. mass production industries in the 1930s and 1940s provide much of the explanation for the superb productivity growth of the 1950s and 1960s. (The absence of pressure effects may help explain why many past and present state socialist countries have seen slow growth, since they tend to offer numerous protections for workers but no right to organize independent unions.) Similarly, if a government buys out large land-holdings in order to break them up, wealthy families who simply kept their fortunes tied up in land for generations will look for new, productive investments. Industrialization in Asian "tigers" South Korea and Taiwan took off in the 1950s on the wings of funds freed up in exactly this way.

Inequality, Conflict, and Growth

Inequality hinders growth in another important way: it fuels social conflict. Stark inequality in countries such as Bolivia and Haiti has led to chronic conflict that hobbles economic growth. Moreover, inequality ties up resources in unproductive uses such as paying for large numbers of police and security guards—attempts to prevent individuals from redistributing resources through theft.

Ethnic variety is connected to slower growth because,on the average, more ethnically diverse countries are also more likely to be ethnically divided. In other words, the problem isn't ethnic variety itself, but racism and ethnic conflict that can exist among diverse populations. In nations like Guatemala, Congo, and Nigeria, ethnic strife has crippled growth—a problem alien to ethnically uniform Japan and South Korea. The reasons are similar to some of the reasons that large class divides hurt growth. Where ethnic divisions (which can take tribal, language, religious, racial, or regional forms) loom large, dominant ethnic groups seek to use government power to better themselves at the expense of other groups, rather than making broad-based investments in education and infrastructure. This can involve keeping down the underdogs—slower growth in the U.S. South for much of the country's history was linked to the Southern system of white supremacy. Or it can involve seizing the surplus of ethnic groups perceived as better off—in the extreme, Nazi Germany's expropriation and genocide of the Jews, who often held professional and commercial jobs.

Of course, the solution to such divisions is not "ethnic cleansing" so that each country has only one ethnic group—in addition to being morally abhorrent, this is simply impossible in a world with 191 countries and 5,000 ethnic groups. Rather, the solution is to diminish ethnic inequalities. Once the 1964 Civil Rights Act forced the South to drop racist laws, the New South's economic growth spurt began. Easterly reports that in countries with strong rule of law, professional bureaucracies, protection of contracts, and freedom from expropriation—all rules that make it harder for one ethnic group to economically oppress another—ethnic diversity has no negative impact on growth.

If more equality leads to faster growth so everybody benefits, why do the rich typically resist redistribution? Looking at the ways that equity seeds growth helps us understand why. The importance of pressure effects tells us that the wealthy often don't think about more productive ways to invest or reorganize their businesses until they are forced to. But also, if a country becomes very unequal, it can get stuck in an "inequality trap." Any redistribution involves a tradeoff for the rich. They lose by giving up part of their wealth, but they gain a share in increased economic growth. The bigger the disparity between the rich and the rest, the more the rich have to lose, and the less likely that the equal share of boosted growth they'll get will make up for their loss. Once the gap goes beyond a certain point, the wealthy have a strong incentive to restrict democracy, and to block spending on education which might lead the poor to challenge economic injustice—making reform that much harder.

Does Economic Growth Reduce Inequality?

If inequality isn't actually good for the economy, what about the second part of the conservatives' argument—that growth itself promotes equality? According to the conservatives, those who care about equality should simply pursue growth and wait for equality to follow.

"A rising tide lifts all boats," President John F. Kennedy famously declared. But he said nothing about which boats will rise fastest when the economic tide comes in. Growth does typically reduce poverty, according to studies reviewed by economist Gary Fields, though some "boats"—especially families with strong barriers to participating in the labor force—stay "stuck in the mud." But inequality can increase at the same time that poverty falls, if the rich gain even faster than the poor do. True, sustained periods of low unemployment, like that in the late 1990s United States, do tend to raise wages at the bottom even faster than salaries at the top. But growth after the recessions of 1991 and 2001 began with years of "jobless recoveries"— growth with inequality.

For decades the prevailing view about growth and inequality within countries was that expressed by Simon Kuznets in his 1955 presidential address to the American Economic Association. Kuznets argued that as countries grew, inequality would first increase, then decrease. The reason is that people will gradually move from the low-income agricultural sector to higher-income industrial jobs—with inequality peaking when the workforce is equally divided between low- and high-income sectors. For mature industrial economies, Kuznets's proposition counsels focusing on growth, assuming that it will bring equity. In developing countries, it calls for enduring current inequality for the sake of future equity and prosperity.

But economic growth doesn't automatically fuel equality. In 1998, economists Klaus Deininger and Lyn Squire traced inequality and growth over time in 48 countries. Five followed the Kuznets pattern, four followed the reverse pattern (decreasing inequality followed by an increase), and the rest showed no systematic pattern. In the United States, for example:

- incomes became more equal during the 1930s through 1940s New Deal period (a time that included economic decline followed by growth);
- from the 1950s through the 1970s, income gaps lessened during booms and expanded during slumps;
- from the late 1970s forward, income inequality worsened fairly consistently, whether the economy was stagnating or growing.

The reasons are not hard to guess. The New Deal introduced widespread unionization, a minimum wage, social security, unemployment insurance, and welfare. Since the late 1970s, unions have declined, the inflation-adjusted value of the minimum wage has fallen, and the social safety net has been shredded. In the United States, as elsewhere, growth only promotes equality if policies and institutions to support equity are in place.

Trapped?

Let's revisit the idea of an inequality trap. The notion is that as the gap between the rich and everybody else grows wider, the wealthy become more willing to give up overall growth in return for the larger share they're getting for themselves. The "haves" back policies to control the "have-nots," instead of devoting social resources to educating the poor so they'll be more productive.

Sound familiar? It should. After two decades of widening inequality, the last few years have brought us massive tax cuts that primarily benefit the wealthiest, at the expense of investment in infrastructure and the education, child care, and income supports that would help raise less well-off kids to be productive adults. Federal and state governments have cranked up expenditures on prisons, police, and "homeland security," and Republican campaign organizations have devoted major resources to keeping blacks and the poor away from the polls. If the economic patterns of the past are any indication, we're going to pay for these policies in slower growth and stagnation unless we can find our way out of this inequality trap. ❑

Article 3.2

THE DEATH OF HORATIO ALGER

BY PAUL KRUGMAN
January 2004; The Nation

The other day I found myself reading a leftist rag that made outrageous claims about America. It said that we are becoming a society in which the poor tend to stay poor, no matter how hard they work; in which sons are much more likely to inherit the socioeconomic status of their fathers than they were a generation ago.

The name of the leftist rag? *BusinessWeek*, which published an article titled "Waking Up From the American Dream." The article summarizes recent research showing that social mobility in the United States (which was never as high as legend had it) has declined considerably over the past few decades. If you put that research together with other research that shows a drastic increase in income and wealth inequality, you reach an uncomfortable conclusion: America looks more and more like a class-ridden society.

And guess what? Our political leaders are doing everything they can to fortify class inequality, while denouncing anyone who complains—or even points out what is happening—as a practitioner of "class warfare."

Let's talk first about the facts on income distribution. Thirty years ago we were a relatively middle-class nation. It had not always been thus: Gilded Age America was a highly unequal society, and it stayed that way through the 1920s. During the 1930s and '40s, however, America experienced what the economic historians Claudia Goldin and Robert Margo have dubbed the Great Compression: a drastic narrowing of income gaps, probably as a result of New Deal policies. And the new economic order persisted for more than a generation. Strong unions, taxes on inherited wealth, corporate profits and high incomes, and close public scrutiny of corporate management all helped to keep income gaps relatively small. The economy was hardly egalitarian, but a generation ago the gross inequalities of the 1920s seemed very distant.

Now they're back. According to estimates by the economists Thomas Piketty and Emmanuel Saez—confirmed by data from the Congressional Budget Office—between 1973 and 2000 the average real income of the bottom 90% of American taxpayers actually fell by 7%. Meanwhile, the income of the top 1% rose by 148%, the income of the top 0.1% rose by 343% and the income of the top 0.01% rose 599%. (Those numbers exclude capital gains, so they're not an artifact of the stock-market bubble.) The distribution of income in the United States has gone right back to Gilded Age levels of inequality.

Never mind, say the apologists, who churn out papers with titles like that of a 2001 Heritage Foundation piece, "Income Mobility and the Fallacy of Class-Warfare Arguments." America, they say, isn't a caste society—people with high incomes this year may have low incomes next year and vice versa, and the route to wealth is open to all. That's where those commies at *BusinessWeek* come in. As they point out (and as economists and sociologists have been pointing out for some time), America actually is more of a caste society than we like to think. And the caste lines have lately become a lot more rigid.

The myth of income mobility has always exceeded the reality. As a general rule, once they've reached their 30s, people don't move up and down the income ladder very much. Conservatives often cite studies like a 1992 report by Glenn Hubbard, a Treasury official under the elder Bush who later became chief economic adviser to the younger Bush, that purport to show large numbers of Americans moving from low-wage to high-wage jobs during their working lives. But what these studies measure, as the economist Kevin Murphy put it, is mainly "the guy who works in the college bookstore and has a real job by his early 30s." Serious studies that exclude this sort of pseudo-mobility show that inequality in average incomes over long periods isn't much smaller than inequality in annual incomes.

It is true, however, that America was once a place of substantial intergenerational mobility—sons often did much better than their fathers. A classic 1978 survey found that among adult men whose fathers were in the bottom 25% of the population as ranked by social and economic status, 23% had made it into the top 25%. In other words, during the first thirty years or so after World War II, the American dream of upward mobility was a real experience for many people.

Now for the shocker: The *BusinessWeek* piece cites a new survey of today's adult men, which finds that this number has dropped to only 10%. That is, over the past generation upward mobility has fallen drastically. Very few children of the lower class are making their way to even moderate affluence. This goes along with other studies indicating that rags-to-riches stories have become vanishingly rare, and that the correlation between fathers' and sons' incomes has risen in recent decades. In modern America, it seems, you're quite likely to stay in the social and economic class into which you were born.

BusinessWeek attributes this to the "Wal-Martization" of the economy, the proliferation of dead-end, low-wage jobs and the disappearance of jobs that provide entry to the middle class. That's surely part of the explanation. But public policy plays a role—and will, if present trends continue, play an even bigger role in the future.

Put it this way: Suppose that you actually liked a caste society, and you were seeking ways to use your control of the government to further entrench the advantages of the haves against the have-nots. What would you do?

One thing you would definitely do is get rid of the estate tax, so that large fortunes can be passed on to the next generation. More broadly, you would seek to reduce tax rates both on corporate profits and on unearned income such as dividends and capital gains, so that those with large accumulated or inherited wealth could more easily accumulate even more. You'd also try to create tax shelters mainly useful for the rich. And more broadly still, you'd try to reduce tax rates on people with high incomes, shifting the burden to the payroll tax and other revenue sources that bear most heavily on people with lower incomes.

Meanwhile, on the spending side, you'd cut back on healthcare for the poor, on the quality of public education and on state aid for higher education. This would make it more difficult for people with low incomes to climb out of their difficulties and acquire the education essential to upward mobility in the modern economy.

And just to close off as many routes to upward mobility as possible, you'd do everything possible to break the power of unions, and you'd privatize government functions so that well-paid civil servants could be replaced with poorly paid private employees.

It all sounds sort of familiar, doesn't it?

Where is this taking us? Thomas Piketty, whose work with Saez has transformed our understanding of income distribution, warns that current policies will eventually create "a class of rentiers in the U.S., whereby a small group of wealthy but untalented children controls vast segments of the US economy and penniless, talented children simply can't compete." If he's right—and I fear that he is—we will end up suffering not only from injustice, but from a vast waste of human potential.

Goodbye, Horatio Alger. And goodbye, American Dream. ❏

Article 3.3

UNIONS AND INCOME INEQUALITY

BY ARTHUR MacEWAN
November/December 2011

Dear Dr. Dollar:
I know unions have shrunk in the United States, but by how much? And how best to respond to my right-wing friends who claim that unions are bad for the economy? —Rich Sanford, Hardwick, Mass.

Take a look at the graph below. The two lines on the graph show for the period 1917 through 2007 (1) labor union membership as a percentage of the total U.S. work force and (2) the percentage of all income obtained by the highest 1% of income recipients. So the lines show, roughly, the strength of unions and the distribution of income for the past century. (John Miller and I developed this graph for our book *Economic Collapse, Economic Change.*)

The picture is pretty clear. In periods when unions have been strong, income distribution has been less unequal. In periods when unions have been weak, income distribution has been more unequal. In the post-World War II era, union members were about 25% of the labor force; today the figure is about 10%. In those postwar years, the highest-income 1% got 10% to 12% of all income; today they get about 25%.

UNION MEMBERSHIP AND INCOME INEQUALITY, 1917-2007

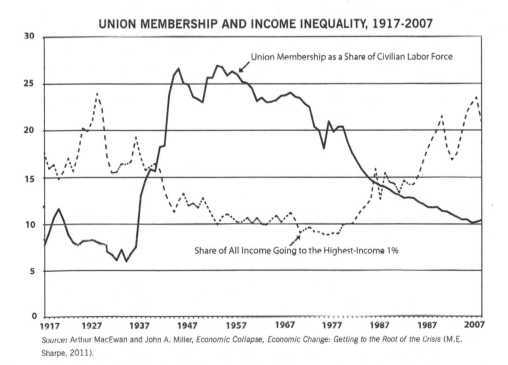

Source: Arthur MacEwan and John A. Miller, *Economic Collapse, Economic Change: Getting to the Root of the Crisis* (M.E. Sharpe, 2011).

The causation between union strength and income distribution is not simple. Nonetheless, there are some fairly direct connections. For example, when unions are strong, they can push for higher wages and thus we see a more equal distribution of income. Also, strong unions can have an impact on the political process, bringing about policies that are more favorable to workers.

But causation can work in the other direction as well. Great income inequality puts more power in the hands of the rich, and they can use that power to get policies put in place that weaken unions—for example, getting people who are hostile to unions appointed to the National Labor Relations Board.

And then there are other factors that affect both union strength and income distribution—for example, the changing structure of the global economy, which places U.S. workers in competition with poorly paid workers elsewhere. Yet the structure of the global economy is itself affected by the distribution of political power. For example, the "free trade" agreements that the United States has established with other countries generally ignore workers' rights (to say nothing of the environment) and go to great lengths to protect the rights of corporations. So, again, causation works in complex ways, and there are certainly other factors that need to be taken account of to explain the relationship shown in the graph.

However one explains the relationship, it is hard to imagine that we can return to a more equal distribution of income while unions remain weak. This means, at the very least, that the interests of unions and of people at the bottom of the income distribution are bound up with one another. Building stronger unions is an important part of fighting poverty—and the hunger and homelessness that are the clear manifestations of poverty.

One important thing to notice in the graph: In the post-World War II years, economic growth was the best we have seen. Certainly no one can claim that it is impossible for strong unions and a more equal distribution of income to co-exist with fairly rapid economic growth. Indeed, we might even argue that strong unions and a more equal distribution of income create favorable conditions for economic growth!

Stronger unions, it turns out, could be good preventive medicine for much of what ails our economy. ❑

Article 3.4

BLACK-WHITE INCOME DIFFERENCES: WHAT'S HAPPENED?

BY ARTHUR MacEWAN
July/August 2013

Dear Dr. Dollar:
There is a great deal of awareness of the general increase of income inequality in the United States. But what's happened to the income inequality between African Americans and European Americans (the "Black-White" inequality)?
 —Andy Druding, Richmond, Calif.

With a president who is African-American and talk of a "post-racial" society, one might think that the economic position of African Americans relative to European Americans had improved significantly over the last 40 or so years. One would be wrong.

In 2011, the median income of Black households was about $32,000; that is, half of Black households had income above this figure, and half had incomes below this figure. This was 61.7% of the 2011 median income of White households. In 1970, before the general increase of income inequality, the figure was 60.9%, just a smidgen lower. Not much change. Also, there has been virtually no change if mean incomes are used for the Black-White comparison. (The "mean" is the average—the total income all households in the group divided by the number of households.)

This lack of change over the last 40 years might come as a surprise, contrary to visible indicators of improvement in the position of Black people. We see, for example, many Black professionals in fields where 40 years ago there were few. There are also more Black executives—even a few CEOs of major corporations. And there is Barack Obama. How do these visible changes square with the lack of change in the relative income positions of Blacks and Whites?

The answer to this question is largely that the distribution of income among Black households is very unequal, even more unequal than the distribution of income among White households. So many of the prominent Black people who appear to be doing so well are indeed doing well. At the other end are the Black households that are doing worse. Between 1970 and 2011, the upper 5% of Black households saw their average (mean) incomes rise from about $114,000 to about $215,000 (measured in 2011 dollars), while the incomes of Black households in the bottom 20% saw their average income fall from $6,465 to $6,379.

Among White households, the pattern of change was similar but not quite so extreme. The average income of the top 5% of White households rose by 83% in this period, as compared to the 88% increase for the top Black households—though that elite White group was still taking in 50% per household more than their Black counterparts. The bottom 20% of White households saw a 13% increase per household in their inflation-adjusted incomes between 1970 and 2011.

So high-income Blacks have done pretty well—even slightly improved relative to the top White households. They have to a degree benefited from the social changes of recent decades. But for a very large segment of the Black population, not only that bottom 20%, their relative position has gotten somewhat worse, and for many their absolute incomes have actually fallen. The long-term reduction of the minimum wage (in real terms) has had an especially harsh impact on low-income Blacks, and the weakening of labor unions has also harmed a broad swath of the Black community. Add the mass incarceration of young Black men and their consequent exclusion from the economic mainstream, and it is not hard to understand continuing Black-White inequality.

Two other points should be kept in mind: First, the changes between 1970 and 2011 have not been smooth. Measured by either the mean or the median, the income position of Black households relative to White households was fairly stable in the 1970s, fell off sharply in the early 1980s, and rose again to a peak in the late 1990s before falling off to its current level.

Second, income distribution is only one measure of economic inequality. The Great Recession had a devastating impact on the wealth of Black households, largely explained by the impact of the housing crisis (see Jeannette Wicks-Lim, "The Great Recession in Black Wealth," D&S, Jan/Feb 2012). In 2004, the net worth of White households was about eleven times that of Black households (bad enough), about the same as it had been since the early 1980s (with a slight improvement in the mid-1990s). But by 2009, though both Black and White net worth fell from 2004, White net worth was 19 times Black net worth.

The more things change, the more they stay the same—or get worse! ❏

Sources: U.S. Census Bureau, Historical Income Tables: Income Inequality (census.org).

Article 3.5

THE 99%, THE 1%, AND CLASS STRUGGLE

BY ALEJANDRO REUSS
November/December 2011

Between 1979 and 2007, the income share of the top 1% of U.S. households (by income rank) more than doubled, to over 17% of total U.S. income. Mean while, the income share of the bottom 80% dropped from 57% to 48% of total income. "We are the 99%," the rallying cry of the Occupy Wall Street movement, does a good job at calling attention to the dramatic increase of incomes for those at the very top—and the stagnation of incomes for the majority.

This way of looking at income distribution, however, does not explicitly focus on the different *sources* of people's incomes. Most people get nearly all of their incomes— wages and salaries, as well as employment benefits—by working for someone else. A few people, on the other hand, get much of their income not from work but from ownership of property—profits from a business, dividends from stock, interest income from bonds, rents on land or structures, and so on. People with large property incomes may also draw large salaries or bonuses, especially from managerial jobs. Executive pay, though treated in official government statistics as labor income, derives from control over business firms and really should be counted as property income.

Over the last forty years, the distribution of income in the United States has tilted in favor of capitalists (including business owners, stock- and bond-holders, and corporate executives) and against workers. Between the 1940s and 1960s, U.S. workers' hourly output ("average labor productivity") and workers' real hourly compensation both grew at about 3% per year, so the distribution of income between workers and capitalists changed relatively little. (If the size of a pie doubles and the size of

GROWING GAP BETWEEN PRODUCTIVITY AND PAY, 1947-2010

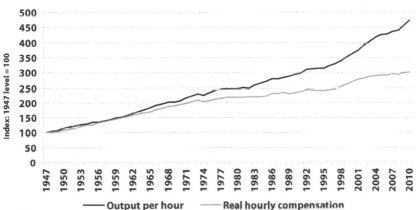

——— Output per hour   ——— Real hourly compensation

Source: Bureau of Labor Statistics, Real Hourly Compensation, Private Business Sector, Series ID number: PRS84006153; Bureau of Labor Statistics, Output Per Hour, Private Business Sector, Series ID number: PRS84006093.

your slice also doubles, your share of the pie does not change.) Since the 1970s, productivity has kept growing at over 2% per year. Average hourly compensation, however, has stagnated—growing only about 1% per year (see figure below). As the gap between what workers produce and what they get paid has increased, workers' share of total income has fallen, and capitalists' share has increased. Since income from property is overwhelmingly concentrated at the top of the income scale, this has helped fuel the rising income share of "the 1%."

The spectacular rise in some types of income—like bank profits or executive compensation—has provoked widespread outrage. Lower financial profits or CEO pay, however, will not reverse the trend toward greater inequality if the result is only to swell, say, profits for nonfinancial corporations or dividends for wealthy shareholders. Focusing too much on one or another kind of property income distracts from the fact that the overall property-income share has been growing at workers' expense.

Workers and employers—whether they like it or not, recognize it or not, prepare for it or not—are locked in a class struggle. Employers in the United States and other countries, over the last few decades, have recognized that they were in a war and prepared for it. They have been fighting and winning. Workers will only regain what they have lost if they can rebuild their collective fighting strength. In the era of globalized capitalism, this means not only building up labor movements in individual countries, but also creating practical solidarity between workers around the world.

A labor resurgence could end workers' decades-long losing streak at the hands of employers and help reverse the tide of rising inequality. Ultimately, though, this struggle should be about more than just getting a better deal. It should be—and can be—about the possibility of building a new kind of society. The monstrous inequalities of capitalism are plain to see. The need for an appealing alternative—a vision of a cooperative, democratic, and egalitarian way of life—is equally stark. ❑

Sources: Bureau of Labor Statistics, Real Hourly Compensation, Private Business Sector, Series ID number: PRS84006153; Bureau of Labor Statistics, Output Per Hour, Private Business Sector, Series ID number: PRS84006093; Congressional Budget Office, Trends in the Distribution of Household Income Between 1979 and 2007 (October 2011) (www.cbo.gov); James Heintz, "Unpacking the U.S. Labor Share," *Capitalism on Trial: A Conference in Honor of Thomas A. Weisskopf,* Political Economy Research Institute, University of Massachusetts-Amherst (September 2011).

Article 3.6

RICH AND POOR IN THE GLOBAL ECONOMY
An Interview with Bob Sutcliffe

March/April 2005

Whether economic inequality is rising or falling globally is a matter of intense debate, a key question in the larger dispute over how three decades of intensified economic global ization have affected the world's poor. Bob Sutcliffe is an economist at the University of the Basque Country in Bilbao, Spain, and the author of 100 Ways of Seeing an Unequal World. *He has been analyzing both the statistical details and the broader political-economic import of the debate and shared some of his insights in a recent interview with* Dollars & Sense.

DOLLARS & SENSE: If someone asked you whether global inequality has grown over the past 25 years, I assume you'd say, "It depends—on how inequality is defined, on what data is used, on how that data is analyzed." Is that fair?

BOB SUTCLIFFE: Yes, it's fair, but it's not enough. First, the most basic fact about world inequality is that it is monstrously large; that result is inescapable, whatever the method or definition. As to its direction of change in the last 25 years, to some extent there are different answers. But also there are different questions. Inequality is not a simple one-dimensional concept that can be reduced to a single number. Single overall measures of world inequality (where all incomes are taken into account) give a different result from measures of the relation of the extremes (the richest compared with the poorest). Over the last 25 years, you find that the bottom half of world income earners seems to have gained something in relation to the top half (so, in this sense, there is less inequality), but the bottom 10% have lost seriously in comparison with the top 10% (thus, more inequality), and the bottom 1% have lost enormously in relation to the top 1% (much more inequality). None of these measures is a single true measure of inequality; they are all part of a complex structure of inequalities, some of which can lessen as part of the same overall process in which others increase.

We do have to be clear about one data-related question that has caused huge confusion. To look at the distribution of income in the world, you have to reduce incomes of different countries to one standard. Traditionally it has been done by using exchange rates; this makes inequality appear to change when exchange rates change, which is misleading. But now we have data based on "purchasing power parity" (the comparative buying power, or real equivalence, of currencies). Using PPP values achieves for comparisons over space what inflation-adjusted index numbers have achieved for comparisons over time. Although many problems remain with PPP values, they are the only way to make coherent comparisons of incomes between countries. But they produce estimates that are astonishingly different from exchange rate-based calculations. For instance, U.S. income per head is 34 times Chinese income per head using exchange rates, but only 8 times as great using PPP values.

(And, incidentally, on PPP estimates the total size of the U.S. economy is now only 1.7 times that of China, and is likely to be overtaken by it by 2011.) So when you make this apparently technical choice between two methods of converting one currency to another, you come up not only with different figures on income distribution but also with two totally different world economic, and thus political, perspectives.

D&S: So even if some consensus were reached on the choices of definition, data, and method, you're urging a complex, nuanced portrait of what is happening to global inequality, rather than a yes or no answer. Could you give a brief outline of what you think that portrait looks like?

BS: Most integral measures—integral meaning including the entire population rather than comparing the extremes—that use PPP figures suggest that overall income distribution at the global level during the last 25 years has shown a slight decline in inequality, though there is some dissent on this. In any event this conclusion is tremendously affected by China, a country with a fifth of world population which has been growing economically at an unprecedented rate. Second, there seems to me little room for debate over the fact that the relative difference between the very rich and the very poor has gotten worse. And the smaller the extreme proportions you compare, the greater the gap. So the immensely rich have done especially well in the last 25 years, while the extremely poor have done very badly. The top one-tenth of U.S. citizens now receive a total income equal to that of the poorest 2.2 billion people in the rest of the world.

There have also been clear trends within some countries. Some of the fastest growing countries have become considerably more unequal. China is an example, along with some other industrializing countries like Thailand. The most economically liberal of the developed countries have also become much more unequal—for instance, the United States, the United Kingdom, and Australia—and so have the post-communist countries. The most extreme figures for inequality are found in a group of poor countries including Namibia and Botswana in southern Africa and Paraguay and Panama in Latin America.

Finally, the overall index of world inequality (measured by the Gini coefficient, a measure of income distribution) is about the same as that for two infamously unequal countries, South Africa and Brazil. And in the last few years it has shown no signs of improvement whatsoever.

D&S: People use the terms "unimodal" and "bimodal" to describe the global distribution of income. Can you explain what these mean? Also, you have referred elsewhere to a possible trimodal distribution—what does that refer to?

BS: The mode of a distribution is its most common value. In many countries there is one level of income around which a large proportion of the population clusters; at higher or lower levels of income there are progressively fewer people, so the distribution curve rises to a peak and then falls off. That is a unimodal distribution. But in South Africa, for example, due to the continued existence of entrenched ethnic division and economic inequality, the curve of distribution has two peaks—a low one, the most common income received by black citizens, and another, higher one, the the most common received by whites. This is a bimodal distribution because there are two values that are relatively more common than those above or below them. Because of its origins you could call it the "Apartheid distribution." The world distribution is in many respects uncannily like that of South Africa. It could be becoming trimodal in the sense that the frequency distribution of income has three peaks—one including those in very poor countries which have not been growing economically (e.g., parts of Africa), one in those developing countries which really have been developing (e.g., in South and East Asia), and one in the high-income industrialized countries. It's a kind of "apartheid plus" form of distribution.

D&S: In 2002, you wrote that many institutions, like the United Nations and the World Bank, were not being exactly honest in this debate—for example, emphasizing results based on data or methods that they elsewhere acknowledged to be poor. Has this changed over the past few years? Has the quality of the debate over trends in global income inequality improved?

BS: The most egregious pieces of statistical opportunism have declined. But I think there is a strong tendency in general for institutions to seize on optimistic conclusions regarding distribution in order to placate critics of the present world order. This increasingly takes the form of putting too much weight on measures of welfare other than income, for instance, life expectancy, for which there has been more international convergence than in the case of income. But there has been very little discussion of the philosophical basis for using life expectancy instead of or combined with income to measure inequality. If poor people live longer but in income terms remain as relatively poor as ever, has the world become less unequal?

The problem of statistical opportunism is not confined to those who are defending the world economic order; it also exists on the left. So, on the question of inequality, there is a tendency to accept whatever numerical estimate shows greatest inequality on the false assumption that this confirms the wickedness of capitalism. But capitalist inequality is so great that the willful exaggeration of it is not needed as the basis of anti-capitalist propaganda. It is more important for the left to look at the best indicators of the changing state of capitalism, including indicators of inequality, in order to intervene more effectively.

Finally, the quality of the debate, regardless of the intentions of the participants, is still greatly restricted by the shortage of available statistics about inequalities. That has improved somewhat in recent years although there are many things about past and present inequalities which we shall probably never know.

D&S: Do you see any contexts in which it's more important to focus on absolute poverty levels and trends in those levels rather than on inequality?

BS: The short answer is no, I do not. Plans for minimum income guarantees or for reducing the number of people lacking basic necessities can be important. But poverty always has a relative as well as an absolute component. It is a major weakness of the Millenium Development Goals, for example, that they talk about halving the number of people in absolute extreme poverty without a single mention of inequality. [The Millenium Development Goals is a U.N. program aimed at eliminating extreme poverty and achieving certain other development goals worldwide by 2015. —*Eds.*] And there is now a very active campaign on the part of anti-egalitarian, pro-capitalist ideologues in favor of the complete separation of the two. That is wrong not only because inequality is what partly defines poverty but more importantly because inequality and poverty reduction are inseparable. To separate them is to say that redistribution should not form part of the solution to poverty. Everyone is prepared in some sense to regard poverty as undesirable. But egalitarians see riches as pathological too. The objective of reducing poverty is integrally linked to the objective of greater equality and social justice.

D&S: Can you explain the paradox that China's economic liberalization since the late 1970s has increased inequality within China and at the same time reduced global inequality? Some researchers and policymakers interpret China's experience over this period as teaching us that it may be necessary for poor countries to sacrifice some equality in order to fight poverty. Do you agree with this—if not, how would you respond?

BS: When you measure *global* inequality, you are not just totalling the levels of inequality in individual countries. In theory all individual countries could become more unequal and yet the world as a whole become more equal, or vice versa. In China, a very poor country in 1980, average incomes have risen much faster than the world average and this has reduced world inequality. But different sections of the population have done much better than others so that inequality within China has grown. If and when China becomes on average a richer country than it is now, further unequal growth there may contribute to increasing rather than decreasing world inequality.

China's growth has been very inegalitarian, but it has been very fast. And the proportion of the population in poverty seems to have been reduced. But it is possible to envisage a more egalitarian growth path which would have been slower in aggregate but which would have reduced the number of poor people at least as much if not more than China's actual record. So I do not think it is right to say that higher inequality is the cause of reduced poverty, though it may for a time be a feature of the rapid growth which in turn creates employment and reduces poverty.

This does not mean that all increases in inequality are necessarily pathological. The famous Kuznets curve sees inequality first rising and then falling during economic growth as an initially poor population moves by stages from low-income, low-productivity work into high-income, high-productivity work, until at the end of the process 100% of the population is in the second group. If you measure inequality during such a process, it does in fact rise and then fall again to its original level—in this example at the start everyone is equally poor, at the end everyone is equally richer. That might be called transitional inequality; many growth processes may include an element of it. In that case equality is not really being "sacrificed" to reduce poverty—poverty is reduced by a process which increases inequality and then eliminates it again. But at the same time inequality may be growing for many other reasons which are not, like the Kuznets effect, self-eliminating, but rather cumulative. When inequality grows, this malign variety tends to be more important than the self-eliminating variety. But many economists are far too ready to see growing inequality as the more benign, self-eliminating variety.

D&S: Where do you think the question of what is happening to global income inequality fits into the broader debate over neoliberalism and globalization?

BS: Many people say that since some measures of inequality started to improve in about 1980 and that is also when neoliberalism and globalization accelerated, it is those processes which have produced greater equality. There are many problems with this argument, among them the fact that at least on some measures global inequality has grown since 1980. In any case, measures which show global inequality falling in this period are, as we have seen, very strongly influenced by China. China's extraordinary growth has, of course, in part been expressed in and permitted by greater globalization (its internationalization has grown faster than its production), and it is also clear that liberalization of economic policy has played a role, though China hardly has a neoliberal economy. But to permit is not to cause. The real cause is surely to be found not so much in economic policy as in a profound social movement in which a new and highly dynamic capitalist class (combined with a supportive authoritarian state) has once again become an agent of massive capitalist accumulation, as seen before in Japan, the United States, and Western Europe. So, an important part of what we are observing in figures which show declining world inequality is not any growth of egalitarianism, but the dynamic ascent of Chinese and other Asian capitalisms. ❑

This interview also appears on the website of the Political Economy Research Institute at the University of Massachusetts-Amherst, along with Bob Sutcliffe's working paper "A More or Less Unequal World? World Income Distribution in the 20th Century." See www.umass.edu/peri.

Article 3.7

THE RISE OF THE GLOBAL BILLIONAIRES

BY ROBIN BROAD AND JOHN CAVANAGH

October 2013

With the help of Forbes magazine, we and colleagues at the Institute for Policy Studies have been tracking the world's billionaires and rising inequality the world over for several decades. Just as a drop of water gives us a clue into the chemical composition of the sea, these billionaires offer fascinating clues into the changing face of global power and inequality.

After our initial gawking at the extravagance of this year's list of 1,426, we looked closer. This list reveals the major power shift in the world today: the decline of the West and the rise of the rest. Gone are the days when U.S. billionaires accounted for over 40% of the list, with Western Europe and Japan making up most of the rest. Today, the Asia-Pacific region hosts 386 billionaires, 20 more than all of Europe and Russia combined.

In 2013, of the nine countries that are home to over 30 billionaires each, only three are traditional "developed" countries: the United States, Germany, and the United Kingdom.

Next in line after the United States, with its 442 billionaires today? China, with 122 billionaires (up from zero billionaires in 1995), and third place goes to Russia with 110. China's billionaires have made money from every possible source. Consider the country's richest man, Zong Qinghou, who made his $11.6 billion through his ownership of the country's largest beverage maker. Russia's

The *Forbes* Billionaires List in 1995 ...

- ■ 100-199
- ▨ 50-99
- ▧ 20-49
- ▢ 6-19

Note: This map and the one on p. 8 both show the number of billionaires, by country, on the *Forbes* list for that year. The lists have not been adjusted for inflation, so the two maps are not strictly comparable. In addition, *Forbes* noted in 1995 that the figure for India (2 billionaires) might have been higher if translated into dollars on a purchasing-power rather than exchange-rate basis, and that the one for Russia (0 billionaires) was likely affected by lack of disclosure.

lengthy billionaire list is led by men who reaped billions from the country's vast oil, gas and mineral wealth with devastating consequences to the environment.

Germany is fourth on the list with 58 billionaires, followed by India (55), Brazil (46), Turkey (43), Hong Kong (39), and the United Kingdom (38). Yes, Turkey has more billionaires than any other country in Europe save Germany.

Moving beyond these top 9 countries, Taiwan has more billionaires than France. Indonesia has more billionaires than Italy or Spain. South Korea now has more billionaires than Japan or Australia.

This surging list of billionaires is tribute to the growing inequality in almost all nations on earth. The richest man in the world, for example, is Carlos Slim of Mexico—with a net worth of $73 billion, comparable to a whopping 6.2% of Mexico's GDP. The world's third richest person is Spain's retail king, Amancio Ortega, who has accumulated a net worth of $57 billion in a country where over a quarter of the people are now unemployed.

U.S. billionaires still dominate. The United States' 442 billionaires represent 31% of the total number. Bill Gates and Warren Buffett remain numbers 2 and 4, and are household names given the combination of their wealth, their philanthropy, and their use of their power and influence to convince other billionaires to increase their own charitable giving.

But, also among the 12 U.S. billionaires in the top 20 richest people in the world are members of two families who have used their vast wealth and concomitant power to corrupt our politics. Charles and David Koch stand at numbers 6 and 7 in the world; they have drawn on a chunk of their combined $68 billion to fund not only candidates of the far right but also political campaigns against environmental and other regulation. So too do four Waltons stand among the top 20; their combined wealth of $107.3 billion has skyrocketed thanks to Wal-

... and the *Forbes* list in 2013.

- 200+
- 100-199
- 50-99
- 20-49
- 6-19

Source: *Forbes*, March 25, 2013.

mart's growing profits as the company pressures cities and states to oppose raising wages to livable levels.

How have the numbers changed over the years? Let's travel back to1995, a time of surging wealth amidst the deregulation under the Clinton administration in the United States, and the widespread pressure around the world to deregulate, liberalize, and privatize markets.

In 1995, Forbes tallied 376 billionaires in the world. Of these, 129 (or 34%) were from the United States. The fact that the number of U.S. billionaires rose to 442 over the next 18 years while the percentage of U.S. billionaires fell only from 34% to 31% of the global total is testimony to how the deregulatory and tax-cutting atmosphere in the United States under Clinton and Bush proved so favorable to the super-rich.

Notable over these past 18 years is that the so-called developed world has been eclipsed by the so-called developing world. In 1995, the billionaire powerhouses were the United States (129), Germany (47), and Japan (35). These three countries were home to 56% of the world's billionaires. No other country came close, with France, Hong Kong, and Thailand tied in fourth place, with 12 billionaires each. Russia and China didn't have a single billionaire in 1995, although for Russia, Forbes admitted that financial disclosure in that country in the years after the Berlin Wall fell was sketchy. And, in 1995, Brazil had only 8 billionaires and India only 2.

Today, these four countries (Russia, China, Brazil, and India) host 333 of the world's 1,426 billionaires—23% of the total. And, Japan's total number of billionaires has actually fallen in the last 18 years, from 35 to 22.

The figures offer a dramatic snapshot of the relative decline of the United States, Europe, and Japan in less than two decades and the stunning rise of Brazil, Russia, India, and China, as well as the rest of Asia. And, they remind us that countries where income was relatives equal twenty years ago, like China and Russia, have rushed into the ranks of the unequal. Across the globe, the rapid rise of billionaires in dozens of countries (again, with Japan as the notable exception) is testimony to how the deregulatory climate of these past two decades sped the rise of the super-rich, while corporations kept workers' wages essentially flat.

Suffice it to say: More equal and more healthy societies require a vastly different approach to public policy. As IPS associate fellow Sam Pizzigati has chronicled, fair taxes created a vast middle class in the United States between the 1940s and 1960s. Such fair tax policies are needed today the world over if the gap between the super-haves and the have-nots is to be narrowed rather than widened. ❑

Sources: "The World's Billionaires," *Forbes*, March 25, 2013 (forbes.com); "Bill Gates Again at No. 1 on Forbes Wealthiest List," *Los Angeles Times*, October 2, 1995 (latimes.com); World/ Global Inequality, Inequality.org (inequality.org); "Change Walmart, Change America," Jobs with Justice (jwj.org); Mexico GDP, Trading Economics (tradingeconomics.com); "Spanish Jobless Rate Dips to 25.98% as Recession Ends," Yahoo News, October 24, 2013 (news.yahoo.com); Robin Broad and John Cavanaugh, "A Tax System for the 99%," Yes! magazine blog, April 17, 2013; Koch Cash (website), International Forum on Globalization (kochcash.org), Sam Pizzigati, *The Rich Don't Always Win: The Forgotten Triumph over Plutocracy that Created the American Middle Class, 1900–1970* (Seven Stories Press, 2012).

Article 3.8

VICE VERSA

Rising Inequality is the Root Cause of our Economic Problems

BY JOHN MILLER
November/December 2013

> ...President Obama and his supporters have been talking about "an economy that grows from the middle out"...
>
> The key causal factor of the middle-out view is that a wider income distribution slows economic growth by lowering consumption demand. The data for the recovery since mid-2009 do not support this view.
>
> Moreover, data do not support the view that tax cuts in the past 30 years are responsible for the widening income distribution.
>
> —John B. Taylor, "The Weak Recovery Explains Rising Inequality, Not Vice Versa" *Wall Street Journal,* Sept. 9, 2013

Vice versa back at you, John Taylor. Rising inequality is not just bad for us, but is the root cause of today's economic problems.

A Stanford economist and Senior Fellow at the conservative Hoover Institute, Taylor readily admits that inequality is on the rise. But he never spells out the degree to which the widening gulf between the best off and the rest of us has concentrated economic gains nearly exclusively among the super rich. Had he done so, he would have found it far harder to dismiss the role pro-rich economic policies and worsening inequality have played in causing today's economic maladies.

The most recent data, drawn of from a variety of highly credible sources, show what the concentration of income "more at the upper end," as Taylor puts it, has meant in practice. As of 2012, the richest 1% of families, all with incomes above $394,000, receive more than one-fifth of the income of the nation, some 22.5%, according the latest data compiled by economists Emmanuel Saez and Thomas Piketty. That's nearly equal to the their 23.5% share of income in 2007, before the onset of the Great Recession, and their 24% share during the late 1920s, on the eve of the Great Depression—the two highest concentrations of income since 1913. And, as Saez and Piketty document, a stunning 95% of what income gains there have been during the current recovery (from 2009 to 2012) have gone to richest 1%.

Not surprisingly, by 2012 only the income of the top 5% had returned to its pre-recession level in 2007, as the latest figures from the Bureau of the Census confirm. The inflation-adjusted income of the median family, on the other hand, was still 8.3% below its pre-recession level, and no higher than in 1989, nearly a generation earlier.

College Graduates and the Super Rich

What accounts for today staggering inequality? Taylor claims that changes in the private economy have driven up the wages of the well-educated and have left those with fewer years of education behind.

The distance between the economic position of workers with college degrees and those without has, indeed, widened considerably over the last three decades. In 1979, the "college premium" was 1.41. That is, the median wage of a college graduate was 41% greater than that of a worker with only a high-school diploma. By 2007, the college premium had reached 1.75. In addition, since the onset of the Great Recession in December 2007, the number of jobs held by college graduates has increased, while the number of jobs held by those without a college degree has fallen.

But that is hardly enough evidence to support Taylor's claim. First off, nearly all of the increase in the college premium occurred before the last decade, but inequality has continued to worsen. In addition, the inequality among wage earners, especially between the top wage earners and the rest of the workforce, a large and increasing number of whom hold a college degree, is far greater than the college premium data suggest. For instance, looking at the ranking of wage and salary earners between 1979 and 2007, the wages and salaries of the top 1% rose by 156%, while those of the bottom 90% went up by just 17%. At the end of that period, the ratio of the wages and salaries of the top 1% to those of the bottom 90% stood at over 20-to-1, more than double the 9.7-to-1 ratio in 1979.

When investment income is added to wage and salary income, the economic gulf between the elites and the vast majority becomes even greater and increases even more quickly than the wage gap alone. Over the same 1979-to-2007 period, the ratio of total income of the top 1% to that of the bottom 90% tripled from 14-to-1 to 42-to-1. And, even among the richest 1%, income became considerably more concentrated. The ratio of income of the top one-tenth of 1% to that of the top 1% was 3.4-to-1 in 1979, but reached to 5.2-to-1 by 2007.

These vast differences cannot be attributed solely, or even primarily, to differences in years of education among wage earners.

Pro Rich Tax Cuts and Inequality

Taylor also emphatically disagrees with the "middle-out view" that the pro-rich tax cuts and economic policies that began in early1980s are the cause of the ever widening gulf between the haves and the have-nots. But the very evidence he uses to support his position suggests otherwise.

Taylor's argument rests on data published by the Congressional Budget Office (CBO) showing that "the distribution of market income before taxes widened in the 1980s and '90s by about as much as the distribution of income after taxes." But that hardly makes his case.

Rather, the fact that after-tax income and before-tax income are widening at about the same rate offers powerful testimony to how pro-rich tax cuts have wiped out whatever government taxing policies had done in the past to mitigate the effects of widening economic differences in the private sector. "Market income inequality rose almost continually over the period [from 1979 to 2009]," write CBO tax analysts Ed Harris and Frank Sammartino. "Taxes and transfers did not offset market inequality."

Federal taxes are considerably less progressive than in the past and no match for three decades of ever widening inequality. In 1979, the richest 1% paid an effective federal tax rate of 35%—handing over a little over one-third of their total income in federal taxes. By 2009, the effective tax rate of the top 1% had fallen to 28.9%, according to the CBO. And when a less progressive federal tax code was combined with a regressive state and local tax code, taxes could no longer combat widening inequality.

Inequality and Economic Growth

Finally, there are also several reasons to reject Taylor's claim that inequality is not the cause of the weak recovery and sluggish economic growth since the official end of the Great Recession in June 2009.

Taylor's argument is that inequality has not retarded spending because today's saving rate of 5.4% is not especially high by historical standards. That's true. But after the 1980s, the saving rate dropped steadily as consumption, boosted by a stock market boom, rose during the 1990s and, fueled by a housing bubble, rose still more during the last decade. Today's savings rate is considerably higher than the 3% savings rate that prevailed in the middle of the last decade.

While spending by the rich, if high enough, could hypothetically power economic growth, several prominent economists are convinced that the redistribution of income toward the upper end has diminished spending and stood in the way of more rapid economic growth. Alan Krueger, current chair of the Council of Economic Advisors, thinks the drag on spending from this upper redistribution "could be substantial." He estimates that, by 2007, increased income inequality put an additional $1.1 trillion a year into the hands of the top 1%, who spend only about one-half of additional income. Had that $1.1 trillion remained in the hands of the bottom 99%, who have a general savings rate of about 10%, Krueger calculates that total consumption spending would have been 5% higher.

On top of its retarding effect on consumer spending, the concentration of income enhanced the political power of the super rich. Political scientists Adam Bonica, Nolan McCarty, Keith Poole, and Howard Rosenthal report that the share of individual campaign contributions made by the richest 0.01% rose from about 15% in 1980 to 40% in 2012.

And the political outcomes of the last three decades have surely conformed to the political interests of the most well to do—from the deregulation of the financial sector to pro-rich taxes to constraints on federal spending since the end of the Great Recession. Government spending and investment has been falling since 2010. Cuts in discretionary spending have reduced economic growth by 0.7 percentage points since 2010 and raised the unemployment rate by 0.8 percentage points, according to a recent report prepared for the conservative Peter G. Peterson Foundation.

Taylor claims that three decades of rising inequality are explained by market forces. The lesson here, as Joseph Stiglitz has argued, is that "market forces don't exist in a vacuum—we shape them." In the last three decades, the very policies Taylor is determined to absolve have, in fact, shaped market forces in a way that has brought us ever-widening economic inequality, economic crisis, and now unrelenting economic stagnation. ❏

Sources: Lawrence Mishel and Josh Bivens, "Occupy Wall Streeters Are Right About Skewed Economic Rewards in the United States," Economic Policy Institute Briefing Paper, Oct. 26, 2011;

Congressional Budget Office, "The Distribution of Household Income and Federal Taxes, 2008 and 2009," July 2012; Adam Bonica, Nolan McCarty, Keith T. Poole, andHoward Rosenthal, "Why Hasn't Democracy Slowed Rising Inequality?" *Journal of Economic Perspectives*, Summer 2013; Emmanuel Saez, "Striking it Richer," University of California-Berkeley, Sept. 3, 2013; Ed Harris and Frank Sammartino, "Trends in the Distribution of Household Income, 1979-2009," Congressional Budget Office, Aug. 6, 2012; Jonathan James, "The College Wage Premium," Economic Commentary, Aug. 8, 2012; Carmen DeNavas-Walt, Bernadette D. Proctor, Jessica C. Smith, Income, Poverty, and Health Insurance Coverage in the United States: 2012, September 2013; Paul Krugman, "The Damage Done," *New York Times*, Oct. 17, 2013; Joseph Stiglitz, "Inequality Is Holding Back the Recovery," *New York Times*, Jan. 19, 2013; Dean Baker, "Krugman versus Stiglitz on Inequality and Economic Growth," Center For Economic and Policy Research, Jan. 20.2013;The Cost of Crisis-Driven Fiscal Policy, Prepared by Macroeconomic Advisers, LLC for the Peter G. Peterson Foundation;Alan Krueger, "The Rise and Consequence of Inequality in the United States," Jan. 12, 2012.

Chapter 4

SAVINGS AND INVESTMENT

INTRODUCTION

Never a slip from the savings "cup" to the investment "lip." That is the orderly world of classical macroeconomics, where every cent of household savings is neatly transferred to business investment. In the classical world, capital markets—governed by all-powerful interest rates—work seamlessly to assure that savings are matched by investments, fueling growth in the private economy, which in turn guarantees full employment. Should the flow of savings exceed the uptake of investment, falling interest rates automatically solve the problem.

In the real world, macroeconomies are far messier than classical macroeconomists suggest. Keynes argued that there is no neat connection, or "nexus," between savings and investment in a modern financial economy. Savings often sit, hoarded and uninvested. And interest rates, no matter how low, seldom coax balky investors to lay out their money in a weak economy. In the Keynesian world, economies regularly suffer from investment shortfalls that lead to recessions and cost workers their jobs.

In this chapter, Gretchen McClain and Randy Albelda report on one critical test of the classical and Keynesian visions, conducted by economist Steven Fazzari. In a massive study of 5,000 manufacturing firms, Fazzari rated the influence of interest rates, business-cycle conditions, and firms' financial conditions on their investment in plant and equipment. He concluded that the influence of interest rates is overrated, putting him squarely in the Keynesian camp (Article 4.1).

The next three articles look at the financial system that is supposed, in the mainstream view, to channel savings into productive investment

Economist Marty Wolfson gives a down-to-earth description of the financial instruments and deregulatory measures at the heart of the current economic crisis. He calls for a regulatory structure that puts limits on financial risk and manipulation (Article 4.2).

Ramaa Vasudevan provides a primer on the increased importance of financial markets, financial institutions, and financial elites in today's economy and its governing institutions. The fact that failed financial corporations have received massive bailouts, for Vasudevan, only underlines the power they wield in the era of "financialization" (Article 4.3)

Doug Orr sorts out the confusion caused by applying the term "investor" both to those making productive investments in businesses and to speculators on Wall Street (Article 4.4). He likens the stock market to a "big casino," in which a great deal of money changes hands, but scarcely any goes to the expansion of productive capacity. Stock market speculation, Orr argues, has little effect on most people in boom times, but can have deeply destructive effects in a crisis.

Arthur MacEwan turns to the housing sector, whose output counts directly as part of investment, but which has been plagued by instability in recent years. He explains why the recent housing bubble—despite the role of fraud and deception—was no Ponzi scheme (Article 4.5). In many ways, its ramifications were far worse.

Gerald Friedman tracks trends in private investment before, during, and after the Great Recession (Article 4.6). He finds that profits are not being recycled into new investment, and as investment remains low, unemployment remains high.

Discussion Questions

1. (Article 4.1) Keynes argued that savings and investment were not balanced by the interest rate but by changes in the level of aggregate output. How does the essay by McClain and Albelda support this claim? How does this help us understand the slow recovery from the Great Recession?

2. (Article 4.1) According to McClain and Albelda, how did Fazzari rate the influence of interest rates, business-cycle conditions, and firms' financial conditions on corporate investment? What do his findings suggest about Keynesian and classical theories of investment? Based on his findings, what stabilization policies might be appropriate to promote investment?

3. (Article 4.2) What exactly is a derivative and what role did derivatives play in the financial crisis?

4. (Article 4.3) What is "financialization"? How does it manifest itself in today's economy? How did it contribute to the recent financial crisis?

5. (Article 4.4) What's in a name? Why does Orr dispute the use of the term "investor" to describe those who engage in stock-market trading?

6. (Article 4.5) What role did deception play in the recent housing bubble? What role did the bubble play in fueling a broader economic boom? How did its collapse contribute to the Great Recession?

7. (Article 4.6) Figure 1 shows a widening gap between net after-tax profits and net private investment. If firms can be profitable with a low level investment, why should this gap concern us?

Article 4.1

BOOSTING INVESTMENT
The Overrated Influence of Interest Rates

BY GRETCHEN McCLAIN AND RANDY ALBELDA
July 1993; revised April 2001

Few economists or politicians would disagree that an economy's prospects for long-term growth depend on the productive capacity of its people and its physical equipment. But what to invest in—and how to get the appropriate economic actors to invest—is a matter of much debate.

All economies face a choice between using their productive resources to produce goods and services to be consumed now, and forsaking today's consumption to produce more goods for the future. While catering to consumption today may be more satisfying for wealthier countries and absolutely vital for poor countries, it fails to provide for future growth.

Investing in new plant and equipment can stimulate growth over time, as it provides the physical capacity for new production. Moreover, new plant and equipment tend to be better designed than the existing capital stock, and the improvement usually helps to boost output per worker. If this new productivity translates into higher wages, investment can also increase a country's standard of living and improve employment possibilities. In turn, improving human productive capacity—through training and education—can lead to growth and increased productivity in the long run.

Investment, and the consequent increase in productivity, is critical for international economic success. The more efficiently a country can produce a product, the more competitive that country will be in the world market. Since international markets provide an avenue of demand for our goods, the more domestically produced products and services we can sell abroad, the more jobs we can support here.

Investment can also help stimulate the economy in the short run. During an economic downturn, increased investment will yield more jobs and income for workers who would otherwise be unemployed. They will then return their income to the market when they purchase goods and services, which will boost demand for those products. Economists call this the "multiplier effect." The increase in demand in turn encourages firms to invest more so that they can meet that demand—known to economists as the "accelerator effect." All in all, such a cycle creates more jobs, income, and spending.

While few economists dispute the importance of investment, many disagree on what type is needed, which sectors of the economy are best able to provide it, and what are the best ways to encourage investment. Typically, these debates have revolved around the government's role in encouraging private investment in new plant and equipment. But the role that public investment in infrastructure and education plays in promoting not only our economic well-being and growth, but also in encouraging private investment, could and should widen the terms of the debate.

The Backdrop

The traditional economic argument about investment—and the prevailing conservative line espoused by elected officials at the federal and state levels—has been that the most important fiscal policies to encourage privately owned firms to invest are those which boost profits. If the government helps provide the conditions for profitability, the argument goes, firms will be encouraged to make the right types of investment.

Government tax-and-spend policies during the 1980s and 1990s have often tried to promote investment by reducing corporate taxes, in order to boost profits and stimulate savings. Such measures were supposed to leave firms with a bigger bottom line, in the hope that they would turn profits into new plant and equipment. Cuts in personal income tax rates—especially for the wealthiest—were intended to leave people with more after-tax income that they could save. Higher savings, according to this logic, translates into lower interest rates which in turn lead to more investment. While such policies have been very effective in redistributing money from the poor to the wealthy, they did not do much for investment. For example, the amount of new fixed investment (i.e., new plant and equipment) relative to the total amount of plant and equipment actually sank to its lowest post-World War II mark between 1989 and 1991.

Merely providing the conditions for profit-making does not mean that private firms will plow those profits back into new plant and equipment. Speculation on real-estate markets, the value of foreign currencies, or the price of silver and gold could easily eat up new profits. Much of the money generated for investment in the 1980s financed mergers and acquisitions, which generally resulted in less employment and little new physical productive capacity. And, perhaps even more important, new investment by U.S. firms may not take place in the United States. Investing abroad has been the trend since the 1970s. Finally, even if there is domestic investment and it increases productivity, unless workers share in those gains it may not promote robust growth or increase the standard of living of the country as a whole.

In the face of the failure of the 1980s policies to promote investment, conservatives came up with a new explanation of why the economy was so sluggish: the deficit. Ironically, the conservative policies mentioned above were largely responsible for the public debt, but nonetheless Republicans, along with many Democrats galvanized by billionaire Ross Perot, latched onto deficit reduction as the most important fiscal policy of the 1990s.

The deficit, they argued, kept long-term interest rates high because it created competition for precious funds. The result was that federal borrowing, necessitated by debt-financed government spending and tax cuts, "crowded out" private investment. The best solution, they said, was to reduce the deficit and bring down long-term interest rates so that private investment would thrive.

Identifying Influence

Economist Steven Fazzari tackled these assumptions in a study of the influence of the federal government's taxing and spending policies on private investment. Using a large data base from Standard and Poor on over 5,000 manufacturing firms from 1971 to 1990, Fazzari tested three different factors for their effects on levels of investment in plant and equipment: interest rates, the business cycle, and the financial conditions of the firms.

According to Fazzari, these three "channels of influence" shape patterns of investment. First, he takes on the traditionalists, by addressing the costs associated with investment: the price of borrowing money (i.e., interest rates), depreciation (how fast the new piece of equipment or building will lose its value), and taxes affecting both corporate profits and dividends. To measure this channel, Fazzari employs the interest rate on one type of corporate bond.

Next, he considers the influence of the business cycle by looking at sales growth. Traditional economic theory tends to assume a ready market, but Fazzari suggests instead that firms make investment decisions based on their perception of their ability to sell their products. The more robust current sales are and are expected to be, the more likely firms will be willing to risk new investment—regardless of the interest rate. Since the general condition of the economy influences sales levels, it also has an impact on investment.

In Fazzari's examination of the third channel of influence—the financial condition of firms—he again questions conventional wisdom, this time about the supply and demand for loans. Most economists assume that if the expected return on an investment exceeds the interest rate, then the project is profitable and will be undertaken. This is most likely to be true when the firm in question has enough cash on hand from prior profits to make the investment without asking a bank for a loan. Many firms, though, need to borrow money, and some are unable to persuade banks to loan it to them. Banks often refuse loan applications from new businesses with few assets, or charge them prohibitively high interest rates. Even if a young firm finds a potentially profitable investment, severe constraints on raising capital may prevent the firm from pursuing it. A firm's financial condition—not the projected rate of return on the new investment—can thus end up determining whether or not investment takes place.

Perfecting Policy

After looking at the importance of interest rates, the business cycle, and the financial conditions of firms in determining investment, Fazzari found that interest rates exert the weakest influence of the three factors. He concludes that there is no evidence that interest rates significantly affect investment for the fastest growing firms in his sample. Based on these findings, Fazzari claims that "it would be speculative to base policy on the assumption that interest rates drive investment to an important extent, especially for growing firms."

So, what kinds of fiscal policies should we adopt? If we believe Fazzari's results, we should be looking for those that attend to the financial conditions of firms and stimulate demand for products.

A tax cut targeted not at the very rich but at the "middle class" would probably give investment at least a temporary boost by generating increased consumption. Increased sales from a temporary tax cut create the illusion of a permanent increase in demand, and the multiplier and accelerator effects discussed earlier come into play. In order to meet what firms believe is a permanent increase in demand for their goods, they make investments in more equipment, more factories, and more employees.

Another means of encouraging investment that Fazzari evaluates is cutting corporate income taxes. Such cuts increase firms' after-tax profits, leaving them with a larger pool of funds to invest if they so choose. Since there is no guarantee that they will invest the savings from reduced taxes, though, Fazzari prefers investment tax credits (ITCs) to cuts in taxes for all firms. Only if firms invested would they be able to reduce their corporate tax bills. In Fazzari's view, ITCs will effectively encourage investment whether it is sensitive to interest rates or not.

The most important lesson from Fazzari's analysis is that concerns about investment should not stand in the way of policy initiatives that are important for society, such as spending on education and job training, simply because they may increase the federal budget deficit and cause interest rates to rise. Government investments in public works and education will likely increase productivity in the long run, and this can only be good for investment. Moreover, if investment is not sensitive to interest rates, then the much-discussed "crowding out" effect of deficit spending on private business is bound to be very small. And as Fazzari points out, when unemployment is high, the stimulative effects of deficit spending on sales may far outweigh the impacts of increased interest rates.

The focus on balanced budgets should be tempered by a thorough analysis of what this policy implies for society's immediate and long-term welfare. When we underinvest in the economy during a recession by eliminating educational and social investments, the foregone technical innovation resulting from this underinvestment may lead to less efficient workers, and lower productivity, for many years.

Fazzari's results not only repudiate the traditional answer to lagging investment—tax cuts for the wealthy and the lowering of interest rates. Instead, the government should be trying to stimulate the economy through improved physical and social infrastructure, which will boost not only sales but investment and incomes. ❑

Article 4.2

DERIVATIVES AND DEREGULATION

BY MARTY WOLFSON
November/December 2008

It has become commonplace to describe the current financial crisis as the most serious since the Great Depression. Although we have more tools now to avoid a depression, the current crisis presents in some ways more significant challenges than did the banking crises of the 1930s.

And it's not over.

The form of the current crisis is similar to others we have seen in the past: a speculative increase in asset prices, overly optimistic expectations, and an expansion of debt sustainable only if the speculative bubble continues. Then the bubble pops, debt can't be repaid, and losses mount at financial institutions. The risk of bank failures rises and lenders get scared. They panic, refuse to lend to anyone that seems at all risky, and seek safety in cash or super-safe assets.

In the early 1930s, there was no federal deposit insurance and little federal government intervention. Depositor runs took down the banking system.

In more recent crises, though, the Federal Reserve successfully developed and used its powers as a lender of last resort. Deposit insurance helped to reassure small depositors and, if needed, the Federal Deposit Insurance Corporation stepped in and bailed out threatened banks. It could guarantee all liabilities of a failing bank and arrange mergers with healthier banks. These tools generally worked to reduce panicked reactions and prevent the freezing up of credit.

But this time, after the collapse of the speculative bubble in housing prices, the course of events has been different. The Federal Reserve was forced to expand the concept of a lender of last resort in unprecedented ways. It has lent to investment banks and insurance companies, not just regulated depository institutions. It has taken all kinds of assets as collateral for its loans, not just the high-grade securities it traditionally accepted. It has even lent to nonfinancial corporations (by buying their commercial paper).

What is surprising is that these dramatic actions and expensive bailouts of financial institutions, such as American International Group (AIG) and even Fannie Mae and Freddie Mac, were insufficient to reassure lenders about the ability of financial institutions to honor their repayment commitments. Treasury Secretary Paulson's plan to use $700 billion to buy "toxic assets" from financial institutions, signed into law by President Bush on October 3rd, failed to stop what had become by then a generalized panic and freeze-up of credit. It took a coordinated global initiative to inject capital directly into financial institutions, plus a federal guarantee on bank debt and unlimited FDIC insurance on non-interest-bearing (mostly business) accounts at banks, announced on October 12th, to begin to have an effect on unfreezing credit markets.

The "TED spread," a widely watched measure of credit risk that had spiked sharply during the panic, began to reverse its path following the October 12 announcement. The TED spread measures the difference between an interest rate that banks charge when lending to each other (the London Interbank Offered Rate, or Libor) and the interest rate on U.S. Treasury bills. Because the Treasury is assumed to be "risk-free," the difference between it and Libor measures the perceived relative risk of lending to banks.

Why has this panic been so much more difficult to control? The answer has to do with the widespread use of complicated and opaque securities, known as derivatives, in a deregulated, interconnected, and global financial system.

A derivative is a financial contract that derives its value from something else, such as an asset or an index. At the root of the current crisis are derivatives known as mortgage-backed securities (MBSs). MBSs are claims to payments from an underlying pool of mortgages. The ability of MBS issuers to repay their debt, and thus the value of the MBS, is derived from the ability of homeowners to meet their mortgage payments.

In the process leading up to the crisis, a mortgage broker typically extended a mortgage to a borrower, and then turned to a commercial bank to fund the loan. The bank might sell the loan to Fannie Mae, which would pool a group of mortgages together and sell the resulting MBS to an investment bank like Lehman Brothers. Lehman, in turn, repackaged the MBS in various ways, and issued even more complicated derivatives called collateralized debt obligations (CDOs). Buyers of the CDOs might be other banks, hedge funds, or other lenders.

At the base of this complicated pyramid of derivatives might be a subprime borrower whose lender did not explain an adjustable-rate loan, or another borrower whose ability to meet mortgage payments depended on a continued escalation of home prices. As subprime borrowers' rates reset, and especially as housing price speculation collapsed, the whole house of cards came crashing down.

Why were mortgage loans made that could not be repaid? And why did supposedly sophisticated investors buy MBSs and CDOs based on these loans? First of all, the mortgage brokers and commercial banks that made and funded these loans quickly sold them off and no longer had any responsibility for them. Second, rating agencies like Moody's and Standard & Poor's gave these derivatives stellar AAA ratings, signifying a credit risk of almost zero. Recent Congressional hearings have highlighted the conflict of interest that these rating agencies had: they were being paid by the issuers of the derivatives they were rating. Third, financial institutions up and down the line were making money and nobody was limiting what they could do. In the deregulated financial environment, federal regulators stood aside as housing speculation spun out of control and did little to regulate, or even document, the growth of complicated derivatives.

Finally, financial institutions' concerns about the creditworthiness of the derivatives they held were eased because they thought they could protect themselves against possible loss. For example, by using another type of derivative known as a credit default swap, holders of MBSs and CDOs could make periodic premium payments to another financial institution, like American International Group (AIG), to insure themselves against default by the issuers of the MBSs and CDOs. (This insurance contract was technically classified as a derivative rather than insurance in order to escape regulation.) However, if an insurer like AIG is unable to honor all its insurance contracts, then the protection against loss is illusory.

The total value of all the securities insured by credit default swaps at the end of 2007 was estimated by the Bank of International Settlements to be $58 trillion, and by the International Swaps and Derivatives Association to be $62 trillion. (The estimates could vary by as much as $4 trillion because unregulated credit default swaps do not have to be officially reported to regulatory agencies. Moreover, even greater ambiguity surrounds these contracts because insurers can transfer their liability to other parties, and the insured party may be unaware of the creditworthiness or even the identity of the new insurer.)

Surprisingly, though, the value of the actual securities that form the basis of these credit default swaps was only about $6 trillion. How could $6 trillion worth of assets be insured at ten times that amount? The discrepancy is due to the fact that it is possible to speculate on the likelihood of default of a security without actually owning the security: all the speculator has to do is enter into a credit default swap contract with an insurer. The total volume of "insured securities" can thus escalate dramatically.

Because derivatives are so complex, because so much speculation and debt are involved, and because it is so hard to know how much is at risk (and exactly who is at risk), regulators are unsure of the implications of the failure of a particular financial institution. That is why they have been so fearful of the consequences of letting a troubled institution fail.

The exception that did indeed prove the rule was Lehman Brothers. The Federal Reserve and Treasury did not bail it out, and its failure led to an intensification of the problems in credit markets. A money market fund, the Reserve Primary Fund, announced that it would only pay 97 cents on the dollar to its investors, because its investments in Lehman Brothers could not be redeemed. The Treasury moved quickly to announce that it would insure money market funds, in order to prevent a run on the funds. However, the Lehman failure raised further concerns that lenders had about the derivatives portfolios of other banks, and about the possibility that the banks would not have enough capital to cover potential losses.

Secretary Paulson's initial plan to buy "toxic" assets (including MBSs and CDOs) from financial institutions was designed to address these concerns about bank capital. However, his plan was probably also negatively affected by uncertainty. Because these "toxic" assets are complex and nobody wants to buy them, there is no market for them and their value is uncertain. And because the Paulson plan's unstated objective was to boost bank capital by overpaying for these assets, the difficulties in pricing the assets raised the prospects of long delays and questions about whether the plan to increase bank capital would be successful. Lenders continued to hold back. They may also have hesitated because of concern about a political backlash against a taxpayer subsidy for the very banks that many people blamed for the crisis.

By injecting capital directly into the banks, the global initiative announced on October 12th 2008 raised the prospect of returns on the capital investment for taxpayers. It also avoided the uncertainties of buying individual assets and helped to reduce the panic.

But the crisis isn't over. Reducing the panic is only the first step. There is now likely to be a longer-term credit crunch that will continue to threaten the broader economy. Banks and other lenders will be wary for quite some time. Losses on mortgage-related assets will continue as years of housing speculation—financed with heaps of borrowed money—continues to unwind. Bank lending will lag as banks rebuild their capital and overcome their pessimistic expectations.

It will be up to the federal government to pick up the slack that the banks will leave. We will need programs to enable people to stay in their homes and stabilize their communities. We will need to create jobs by investing in infrastructure, renewable energy, and education. We will need a "trickle-up" approach that puts people first and raises living standards and opportunities.

At the same time, we need a regulatory structure for the financial system that puts limits on risk and manipulation. It is clear that deregulation, and the entire neoliberal model that has dominated economic policy for the past 30 years, has run aground. It has sown the seeds of financial crisis, and this crisis has led us to the edge of an abyss. Only by dramatically reorienting our economic and financial structure can we avoid the abyss and create the kind of society that meets our needs. The nature of that new structure should be the subject of intensive democratic discussion and debate in the days to come. ❏

Article 4.3

FINANCIALIZATION: A PRIMER

BY RAMAA VASUDEVAN
November/December 2008

You don't have to be an investor dabbling in the stock market to feel the power of finance. Finance pervades the lives of ordinary people in many ways, from student loans and credit card debt to mortgages and pension plans.

And its size and impact are only getting bigger. Consider a few measures:

- U.S. credit market debt—all debt of private households, businesses, and government combined—rose from about 1.6 times the nation's GDP in 1973 to over 3.5 times GDP by 2007.
- The profits of the financial sector represented 14% of total corporate profits in 1981; by 2001-02 this figure had risen to nearly 50%.

These are only a few of the indicators of what many commentators have labeled the "financialization" of the economy—a process University of Massachusetts economist Gerald Epstein succinctly defines as "the increasing importance of financial markets, financial motives, financial institutions, and financial elites in the operation of the economy and its governing institutions."

In recent years, this phenomenon has drawn increasing attention. In his latest book, pundit Kevin Phillips writes about the growing divergence between the real (productive) and financial economics, describing how the explosion of trading in myriad new financial instruments played a role in polarizing the U.S. economy. On the left, political economists Harry Magdoff and Paul Sweezy had over many years pointed to the growing role of finance in the operations of capitalism; they viewed the trend as a reflection of the rising economic and political power of "rentiers"—those whose earnings come from financial activities and from forms of income arising from ownership claims (such as interest, rent, dividends, or capital gains) rather than from actual production.

From Finance to Financialization

The financial system is supposed to serve a range of functions in the broader economy. Banks and other financial institutions mop up savings, then allocate that capital, according to mainstream theory, to where it can most productively be used. For households and corporations, the credit markets facilitate greatly increased borrowing, which should foster investment in capital goods like buildings and machinery, in turn leading to expanded production. Finance, in other words, is supposed to facilitate the growth of the "real" economy—the part that produces useful goods (like bicycles) and services (like medical care).

In recent decades, finance has undergone massive changes in both size and shape. The basic mechanism of financialization is the transformation of future streams of income (from profits, dividends, or interest payments) into a tradable asset like a stock or a bond. For example, the future earnings of corporations are transmuted into equity stocks that are bought and sold in the capital market. Likewise, a loan, which involves certain fixed interest payments over its duration, gets a new life when it is converted into marketable bonds. And multiple loans, bundled together then "sliced and diced" into novel kinds of bonds ("collateralized debt obligations"), take on a new existence as investment vehicles that bear an extremely complex and opaque relationship to the original loans.

The process of financialization has not made finance more effective at fulfilling what conventional economic theory views as its core function. Corporations are not turning to the stock market as a source of finance for their investments, and their borrowing in the bond markets is often not for the purpose of productive investment either. Since the 1980s, corporations have actually spent more money buying back their own stock than they have taken in by selling newly issued stock. The granting of stock options to top executives gives them a direct incentive to have the corporation buy back its own shares—often using borrowed money to do so—in order to hike up the share price and allow them to turn a profit on the sale of their personal shares. More broadly, instead of fostering investment, financialization reorients managerial incentives toward chasing short-term returns through financial trading and speculation so as to generate ballooning earnings, lest their companies face falling stock prices and the threat of hostile takeover.

What is more, the workings of these markets tend to act like an upper during booms, when euphoric investors chase the promise of quick bucks. During downturns these same mechanisms work like downers, turning euphoria into panic as investors flee. Financial innovations like collateralized debt obligations were supposed to "lubricate" the economy by spreading risk, but instead they tend to heighten volatility, leading to amplified cycles of boom and bust. In the current crisis, the innovation of mortgage-backed securities fueled the housing bubble and encouraged enormous risk-taking, creating the conditions for the chain reaction of bank (and other financial institution) failures that may be far from over.

Financialization and Power

The arena of finance can at times appear to be merely a casino—albeit a huge one—where everyone gets to place her bets and ride her luck. But the financial system carries a far deeper significance for people's lives. Financial assets and liabilities represent claims on ownership and property; they embody the social relations of an economy at a particular time in history. In this sense, the recent process of financialization implies the increasing political and economic power of a particular segment of the capitalist class: rentiers. Accelerating financial transactions and the profusion of financial techniques have fuelled an extraordinary enrichment of this elite.

This enrichment arises in different ways. Financial transactions facilitate the reallocation of capital to high-return ventures. In the ensuing shake-up, some sectors of capital profit at the expense of other sectors. More important, the capitalist class as a whole is able to force a persistent redistribution in its favor, deploying its newly expanded wealth to bring about changes in the political-economy that channel even more wealth its way.

The structural changes that paved the way for financialization involved the squashing of working-class aspirations during the Reagan-Thatcher years; the defeats of the miners' strike in England and of the air traffic controllers' (PATCO) strike in the United States were perhaps the most symbolic instances of this process. At the same time, these and other governments increasingly embraced the twin policy mantras of fighting inflation and deregulating markets in place of creating full employment and raising wages. Corporations pushed through legislation to dismantle the financial regulations that inhibited their profitmaking strategies.

Financialization has gathered momentum amid greater inequality. In the United States, the top 1% of the population received 14.0% of the national after-tax income in 2004, nearly double its 7.5% share in 1979. In the same period the share of the bottom fifth fell from 6.8% to 4.9%.

And yet U.S. consumption demand has been sustained despite rising inequality and a squeeze on real wages for the majority of households. Here is the other side of the financialization coin: a massive expansion of consumer credit has played an important role in easing the constraints on consumer spending by filling the gap created by stagnant or declining real wages. The credit card debt of the average U.S. family increased by 53% through the 1990s. About 67% of low-income families with incomes less than $10,000 faced credit card debt, and the debt of this group saw the largest increase—a 184% rise, compared to a 28% increase for families with incomes above $100,000. Offered more and more credit as a privatized means of addressing wage stagnation, then, eventually, burdened by debt and on the edge of insolvency, the working poor and the middle class are less likely to organize as a political force to challenge the dominance of finance. In this sense, financialization becomes a means of social coercion that erodes working-class solidarity.

As the structures created by financial engineering unravel, the current economic crisis is revealing the cracks in this edifice. But even as a growing number of U.S. families are losing their homes and jobs in the wake of the subprime meltdown, the financial companies at the heart of the crisis have been handed massive bailouts and their top executives have pocketed huge pay-outs despite their role in abetting the meltdown—a stark sign of the power structures and interests at stake in this era of financialization. ❑

Sources: Robin Blackburn, "Finance and the Fourth Dimension," *New Left Review* 39 May-June 2006; Robert Brenner, "New Boom or Bubble," *New Left Review* 25 Jan-Feb 2004; Tamara Draut and Javier Silva, "Borrowing to make ends meet," *Demos*, Sept 2003; Gerald Epstein, "Introduction" in G. Epstein, ed., *Financialization and the World Economy*, 2006; John Bellamy Foster, "The Financialization of Capitalism," *Monthly Review*, April 2007; Gretta Krippner, "The financialization of the US economy," *Socio-Economic Review* 3, Feb. 2005; Thomas Palley, "Financialization : What it is and why it matters," Political Economy Research Institute Working Paper #153, November 2007; A. Sherman and Arin Dine, "New CBO data shows inequality continues to widen," Center for Budget Priorities, Jan. 23, 2007; Kevin Phillips, *Bad Money: Reckless Finance, Failed Politics, and the Global Crisis of American Capitalism*, 2008.

Article 4.4

THE BIG CASINO

BY DOUG ORR
May/June 2014

> *Speculators may do no harm as bubbles on a steady stream of enterprise. But the position is serious when enterprise becomes the bubble on a whirlpool of speculation. When the capital development of a country becomes a by-product of the activities of a casino, the job is likely to be ill-done.*
> — John Maynard Keynes (1936)

O n December 31, 2013, the Dow-Jones Industrial Average hit a new record high of 16,577. The media cheered this result and proclaimed that happy days are here again. Yet that same day, they reported that income inequality is continuing to increase, median family income is still 9% below what it was at the start of the recession, and the index of consumer sentiment is still 25% below pre-recession levels. Millions of people are still unemployed and Congress let long-term unemployment benefits expire. It appears that all of this suffering on Main Street is good for the stock market.

The media's constant reporting of stock market numbers so prominently and giving supposed links to the events of the day gives the impression that the stock market plays a central role in moving the economy forward and that everyone has a stake in these daily changes. In fact, the movement of these stock indices on a day-to-day basis has very little to do with the actual economy and, except in times of economic crisis, the stock market has almost no impact on the lives of most Americans. Fewer than half of American families own a single share of stock, and only about a third own shares totaling more than $5000. The stock market is the realm of the elite, and for the past several decades has had a negative impact on the real economy.

Who Are the "Investors"?

Economics textbooks tell us that financial markets play an important role in the economy, linking saving to investment. Some individuals have more income than they currently want to spend, so they engage in saving. Other individuals need money to engage in investment. "Investment" in this context means the creation of new, physically productive resources. If a firm builds a new factory, installs new machines, or buys new software to do its accounting, that is investment. When students spend time and money to acquire new skills that make them more productive, that is investment. So when a bank takes people's savings and lends it to the owner of a restaurant to buy a new stove, the bank plays an important economic role. Further, savers can get their money back if they need it in the future, because loans get repaid.

When you put money in the bank you receive interest. This is your reward for saving and giving the bank the use of your money. But you are not engaging in investment. The person who borrows the money and puts it to productive use is the investor. When you put money in the bank, you are a saver, not an investor.

Corporations, however, can bypass banks and gain access to financial capital by issuing stock. When a company issues new shares of stock, the money raised from the sale can be used to engage in productive investment. The issuing of new shares is called an "initial public offering," or IPO. IPOs are not done on stock exchanges. They are handled by investment banks. These IPOs transfer saving to firms and the firms can use the money for real investment. If these investments are successful, GDP will rise as consumers gain access to new products, the firm will grow and become more profitable, the price of their shares will rise, which provides savers a long-term capital gain as a return on their saving. This usually occurs over an extended period of time. But no one would buy a share of stock if they could not get their money back when they needed it. The useful role of the stock exchanges, what we call the "stock market," is to provide "liquidity." One individual who has money to save today can buy a share of stock from someone who needs to get their past savings back.

The words we use to describe things matter. Investors are usually seen as contributing to the economy because they hire workers to build new factories, new machines, and other productive assets, and these assets can make the real economy more productive. Workers create the assets, and the investors are given the credit. On the other hand, gamblers and speculators are usually seen as frivolous and destructive.

The biggest propaganda coup of the 20th century was convincing the media and the general public to call the speculators on the New York Stock Exchange (NYSE) "investors." They did it by blurring the positive role of the stock market with the speculative role. If you buy a share of Pacific Gas and Electric (PG&E) stock on the stock exchange, you will get a quarterly dividend payment, just like the interest you get from the money you put in a bank. But, PG&E does not get any new money to use for actual investment. The price you pay for the stock goes to the previous owner of the stock, not PG&E. Buying stock on the NYSE is not investing, but rather seeking a return on saving. But unlike saving at a bank, this saving involves a risk and is a form of speculation.

When the Dow-Jones index hit a record high of 16,577, that day NYSE market volume was 461 million shares, and another 1.34 billion shares were traded on the NASDAQ. That was a slow day because of the holidays. More than $50 billion changed hands, yet not a penny of all this money went to a corporation for use as productive investment.

The biggest casino in the world is located at the corner of Wall Street and Broad Street in New York City. Calling the players on the NYSE "investors" completely changes our understanding of the role they play. Consider rewording some recent stories: "Gamblers bet big on new Genentech drug," or "Speculators made 73% in one day buying Twitter's IPO in the morning and reselling later in the day to suckers caught up in the excitement." The Wall Street Journal does occasionally tell us the truth when they report on the "bets" made by "players" on the NYSE. Speculators betting that the price of a share will rise want to buy it and those betting that the price will fall want to sell it. If there are more buyers than sellers, the price will rise, regardless of anything that is happening in the real economy. Reporting a record high for the NYSE has about as much importance as reporting a record amount of gambling in Las Vegas. Except the gambling on the NYSE can have a much larger negative impact on the real economy.

Big Gambling Does Big Damage

The reason why the volume on the NYSE is so high is because speculators engage in high-frequency trading. An analyst predicts that, based on breaking news, the price of a particular stock may go up. If you can be the first to buy the stock before the price goes up, you can sell it a few minutes later (or even seconds, or fractions of a second, later) and make a profit. This is why brokerage houses now rely on "program trading." Computers can see price differentials and make trades much faster than humans can. Brokerage firms need to have the fastest possible computers and the fastest network connections because milliseconds matter. By 2010, this type of high-frequency, or "quant" trading made up 70% of the bloated stock trading volume.

If you buy a share of stock for $100 and sell it 30 minutes later for $100.50, you make a return of 50 cents, or 0.5%. If you buy a million shares, you make half a million dollars for a half an hour of "work." But the "work" was done by a computer program and you have done nothing to make the economy more productive, to create jobs, or to increase GDP. All you have done is to bring a large pile of money to the table at the casino. You have redistributed money from one person at the table to another, and for this, the Wall Street Journal calls you an "investor." You can use your winnings to hire the best and brightest minds to give you an edge at the table, and you will pay them well.

We are being told how important it is to get students into STEM fields (science, technology, engineering and math). Yet government funding for these fields is being cut and jobs prospects are uncertain. Stock market speculation diverts the best and brightest minds away from solving the real problems facing the world. Instead they are writing software to "read" news feeds looking for key phrases that might indicate a change in speculators' sentiment toward a particular stock, so that instantaneous trades can be made. They are writing algorithms to find the minutest correlations between economic indicators and changes in share prices. Landing a job at a big Wall Street firm can lead to annual bonuses in the millions of dollars. Jobs in basic scientific research and engineering cannot hope to compete.

Corporate managers are rewarded with bonuses for increases in stock prices, regardless of the long-term impacts on the firm. It forces managers to focus on quarterly profits and not on long-term economic growth. Cutting jobs and driving down wages can increase stock prices, but this has devastating impacts on the lives of ordinary people and reduces demand for products. If the price of a company's stock starts to fall, management may use the cash held by the company to buy back shares in order to prop up the price. This diverts resources that could have been used for productive investment into the hands of stock market speculators.

If enough of these speculators believe prices will continue to rise, they will pour more money into stocks, and share prices will rise. Speculation can be self-fulfilling and create price bubbles. The Dow-Jones was up by more than 35% for the year 2013. This run up in stock prices had several causes. Economists tell us that stock prices should reflect expected profitability, and despite the anemic recovery, corporate profits are soaring. The share of total national income going the owners of capital is now higher than at any point in modern U.S. history. But this is at the expense of the vast majority of the population. The share of national income going to wages and salaries continues to fall and is lower than in 1960. In the thirty three years since 1980, adjusted for inflation, labor productivity has gone up by 141% and wages have stagnated, going up by only 8%. The idea that each generation is better off than their parents' is no longer true. In the current recovery, 95% of the income gains have been taken by the top 1% of the population. The rise in stock prices is a reflection of the declining standard of living of the majority of Americans and the increasing incomes of the already wealthy. A recent Pew Center poll revealed that 64% of the population responded "no" when asked "does the U.S. offer everyone the same chance to get ahead." The share of income going to the richest 10% is higher than at any time since 1917. It is this richest 10% that own 91% all stocks, including all 401(k) accounts and mutual funds and 94% of other financial securities.

Some of the run up in stock prices may reflect this rise in profit, but another larger part is the result of speculation. Since the start of the recession, the Federal Reserve has pumped almost $4 trillion into the financial markets. All of this money has to go somewhere and banks are not lending it to businesses to engage in real investment. Some of it is being used by speculators to buy up foreclosed houses and either turning them into rentals or doing minor maintenance and then "flipping" them for a tidy profit (See Darwin BondGraham, "Whose Housing Recovery?" D&S March/April 2013). This is resulting in a massive redistribution of wealth from the middle class to the top 10% of wealth holders. In some cities, this is reigniting the housing bubble. But much of the money is finding its way into the stock market and this flood of money is driving up stock prices.

When speculators are optimistic they create bubbles. But if speculators turn pessimistic, they can also create stock market crashes. If this only affected the gamblers it would not be a problem. But as a company's stock price falls, it may be harder for the firm to borrow from banks or the bond market to pay for day-to-day operations. If this happens to enough companies, this can crash the real economy and drive up unemployment. As stock prices fall, the retirement savings of millions of workers (who have seen their defined-benefit pensions stolen and converted into 401(k) savings accounts) will also decline. Ordinary people reap little benefit from the daily speculation on the stock market, but millions experience real losses when the bets go bad. The Big Casino does very real damage to the real economy.

A Small Step Toward Taming the Casino

One way to reduce the damage would be to put a tax on the socially destructive behavior. We tax cigarettes and alcohol because of the damage they do. We tax gambling in Atlantic City at 8% and in Las Vegas at 6.25%. The sales taxes on socially useful items like shoes and computers are often more than 7%. There should also be a sales tax on the speculative buying and selling of stock.

To be sure, Wall Street lobbyists will try to scare the pubic in thinking that taxing speculation will somehow kill "investment" and jobs. Because unemployment is still high, anything that reduces employment growth will be seen as negative. But

SPECULATIVE TRADING VERSUS PRODUCTIVE FINANCING (FIGURES FOR 2007)		
EXISTING STOCKS TRADED	NEW STOCKS ISSUED	RATIO OF TRADING TO NEW ISSUES
$43.8 TRILLION	$65.1 BILLION	673:1
PERCENT OF TRADES GOING TO PRODUCTIVE FINANCING = 0.15%		

this tax will not reduce job creation. In fact, it is stock market speculation that does that. Between 2008 and 2013, the dollar value of shares repurchased by corporations was higher than the amount raised by IPOs. So the stock market has actually drained resources away from real investment and job creation.

In 2007, the year before the most recent collapse of a speculative bubble, $43.8 trillion in stocks changed hands on just the NYSE and the NASDAQ. That same year, only $65.1 billion was raised in IPOs. That is $673 dollars of speculation for every $1 allocated from savers to real investors. Putting a tax on stock speculation will have almost no impact on productive investment by businesses, but it will raise much needed revenue for public investments in education and infrastructure.

What we need is a "speculation-reduction tax." Some proponents of this type of tax call it a "financial transactions tax," or FTT. But the tax would not be on all financial transactions, just on speculation in the stock and bond markets. Gamblers and speculators are seen as frivolous and destructive, and a tax that would restrict their behavior would be positively received. To be fully effective, the tax should be "progressive" with respect to time. If a stock is held for less than a day, the tax on the trade should be 5% of the value of the trade. The tax on a stock held for a week would be 2%; for a month, 1%; and, for a year, 0.5%. But opponents will make the case that this is too complex and too costly, so a flat-rate tax is more feasible.

The European Union is likely to implement a FTT rate of 0.1% in 2014. This rate is too small to have much of an impact on speculation. The UK has had a tax rate of 0.5% since 1986. It has not restricted the basic functioning of their stock market, but a tax of this amount makes the short-term trade described above unprofitable. Since 2009, ten different FTT bills have been introduced in the U.S. House and four in the Senate, most at a rate less than 0.5%. If a 0.5% tax were implemented in the United States, the Congressional Research Service estimates revenue generation of $164 to $264 billion per year, depending on the decline in speculative trading. The left-leaning Center for Economic and Policy Research (CEPR) estimates revenues would be between $110 to $220 billion.

If the U.S. government implements this type of speculation-reduction tax, it will reallocate much needed resources to productive public investment and away from job-killing stock speculation. This idea, first proposed by John Maynard Keynes in 1936, is long over-due. As CEPR co-director Dean Baker put it in 1994, "Government is perfectly willingly to tax Las Vegas, Atlantic City and the lotteries, where working people place their bets with virtually no consequence to the country's economic future. Why then should it not also tax the preferred gambling venue of the wealthy, especially given the serious costs their activities impose on the economic prospects of the majority?" ❑

Sources: Dean Baker, et.al., "The Potential Revenue from Financial Transactions Taxes," Center for Economic and Policy Research, Dec. 2009; "A securities Transactions Tax: Brief Analytic Overview with Revenue Estimates," Congressional Research Service, June 2012; Robert Pollin and James Heintz, "Transaction Costs, Trading Elasticities and the Revenue Potential of Financial Transaction Taxes for the United States," Political Economy Research Institute, Dec. 2011; Dean Baker, Robert Pollin, and Marc Schaberg, "Taxing the Big Casino," The Nation, May 1994; Edward N. Wolff, The Asset Price Meltdown and the Wealth of the Middle Class, August 2012;NYSE Technologies Market Data (nyxdata.com); NASDAQ Trader (NASDAQtrader.com); PriceWaterhouse IPO Watch (pwc.com).

Article 4.5

WAS THE HOUSING BUBBLE A PONZI SCHEME?

BY ARTHUR MacEWAN
July/August 2009

> Dear Dr. Dollar:
> *What is the difference between a Ponzi scheme and the way the banks and other investors operated during the housing bubble?*
> —Leela Choiniere, Austin, Texas

As badly as our banking system operated in recent years, the housing bubble was not a Ponzi scheme. In some respects, however, it was even worse than a Ponzi scheme!

A Ponzi scheme is based on fraud. The operators of the scheme deceive the participants, telling them that their money is being used to make real or financial investments that have a high return. In fact, no such investments are made, and the operators of the scheme are simply paying high returns to the early participants with the funds put in by the later participants. A Ponzi scheme has to grow—and grow rapidly—in order to stay viable. When its growth slows, the early participants can no longer be paid the returns they expect. At this point, the operators disappear with what's left of the participants' funds—unless the authorities step in and arrest them, which is what happened with Charles Ponzi in 1920 and Bernard Madoff this year.

Fraud certainly was very important in the housing bubble of recent years. But the housing bubble—like bubbles generally—did not depend on fraud, and most of its development was there for everyone to see. With the principal problems out in the open and with the authorities not only ignoring those problems but contributing to their development, one might say that the situation with the housing bubble was worse than a Ponzi scheme. And Madoff bilked his marks out of only $50 billion, while trillions were lost in the housing bubble.

Bubbles involve actual investments in real or financial assets—housing in the years since 2000, high-tech stocks in the 1990s, and Dutch tulips in the 17th century. People invest believing that the price of the assets will continue to rise; as long as people keep investing, the price does rise. While some early speculators can make out very well, this speculation will not last indefinitely. Once prices start to fall, panic sets in and the later investors lose.

A bubble is similar to a Ponzi scheme: early participants can do well while later ones incur losses; it is based on false expectations; and it ultimately falls apart. But there need be no fraudulent operator at the center of a bubble. Also, while a Ponzi scheme depends on people giving their money to someone else to invest (e.g., Madoff), people made their own housing investments—though mortgage companies and banks made large fees for handling these investments.

Often, government plays a role in bubbles. The housing bubble was in part generated by the Federal Reserve maintaining low interest rates. Easy money meant readily obtainable loans and, at least in the short run, low monthly payments. Also, Fed Chairman Alan Greenspan denied the housing bubble's existence—not fraud exactly, but deception that kept the bubble going. (Greenspan, whose view was ideologically driven, got support in his bubble denial from the academic work of the man who was to be his successor, Ben Bernanke.)

In addition, government regulatory agencies turned a blind eye to the highly risky practices of financial firms, practices that both encouraged the development of the bubble and made the impact all the worse when it burst. Moreover, the private rating agencies (e.g., Moody's and Standard and Poor's) were complicit. Dependent on the financial institutions for their fees, they gave excessively good ratings to these risky investments. Perhaps not fraud in the legal sense, but certainly misleading.

During the 1990s, the government made tax law changes that contributed to the emergence of the housing bubble. With the Taxpayer Relief Act of 1997, a couple could gain up to $500,000 selling their home without any capital gains tax liability (half that for a single person). Previously, capital gains taxes could be avoided only if the proceeds were used to buy another home or if the seller was over 55 (and a couple could then avoid taxes only on the first $250,000). So buying and then selling houses became a more profitable operation.

And, yes, substantial fraud was involved. For example, mortgage companies and banks used deceit to get people to take on mortgages when there was no possibility that the borrowers would be able to meet the payments. Not only was this fraud, but this fraud depended on government authorities ignoring their regulatory responsibilities.

So, no, a bubble and a Ponzi scheme are not the same. But they have elements in common. Usually, however, the losers in a Ponzi scheme are simply the direct investors, the schemer's marks. A bubble like the housing bubble can wreak havoc on all of us. ❑

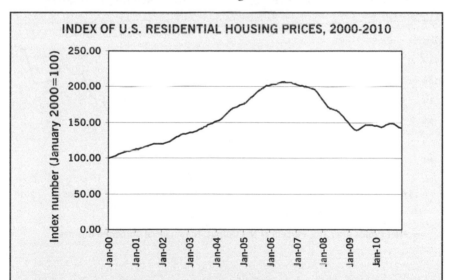

INDEX OF U.S. RESIDENTIAL HOUSING PRICES, 2000-2010

As the housing bubble inflated, the index of residential housing prices in the United States more than doubled in value, from 100 in 2000 to over 200 in 2006. Since then, the bubble has burst, and the housing index has dropped back below 150. The real estate bubble helped fuel an economic boom in the United States. As people saw their homes increase in value, many spent more freely. Many borrowed against the rising value of their houses. The collapse of the bubble had the opposite effect. As people saw the value of their homes plummet, they cut back on their spending. The collapse in demand resulted in dropping output and employment. – *Alejandro Reuss*

Article 4.6

COLLAPSING INVESTMENT AND THE GREAT RECESSION

BY GERALD FRIEDMAN
July/August 2013

Investment in real inputs—structures and machinery used to boost future output and productivity—is one of the ways that an economy grows over time. In a capitalist economy, such investments are also crucial for macroeconomic stability and full employment because they provide an "injection" of demand to balance the "leakage" caused by personal and institutional savings. The Great Recession that began in 2007 was marked by a collapse of investment unprecedented since the Great Depression, as well as a dramatic drop in overall production and a sharp jump in unemployment. Since 2009, overall output has been growing again, but we have seen a much slower recovery of investment than after other recessions since 1947. The worst economic crisis since the 1930s, the Great Recession came after a long period of declining investment, and a break in the linkage between corporate profits and new investment.

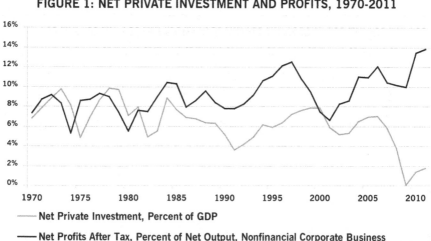

FIGURE 1: NET PRIVATE INVESTMENT AND PROFITS, 1970-2011

——— Net Private Investment, Percent of GDP

—— Net Profits After Tax, Percent of Net Output, Nonfinancial Corporate Business

The share of national income going to investment (net of depreciation of existing plant and machinery) has been declining since the beginning of the "neoliberal" era, around 1980. Since the start of the Great Recession, net investment as a share of GDP has plummeted to its lowest level since the 1930s. This sharp drop in investment comes despite sharply rising profits.

FIGURE 2: NET PRIVATE INVESTMENT AND INTEREST RATES, 1946-2011

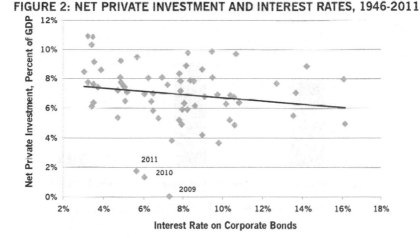

The Federal Reserve has helped to shorten past recessions by driving down interest rates to lower the cost of borrowing and so spur investment. During the current crisis, the Fed has conducted an aggressive monetary policy, raising the money supply to lower interest rates. But it has had little effect on investment. While lower interest rates have had only a weak effect on investment in the past, monetary policy has had no discernible effect in the last few years, as investment rates are dramatically lower than would have been expected given the level of interest rates. Substantial excess capacity, weak expectations of future sales, and corporate strategies to shift production outside the United States all may be contributing to the lack of investment demand

FIGURE 3: INVESTMENT AND UNEMPLOYMENT, 1947-2011

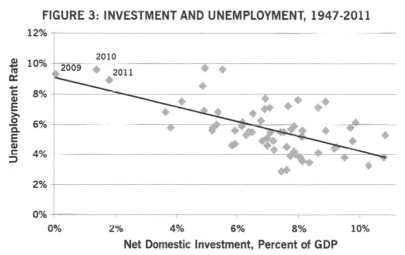

In one respect, the current recession resembles past experience. Low rates of investment are associated with high rates of unemployment, just as in previous economic downturns. The difference is that, three years after the official end of the Great Recession, the unemployment rate remains persistently high, and investment remains dramatically lower than in past recoveries.

FIGURE 4: WHAT RECOVERY?

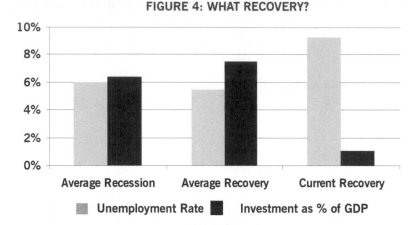

During the current "recovery" (2009-present), the unemployment rate has remained higher and investment as a share of GDP has remained lower than the average not only for past recoveries, but even for past recessions (since 1947). No wonder the current situation seems more like a continuation of the Great Recession than a genuine recovery.

FIGURE 5: CORPORATE PROFITS AND INVESTMENT, 1947-2011

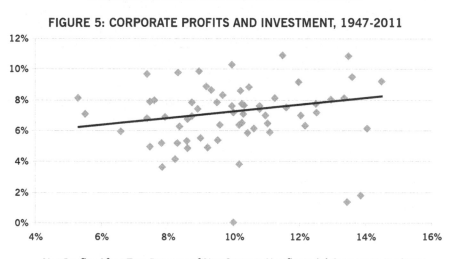

Net Profits After Tax, Percent of Net Output, Nonfinancial Corporate Business

Note: Trendline excludes years 2009-2011.

In the past, higher corporate profits were associated with higher rates of investment, as businesses have rushed to take advantage of profitable opportunities. In the current crisis, however, the link between profit and investment has been broken and investment rates have been very low despite high rates of profitability (especially in 2010 and 2011). Businesses are holding back on investing, either because they anticipate continued low levels of demand (perhaps due to high unemployment and low wages) or because they plan to shift more production outside the United States. ❏

Sources: Investment: Bureau of Economic Analysis (BEA, bea.gov), Table 5.2.5, Gross and Net Domestic Investment by Major Type; GDP: BEA, Current-Dollar and "Real" Gross Domestic Product; Profits: BEA, Table 1.15, Price, Costs, and Profit Per Unit of Real Gross Value Added of Nonfinancial Domestic Corporate Business; Unemployment: Bureau of Labor Statistics, Unemployment rate, 16 years and over, Not seasonally adjusted, Series ID LNU04000000; Interest rate: St. Louis Federal Reserve, Moody's Seasoned Baa Corporate Bond Yield.

Chapter 5

FISCAL POLICY, DEFICITS, AND AUSTERITY

INTRODUCTION

Most textbooks, at least to the extent that they are influenced by Keynesian economics, depict a macroeconomy stabilized by government intervention. They look at ways the government can use fiscal policy—government spending and taxation—to bolster a flagging economy. Today's economy, yet to recover from the worst economic crisis since the Great Depression, is still flagging. Worse yet, this lingering crisis comes on the heels of a feeble economic expansion that created fewer jobs and did less to raise wages than any other economic expansion since World War II.

What is the role of fiscal policy in this context? As the crisis worsened in the fall of 2008, the federal government dramatically increased spending. First, Congress passed the Troubled Asset Relief Program (TARP), which bailed out giant investment banks and insurance companies. It then passed the Obama stimulus package and budget, which provided some much-needed domestic spending but also boosted military spending. At the same time, the Federal Reserve and the Federal Deposit Insurance Corporation (which insures bank deposits) issued loans, lines of credit, and loan guarantees, and pledged an emergency fund to clean up losses on Wall Street. All told, the federal government, the Fed, and FDIC sank nearly the value of a year's total U.S. national output into propping up the failed financial sector and rescuing the economy. That was enough to prevent a repeat of the Great Depression, but not enough to ignite the rapid economic growth necessary to put those who lost their jobs back to work. (See Chapter 6 for more on the financial bailout.)

While the increased spending played a role, it was mainly the collapse of the economy and the Bush administration's tax cuts and war spending that pushed the federal budget far into the red. Today, U.S. government debt is equal to just over one year's Gross Domestic Product (GDP). (Though it is less than 75% of GDP if we exclude the debt held by the Federal Reserve, the Social Security Trust Fund, and other government agencies.) The surge in government deficits and debt has somehow become the focus of macroeconomic policy debates in the United States, despite the persistence of historically high unemployment. The articles in this chapter contest the orthodox view that short-term deficit-reduction should be the focus of macroeconomic policy, arguing that fiscal stimulus is necessary to tackle the still-raging unemployment crisis.

In Article 5.1, economist Marty Wolfson debunks the widespread myth, parroted by mainstream politicians and media commentators, that government spending cannot create jobs. He sees this as part of a conservative ideological campaign to prevent government from doing just that. Government spending, he argues, need not be wasteful, and in fact is not necessarily less valuable than private spending. The government, he concludes, can and should be creating jobs.

Alejandro Reuss (Article 5.2) takes a close look at what Keynes actually had to say about the efficacy of fiscal policy in his most famous book, *The General Theory of Employment, Interest, and Money*. Keynes was a strong advocate of fiscal policy, especially government spending, as a response to business-cycle downturns. Reuss explains how Keynes challenged the "Treasury view" that government spending could not get the economy going because it would "crowd out" private investment, the same argument conservatives have invoked against fiscal stimulus policies today.

The Great Recession didn't just blow a massive hole in federal government finances, but state and municipal government finances as well. The effects have been devastating. As economists Robert Pollin and Jeffrey Thompson point out, state and local government is the single largest employer in the U.S. economy. The authors make the case that public employees are not responsible for today's budget problems. They also find, contrary to what is often reported by the mainstream and business press, that state and local government employees are not overpaid (Article 5.3).

Two articles by economist Gerald Friedman tackle current controversies about federal tax and spending policies. Friedman shows that cutting taxes on the very rich, as the U.S. government has been doing for decades, has not led to the investment or economic growth that conservative economists promised (Article 5.4). Next, he refutes the myth that "runaway" federal spending is the cause of today's large budget deficits (Article 5.5).

To round out the chapter, two articles show that the U.S. government debt is not the looming crisis that many politicians and commentators claim. Economist Marty Wolfson (Article 5.6) clarifies the link between Social Security benefit payments and the gross federal debt. Of the $17 trillion in federal debt, $2.7 trillion are in the form of treasury bonds held by the Social Security Trust Fund. That slice of the federal debt is not a result of overly generous benefits that we cannot afford. Rather, an entire generation of workers paid more into Social Security than they have withdrawn in benefits, and the surplus has been invested in treasury bonds. Finally, Robert Pollin explains why a hugely influential study by two prominent economists—claiming that high levels of government debt diminish future growth—is fatally flawed (Article 5.7). Therefore, he concludes, urgent calls for fiscal "belt-tightening" are unjustified.

Discussion Questions

1. (Article 5.1) What are the main arguments made by opponents of government "stimulus" spending? How does Wolfson refute each of these points?

2. (Article 5.2) Why did Keynes think that the dollar-for-dollar crowding-out argument (the "Treasury view") was mistaken? And how might Keynes respond to the arguments conservatives have leveled against fiscal stimulus policies during the Great Recession?

3. (Article 5.3) What evidence do Pollin and Thompson present to show that state and local government workers are not overpaid and that their pension funds are not about to collapse?

4. (Article 5.4) When it comes to promoting investment and economic growth, what is the track record of tax cuts for high-income individuals?

6. (Article 5.5) What are the main reasons that federal government spending increased during the Great Recession? Is increasing spending to blame for today's budget deficits? Why does Friedman argue that federal spending is actually too low?

7. (Article 5.6) Why is the $17 trillion figure for gross federal debt a misleading measure of our future obligations? Wolfson argues that reducing Social Security benefits would increase federal debt. How could this be so?

8. (Article 5.7) Pollin argues that it is not just the size of the debt that matters, but what kind of spending we do with the borrowed money. What do you think our spending priorities should be? What affects our ability to borrow to meet our spending needs?

Article 5.1

THE IDEOLOGICAL ATTACK ON JOB CREATION
Responding to Anti-Government Arguments

BY MARTY WOLFSON
May/June 2012

> "Government doesn't create jobs. It's the private sector that creates jobs."
> —presidential candidate Mitt Romney, speaking at Wofford College,
>   Spartenburg, S.C., January 18, 2012

It is jarring to hear pundits say that the government can't create jobs. It is even more jarring to hear the same refrain from someone whose job was created by the government! Perhaps Mr. Romney has forgotten, or would like to forget, that he used to have a government job as governor of Massachusetts.

But surely those currently on the government payroll have not forgotten, like the chairman of the House Republican Policy Committee, Rep. Tom Price (R-Ga.). He used the same talking points, "The government doesn't create jobs. It's the private sector that creates jobs," speaking on MSNBC's "Andrea Mitchell Reports" last June.

Rep. Price apparently thinks he doesn't have a real job, but what about teachers, firefighters, police officers, and school cafeteria workers? And what about the 2 to 4.8 million jobs—in both the public and private sectors—the U.S. Congressional Budget Office estimated were created by the 2009 U.S. economic stimulus package?

The "government doesn't create jobs" mantra is part of a coordinated right-wing campaign to *prevent* the government from creating jobs and promoting the interests of working families, and to instead encourage a shift in the distribution of income towards the wealthy. It is supported by ideologically motivated arguments and theories from conservative economists and anti-government think tanks. In what follows, these arguments are addressed and criticized, in the hopes of clearing away some of the confusion undermining a vigorous government program to put people back to work.

The Argument That Government Spending Can't Increase Jobs

A Senior Fellow at the Cato Institute says the idea that government spending can create jobs "has a rather glaring logical fallacy. It overlooks the fact that, in the real world, government can't inject money into the economy without first taking money out of the economy." This argument is wrong for several reasons.

First, the government *can* inject money into the economy. It does so whenever it finances its spending by selling bonds to the Federal Reserve. In this case, money is created by the Federal Reserve when it buys the bonds. It creates a reserve account on its books; money is thus created without any reduction in money elsewhere in the economy.

Alternatively, the government can finance its spending by taxes or by selling bonds to the public. This is the case envisioned by the Cato analysis. The argument is that the money spent by the government is exactly balanced by a reduction in money in the pockets of taxpayers of bond buyers. However, if the taxpayers' or the bond buyers' money would otherwise have been saved and not spent, then there is a net injection into the economy of funds that can put people to work.

The argument made by the Cato Institute is actually a variation of another theory, known as "crowding out." In this theory, government spending creates competition for real resources that "crowds out," or displaces, private investment; private companies are unable to obtain the workers and capital they need for investment, so that any jobs due to government spending are offset by a decrease of jobs in the private sector.

This theory is valid only when there is full employment because there would be no idle resources, labor or capital, to put to use. In that case, though, neither the government nor the private sector would be able to create net new jobs. In contrast, in a situation of unemployment, it is precisely because the government can access otherwise idle resources that it can create jobs.

And, of course, that is exactly the situation we are in. As of March, the official unemployment rate stood at 8.2 %. Adjusted for underemployment, e.g., by counting those discouraged workers who have dropped out of the labor force and those workers who are working part-time but would like to work full-time, the more accurate unemployment rate was 14.5%.

The Argument That Cutting Government Spending Creates Jobs

Consistent with anti-government ideology, conservative economics asserts not only that government spending can't create jobs, but also that cutting government spending creates jobs. Here's how the argument goes: less government spending will reduce the government deficit; smaller deficits will increase the confidence of businesses that will invest more and in that way create more jobs. According to John B. Taylor, an economist affiliated with Stanford's conservative Hoover Institution, "Basic economic models in which incentives and expectations of future policy matter show that a credible plan to reduce gradually the deficit will increase economic growth and reduce unemployment by removing uncertainty and lowering the chances of large tax increases in the future." (Interestingly, an analysis by economist Robert Pollin of the Political Economy Research Institute at the University of Massachusetts-Amherst finds that Taylor's empirical model concludes that the stimulus bill was ineffective—but only because it included too much in tax cuts as opposed to direct government spending.)

This assertion is based more on wishful thinking than empirical validity, and has been criticized by Paul Krugman as depending on belief in a "confidence fairy." But it is not just liberal economists like Krugman who are critical of this theory. A confidential report prepared for clients by the investment bank Goldman Sachs concluded that a $61 billion cut in government spending from a bill passed by the House of Representatives in February 2011 (but not enacted into law) would lead to a decline in economic growth of 2%. And economist Mark Zandi, formerly an advisor to Republican presidential candidate John McCain, concluded that this $61 billion reduction in government spending could result in the loss of 700,000 jobs by 2012.

Ben Bernanke, chairman of the Board of Governors of the Federal Reserve System, stated that "the cost to the recovery [of steep reductions in government outlays now] would outweigh the benefits in terms of fiscal discipline." Even the International Monetary Fund, in its semiannual report on the world economic outlook, concluded that "the idea that fiscal austerity triggers faster growth in the short term finds little support in the data."

Also, in a review of studies and historical experience about the relationship between budget-cutting and economic growth, economists Arjun Jayadev and Mike Konczal concluded that countries historically did not cut government spending and deficits in a slump and that there is no basis to conclude that doing so now, "under the conditions the United States currently faces, would improve the country's prospects."

The Argument That Private Spending Is Always Better than Public Spending

Another way that right-wing economics tries to discredit the idea that the government can create jobs is to assert that private spending is always to be preferred to public spending. There are several rationalizations for this view.

One is that private spending is more efficient than public spending. This ideological refrain has been repeated consistently, and gained a following, over the past thirty years. But repetition does not make it correct. Of course, the proponents of this argument can point to examples of government mismanagement, such as that following Hurricane Katrina. However, government bungling and inefficiency by an administration that did not believe in government does not prove the point. A much more grievous example of inefficiency and misallocation of resources is the housing speculation and financial manipulation—and eventual collapse that brought us to the current recession—due to a deregulated private financial system. Yet for free-market ideologues, this somehow does not discredit the private sector.

Some people think that economists have "proven" that "free" markets are efficient. The only thing that has been proven, however, is that you can arrive at any conclusion if your assumptions are extreme enough. And the assumptions that form the basis for the free-market theory are indeed extreme, if not totally unrealistic and impossible. For example: orthodox free-market economics assumes perfectly competitive markets; perfect information; no situations, like pollution, in which private decision-makers do not take account of the societal effects of their actions; even full employment. But none of these assumptions hold true in the real world. Also, the distribution of income is irrelevant to the conclusions of this theory. The distribution of income is simply taken as given, so that the results of the theory are consistent with a relatively equal distribution of income as well as a very unequal distribution. As economist Joseph Stiglitz has said, "Today, there is no respectable intellectual support for the proposition that markets, by themselves, lead to efficient, let alone equitable outcomes."

A second reason for supposing that private spending is to be preferred to public spending is the notion that public spending is less worthwhile than private spending. This means, for many people, reducing government spending as much as possible. For example, Grover Norquist, founder and president of Americans for Tax Reform and author of the anti-tax pledge signed by many members of Congress, said that he wanted to "shrink [the government] down to the size where we can drown it in the bathtub." The anti-tax, anti-spending crusade has in many cases been successful in reducing government budgets, on the national as well as the local level. This has resulted in a significant decrease in government services. Although some people are attracted to the view that government spending should always be reduced, they probably at the same time don't want to drive on roads and bridges that aren't repaired and they probably want fire trucks to arrive if their house is on fire. Perhaps, too, they wouldn't automatically prefer twelve kinds of toothpaste to schools, parks, and libraries.

The Argument That Government Spending Is Wasteful

Another argument contends that public spending is wasteful. Discussions of government accounts generally do not take account of public investment, so all public spending is essentially treated as consumption. As such, it is considered unproductive and wasteful by those who wish to disparage government spending. In other words, the government budget does not make a distinction between long-term investments and other spending as corporate budgets do.

One implication of treating all government spending as consumption is the notion that the federal government should maintain a balanced budget. To put this in accounting terms, on this view government accounts are considered to only have an income statement (which shows current revenues and current expenditures), not a balance sheet (which shows assets and liabilities).

Corporations, in contrast, maintain balance sheets. They don't balance their budgets in the way that the budget hawks want the government to do. Private investment in plant and equipment, for example, is accounted for on the asset side of the balance sheet; borrowing to finance this investment is accounted for on the liability side. Interest on the debt is accounted for on the income statement, and it is only the interest, not the outstanding debt balance, that has to be covered by cur-

---

The Ryan Budget: A Path to Prosperity?

On March 29, the House of Representatives passed Rep. Paul Ryan's budget proposal, called the "FY2013 Path to Prosperity Budget." It would be a disaster for working Americans. It shreds the safety net; according to the Center for Budget and Policy Priorities, 62% of Ryan's trillions in spending cuts come from programs affecting low-income Americans. The vast majority of tax cuts would go to corporations and upper-income Americans. Yet Ryan claims that his budget brings the "size of government to 20 percent of [the] economy by 2015, allowing the private sector to grow and create jobs." But an independent analysis by Ethan Pollack, a researcher at the Economic Policy Institute, concludes that Ryan's budget would result in the loss of 4.1 million jobs by 2014.

rent revenues. The assumption behind this accounting is that borrowing to finance productive investment will generate the revenue to pay off the borrowing.

In other words, corporations borrow on a regular basis to finance investment. So they only attempt to balance their current expenditures and revenues and not their capital budget.

Much confusion about private and public spending, and also about budget deficits, could be avoided if discussion focused on a federal government balance sheet. In that way, current spending that needs to be balanced with current revenue could be separated from long-term investments that will increase the productivity of the American economy. Such investments, in areas like infrastructure and education, can increase future economic growth and income, and thus generate more tax revenue to pay off the debt. Just like a private company's investments, they are legitimately financed by borrowing.

Government Can Indeed Create Jobs

The main point, though, is this: whether financed by borrowing or taxes, whether consumption or investment, government spending that increases the demand for goods and services in the economy is not wasteful. It has the ability to employ underutilized resources and create jobs.

Ultimately, a job is a job, whether created by the private or public sector. A job has the potential to enable workers to support themselves and their families in dignity. We should not let ideological arguments keep us from using every available means to promote the basic human right of employment. ❑

Sources: Congressional Budget Office, "Estimated Impact of the American Recovery and Reinvestment Act on Employment and Economic Output From April 2010 Through June 2010," August 2010; Daniel J. Mitchell, "The Fallacy That Government Creates Jobs," The Cato Institute, 2008; John B. Taylor, "Goldman Sachs Wrong About Impact of House Budget Proposal," Economics One blog, February 28, 2011; Paul Krugman, "Myths of austerity," *The New York Times.* July 1, 2010; Jonathan Karl, "Goldman Sachs: House Spending Cuts Will Hurt Economic Growth," The Note, 2011; Mark Zandi, "A federal shutdown could derail the recovery," Moody's Analytics, February 28, 2011; Pedro da Costa and Mark Felsenthal, "Bernanke warns against steep budget cuts," Reuters, February 9, 2011; International Monetary Fund, *World Economic Outlook: Recovery, Risk, and Rebalancing,* 2010; Arjun Jayadev and Mike Konczal, "When Is Austerity Right? In Boom, Not Bust," *Challenge,* November-December 2010, pp. 37-53; Joseph Stiglitz, Foreword, in Karl Polanyi, *The Great Transformation: The Political and Economic Origins of Our Times,* 2001; David Aschauer, "Is Public Expenditure Productive?" *Journal of Monetary Economics,* 1989, pp. 177-200; Robert Pollin, "US government deficits and debt amid the great recession: what the evidence shows, *Cambridge Journal of Economics,* 2012, 36, 161-187; Kelsey Merrick and Jim Horney, "Chairman Ryan Gets 62 Percent of His Huge Budget Cuts from Programs for Lower-income Americans," Center on Budget and Policy Priorities, March 23, 2012; Paul Ryan, The Path to Prosperity, March 20, 2012; Ethan Pollack, "Ryan's Budget Would Cost Jobs," The Economic Policy Institute, March 21, 2012.

Article 5.2

FISCAL POLICY AND "CROWDING OUT"

BY ALEJANDRO REUSS
May/June 2009

In response to the deepest recession in the United States since the Great Depression, the Obama administration proposed a large fiscal "stimulus" plan. (Fiscal policies involve government spending and taxation. A fiscal stimulus involves increases in government spending or tax cuts, or both.) The current stimulus plan, after some compromises between the Obama administration and Republicans in Congress, included both substantial tax cuts and increases in government spending. Together, they would increase the federal government deficit by over $700 billion.

A fiscal stimulus is a standard "Keynesian" response to a recession. The logic behind these policies is that recessions can be caused by insufficient total demand for goods and services. If saving (a "leakage" from demand) exceeds investment (an "injection" of demand), there will not be enough demand to buy all the goods and services that the economy is capable of producing at the "full employment" level. Some goods will go unsold, and firms will reduce output. They will cut jobs, cancel supply orders, and even close production facilities. The economy will spiral into a recession.

In standard Keynesian models, either tax cuts or increased government spending can increase total demand, and therefore total output and employment. An initial increase in spending (by either the government or the recipients of the tax cuts) results in new income for other individuals, who then go on to spend part (not all) of this income, which results in new income for still other individuals, and so on. Ultimately, this series of additions to income results in a total increase in GDP greater than the original increase in government spending or reduction in taxes. The increase in real GDP divided by the initial spending increase is called the "multiplier." The standard Keynesian view implies a multiplier greater than one.

The Conservative Critique

Conservative economists, whose intellectual heritage includes decades-old attempts to refute Keynesian theory, disagree with this view. They argue that government spending cannot possibly increase overall economic activity, and that the stimulus plan is therefore doomed to fail. This position is sometimes known as the "Treasury view" (because it mirrors the arguments of the British Treasury Department during the Great Depression) or the theory of "crowding out." The new government spending, these economists argue, "has to come from somewhere," either from higher taxes or increased government borrowing. Either way, the increase in government spending will come at the expense of private spending.

If the spending is financed by tax increases, conservative economists argue, this will reduce individuals' after-tax incomes and therefore reduce their spending. If it is financed through borrowing, the increased government demand for loans will drive up interest rates, and this will "crowd out" private investment. (Some private investment projects that would have been profitable at lower interest rates would not be profitable at the higher rates, and therefore would not be undertaken.) Extreme versions of this theory, known as "dollar-for-dollar" crowding out, argue that the decrease in private investment will exactly offset the increase in government spending, and there will be no change in the overall output of goods and services.

Government intervention is not only incapable of pulling the economy out of a recession, conservative economists argue, it is also unnecessary. If there is more saving than investment, the quantity of funds people are willing to loan out will exceed the quantity that people are willing to borrow at the current interest rate. The surplus of loanable funds will drive down the interest rate. People will save less (since the reward to saving is lower) and borrow more and invest more (since the cost of borrowing is lower), until the injection of investment and the leakage of saving are equal. In short, if insufficient demand ever caused a recession, the economy would quickly pull itself back to full employment without any need for government intervention.

Keynes' Rejoinder

Keynes agreed with the idea that saving equals investment. In his view, however, this is true not only when the economy is producing at its full-employment capacity, but also when it is producing at far less than its capacity. Keynes argued that the "classical" economists (as he called the conservative orthodoxy of his time) had an incorrect view of the relationship between interest rates and savings, and that this was at the heart of their errors about the possibility of prolonged recessions.

The classicals believed that as interest rates increased, savings would increase, and that as interest rates declined, savings would decline. Keynes agreed that this was true at "a given income," but that a change in the interest rate would also affect the amount investment and therefore the level of income. A higher interest rate, he argued, was associated with lower investment, lower incomes, and therefore lower saving; a lower interest rate, with higher investment, higher incomes, and therefore higher saving. (As people's incomes increase, they spend more *and* save more; as their incomes decline, they spend less *and* save less.) In Keynes' view, saving will equal investment whether investment and saving are both high (at or near the full employment level of output) or if investment and saving are both low (in a low-output, high-unemployment economy). In the latter case, Keynes believed, there was no guarantee that the economy would pull itself back to full employment.

Keynes was also well aware, long before his critics, that government borrowing could crowd out some private investment. In *The General Theory* itself, he noted that the effects of the government directly increasing employment on public works may include "increasing the rate of interest and so retarding investment in other directions." This does not imply, however, dollar-for-dollar crowding out. Keynes still believed, and the empirical evidence confirms, that under depression conditions an increase in government spending can result in an increase in total output larger than the initial spending increase (a multiplier greater than one).

Of Spending and Multipliers

In a January 2009 article in the *Wall Street Journal*, conservative economist Robert Barro declares, as a "plausible starting point," that the multiplier actually equals zero. That's what the dollar-for-dollar crowding-out theory means—an increase in government spending will be matched by equal decreases in private spending, and so will have zero effect on real GDP. When it comes to estimating the multiplier, based on historical data from 1943-1944, however, Barro finds that it is not zero, but 0.8.

First, contrary to Barro's intent, this is actually a disproof of dollar-for-dollar crowding out. It means that increased government spending brought about increased real GDP, though not by as much as the spending increase. It increased the production of public-sector goods by (much) more than it reduced the production of private-sector goods. Unless one views private-sector goods as intrinsically more valuable than public-sector goods, this is not an argument against government spending.

Second, Barro chose to base his study on two years at the height of the U.S. mobilization for World War II. When the economy is at or near full employment, the multiplier is bound to be small. If all resources are already being used, the only way to produce more of some kinds of goods (say, tanks and war planes) is to produce less of some others (say, civilian cars). Keynesian economists certainly understand this. Their point, however, is that government spending creates a large multiplier effect when the economy is languishing in a recession, not when it is already at full employment.

Economist Mark Zandi of Moody's Economy.com reports much higher multipliers for government spending. Zandi estimates multipliers between 1.3 and 1.6 for federal aid to states and for government infrastructure expenditures. The multipliers are even larger for government transfers (such as food stamps or unemployment compensation) to the hardest-hit, who are likely to spend all or almost all of their increase in income. Zandi estimates these multipliers at between 1.6 and 1.8. Tax cuts for high income individuals and corporations, who are less likely to spend their additional disposable income, have the lowest multipliers—between 0.3 and 0.4.

Why the *General* Theory?

The conservative case against standard Keynesian fiscal stimulus policy rests on the assumption that all of the economy's resources are already being used to the fullest. Keynes titled his most important work *The General Theory* because he thought that the orthodox economics of his time confined itself to this special case, the case of an economy at full employment. He did not believe that this was generally the case in capitalist economies, and he sought to develop a theory that explained this.

The argument conservatives make against government spending—"it has to come from somewhere"—is actually no less true for private investment. If dollar-for-dollar crowding out were true, therefore, it would be just as impossible for private investment to pull the economy out of a recession. This, of course, would be nonsense unless the economy was already at full employment (and an increase in one kind of production would have to come at the expense of some other kind of production).

If the economy were already operating at full capacity—imagine a situation in which all workers are employed, factories are humming with activity 24/7, and no unused resources would be available to expand production if demand increased—the argument that increased government spending could not increase overall economic output might be plausible. But that is manifestly not the current economic situation.

Real GDP declined at an annual rate of 6.3% in the fourth quarter of 2008. The official unemployment rate surged to 8.5%, the highest rate in 30 years, in March 2009. Over 15% of workers are unemployed, have given up looking for work, or can only find part-time work. Employment is plummeting by more than half a million workers each month. A theory that assumes the economy is already at full employment can neither help us understand how we got into this hole—or how we can get out. ❑

Sources: John Maynard Keynes, *The General Theory of Employment, Interest, and Money*, 1964; Associated Press, "Obama: Stimulus lets Americans claim destiny," February 17, 2009; Paul Krugman, "A Dark Age of macroeconomics (wonkish)," January 27, 2009 (krugman.blogs. nytimes.com); J. Bradford DeLong, "More 'Treasury View' Blogging," February 5,2009 (delong. typepad.com); J. Bradford DeLong, "The Modern Revival of the 'Treasury View,'" January 18, 2009 (delong.typepad.com); Robert J. Barro,"Government Spending is No Free Lunch," *Wall Street Journal*, January 22, 2009 (wsj.com); Paul Krugman, "War and non-remembrance," January 22, 2009 (krugman.blogs.nytimes.com); Paul Krugman, "Spending in wartime," January 23, 2009 (krugman.blogs.nytimes.com); Mark Zandi, "The Economic Impact of a $750 Billion Fiscal Stimulus Package," Moody'sEconomy.com, March 26, 2009; Bureau of Labor Statistics, Alternative measures of labor underutilization; Bureau of Labor Statistics Payroll Employment.

Article 5.3

THE BETRAYAL OF PUBLIC WORKERS

It's not only bad politics for states to use their budget crises to bust unions—it's bad economics.

BY ROBERT POLLIN AND JEFFREY THOMPSON
March 2011; The Nation

The Great Recession and its aftermath are entering a new phase in the United States, which could bring even more severe assaults on the living standards and basic rights of ordinary people than we have experienced thus far. This is because a wide swath of the country's policy- and opinion-making elite have singled out public sector workers—including schoolteachers, healthcare workers, police officers and firefighters—as well as their unions and even their pensions as deadweight burdens sapping the economy's vitality.

The Great Recession did blow a massive hole in state and municipal government finances, with tax receipts—including income, sales and property taxes—dropping sharply along with household incomes, spending and real estate values. Meanwhile, demand for public services, such as Medicaid and heating oil assistance, has risen as people's circumstances have worsened. But let's remember that the recession was caused by Wall Street hyper-speculation, not the pay scales of elementary school teachers or public hospital nurses.

Nonetheless, a rising chorus of commentators charge that public sector workers are overpaid relative to employees in comparable positions in the private sector. The fact that this claim is demonstrably false appears not to matter. Instead, the attacks are escalating. The most recent proposal gaining traction is to write new laws that would allow states to declare bankruptcy. This would let them rip up contracts with current public sector employees and walk away from their pension fund obligations. Only by declaring bankruptcy, Republican luminaries Jeb Bush and Newt Gingrich argued in the *Los Angeles Times*, will states be able to "reform their bloated, broken and underfunded pension systems for current and future workers."

But this charge is emanating not only from the Republican right; in a front-page story on January 20, 2011, the *New York Times* reported on a more general trend spreading across the country in which "policymakers are working behind the scenes to come up with a way to let states declare bankruptcy and get out from under crushing debts, including the pensions they have promised to retired public workers."

Considered together, state and local governments are the single largest employer in the US economy. They are also the country's most important providers of education, healthcare, public safety and other vital forms of social support. Meanwhile, the official unemployment rate is stuck at 9%—a more accurate figure is 16.1%—a full eighteen months after the recession was declared over. How have we reached the point where the dominant mantra is to dismantle rather than shore up state and local governments in their moment of crisis?

Why States Need Support During Recessions

The Wall Street–induced recession clobbered state and local government budgets. By 2009, state tax revenues had fallen by fully 13% relative to where they were in 2007, and they remained at that low level through most of last year. By comparison, revenues never fell by more than 6% in the 2001 recession. Even during the 1981–82 recession, the last time unemployment reached 9%, the decline in state tax revenues never exceeded 2%. These revenue losses, starting in 2008, when taken together with the increased demand for state services, produced an average annual budget gap in 2009–11 of $140 billion, or 21% of all state spending commitments.

Unlike the federal government, almost all state and local governments are legally prohibited from borrowing money to finance shortfalls in their day-to-day operating budgets. The state and local governments do borrow to finance their long-term investments in school buildings, roads, bridges, sewers, mass transit and other infrastructure projects. They have established a long record of reliability in repaying these debt obligations, even during the recession. Nevertheless, these governments invariably experience a squeeze in their operating budgets during recessions, no matter how well they have managed their finances during more favorable economic times.

If, in a recession, states and municipalities are forced to reduce their spending in line with their loss in tax revenues, this produces layoffs for government employees and loss of sales for government vendors. These cutbacks, in turn, will worsen conditions in the private market, discouraging private businesses from making new investments and hiring new employees. The net impact is to create a vicious cycle that deepens the recession.

As such, strictly as a means of countering the recession—on behalf of business interests as well as everyone else in the community—the logic of having the federal government providing stimulus funds to support state and local government spending levels is impeccable. The February 2009 Obama stimulus—the American Recovery and Reinvestment Act (ARRA)—along with supplemental funds for Medicaid, has provided significant support, covering about one-third of the total budget gap generated by the recession. But that leaves two-thirds to be filled by other means. ARRA funds have now run out, and the Republican-controlled House of Representatives will almost certainly block further funding.

In 2010 roughly another 15% of the budget gap was covered by twenty-nine states that raised taxes and fees-for-services. In general, raising taxes during a recession is not good policy. But if it must be done to help fill deepening budgetary holes, the sensible way to proceed is to focus these increases on wealthier households. Their ability to absorb such increases is obviously strongest, which means that, unlike other households, they are not likely to cut back on spending in response to the tax hikes. In fact, ten states—New York, Illinois, Connecticut, North Carolina, Wisconsin, Oregon, Hawaii, Vermont, Rhode Island and Delaware—have raised taxes progressively in some fashion.

Of course, the wealthy do not want to pay higher taxes. But during the economic expansion and Wall Street bubble years of 2002–07, the average incomes of the richest 1% of households rose by about 10% per year, more than three times that for all households. The richest 1% received fully 65% of all household income growth between 2002–07.

One charge against raising state taxes in a progressive way is that it will encourage the wealthy to pick up and leave the state. But research on this question shows that this has not happened. We can see why by considering, as a hypothetical example, the consequences of a 2% income tax increase on the wealthiest 5% of households in Massachusetts. This would mean that these households would now have $359,000 at their disposal after taxes rather than $370,000—hardly enough to affect spending patterns significantly for these households, much less induce them to relocate out of the state. At the same time, a tax increase such as this by itself will generate about $1.6 billion for the state to spend on education, healthcare and public safety.

But even with the ARRA stimulus funds and tax increases, states and municipalities have had to make sharp cuts in spending. More severe cuts will be coming this year, with the ARRA funds now gone. These include cuts that will reduce low-income children's or families' eligibility for health insurance; further cuts in medical, homecare and other services for low-income households, as well as in K–12 education and higher education; and layoffs and furloughs for employees. The proposed 2012 budgets include still deeper cuts in core areas of healthcare and education. In Arizona, the governor's budget would cut healthcare for 280,000 poor people and reduce state support for public universities by nearly 20%. In California, Governor Brown is proposing to bring spending on the University of California down to 1999 levels, when the system had 31% fewer students than it does today.

State and Local Government Workers Are Not Overpaid

Even if state and local government employees are not responsible for the budgetary problems that emerged out of the recession, are they nevertheless receiving bloated wage and benefits packages that are holding back the recovery? Since the recession began, there has been a steady stream of media stories making such claims. One widely cited 2009 Forbes cover article reported, "State and local government workers get paid an average of $25.30 an hour, which is 33% higher than the private sector's $19.... Throw in pensions and other benefits and the gap widens to 42%."

What figures such as these fail to reflect is that state and local government workers are older and substantially better educated than private-sector workers. Forbes is therefore comparing apples and oranges. As John Schmitt of the Center for Economic Policy Research recently showed, when state and local government employees are matched against private sector workers of the same age and educational levels, the public workers earn, on average, about 4% less than their private counterparts. Moreover, the results of Schmitt's apples-to-apples comparison are fully consistent with numerous studies examining this same question over the past twenty years. One has to suspect that the pundits who have overlooked these basic findings have chosen not to look.

State Pension Funds Are Not Collapsing

Not surprisingly, state and local government pension funds absorbed heavy losses in the 2008–09 Wall Street crisis, because roughly 60% of these pension fund assets were invested in corporate stocks. Between mid-2007 and mid-2009, the total value of these pension funds fell by nearly $900 billion.

This collapse in the pension funds' asset values has increased their unfunded liabilities—that is, the total amount of benefit payments owed over the next thirty years relative to the ability of the pension funds' portfolio to cover them. By how much? In reality, estimating the total level of unfunded liabilities entails considerable guesswork. One simply cannot know with certainty how many people will be receiving benefits over the next thirty years, nor—more to the point—how much money the pension funds' investments will be earning over this long time span. The severe instability of financial markets in the recent past further clouds the picture.

Thus, these estimates vary by huge amounts, depending on the presumed rate of return for the funds. The irony is that right-wing doomsayers in this debate, such as Grover Norquist, operate with an assumption that the fund managers will be able to earn returns only equal to the interest rates on riskless U.S. Treasury securities. Under this assumption, the level of unfunded liabilities balloons to the widely reported figure of $3 trillion. To reach this conclusion, the doomsayers are effectively arguing that the collective performance of all the Wall Street fund managers—those paragons of free-market wizardry—will be so anemic over the next thirty years that the pension funds may as well just fire them and permanently park all their money in risk-free government bonds. It follows that the profits of private corporations over the next thirty years will also be either anemic or extremely unstable.

But it isn't necessary to delve seriously into this debate in order to assess the long-term viability of the public pension funds. A more basic consideration is that before the recession, states and municipalities consistently maintained outstanding records of managing their funds. In the 1990s the funds steadily accumulated reserves, such that by 2000, on average, they were carrying no unfunded liabilities at all. Even after the losses to the funds following the previous Wall Street crash of 2001, the unfunded share of total pension obligations was no more than around 10%. By comparison, the Government Accountability Office holds that to be fiscally sound, the unfunded share can be as high as 20% of the pension funds' total long-term obligations.

A few states are facing more serious problems, including New Jersey, Illinois and California. New Jersey is in the worst shape. But this is not because the state has been handing out profligate pensions to its retired employees. The average state pension in New Jersey pays out $39,500 per year. The problem is that over the past decade, the state has regularly paid into the system less than the amount agreed upon by the legislature and governor and stipulated in the annual budgets. For 2010 the state skipped its scheduled $3.1 billion payment altogether. However, even taking New Jersey's worst-case scenario, the state could still eliminate its unfunded pension fund liabilities—that is, begin running a 100% fully funded pension fund—if it increased the current allocation by about 4% of the total budget, leaving 96% of the state budget allocation unchanged.

In dollar terms, this worst-case scenario for New Jersey would require the state to come up with roughly $4 billion per year to cover its pension commitments in an overall budget in the range of $92 billion. Extracting this amount of money from other programs in the budget would certainly cause pain, especially when New Jersey, like all other states, faces tight finances. But compare this worst-case scenario with the bankruptcy agenda being discussed throughout the country.

To begin with, seriously discussing a bankruptcy agenda will undermine the confidence of private investors in all state and municipal bonds—confidence that has been earned by state and municipal governments. When the markets begin to fear that states and municipalities are contemplating bankruptcy, this will drive up the interest rates that governments will have to pay to finance school buildings, infrastructure improvements and investments in the green economy.

Then, of course, there is the impact on the pensioners and their families. For the states and municipalities to walk away from their pension fund commitments would leave millions of public sector retirees facing major cuts in their living standards and their sense of security. Something few Americans understand is that roughly one-third of the 19 million state and local employees—i.e., those in fifteen states, including California, Texas and Massachusetts—are not eligible for Social Security and will depend exclusively on their pensions and personal savings in retirement. In addition, public sector pensions are not safeguarded by the federal Pension Benefit Guaranty Corporation. Unlike Wall Street banks, state pensioners will receive no bailout checks if the states choose to abrogate their pension fund agreements.

Getting Serious About Reforming State Finances

Of course, there are significant ways the public pension systems, as well as state and local finances more generally, can be improved. The simplest solution, frequently cited, involves "pension spiking"—that is, practices such as allowing workers to add hundreds of hours of overtime at the end of their careers to balloon their final year's pay and their pensions. This has produced serious additional costs to pension obligations in some states and municipalities, but it is still by no means a major factor in explaining states' current fiscal problems.

But states and municipalities also have to follow through on the steps they have taken to raise taxes on the wealthy households that are most able to pay. They should also broaden their sources of tax revenue by taxing services such as payments to lawyers, as well as by taxing items purchased over the Internet. And they have to stop giving out large tax breaks to corporations as inducements to locate in their state or municipality instead of neighboring locations. This kind of race to the bottom generates no net benefit to states and municipalities.

Finally, state and local governments are in the same boat as the federal government and private businesses in facing persistently rising healthcare costs. As was frequently noted during the healthcare debates over the past two years, the United States spends about twice as much per person on healthcare as other highly developed countries do, even though these other countries have universal coverage, longer life expectancies and generally healthier populations. These costs weigh heavily on the budgets of state and local governments, which finance a large share of Medicaid and health benefits for state employees. The problem is that we spend far more than other countries on medications, expensive procedures and especially insurance and administration. We also devote less attention to prevention. It remains to be seen how much the Obama healthcare reform law—the 2010 Patient Protection and Affordable Care Act—will remedy this situation. It is certainly the case that more must be done, especially in establishing effective controls on the drug and insurance industries.

These are some of the long-run measures that must be taken to bolster the financing of education, healthcare, public safety and other vital social services, as well as to support investments in infrastructure and the green economy. If states declare bankruptcy they will break their obligations to employees, vendors, pensioners and even bondholders, which will undermine the basic foundations of our economy. As we emerge, if only tentatively, from the wreckage of the Great Recession, this is precisely the moment we need to strengthen, not weaken, the standards of fairness governing our society. ❑

Article 5.4

THE GREAT TAX-CUT EXPERIMENT

Has cutting tax rates for the rich helped the economy?

BY GERALD FRIEDMAN
January/February 2013

S ince the late 1970s, during the Carter Administration, conservative economists have been warning that high taxes retard economic growth by discouraging productive work and investment. These arguments have resonated with politicians, who have steadily cut income taxes, especially those borne by the richest Americans. The highest marginal tax rate, which stood at 70% by the end of the 1970s, was cut to less than 30% in less than a decade. (The marginal rate for a person is the one applied to his or her last dollar of income. A marginal rate that applies to, say, the bracket above $250,000, then, is paid only on that portion of income. The portion of a person's income below that threshold is taxed at the lower rates applying to lower tax brackets.) Despite increases in the early 1990s, the top marginal rate remained below 40%, when it was cut further during the administration of George W. Bush. These dramatic cuts in tax rates, however, have not led to an acceleration in economic growth, investment, or productivity.

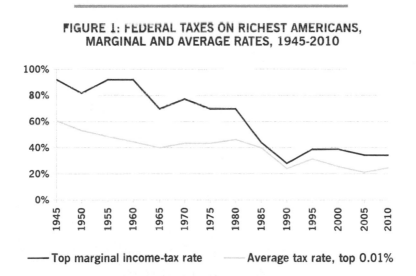

FIGURE 1: FEDERAL TAXES ON RICHEST AMERICANS,
MARGINAL AND AVERAGE RATES, 1945-2010

——— Top marginal income-tax rate   ——— Average tax rate, top 0.01%

The federal government has been cutting taxes on the richest Americans since the end of World War II. The average tax paid by the richest taxpayers, as a percentage of income, is typically less than the top marginal rate. Some of their income (the portion below the threshold for the top marginal rate, any capital-gains income, etc.) is taxed at lower rates. Some is not subject to federal income tax because of deductions for state and local taxes, health-care costs, and other expenses. The decline in the average tax rate for the richest, however, does follow the cuts in the top marginal income-tax rate.

FIGURE 2: TAX REVENUE AS A PERCENTAGE OF GDP, 2008

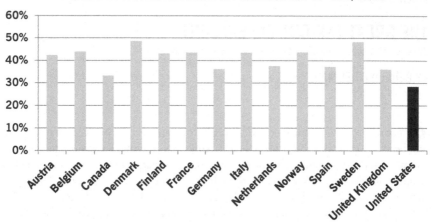

Americans pay a smaller proportion of total income in taxes than do people in any other advanced capitalist economy. As recently as the late 1960s, taxes accounted for as high a share of national income in the United States as in Western European countries. After decades of tax cuts, however, the United States now stands out for its low taxes and small government sector.

FIGURE 3: AVERAGE TAX RATES ON RICHEST AND REAL GDP GROWTH, BY PRESIDENT, 1947-2010

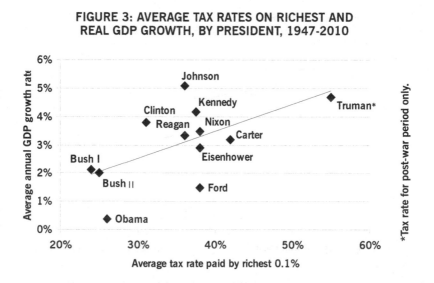

On average, the economy has grown faster during presidential administrations with higher tax rates on the richest Americans. Growth was unusually slow during George W. Bush's two terms (Bush II) and during Obama's first term, when the Bush tax cuts remained in effect. On average, every 10 percentage-point rise in the average tax rate on the richest has been associated with an increase in annual GDP growth of almost one percentage point.

FIGURE 4: TOP MARGINAL TAX RATE AND INVESTMENT, 1963-2011

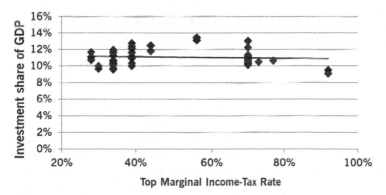

Cutting taxes on the richest Americans has not led them to invest more in plant and equipment. Over the past 50 years, as tax rates have declined, there has been no increase in investment spending as a percentage of GDP. (The flat trend line shows that changes in the highest marginal income-tax rate have not affected investment much, one way or the other.) Instead, the investment share of the economy has been determined by other factors, such as aggregate demand, rather than tax policy.

FIGURE 5: TAX SHARE OF GDP AND PRODUCTIVITY GROWTH

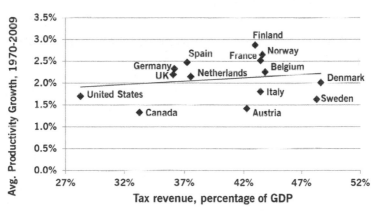

Despite lower and declining tax rates, especially on the rich, the United States has had slower productivity growth over the last several decades than other advanced economies. Overall, lower taxes are associated with slower growth in GDP per hour worked. A 10 percentage point increase in taxes as a share of GDP is associated with an increase in the productivity growth rate of 0.2 percentage points. ❑

Sources: Tom Petska and Mike Strudler, "Income, Taxes, and Tax Progressivity: An Examination of Recent Trends in the Distribution of Individual Income and Taxes" (Statistics of Income Division, Internal Revenue Service, 1997); Thomas Hungerford, "Taxes and the Economy: An Economic Analysis of the Top Tax Rates Since 1945" (Congressional Research Service, 2012); Economic Report of the President, 2012; Bureau of Economic Analysis (bea.gov); Organization of Economic Cooperation and Development, OECD STAT.

Article 5.5

MYTHS AND REALITIES OF GOVERNMENT SPENDING

BY GERALD FRIEDMAN
March/April 2013

Conservatives claim that massive government spending threatens the economy. The corporate-funded Fix the Debt coalition, for example, warns that, under President Obama, wasteful government spending includes "unsustainable entitlement costs." Swelling government debt, Fix the Debt contends, will force the United States to pay ruinous interest rates that will drive down living standards. While these charges serve the political interests of those who oppose government social programs, they confuse the real fiscal issues in America: the effects of the Great Recession on government revenues and the inadequacy of current levels of government spending to deal with massive unemployment..

Sources: "Citizens' Petition," Fix the Debt (fixthedebt.org); Economic Report of the President, 2012; United States Treasury, "Joint Statement on Budget Results for Fiscal Year 2012," Feb. 12, 2012 (treasury.gov); Bureau of Labor Statistics, "Employment Situation, 2012" Feb. 1, 2013 (bls.gov); Bureau of Economic Activity, "Gross Domestic Product: Fourth Quarter and Annual 2012," Feb. 28, 2013 (bea.gov).

FIGURE 1: FEDERAL SPENDING AND REVENUE AS SHARE OF GDP, 1963-2012

As a share of national income, federal spending peaked during the Reagan administration. There was a brief jump in spending as a share of Gross Domestic Product (GDP) in 2009 due to the fall in national income as well as the Obama stimulus program. Since then, however, spending has fallen sharply as a share of GDP. Large federal deficits since 2001 have been the result of declining revenues, first due to the Bush tax cuts and then due to falling incomes in the Great Recession.

FIGURE 2. FEDERAL SPENDING GROWTH

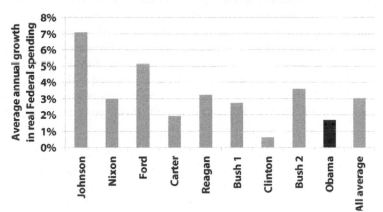

Despite the stimulus program and demands for aid to the unemployed and to distressed local and state governments, inflation-adjusted spending has increased only half as fast under President Obama as under George W. Bush. Spending under Obama has risen at the slowest rate of any presidential administration since the 1960s, except Clinton's. In past administrations, spending increased with higher unemployment. Had federal spending increased with high unemployment as fast under Obama as in the past, spending would have risen two percentage points faster each year. This increase, over $70 billion dollars a year or nearly $300 billion by the end of four years, would be enough to enact another stimulus program leading to over 2.5 million additional jobs.

FIGURE 3: ANNUAL GROWTH IN REAL FEDERAL REVENUE

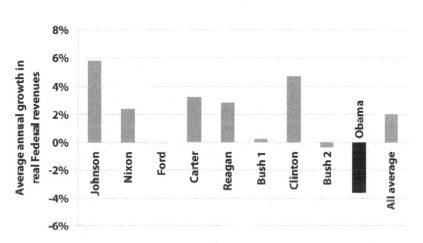

Contrary to the conservative drumbeat about "out of control" spending, it is the decline in revenues, not rising spending, that accounts for the swelling federal deficit under Presidents Bush and Obama. Revenues have fallen dramatically due to the Great Recession because laid off workers and shuttered businesses do not pay income or payroll taxes, and because tax cuts, whether to favor the rich under President George W. Bush or to stimulate the economy under President Obama, have further reduced revenues. The shortfall in revenues compared with earlier administrations explains all of the increase in the federal deficit between the last year of the Bush administration (2008) and the last year of Obama's first term (2012). ❏

Article 5.6

THE $17 TRILLION DELUSION

BY MARTY WOLFSON
January/February 2014

$17,000,000,000,000

President Obama boasted last week that he had signed legislation to lift "the twin threats" to our economy of government shutdown and default. But what was done to fix the problem of growing debt that leads Washington to repeatedly raise the debt ceiling?

Nothing. In fact, by Friday, the U.S. debt had rocketed past $17 trillion. What does this mean?

At $17 trillion, this number has passed total U.S. gross domestic product (GDP), the measure of all that is produced in the economy.

Since Obama took office, the national debt has increased from about $10.6 trillion to more than $17 trillion—a 60 percent increase.

. . . Meanwhile, entitlement spending—the key driver of spending and debt remains unaddressed.

> —"Debt Hits $17 Trillion," The Foundry: Conservative Policy News
> Blog from the Heritage Foundation, October 21, 2013

Shortly after the ceiling on federal debt was raised on October 17, 2013, the conservative Heritage Foundation notified its readers that the outstanding debt of the United States had "rocketed past $17 trillion," and that "entitlement spending—the key driver of spending and debt—remains unaddressed." The three assumptions in that statement—that the true measure of our debt is $17 trillion, that the cause of the buildup of debt is entitlement spending, and that therefore the appropriate policy to "address" this problem is to cut Social Security benefits and other "entitlements"—are endorsed by many politicians and policy pundits in Washington. But they're all wrong as economic analysis and disastrous as policy recommendations.

Seventeen trillion dollars certainly sounds like a big, scary number, especially when national debt clocks tell us that this translates into more than $53,000 for every person in the United States. But it is the wrong number to focus on.

The $17 trillion figure is a measure of "gross debt," which means that it includes debt owed by the U.S. Treasury to more than 230 other U.S. government agencies and trust funds. On the consolidated financial statements of the federal government, this intragovernmental debt is, in effect, canceled out. Basically, this is money the government owes itself. What is left is termed "debt held by the public." It is this measure of debt that is relevant to a possible increase in interest rates due to competition for funding between the private and public sectors. It is also the category of government debt used by the Congressional Budget Office and other analysts. (Of course, the full economic significance of any debt measure needs to be considered in context, in relationship to the income available to service the debt.) The total debt held by the public is $12 trillion.

The Social Security Trust Fund owns $2.7 trillion of the $5 trillion of Treasury securities held in intragovernmental accounts. In fact, Social Security is the largest single owner of Treasury securities in the world, surpassing even China's significant holdings of $1.3 trillion.

Social Security accumulated all these Treasury securities because of the way that its finances are organized. Social Security benefits to retirees (and to the disabled) are paid for by a payroll tax of 12.4 % on workers' wages (with 6.2% paid by the worker and 6.2% paid by the employer), up to a limit, currently $113,700. If, in any year, Social Security revenue is greater than what is needed to pay current retiree benefits, the surplus must, by law, be invested in Treasury securities (most of which are "special obligation bonds" issued only to the Social Security Trust Fund).

Since 1983, workers have been paying more in Social Security taxes than what was needed to pay retiree benefits. A special commission, appointed by President Reagan and chaired by future Federal Reserve Chair Alan Greenspan, recommended several changes to increase the revenue received by the Social Security Trust Fund. Most prominent among these changes was an increase in the payroll tax rate to its current level of 12.4%, although the Commission also recommended reductions in benefits, including a gradual increase in the retirement age from 65 to 67. The effect of the changes would be to create significant surpluses in the Social Security Trust Fund. The thinking was that, if in the future payroll taxes fell below benefits, the Trust Fund could draw upon the accumulated surpluses to pay benefits.

Therefore, the $2.7 trillion of Treasury securities held by the Trust Fund came about not because entitlements are out of control and the government has been forced to borrow to meet retiree benefits, but rather because future retirees have paid more taxes than necessary to meet benefit obligations. Workers have essentially been prepaying into the Trust Fund in order to provide for their future benefits.

So it makes no sense to try to solve the supposed problem of too much government debt by cutting benefits for current and future Social Security recipients. These workers were asked to help keep Social Security solvent by paying increased payroll taxes. As a result, the gross federal debt increased. It would be totally unfair and irrational to cut benefits now because these workers had sacrificed in the past. That would be hitting them with a double burden, the second burden of benefits cuts incurred because there was the first burden of overpaying payroll taxes into the Trust Fund.

What's more, the strategy the Heritage Foundation advocates would make the alleged problem they are claiming to address even worse. That's because cutting benefits would mean that payroll taxes would more easily meet retiree benefits, and so the surplus accumulating in the Social Security Trust Fund would be greater. Since the Trust Fund is required by law to invest its surpluses in Treasury securities, a greater surplus translates into more bonds being accumulated by the Trust Fund, and therefore a higher gross federal debt (assuming that Treasury borrowing from other sources remains the same). So cutting Social Security benefits in order to reduce the $17 trillion debt would produce the contradictory result that the debt would be even higher than it would have been without the benefit cuts.

Despite the 1983 changes to Social Security, the Trustees, the board that over sees Social Security, stated in their 1995 annual report that the 75-year projection of Social Security finances was no longer in "close actuarial balance" and that the long-range deficits should be "addressed." In 2002, they began to be more specific: "Bringing Social Security into actuarial balance over the next 75 years could be achieved by either a permanent 13-percent reduction in benefits or a 15-percent increase in payroll tax income, or some combination of the two."

Of course, the assumptions used by the Trustees, their policy approach, and the need for benefit cuts are all a matter of dispute. However, had benefits been cut by 13% beginning in 1996, total reductions would have totaled $1.2 trillion by 2012. So the Trust Fund would have accumulated that much more in Treasury securities, and the gross debt would actually have increased to $18.2 trillion.

In reality, the bonds in the Social Security Trust Fund are primarily a political accounting device to remind us that we as a society have promised a certain level of benefits to Social Security retirees. It is true that at some point the Trust Fund will most likely need to redeem the bonds in order to pay full benefits to retirees. And it is true that the government will need to raise the funds to do this, either by borrowing from the public (selling Treasury bonds) or through increased tax revenue. But this is the case because we promised benefits to these retirees, not because there is a certain level of bonds in the Trust Fund. The benefits would be due retirees whether or not there are bonds in the Trust Fund.

So the real issue is whether or not society will keep its commitment to retirees. The agenda of those who say we have to cut benefits is really that they don't want to meet this commitment. We should recognize that this is their agenda, and not let them hide behind the smokescreen of supposedly out-of-control federal debt.

Sources: Congressional Budget Office, "Federal Debt and the Statutory Limit," November 20, 2013; Financial Management Service, United States Department of the Treasury, "Monthly Treasury Statement," October 2013; United States Department of the Treasury, "Treasury International Capital System, Monthly Foreign Holders of Treasury Securities," October 2013; The Annual Report of the Board of Trustees of the Federal Old-Age and Survivors Insurance and Federal Disability Insurance Trust Funds, various years; Office of the Chief Actuary, Social Security Administration, Statistical Tables, Benefit Payments by Calendar Year.

Article 5.7

BEYOND DEBT AND GROWTH

An Interview with Robert Pollin

July/August 2013

Nothing warms the heart quite like a story of the high and mighty brought low. Harvard economists Carmen Reinhart and Kenneth Rogoff were the high and mighty—prestigious academics whose influential paper on government debt and economic growth was widely cited by policymakers and commentators to justify painful austerity policies. The underdogs who brought them down were three members of the UMass-Amherst economics department: graduate student Thomas Herndon and professors Michael Ash and Robert Pollin. As Dean Baker of the Center for Economic and Policy Research (CEPR) argues, it is no accident that UMass economists were the ones to debunk Reinhart and Rogoff. The department, Baker notes, "stands largely outside the mainstream" of the economics profession and so is "more willing to challenge the received wisdom."

Reinhart and Rogoff had claimed that countries with government-debt-to-GDP ratios of over 90% could expect dramatically lower future economic growth than other countries. But when Herndon attempted to replicate this result for a course in applied econometrics taught by Ash and Pollin, he found that he couldn't. In fact, as the Herndon-Ash-Pollin published paper would report, there was no dramatic growth dropoff above the supposedly critical 90% threshold. The reasons behind the faulty finding? Well, there was the world's most famous spreadsheet error—which has received extraordinary media attention mainly because it is so embarrassing, so all the more delicious given the lofty position of the authors. More importantly, however, was Reinhart and Rogoff's questionable treatment of the data. Most of the difference between their results and Herndon-Ash-Pollin's was due to no mere error, careless or otherwise, but to deliberate (and, in Pollin's view, "indefensible") decisions about how to average the data, how to divide it into different categories, and so on.

Pollin is the co-director of the Political Economy Research Institute (PERI) at UMass-Amherst and is well-known for his work on minimum-wage and living-wage laws as well as the project of building a green economy. Dollars & Sense co-editor Alejandro Reuss sat down with him to talk not only about the Reinhart-Rogoff paper and the Herndon-Ash-Pollin takedown, but also larger issues about the economic crisis and austerity: the role economists have played in abetting austerity, the reasons behind policymakers' determination to impose austerity policies, and the diverging paths before us—the profit-led recovery promised by neoliberal economists versus a wage-led recovery pointing toward a more egalitarian social-democratic system. (Full disclosure: Pollin is a Dollars & Sense Associate, and was Reuss's professor and dissertation advisor at UMass-Amherst.) —Eds.

D&S: While Reinhart and Rogoff's now-famous Excel error got a lot of attention in the media, this was a relatively small factor in the findings they reported. What do you think are the key critiques of the view that high debt-to-GDP ratios doom growth, both in terms of the figures and interpretation?

RP: I recall one commentator said that the Excel coding error was the equivalent of a figure skater who was not doing well, but it wasn't entirely clear until he or she fell. Even though the fall itself wasn't the most significant thing, it dramatized the broader set of problems. I think that's true of the Reinhart-Rogoff paper. The main things that were driving their results were, first, that they excluded data on some countries, which they have continued to defend. Second, and most importantly, was the way that they weighted data. They took each country as a separate observation, no matter how many years the country had a high public-debt-to- GDP ratio. For example, New Zealand had one year, 1951, in which they had a public-debt-to-GDP ratio over 90%. And in that year New Zealand had a depression. GDP growth was negative 7.6%. The UK, by contrast, had 19 years in which the debt-to-GDP ratio was over 90%, and over those 19 years GDP growth averaged 2.5% per year, which is not spectacular, but not terrible. Now, according to the way Reinhart and Rogoff weighted the data, one year in New Zealand was equally weighted with 19 years in the UK, which I find completely indefensible.

D&S: So when you correct for these problems, you end up with a modest—maybe not even statistically significant—negative relationship between the debt-to-GDP ratio and future growth. What are the main arguments about how to interpret this relationship?

RP: Reinhart and Rogoff have been making the defense that even the Herndon-Ash-Pollin results still showed public-debt-to-GDP over 90% being associated with a GDP growth rate of 2.2%. Meanwhile, at less than 90% debt-to-GDP, growth is between 3 and 4%. So they're saying, "Well, we made some mistakes but it's still a 1% difference in growth over time, which matters a lot." And I wouldn't disagree with that observation.

But there are other things in here. First, is it statistically significant? One of the other things we [Herndon-Ash-Pollin] did was to create another public-debt-to-GDP category, 90% to 120%, and then above 120% debt-to-GDP. For the 90-120% category there's no difference in future growth rates [compared to the lower debt-to-GDP category]. So it's only when you go way out, in terms of the debt ratio, that you will observe a drop-off in growth. Second, what happens when you look over time? In their data, for 2000 to 2009, the growth rate for the highest public-debt-to-GDP category was actually a little bit higher than in the lower categories. So what's clear is that there really is no strong association.

In addition, some people have then taken their findings and asked which way causality is running. Is it that when you have a recession, and you're at lower growth, you borrow more? Well, that's certainly part of the story. And Reinhart and Rogoff have now backpedaled on that. But to me, even that is not nearly getting at the heart of the matter. The heart of the matter is that when you're borrowing money you can use it for good things or bad things. You can be doing it in the midst of a recession. If we're going to invest in green technologies to reduce carbon emissions, that's good.

We also need to ask: what is the interest rate at which the government is borrowing? The U.S. government's debt servicing today—how much we have to pay in interest as a share of government expenditures— is actually at a historic low, even though the borrowing has been at a historic high. The answer obviously is because the interest rate is so low. When you're in an economic crisis and you want to stimulate the economy by spending more, does the central bank have the capacity to maintain a low interest rate? In the United States, the answer is yes. In the UK, the answer is yes. Germany, yes. In the rest of Europe, no. If you can borrow at 0%, go for it. If you have to borrow at 9%, that's a completely different world. And the Reinhart-Rogoff framework doesn't answer the question. It doesn't even ask that question.

D&S: Looking at research touted by policymakers to justify austerity policies, which has now been debunked, do you see the researchers putting a "thumb on the scale" to get the results that they wanted? Is that something you want to address, as opposed to simply getting the data, seeing what's driving the results, and debunking the interpretation when it is not justified?

RP: It's clear that politicians seized on these findings without questioning whether the research was good. That's what you'd expect them to do. Politicians are not researchers. The only research Paul Ryan cited in the 2013 Republican budget was the Reinhart- Rogoff paper. George Osborne, the Chancellor of the Exchequer in the UK—same thing. People at the European Commission—same thing. Now, speaking about Reinhardt and Rogoff themselves, I don't know. In general, it is certainly a tendency that if someone gets a result that they like they may just not push any further. I think that may have happened in their case, without imput-

---

Who, Me?

Since the publication of the Herndon-Ash-Pollin critique of their research, Reinhart and Rogoff have defended their findings while backing off the strongest interpretations. They claimed in the *New York Times* (April 25, 2013) that, far from arguing simply that high debt causes low growth, their "view has always been that causality runs in both directions, and that there is no rule that applies across all times and places." And they have washed their hands of commentators and politicians who "falsely equated our finding of a negative association between debt and growth with an unambiguous call for austerity."

Judge for yourself, based on Rogoff's words back in 2010:

Indeed, it is folly to ignore the long-term risks of already record peacetime debt accumulation. Even where Greek-style debt crises are unlikely, the burden of debt will ultimately weigh on growth due to inevitable fiscal adjustment. ... [A]n apparently benign market environment can darken quite suddenly as a country approaches its debt ceiling. Even the US is likely to face a relatively sudden fiscal adjustment at some point if it does not put its fiscal house in order.

—Kenneth Rogoff, "No need for a panicked fiscal surge," *Financial Times*, July 20, 2010

—Eds.

ing any motives. All I can tell you is that they wrote a paper which does not stand up to scrutiny.

D&S: All this raises the question of why elites in Europe and in the United States have been so determined to follow this austerity course. How much do you see this as being ideologically driven—based on a view of government debt or perhaps government in general being intrinsically bad? And how much should we see this as being in the service of the interests of the dominant class in society? Or should we think of those two things as meshing together?

RP: I think they mesh together. I think part of it comes from our profession, from the world of economics. It's been basically 30 years of pushing neoliberalism. It has become the dominant economic agenda and certainly hegemonic within the profession. When the crisis hit, countries did introduce stimulus policies and one of the criticisms [from economists] was that this is really crude and we don't really know much about multiplier effects and so forth. That's true, and the reason that we have only this crude understanding of how to undertake countercyclical policies is because the mainstream of the profession didn't research this. It was not a question. They spent a generation proving that we didn't need to do these policies—that a market solution is the best. So that's the economics profession and it does filter into the political debates.

But then, beyond that, is the agenda of getting rid of the welfare state and I think a lot of politicians want that to happen. They don't want to have a big public sector. Either they believe that a big public sector is inefficient and that the private sector does things more efficiently, or, whether they believe that or not, they want lower taxes on wealthy people (and wealthy people want lower taxes because that lets them get wealthier). They don't want constraints on their ability to enrich themselves, and they certainly don't want a strong and self-confident working class. They don't want people to have the security of health insurance or pension insurance (i.e., Medicare and Social Security in this country). That's the model of welfare-state capitalism that emerged during the Great Depression and was solidified during the next generation, and these people want to roll it back. The austerity agenda has given them a launching pad to achieve this. I have no idea whether Reinhardt and Rogoff believe this or not, but their research enabled people like Paul Ryan to have the legitimacy of eminent Harvard economists saying we're killing ourselves and we're killing economic growth by borrowing so much money.

D&S: Policymakers in the United States, Europe, and elsewhere, to a great extent, have just tried to "double down" on neoliberal policies. But with the structural problems of neoliberalism, keeping the same structure looks in effect like a way of keeping the same crisis. What do you see as the possible ways out of the impasse, both desirable and undesirable?

RP: I think there are fundamentally only two approaches—basically profit-led models versus wageled models. In the *Financial Times* today [June 10], the well-known columnist Gavyn Davies is saying that the reason the stock market is going up—and it's going up very handsomely—is fundamentally because the current model of capitalism is able to proceed by squeezing workers even harder. The wage share, which had been relatively stable for generations, is going down and the profit share is going up.

Now is that sustainable? Presumably you're going to have a problem of demand at a certain point because if workers don't have enough in their pockets, how are they going to buy the product? One answer is we can export to rising Asian markets and so forth. But the Asian countries themselves are depending on the exact same model. The alternative, which I think makes more sense logically and is also more humane, is to have a more equal distribution of income—a social democratic model of capitalism in which you do have a strong welfare state that acts as a stabilizer to aggregate demand and also enables workers to buy the products that they make. And that's true for China and for the United States.

We have to add into that the issue of environmental sustainability. At the same time that we're building a new growth model it has to be a model in which carbon emissions go down per unit of GDP. I don't think it's that hard to do technically. Whether it happens is another matter. [The 20th-century Polish macroeconomist Michal] Kalecki, of course, recognized this a long time ago, saying you can have a model of capitalism based on repressing workers. (He noted that it's helpful, if you're going to do that, to have a repressive fascist government—not that he was advocating doing that, of course.) After a while, and this was in the *Financial Times* today, workers are going to see that they're not getting any benefit from a recovery, and it's going to create all kinds of political results, and we don't know what they're going to be. But people are going to be pissed off.

D&S: That brings us to a central question, which Kalecki raised, that a social problem may be solved technically and intellectually, but still face barriers of economic and political power. That applies not only to full employment, the issue he was addressing, but also to environmental sustainability and other issues. Can our most serious problems be resolved within the context of capitalism, or do they require a new kind of economy and society, whatever we may call it?

RP: The challenge that Kalecki introduced points to some version of shared egalitarian capitalism, such as a Nordic model. Whether that model works and how long it works is an open question, and it varies for different countries.

Certainly, when we think about environmental infrastructure investments, collective solutions are workable. We know from Europe that initiatives, which are collectively owned and collectively decided, for building renewable energy systems really do work. In large part, this is because it is the community saying, "We don't mind having wind turbines if it's done right, within our community, and we have a stake in it." If some big corporation were to come and say, "We're wiping out 18 blocks here to put up some turbines and we have a right to do it because we own the property"—it doesn't work. We have public utilities and that works just fine in this country.

Expanding the role of the public sector in my view is totally consistent with what's going to happen in the future. So that starts transcending the primacy of corporate capitalism. But we can't get there in ten years. No matter how much anybody wants it, that's not going to happen. We have a problem of mass unemployment and we have an environmental crisis with climate change, and if we're not going to transcend capital-

The Legacy of Michal Kalecki

Michal Kalecki (1899-1970) was a Marxist economist, a scholar at Cambridge and Oxford, and an economic advisor to the governments of his native Poland and other countries. His key insights about the causes of the Great Depression preceded Keynes, but he was not widely recognized for these achievements. (Unlike Keynes, he did not publish mainly in English, was not well-known, and was not connected to elite policymaking circles.) Kalecki is perhaps best remembered for his brief article "Political Aspects of Full Employment" (1943), in which he argued that full-employment policies would erode capitalists' power in the workplace and state, and so would be sure to face capitalist opposition. Robert Pollin calls this "probably the most insightful six pages ever written in economics." —*Eds.*

ism in ten years we have to also figure out ways to address the concerns now within the existing political framework. That's not fun. When I deal with mainstream politics in Washington, it's very frustrating, but that's the world we live in.

I think that if we press the limits of the existing system, that helps me to understand how to move forward into something different than the existing structure. My professor Robert Heilbroner, a great professor who had a beautiful way of expressing things, talked about what he called "slightly imaginary Sweden." So it's not the real Sweden but this notion of some kind of egalitarian capitalism. As you press the limits of that model, you can intelligently ask what's wrong with it. If we're pushing the limits and something is holding us back, let's solve that problem. I think that's a good way forward. ❏

Chapter 6

MONETARY POLICY, BANKING, AND FINANCIAL MARKETS

INTRODUCTION

Ben Bernanke replaced Alan Greenspan as the man behind the curtain of the Federal Reserve Board just in time to oversee the worst financial crisis since the Great Depression.

Bernanke needed all the wizard-like powers the business press sometimes attributed to Greenspan, given that it was Bernanke's job to pull the economy's fat out of the fire. And those powers were in awfully short supply when Greenspan himself confessed before Congress, in October 2008, that the financial crisis had left him "in a state of shocked disbelief" and that he had "made a mistake in presuming that banks ... were capable of protecting their own shareholders."

The Bernanke Fed did help to avert a complete economic meltdown. Limited steps have been undertaken to resolve the nearly intractable mortgage debt crisis and to put in place the measures that might prevent another financial crash. Still, working people have fared no better under Bernanke than they did under maestro Greenspan. Even before the financial crisis, Greenspan worried that, under his tenure, inequality had worsened to levels that threatened our democratic institutions, and that the unprecedented level of U.S. reliance on foreign borrowing had become unsustainable. Bernanke has acknowledged the seriousness of both problems as well, but seems just as incapable as his predecessor of remedying them.

But why should it matter who chairs the Federal Reserve Board? The Fed is charged with using monetary policy to keep inflation in check and provide liquidity to keep the economy going (or bolster a flagging economy). The Fed is supposed to use its three tools—the reserve requirement, the discount and federal funds rates, and open-market operations—to manipulate banking activity, control the money supply, and direct the economy to everyone's benefit.

It all sounds value-free. But what the Fed really does is serve those who hold financial assets. So when it comes to making monetary policy, the Fed puts the interests of bondholders first, well before those of job seekers and workers. Investors look to the Fed to protect the value of their stocks and bonds by keeping inflation low—and if that means keeping a cap on employment growth, so be it.

To begin the chapter, several articles take us through the basics of money and the monetary system. We use money every day, but usually do not stop to think about how money is defined, how it has evolved historically, or how it is created today. Economist Doug Orr explains in everyday language what money is and how the Fed attempts to control the money supply (Article 6.1). Arthur MacEwan compares monetary and fiscal policy, highlighting the greater powers of fiscal policy to counteract recessions (Article 6.2). Next, MacEwan explains how a "fractional reserve banking" system works, and whether it is at the root of our current economic troubles (Article 6.3).

The next two articles address the Fed's recent attempts to spur an economic recovery, by both conventional and less-conventional monetary-policy means. The explosion in the excess reserves held by U.S. banks, as economist Gerald Friedman shows, confirms that the Fed can do little to get the economy going using conventional monetary policy if banks won't make loans (Article 6.4).

The next two articles explain the recent financial crisis in terms of the systemic instabilities of capitalist economies. Economist Gerald Friedman places the financial crisis in a long history of speculative bubbles that have plagued capitalist economies (Article 6.5). He argues that the current crisis, however, could have been avoided with proper regulation. Next, Robert Pollin reviews the insights of economist Hyman Minsky on the tendency toward excessive financial risk-taking during economic booms (Article 6.6). Minsky pointed to government regulation as a substitute for the discipline of the market (which reins in risk-taking only through ruinous financial crashes).

Economist Fred Moseley offers a proposal for what to do about the home-mortgage crisis, the banking industry, and the Fed. Moseley analyzes the bailout of the public mortgage-lending agencies, Fannie Mae and Freddie Mac. He makes the case for a reinvented public home-mortgage agency whose sole purpose would be to provide affordable housing (Article 6.7).

Dean Baker calls for a return to the regulations separating basic banking functions from speculation—rules that were put in place in the wake of the great crash in 1929 but abandoned at the urging of banks in 1999 (Article 6.8).

In the next article, Baker questions the dire predictions bankers made about what would happen if they didn't get their way (Article 6.9). During the financial crisis, Wall Street insisted that without a massive intervention by the Federal Reserve to save them from the consequences of reckless lending, we would fall into a Second Great Depression. That was not a warning of an inevitable consequence, argues Baker. It was a threat.

Lastly, Arthur MacEwan explains "securitization" and its contribution to the financial crisis (Article 6.10). He offers a clear definition and explains the conflicts of interest inherent in the way securities were created and traded.

Discussion Questions

1. (Article 6.1) What are the mechanisms the Fed uses to "control" the creation of money by the banking system? Why, according to Orr, is the Fed's control over the creation of money "limited"?

2. (Article 6.2) What advantage is there in using monetary policy to slow down the economy? Why might fiscal policy be a more effective tool for lifting the economy out of a recession?

3. (Article 6.3) What is "fractional reserve banking"? Do banks "create money out of thin air"? In what ways, according to MacEwan, do U.S. economic problems go deeper than the monetary system?

4. (Article 6.4) Why does Friedman, like others before him, liken monetary policy to "pushing on a string"? What evidence does Friedman offer to show that this analogy is an apt description of monetary policy today?

5. (Article 6.5) What aspects of financial assets make them prone to speculative manias and panics? And what does this pattern suggest about the appropriate public policies for overseeing financial markets?

6. (Article 6.6) Why do financial companies tend to engage in excessive risk-taking during economic booms? If financial crashes are too harmful to tolerate, and bailouts (to prevent or contain a crash) only encourage further risk-taking, what are the alternatives?

7. (Article 6.7) Who is to blame for the financial troubles of Fannie Mae and Freddie Mac? How should Fannie and Freddie be reformed? Should the provision of affordable housing be their sole focus?

8. (Article 6.8) What was the Glass-Steagall Act and why does Dean Baker argue it should be revived?

9. (Article 6.9) At the height of the financial crisis, we heard dire warnings of the potential for a Second Great Depression. The government acted quickly to save the financial sector and we have had only a Great Recession, not a Depression on the scale of the 1930s. Should we conclude that the bailout worked? Or was there an alternative response that could have been better?

10. (Article 6.10) Both the financial firms that issued mortgages and the ratings agencies that evaluated mortgage-backed securities played roles rife with conflicts of interest. What were the conflicts and how did they contribute to the housing bubble?

Article 6.1

WHAT IS MONEY?

BY DOUG ORR
November/December 1993; revised October 2010

We all use money every day. Yet many people do not know what money actually is. There are many myths about money, including the idea that the government "prints" all of it and that it has some intrinsic value. But actually, money is less a matter of value, and more a matter of faith.

Money is sometimes called the universal commodity, because it can be traded for all other commodities. But for this to happen, everyone in society must believe that money will be accepted. If people stop believing that it will be accepted, the existing money ceases to be money. Recently in Poland, people stopped accepting the zloty, and used vodka as money instead.

In addition to facilitating exchanges, money allows us to "store" value from one point in time to another. If you sell your car today for $4,000, you probably won't buy that amount of other products today. Rather, you store the value as money, probably in a bank, until you want to use it.

The "things" that get used as money have changed over time, and "modern" people often chuckle when they hear about some of them. The Romans used salt (from which we get the word "salary"), South Sea Islanders used shark's teeth, and several societies actually used cows. The "Three Wise Men" brought gold, frankincense and myrrh, each of which was money in different regions at the time.

If money does not exist, or is in short supply, it will be created. In POW camps, where guards specifically outlaw its existence, prisoners use cigarettes instead. In the American colonies, the British attempted to limit the supply of British pounds, because they knew that by limiting the supply of money, they could hamper the development of independent markets in the colonies. Today, the United States uses a similar policy, through the International Monetary Fund, in dealing with Latin America.

To overcome this problem, the colonists began to use tobacco leaves as money. This helped the colonies to develop, but it also allowed the holders of large plots of land to grow their own money! When the colonies gained independence, the new government decreed gold to be money, rather than tobacco, much to the dismay of Southern plantation owners. Now, rather than growing money, farmers had to find or buy it.

To aid the use of gold as money, banks would test its purity, put it in storage, and give the depositor paper certificates of ownership. These certificates, "paper money," could then be used in place of the gold itself. Since any bank could store gold and issue certificates, by the beginning of the Civil War, over 7,000 different types of "paper money" were in circulation in the United States, none of it printed by the government.

While paper money is easier to use than gold, it is still risky to carry around large amounts of cash. It is safer to store the paper in a bank and simply sign over its ownership to make a purchase. We sign over the ownership of our money by writing a check. Checking account money became popular when, in an unsuccessful attempt to control the amount of money created by banks, the government outlawed the printing of paper money by private banks in 1864.

How Banks Create Money

Banks are central to understanding money, because in addition to storing it, they help to create it. Bankers realize that not everyone will withdraw their money at the same time, so they loan out much of the money that has been deposited. It is from the interest on these loans that banks get their profits, and through these loans the banking system creates new money.

If you deposit $100 cash in your checking account at Chase Manhattan Bank, you still have $100 in money to use, because checks are also accepted as money. Chase must set aside some of this cash as "reserves," in case you or other depositors decide to withdraw money as cash. Current regulations issued by the Federal Reserve Bank (the Fed) require banks to set aside an average of three cents out of each dollar. So Chase can make a loan of $97, based on your deposit. Chase does not make loans by handing out cash but instead by putting $97 in the checking account of the person, say Emily, taking out the loan. So from your initial deposit of $100 in cash, the economy now has $197 in checking account money.

The borrower, Emily, pays $97 for some product or service by check, and the seller, say Ace Computers, deposits the money in its checking account. The total amount of checking account money is still $197, but its location and ownership have changed. If Ace Computer's account is at Citibank, $97 in cash is transferred from Chase to Citibank. This leaves just $3 in cash reserves at Chase to cover your original deposit. However, Citibank now has $97 in "new" cash on hand, so it sets aside three cents on the dollar ($2.91) and loans out the rest, $94.09, as new checking account money. Through this process, every dollar of "reserves" yields many dollars in total money.

If you think this is just a shell game and there is only $100 in "real" money, you still don't understand money. Anything that is accepted as payment for a transaction is "real" money. Cash is no more real than checking account money. In fact, most car rental companies will not accept cash as payment for a car, so for them, cash is not money!

As of June 2010, there was $883 billion of U.S. currency, i.e. "paper money," in existence. However, somewhere between 50% to 70% of it is held outside the United States by foreign banks and individuals. U.S. $100 bills are the preferred currency of choice used to facilitate illegal international transactions, such as the drug trade. The vast majority of all money actually in use in the United States is not cash, but rather checking account money. This type of money, $1,590 billion, was created by private banks, and was not "printed" by anyone. In fact, this money exists only as electronic "bits" in banks' computers. (The less "modern" South Sea Islanders could have quite a chuckle about that!)

The amount of money that banks can create is limited by the total amount of reserves, and by the fraction of each deposit that must be held as reserves. Prior to

1914, bankers themselves decided what fraction of deposits to hold as reserves. Since then, this fraction has been set by the main banking regulator, the Fed.

Until 1934, gold was held as reserves, but the supply of gold was unstable, growing rapidly during the California and Alaska "gold rushes," and very slowly at other times. As a result, at times more money was created than the economy needed, and at other times not enough money could be created. Starting in 1934, the U.S. government decided that gold would no longer be used as reserves. Cash, now printed by the Fed, could no longer be redeemed for gold, and cash itself became the reserve asset.

Banks, fearing robberies, do not hold all of their cash reserves in their own vaults. Rather, they store it in an account at a regional Fed bank. These accounts count as reserves. What banks do hold in their vaults is their other assets, such as Treasury bonds and corporate bonds.

The Fed and Bank Reserves

The only role of the government in creating money is indirectly through the Fed, which is controlled by neither the Congress nor the executive branch. If the Fed wants to expand the money supply, it must increase bank reserves. To do this, the Fed buys Treasury bonds from a bank, and pays with a check drawn on the Fed itself. By depositing the check in its reserve account at the Fed, the bank now has more reserves, so the bank can now make more loans and create new checking account money.

By controlling the amount of reserves, the Fed attempts to control the size of the money supply. But as recent history has shown, this control is limited. During the late 1970s, the Fed tried to limit the amount of money banks could create by reducing reserves, but banks simply created new forms of money, just like the POW camp prisoners and colonial farmers. In 1979, there was only one form of checking account money. Today, there are many, with odd names such as NOWs, ATSs, repos, and money market deposit accounts. If there is a profit to be made creating money, banks will find a way.

In 2010, we have the opposite problem. The Fed is trying to expand the money supply, but banks are refusing to create new money. In good times, banks hold as few reserves as possible, so they can profit from making loans. In times of crisis, banks fear that we will lose faith in the commercial banking system and all try to take out our "money" as cash. Since there is far more electronic money than cash, this is impossible. But if the bank cannot give us our money in the form we want it, the bank fails and ceases to exist. Since the start of 2007, over 300 banks, with assets totally more than $637 billion, have failed.

Since all banks fear they will be next, they want as many reserves as possible. Excess reserves are any reserves above those required by the Fed. During the 1990s, these averaged about $1 billion for the entire banking system. During the crisis of 2001, they spiked to the then unheard of level of $19 billion. As of June 2010, excess reserves in the banking system were $1,035 billion! This is the classic case of trying to push on a string. The Fed can create reserves, but only banks can create money and they are not yet willing to make any new loans.

These amorphous forms of money function only because we believe they will function, which is why the continued stability of the banking system is so critical. While it is true that the bailout of the banking system was not handled very well, and that many people who created the crisis are still profiting from it, the bailout was a necessary evil. In a modern market economy, banks create the money, and no market economy can function without its money. Money only exists if we believe in it, so we have to maintain the faith. To maintain the faith we need more democratic control over money creation, which can only come if regulation of the financial system is greatly expanded. ❏

Sources: Money supply: Federal Reserve Board, www.federalreserve.gov/releases/h6/current/; excess reserves: St. Louis Federal Reserve Bank, research.stlouisfed.org/fred2/series/EXCRESNS; bank failures: Federal Deposit Insurance Corporation (FDIC), www.fdic.gov/bank/individual/failed/banklist.html.

Article 6.2

HOW DO FISCAL AND MONETARY POLICY COMPARE?

BY ARTHUR MacEWAN

July/August 1997

The Federal Reserve influences the economy through monetary policy—the actions the Fed takes to affect the cost and availability of credit. For example, in March of this year, the Fed, led by its chairman Alan Greenspan, decided that it was time to slow economic growth. So it induced banks and other lenders to raise their interest rates. Higher interest rates mean fewer businesses and individuals will take out loans and spend the borrowed money. Lower spending means slower economic growth.

The federal government can also influence economic growth and the demand for goods and services through fiscal policy—the way it taxes and spends. If the government wants to slow down the economy, for example, it can raise taxes and reduce its own spending. Less money ends up in people's hands if the government hires fewer construction workers to build roads, or if it cuts back on education programs.

One problem with fiscal policy is that changing the budget takes time—except for programs whose spending levels change automatically when the economy does, like unemployment compensation. To slow down the economy, Congress has to pass new laws raising taxes—certainly a "no no" these days—or cutting spending. Then the President has to accept Congress's new law, which might require negotiations, or more legislative action. All this is to say that the political process involves considerable delays and might result in no action at all.

Monetary policy is different because the Fed does not have to bother with this messy political process that we call democracy. It is "independent" since its members, appointed by the President, serve long terms. They decide whether to ease or tighten the availability of credit, without any role for Congress or the President. To be sure, the "independence" of the Fed is not enshrined in the Constitution. Yet for Congress and the President to pass new laws which directed or restricted the Fed's action would be a serious disruption of well-established policy.

The law governing the Fed says that it should pursue both stable prices (low inflation) and full employment. In fact, the Fed focuses almost exclusively on the goal of stable prices. If unemployment has to rise to meet this goal, well, too bad. It is easy to see why the Fed does its work best when it doesn't have to worry about getting democratic approval.

Fiscal policy is somewhat more constrained by democratic processes than is monetary policy. For example, conservative attacks on Medicare and Social Security have not gotten very far because these programs are very popular.

But the recent mania to balance the budget makes it difficult to use fiscal policy to stimulate economic expansion by increasing spending. This may present some serious problems during economic downturns. The monetary policy of the Fed, it turns out, is not nearly so effective in stimulating economic expansion during a recession as it is in slowing growth during relatively good times. In a recession, the Fed can induce commercial banks to lower their interest rates. But if the recession leads investors to worry that demand for products and services will fall, the lower interest rates might not reignite economic growth. What's the point, for example, in building a new office building when it doesn't look like it will be possible to rent out the space in existing buildings for quite a while?

In a recession, then, trying to use monetary policy to get the economy going can be like pushing on a string. It simply won't do any good. Fiscal policy, however, might directly create demand, present businesses with the reality of a new expansion, and generate a new period of investment and growth. ❏

Article 6.3

SHOULD WE BLAME "FRACTIONAL RESERVE" BANKING?

BY ARTHUR MacEWAN
May/June 2013

> Dear Dr. Dollar:
> *I have seen various arguments (on the Internet, for example) that a prime cause of our economic problems (inequality, crises, mass unemployment, the immense power of the banks, etc.) is our montary system. In particular, that it is a "fractional reserve system," in which "money is created out of thin air." Could you comment?*
>
> —Mike Smith, New York, NY

The last several years, when banks and the whole financial system have been at the core of economic disruption, could easily lead one to see the monetary system as central to our economic problems.

Keep in mind, however, that we have had essentially the same monetary system for decades, the Federal Reserve has existed for a hundred years, and the "fractional reserve" system existed before the Fed. During these earlier eras, including periods when we relied on the gold standard as the basis of our monetary system, we have had depressions, inflation, severe inequality, and excessive power in the hands of finance and large corporations generally. We have also had some relatively good times—periods of stable economic growth, less economic inequality, lower unemployment, and less power and profits for the banks. So, whatever is wrong with our monetary system (and there are certainly things wrong), the explanation of our economic problems must be more complex.

But what is the fractional reserve system? Basically, it is the system by which banks keep as reserves only a fraction of the amount of deposits that their customers have with the banks. Banks can do this because at any time their customers will demand only a fraction of those total obligations. When, for example, you deposit $100 in the bank, the bank will loan out to someone else perhaps $90 of that $100. This $90 is new money that the bank has created. The person or business taking this loan then deposits the $90 in another account with the bank or another bank, allowing a new loan of $81 to be generated by the banking system; the remaining $9 (10% of the deposit) will be kept as reserves. And so on.

By this process, if people are willing to take out the loans, the banks can create an additional $900 of money based on an original deposit of $100. This is sometimes called "creating money out of thin air." In fact, it is creating money on the basis of 10% reserves.

If banks were left to their own devices, competition would create pressure to push down the reserve ratio—they could, for example, make twice the amount of loans were they to reduce their reserves from 10% to 5% of obligations. However, the Federal Reserve has a great deal of authority over what the banks can do. It sets the reserve ratio. Banks cannot simply lower the amount of reserves to make more loans. (The actual reserve ratio varies depending on type of obligation; 10% is just an example that makes calculations easy.) Most frequently, the Fed affects the supply of money by buying bonds from the banks, thus increasing the banks' reserves (and enabling them to lend more), or selling bonds to the banks, thus reducing the banks' reserves.

That's the formal way it works. Although critics of a fractional reserve system claim it "debases the currency" (i.e., leads to inflation), it does not automatically allow the banks to create more and more money without limits, which could indeed generate severe inflation. The U.S. economy has experienced mild inflation for most of the last century (averaging 3.2% annually), but fractional reserve banking is not generally associated with high "runaway" inflation. Ironically, in light of the claims of the critics, the Fed has often followed policies that work in exactly the opposite direction—restricting the banks' ability to create money, thus restricting the loans they can make, and restraining economic growth and employment. (After all, neither banks nor other large corporations like severe inflation.)

But of course the formal way the system works is not the whole story. The banks themselves and other big firms have a great deal of influence over what the Fed does. So the Fed usually regulates the banks with a very light hand. In the Great Recession, in particular, the Fed (along with the U.S. Treasury) provided the banks with funds to meet their obligations when many of those banks would have otherwise failed. In this respect, the way the Fed works is not so different from the way the government works in general—money has a great deal of influence over policy.

It would be nice if our economic problems were so simple that they could be solved by some reorganization of our monetary system. But the problems are bigger and deeper. ❑

Article 6.4

PUSHING ON STRINGS

*The explosion of U.S. banks' excess reserves since last fall
illustrates the dramatic failure of monetary policy.*

BY GERALD FRIEDMAN
May/June 2009

Monetary policy is not working. Since the economic crisis began in July 2007, the Federal Reserve has dramatically cut interest rates and pumped out over a trillion dollars, increasing the money supply by over 15% in less than two years. These vast sums have failed to revive the economy because the banks have been hoarding liquidity rather than lending.

The Federal Reserve requires that banks hold money on reserve to back up deposits and other bank liabilities. In the past, beyond these required reserves, banks would hold very small amounts of excess reserves, holdings that they minimized because reserves earn very little or no interest. Between the 1950s and September 2008, U.S. banks held over $5 billion in total excess reserves only once, after the September 11 attacks. This changed with the collapse of Lehman Brothers. Beginning with less than $2 billion in August 2008, excess reserves soared to $60 billion in September and then to $559 billion in November before peaking at $798 billion in January 2009. (They had dropped to $644 billion by the time this article was written.)

This explosion of excess reserves represents a signal change in bank policy that threatens the effectiveness of monetary policy in the current economic crisis. Aware of their own financial vulnerability, even insolvency, frightened bank managers

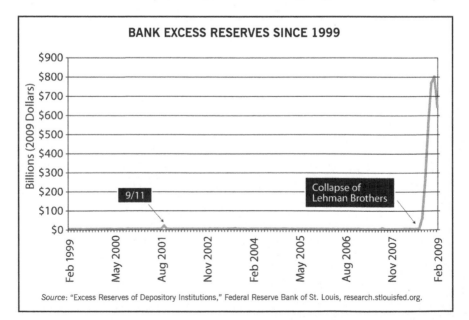

BANK EXCESS RESERVES SINCE 1999

Source: "Excess Reserves of Depository Institutions," Federal Reserve Bank of St. Louis, research.stlouisfed.org.

responded to the collapse of major investment houses like Lehman Brothers by grabbing and hoarding all the cash that they could get. At the same time, a general loss of confidence and spreading economic collapse persuaded banks that there are few to whom they could lend with confidence that the loans would be repaid. Clearly, our banks have decided that they need, or at least want, the money more than consumers and productive businesses do.

Banks could have been investing this money by lending to businesses needing liquidity to buy material inputs or pay workers. Had they done so, monetarist economists would be shouting from the rooftops, or at least in the university halls, about how monetary policy prevented another Great Depression. Instead, even the *Wall Street Journal* is proclaiming that "We're All Keynesians Again" because monetary policy has failed. Monetary authorities, the *Journal* explains, can create money but they cannot force banks to lend or to invest it in productive activities. The Federal Reserve confronts a reality shown in the graph above: it can't "push on a string," as Fed Chair Marriner Eccles famously put it in testimony before Congress in 1935, in the depths of the Great Depression.

If the banks won't lend, then we need more than monetary policy to get out of the current crisis. No bailout, no TARP program, can revive the economy if banks hoard all the cash they receive. The Obama stimulus was an appropriate response to the failure of string-pushing. But much more government stimulus will be needed to solve a crisis this large, and we will need programs to move liquidity from bank vaults to businesses and consumers. It may be time to stop waiting on the banks, and to start telling them what to do with our money. ❑

Article 6.5

FROM TULIPS TO MORTGAGE-BACKED SECURITIES

BY GERALD FRIEDMAN
January/February 2008

Thirty years ago, economist Charles Kindleberger published a little book, *Manias, Panics, and Crashes*, describing the normal tendency of capitalist financial markets to fluctuate between speculative excess (or "irrational exuberance" in the words of a recent central banker) and panic. Kindleberger describes about 40 of these panics over the nearly 260 years from 1720–1975, or one every seven years. Following Kindleberger's arithmetic, we were due for a panic because it had been seven years since the high-tech bubble burst and the stock market panic of 2000-01. And the panic came, bringing in its wake a tsunami of economic woe, liquidity shortages, cancelled investments, rising unemployment, and economic distress.

Of course, more than mechanics and arithmetic are involved in the current financial panic. But there is a sense of inevitability about the manias and panics of capitalist financial markets, a sense described by writers from Karl Marx to John Maynard Keynes, Hyman Minsky, John Kenneth Galbraith, and Robert Shiller. The problem is that financial markets trade in unknown and unknowable future returns. Lacking real information, they are inevitably driven by the madness of crowds.

Unlike tangible commodities whose price should reflect its real value and real cost of production, financial assets are not priced according to any real returns, nor even according to some expected return, but rather according to expectations of what others will pay in the future, or, even worse, expectations of future expectations that others will have of assets' future return. Whether it is Dutch tulips in 1637, the South Sea Bubble of 1720, Florida real estate in the 1920s, or mortgage-backed securities today, it is always the same story of financial markets floating like a manic-depressive from euphoria to panic to bust. When unregulated, this process is made still worse by market manipulation, and simple fraud. Speculative markets like these can make some rich, and can even be exciting to watch, like a good game of poker; but this is a dangerous and irresponsible way to manage an economy.

There was a time when governments understood. Learning from past financial disasters, the United States established rules to limit the scope of financial euphoria and panic by strictly segregating different types of banks, by limiting financial speculation, and by requiring clear accounting of financial transactions. While they were regulated, financial markets contributed to the best period of growth in American history, the "glorious thirty" after World War II. To be sure, restrictions on speculative behavior and strict regulations made this a boring time to be a banker, and they limited earnings in the financial services sector. But, limited to a secondary role, finance served a greater good by providing liquidity for a long period of steady and relatively egalitarian economic growth.

Of course, over time we forgot why we had regulated financial markets, memory loss helped along by the combined efforts of free-market economists and self-interested bankers and others on Wall Street. To promote "competition," we lowered the barriers between different types of financial institutions, widening the scope of financial markets. We moved activities such as home mortgage lending onto national markets and allowed a rash of bank mergers to create huge financial institutions too large to be allowed to fail, but never too large to operate irresponsibly. Despite the growing scope and centralization of financial activity, the government accepted arguments that we could trust financial firms to self-regulate because it was in their interest to maintain credible accounting.

So we reap the whirlwind with a market collapse building to Great Depression levels. Once again, we learn history's lesson from direct experience: capitalist financial markets cannot be trusted. It is time to either re-regulate or move beyond. ❑

Article 6.6

WE'RE ALL MINSKYITES NOW

BY ROBERT POLLIN
October 2008; The Nation

As the most severe financial crisis since the 1930s Depression has unfolded over the past eighteen months, the ideas of the late economist Hyman Minsky have suddenly come into fashion. In the summer of 2007, the Wall Street Journal ran a front-page article describing the emerging crisis as the financial market's "Minsky moment." His ideas have since been featured in the Financial Times, BusinessWeek and The New Yorker, among many other outlets. Minsky, who spent most of his academic career at Washington University in St. Louis and remained professionally active until his death, in 1996, deserves the recognition. He was his generation's most insightful analyst of financial markets and the causes of financial crises.

Even so, most mainstream economists have shunned his work because it emerged out of a dissident left Keynesian tradition known in economists' circles as post-Keynesianism. Minsky's writings, and the post-Keynesian tradition more generally, are highly critical of free-market capitalism and its defenders in the economics profession—among them Milton Friedman and other Nobel Prize-winning economists who for a generation have claimed to "prove," usually through elaborate mathematical models, that unregulated markets are inherently rational, stable and fair. For Friedmanites, regulations are harmful most of the time.

Minsky, by contrast, explained throughout his voluminous writings that unregulated markets will always produce instability and crises. He alternately termed his approach "the financial instability hypothesis" and "the Wall Street paradigm."

For Minsky, the key to understanding financial instability is to trace the shifts that occur in investors' psychology as the economy moves out of a period of crisis and recession (or depression) and into a phase of rising profits and growth. Coming out of a crisis, investors will tend to be cautious, since many of them will have been clobbered during the just-ended recession. For example, they will hold large cash reserves as a cushion to protect against future crises.

But as the economy emerges from its slump and profits rise, investors' expectations become increasingly positive. They become eager to pursue risky ideas such as securitized subprime mortgage loans. They also become more willing to let their cash reserves dwindle, since idle cash earns no profits, while purchasing speculative vehicles like subprime mortgage securities that can produce returns of 10% or higher.

But these moves also mean that investors are weakening their defenses against the next downturn. This is why, in Minsky's view, economic upswings, proceeding without regulations, inevitably encourage speculative excesses in which financial bubbles emerge. Minsky explained that in an unregulated environment, the only way to stop bubbles is to let them burst. Financial markets then fall into a crisis, and a recession or depression ensues.

Here we reach one of Minsky's crucial insights—that financial crises and recessions actually serve a purpose in the operations of a free-market economy, even while they wreak havoc with people's lives, including those of tens of millions of innocents who never invest a dime on Wall Street. Minsky's point is that without crises, a free-market economy has no way of discouraging investors' natural proclivities toward ever greater risks in pursuit of ever higher profits.

However, in the wake of the calamitous Great Depression, Keynesian economists tried to design measures that could supplant financial crises as the system's "natural" regulator. This was the context in which the post-World War II system of big-government capitalism was created. The package included two basic elements: regulations designed to limit speculation and channel financial resources into socially useful investments, such as single-family housing; and government bailout operations to prevent 1930s-style depressions when crises broke out anyway.

Minsky argues that the system of regulations and the bailout operations were largely successful. That is why from the end of World War II to the mid-1970s, markets here and abroad were much more stable than in any previous historical period. But even during the New Deal years, financial market titans were fighting vehemently to eliminate, or at least defang, the regulations. By the 1970s, almost all politicians—Democrats and Republicans alike—had become compliant. The regulations were initially weakened, then abolished altogether, under the strong guidance of, among others, Federal Reserve chair Alan Greenspan, Republican Senator Phil Gramm and Clinton Treasury Secretary Robert Rubin.

For Minsky, the consequences were predictable. Consider the scorecard over the twenty years before the current disaster: a stock market crash in 1987; the savings-and-loan crisis and bailout in 1989-90; the "emerging markets" crisis of 1997-98—which brought down, among others, Long-Term Capital Management, the super-hedge fund led by two Nobel laureates specializing in finance—and the bursting of the dot-com market bubble in 2001. Each of these crises could easily have produced a 1930s-style collapse in the absence of full-scale government bailout operations.

Here we come to another of Minsky's major insights—that in the absence of a complementary regulatory system, the effectiveness of bailouts will diminish over time. This is because bailouts, just like financial crises, are double-edged. They prevent depressions, but they also limit the costs to speculators of their financial excesses. As soon as the next economic expansion begins gathering strength, speculators will therefore pursue profit opportunities more or less as they had during the previous cycle. This is the pattern that has brought us to our current situation—a massive global crisis, being countered by an equally massive bailout of thus far limited effectiveness.

Minsky's Wall Street paradigm did not address all the afflictions of free-market capitalism. In particular, his model neglects the problems that arise from the vast disparities of income, wealth and power that are just as endemic to free market capitalism as are its tendencies toward financial instability, even though he fully recognized that these problems exist.

Yet Minsky's approach still provides the most powerful lens for understanding the roots of financial instability and developing an effective regulatory system.

Minsky understood that his advocacy of comprehensive financial regulations made no sense whatsoever within the prevailing professional orthodoxy of free-market cheerleading. In his 1986 magnum opus, *Stabilizing an Unstable Economy*, he concluded that "the policy failures since the mid-1960s are related to the banality of orthodox economic analysis.... Only an economics that is critical of capitalism can be a guide to successful policy for capitalism." ❏

Article 6.7

THE BAILOUT OF FANNIE MAE AND FREDDIE MAC

BY FRED MOSELEY
September/October 2008

It has been a persistent myth, and an article of faith among "free market" conservatives, that Fannie Mae and Freddie Mac—the two government-sponsored mortgage lending giants—were somehow responsible for the housing-market bubble, its subsequent crash, and therefore the worst U.S. recession since the Great Depression. This is a comforting story, for those who want to believe it, since it indicts government involvement in markets as inherently distorting (something they believe anyway) and lets financial deregulation and the private financial industry off the hook.

As economists like Paul Krugman and Mark Zandi point out, however, the facts do not bear out the view that Fannie and Freddie engaged in irresponsible lending or should be blamed for the bubble. Krugman, a Princeton professor and Nobel laureate in economics, notes that the "serious delinquency" rate of Fannie and Freddie's high risk loans was about the same as the national average for all mortgages—and about one third the rate for the "subprime" loans that became stock-in-trade of private mortgage lenders ("Fannie Freddie Phooey," nytimes.com, July 14, 2011). Zandi, co-founder of Moody's Economy.com, points out that Fannie and Freddie rapidly lost market share as the bubble inflated—that is, as private lenders accelerated their indiscriminate subprime lending. "The two giant housing-finance institutions made many mistakes over the decades ...," Zandi concludes, "but causing house prices to soar and then crater during the past decade weren't among them" ("Fannie and Freddie don't deserve blame for bubble," Washington Post, Jan. 24, 2012).

In this article, economist Fred Moseley takes a retrospective look at the ways Fannie and Freddie have operated over the years, what led to their recent troubles, and the eventual bailouts. Moseley draws opposite conclusions from the conservative critics, pointing to the problems caused by Fannie and Freddie's 1968 privatization (which turned them from government-owned to "government-sponsored" entities, with private shareholders but public loan guarantees). And he points to different solutions from either the conservatives who want to see both abolished and those "reformers" who want to see them turned into mortgage-insurance agencies. He calls, instead, for the formation of a fully public mortgage bank. —Eds.

On Sunday, September 7 [2008], Treasury Secretary Henry Paulson announced that the U.S. government was taking control of Fannie Mae and Freddie Mac, the two giant home mortgage companies, which together either own or guarantee almost half of the mortgages in the United States. This takeover stands in striking contrast to the generally laissez-faire philosophy of the U.S. government, especially the Republican Party. Why did Paulson take this highly unusual action? And what will be the future of Fannie and Freddie? To delve into these questions is to underscore the critical fault line between private profits and public aims—in this case, the aim of making homeownership affordable—a fault line that ran right through the hybrid structure of Fannie and Freddie.

A Brief History

Fannie Mae (short for the Federal National Mortgage Association) was created as an agency of the federal government in 1938 in an attempt to provide additional funds to the home mortgage market and to help the housing industry recover from the Great Depression. Fannie Mae purchased approved mortgages from commercial banks, which could then use the funds to originate additional mortgages. It continued to fulfill this function on a modest scale in the early postwar years.

Fannie Mae was privatized in 1968, in part to help reduce the budget deficit caused by the Vietnam War (a short-sighted goal, if ever there was one). In 1970, Freddie Mac (Federal Home Loan Mortgage Corporation) was created as a private company in order to provide competition for Fannie Mae. Chartered by the federal government, both are (or were, until the takeover) so-called government-sponsored enterprises: private enterprises whose main goal is to maximize profit for the shareholders who own them, but also quasi-public enterprises with a mandated goal of increasing the availability of affordable mortgages to families in the United States. In the end, this dual mandate proved to be untenable.

In order to obtain funds to purchase mortgages, Fannie and Freddie sell short-term bonds. In other words, their business plan involves borrowing short-term and lending long-term, because interest rates are higher on long-term loans than on short-term loans. However, such "speculative finance" is risky because it depends on the willingness of short-term creditors to continue to loan to Fannie and Freddie by rolling over or refinancing their short-term loans. If creditors were to lose confidence in Fannie and Freddie and refuse to do so, then they would be in danger of bankruptcy. This is what almost happened in the recent crisis.

Beginning in the 1970s, Fannie and Freddie began to develop and sell "mortgage-backed securities"—hundreds of mortgages bundled together and sold to investors as a security, similar to a bond. They also guaranteed these securities (so that if a mortgage defaulted, they would repurchase it from the investors) and made money by charging a fee for this guarantee (like an insurance premium). This major financial innovation enabled the two companies to buy more mortgages from commercial banks, thereby increasing the supply of credit in the home mortgage market, which in turn was supposed to push mortgage interest rates lower, making houses more affordable. These early mortgage-backed securities consisted entirely of "prime" mortgages—that is, loans at favorable interest rates, typically made to creditworthy borrowers with full documentation and a substantial down payment.

The securities that Fannie and Freddie sold were widely perceived by investors to carry an implicit government guarantee: if Fannie or Freddie were ever in danger of bankruptcy, then the federal government would pay off their debts (even though this government guarantee was explicitly denied in legislation and in the loan agreements them-selves). This perceived guarantee enabled Fannie and Freddie to borrow money at lower interest rates because loans to them were viewed as less risky.

In the 1980s, Wall Street investment banks also began to package and sell mortgage-backed securities. In the 1990s and 2000s, these "private label" mortgage-backed securities expanded rapidly in volume and also in reach, coming to include "subprime" mortgages—loans at higher interest rates with less favorable terms, geared toward less credit-worthy borrowers and typically requiring little or no documentation and little or no down payment.

The subprime innovation was entirely the work of the investment banks; as of 2000, Fannie and Freddie owned or guaranteed almost no subprime mortgages. This innovation greatly increased the supply of credit for home mortgages and led to the extraordinary housing boom of the last decade, and also eventually to the crisis. As a result of these changes, the share of mortgage-backed securities sold by Fannie and Freddie fell to around 40% by 2005.

In the recent housing boom, the companies—especially Freddie—began to take greater risks. While continuing to bundle prime mortgages into securities and sell them to investors, Fannie and Freddie began to buymortgage-backed securities issued by investment banks, including some based on subprime and Alt-A (between prime and subprime) mortgages. Why did they begin buying as well as selling mortgage-backed securities? Buying these private-label securities gave Fannie and Freddie a way to get in on the subprime action—while still avoiding direct purchases of subprime mortgages from the banks and mortgage companies that originated them. It was a way both to increase their profits at the behest of their shareholders, and, in response to pressure from the government, to make more mortgages available to low- and middle-income families. Of course, it also opened them up to the risks of the subprime arena. Moreover, the prime mortgages they continued to buy and guarantee were increasingly at inflated, bubble prices, making them vulnerable to the eventual bust and the decline of housing prices.

Anatomy of a Crisis

When the subprime crisis began in the summer of 2007, Fannie and Freddie at first appeared to be relatively unaffected, and were even counted on to increase their purchases of mortgages in order to support the mortgage market and help overcome the crisis. Congress facilitated this by relaxing some of its regulations on the two companies: the maximum value of mortgages that they could purchase was increased substantially; their reserve capital requirements, already much lower than for commercial banks, were reduced further; and restrictions on their growth were lifted. As a result of these changes and the drying up of private label mortgage-backed securities, the share of all mortgage-backed securities sold by Fannie and Freddie doubled to approximately 80%. Without Fannie and Freddie, the mortgage and housing crises of the last year would have been much worse.

As the overall crisis unfolded, however, the financial situation of Fannie and Freddie deteriorated. Delinquency and foreclosure rates for the mortgages they own or guarantee, while lower than for the industry as a whole, increased rapidly and beyond expectations. The two companies together reported losses of $14 billion in the last year. Their actual losses have been much worse. As of mid-2008, the two had lost about $45 billion due to the decline in the value of their mortgage-backed securities, mostly those backed by subprime and Alt-A mortgages. But by labeling that decline "temporary," they could leave the losses off their balance sheets. If these losses were counted, as they should be, then Freddie's capital would be completely wiped out (a value of -$5.6 billion), and Fannie's would be reduced to a razor-thin margin of $12.2 billion (less than 2% of its assets), likely becoming negative in the coming quarters. In addition, both Fannie and Freddie count as assets "tax deferred losses" that can be used in future years to offset tax bills—if they make a profit. Without this dubious (but legal) accounting trick, the net assets of both Fannie and Freddie would be below zero, -$20 billion and -$32 billion respectively.

The financial crisis of Fannie and Freddie worsened in early July. The price of their stock, which had already fallen by more than half since last summer, declined another 50% in a few weeks, for a total decline of over 80%. Fear spread that Fannie and Freddie's creditors would refuse to roll over their short-term loans to the two. If that were to happen, then the U.S. home mortgage market and the housing construction industry probably would have collapsed completely, and the U.S. economy would have fallen into an even deeper recession. Furthermore, approximately 20% of the mortgage-backed securities and debt of Fannie and Freddie are owned by foreign investors. Mainly these are foreign governments, most significantly China. If these foreign investors became unwilling to continue to lend Fannie and Freddie money, this would have precipitated a steep fall in the value of the dollar which, on top of recent significant declines, would have dealt another blow to the U.S. economy. Clearly, the potential crisis here was serious enough to spur government action.

In late July, Congress passed a law authorizing the Treasury to provide unlimited amounts of money to Fannie and Freddie, either by buying new issues of stock or by making loans, and also to take over the companies in a conservator arrangement if necessary.

Government Takeover

Through August [2008] the financial condition of Fannie and Freddie continued to deteriorate (especially Freddie), and confidence in their ability to survive waned. Foreign investors in particular reduced their purchases of the companies' debt, and mortgage rates increased. The Treasury concluded that it had to implement a takeover in order to reassure creditors and restore stability to the home mortgage market.

The Treasury plan has three main components:

- It commits up to $200 billion over the next 15 months for purchases of preferred shares of Fannie and Freddie as necessary to keep the companies solvent;

- It establishes a special lending facility that will provide emergency loans in case of a liquidity crisis;

- It commits to purchase unspecified amounts of Fannie and Freddie's mortgage-backed securities "as deemed appropriate."

The day after Paulson's announcement, William Poole, ex-president of the Federal Reserve Bank of St. Louis, estimated that the total cost to taxpayers would be in the neighborhood of $300 billion.

The top managers and the boards of directors of both companies will be dismissed and replaced by new, government-appointed managers. Other than that, the Treasury hopes that day-to-day operations at Fannie and Freddie will be "business as usual." They will continue to borrow money from creditors, now reassured by the government's intervention and more willing to lend to them, and they will continue to purchase and guarantee prime mortgages. In fact, Treasury Department plans call for the volume of mortgages purchased by the two companies to increase over the next year in order to push the supply of mortgage loans up and mortgage interest rates down.

The Treasury plan is a complete bailout of the creditors of Fannie and Freddie, who will be repaid in full, with taxpayer money if necessary. In contrast, owners of Fannie or Freddie stock will lose to some degree: dividends will be suspended for the foreseeable future, and their stock is now worth very little. But their stock was not expropriated. Nor was it wiped out entirely; it could regain value in the future as the home mortgage market recovers. Without the intervention, both companies would have gone bankrupt and the stockowners would have lost everything. So the intervention does represent at least a modest bailout for shareholders.

The most controversial issue in the months ahead will be the future of Fannie and Freddie. Should they become public enterprises permanently? Should they be re-privatized? Should they be sold off in pieces and cease to exist? Secretary Paulson made it clear that the government's current conservatorship is a holding action, and that decisions about the companies' ultimate status will only be made once the next administration and the next Congress are in office. Paulson said that Fannie and Freddie's current structure is unworkable because of its dual and conflicting goals of making housing affordable and maximizing profit—a radical statement, if you think about it! And he suggested that the two should either be fully public enterprises, or else they should be fully private enterprises without any government backing.

In the upcoming debate, the left should advocate forcefully for a public home mortgage agency, one whose sole purpose is to provide affordable housing without the conflicting purpose of maximizing profit. This would stabilize the home mortgage market and help it avoid the boom/bust cycle of private mortgage markets that has brought on the current crisis.

More fundamentally, because decent affordable housing is a basic economic right, providing credit for home purchases should be a function of the government rather than of private businesses whose primary goal is maximum profit. The provision of credit for housing should not be an arena where enormous profits are made, as has been the case in recent years. Without these huge profits, mortgages would be cheaper and houses more affordable. Plus, the kinds of fraudulent lending practices that played a significant role in the recent housing boom would be minimized.

With the presidential election just weeks away, the crisis of Fannie, Freddie, and the whole home lending market is poised to become a major campaign issue. McCain has said that he wants Fannie and Freddie to "go away"—i.e., to be broken up and disappear, leaving the mortgage market entirely to private enterprises. Obama has emphasized the conflict between the public aim of making housing widely affordable and the private aim of making a profit, but so far he has not come down on one side or the other. Now he will have to decide. I hope that he will be a strong advocate of a public home mortgage agency, and I think this would help him to get elected.

Update, October 2010

The current recession has clearly demonstrated that private banks and other investors will flee the mortgage market in a serious recession unless there are government guarantees. Without the government guarantee, investors would generally charge a higher rate of interest to finance 30-year fixed rate mortgages for households, and might not be willing to lend at all in economic downturns.

The interest rate "spread" in normal times between a purely private mortgage system (e.g., jumbo loans which exceed the maximum for Fannie-Freddie mortgages) and a mortgage system with government insurance in recent decades has been between .25% and .5%. However, in the current recession, this spread increased sharply to 1.5% and is still today almost 1%. Only about 10% of new mortgages since the recession began have been without government guarantees.

Where would the mortgage market and the economy be today without Fannie and Freddie? The mortgage market would be about one-tenth of its present size, and the economy would be in correspondingly much worse shape.

In spite of the obvious risks, Republicans want to do away with the government role in the mortgage market altogether. They argue that private banks would increase competition, which would lower costs and lower mortgage rates. But this argument is disingenuous, to say the least; everyone but free-market true-believers recognizes that, without explicit government backing, mortgage rates would be higher and in a crisis would be *much* higher. In such a Republican world, houses would be less affordable and home ownership would decline. And in a crisis, new home ownership would become almost impossible. Because of their blind allegiance to the "free market," Republicans are willing to be reckless with our economy and our lives. Obviously, we should not allow them to do this.

Although a government insurance agency (such as had been proposed by the Obama administration) would be much better than a purely private mortgage market, there is an even better way to reduce interest rates on mortgages: transform Fannie and Freddie into a public mortgage bank (rather than an insurance company) that would buy eligible mortgages from originators and hold them in their own portfolio. Actually, this would be a "return to the past" and to the original structure of Fannie Mae from its beginning in the Great Depression (to provide more affordable mortgages) until its privatization in 1968 (to help pay for the Vietnam War).

Such a public bank could charge lower interest rates than private banks (even with government insurance) because the main goal of private banks is to maximize profit and maximize shareholder value, and also to allow for multimillion-dollar salaries of bank executives. A public mortgage bank would have a different objective: not to maximize profit, shareholder value, and executive salaries, but to increase the availability of affordable housing. This goal would not be pursued to the point of losing money, but the profit margin could be less. And the executive salaries would be more in line with high civil servant salaries. Public bank mortgages would also have an upper limit, perhaps $500,000. The public bank provision of low-interest mortgages would not apply to more expensive houses or to second homes.

A relevant comparison is with student loans. The explicit argument of the Obama administration for a "direct lender" model is that they can provide student loans more cheaply than the private companies they have been subsidizing, and can also use the savings to fund more Pell grants for low-income students. What a great idea! The same logic could be applied to housing.

Another related advantage of a public bank over private banks is that its profit would not have to go to private shareholders (there would be none), but would instead become public income that could be used to pursue public policy goals, such as building more affordable housing.

Another advantage of a public bank over an insurance plan is that it would eliminate the risk (which is probably significant) that the insurance premium charged to banks would be too low, and that in the next serious crisis, taxpayers would once again suffer the losses, rather than the private banks that profited from the mortgages during the good times.

A public bank would raise funds to buy mortgages by borrowing money in the capital market (i.e., by selling bonds), the same way that private banks raise funds to finance their mortgages. But this borrowed money would not add to the government deficit, because the money would be invested in mortgages, which would eventually be recovered, together with a modest profit.

The future of Fannie and Freddie will be one of the most important economic policy issues down the road. The Left should attempt to put the public bank option on the table for discussion, and should advocate its adoption, as the best way to achieve the objective of more affordable housing for all Americans and a more stable economy. ❑

Postscript, November 2013

Five years later, the future of Fannie Mae and Freddie Mac is still undecided. President Obama proposed in a speech in August 2013 that the two government agencies be wound down over five years and replaced by a smaller government agency that would only insure mortgages and would not make mortgage loans themselves, thus leaving the housing mortgage market in the hands of private banks. In my view, this would be a significant step backward from the existing Fannie and Freddie. Therefore, my recommended "second best" option at the present time (since a fully public mortgage bank does not seem to be on the agenda) is to leave Fannie and Freddie as they are—both insuring mortgages and issuing mortgages. Dean Baker of the Center for Economic and Policy Research (CEPR) made a similar recommendation soon after Obama's speech, arguing that the goal of "promot[ing] homeownership ... can be best served with Fannie and Freddie continuing as government companies." —*Fred Moseley*

Article 6.8

GLASS-STEAGALL NOW:
BECAUSE THE BANKS OWN WASHINGTON

BY DEAN BAKER
August 2013, Al Jazeera English

A bipartisan group of senators recently put forward a proposal for new Glass-Steagall legislation that would restore a strict separation between commercial banks and speculative trading. Anyone familiar with the ways of Washington knows that such legislation is badly needed. It is the only way to prevent the Wall Street gang from continuing to rip off the public and subjecting the rest of us to the risks of their speculation.

The idea of the original Glass Steagall was to create two completely distinct types of banks. On the one hand there would be the standard commercial banks with which most of us are familiar. These are the banks where people have checking and savings accounts and where they might go to take out a mortgage or small business loan.

Because of the central role that commercial banks play in the day-to-day workings of the economy, the government established the Federal Deposit Insurance Corporation (FDIC) to guarantee the vast majority of accounts in full. The goal was to let people know that their money is safe in the bank.

Since the government guaranteed the money, people need never worry about racing to the bank to get their money before the bank vault is empty. As a result we have not seen the sort of old-fashioned bank-runs that were a mainstay of the pre-FDIC era.

The quid pro quo for having the government guarantee deposits was that commercial banks were supposed to restrict their loans to a limited number of relatively safe activities, such as mortgage loans, small business loans, car loans and other simple and standardized forms of credit. These restrictions are essential, because if customers know their money is guaranteed by the government, they won't care if their bank is taking enormous risks. The government must act to impose discipline on bank behavior that will not come from the market when deposits are insured.

By contrast, investment banks were set free to engage in whatever risky behavior they liked. Investment banks did not take deposits but rather raised money through issuing bonds or other forms of borrowing. In principle, their potential failure did not pose the same risk to the economy.

The ending of Glass-Steagall removed the separation between investment banks and commercial banks, raising the possibility that banks would make risky investments with government-guaranteed deposits. In principle, even after the ending of Glass Steagall banks were supposed to keep a strict separation between their commercial banking and the risky bets taken by their investment banking divisions, but this depends on the ability of regulators to enforce this restriction.

The Volcker Rule provision in Dodd-Frank was an effort to re-establish a Glass Steagall type separation but the industry is making Swiss cheese out of this regulation in the rule-writing process. Serious people cannot believe that this will keep the Wall Street banks from using their government-guaranteed deposits as a cushion to support their speculative game playing.

If anyone questions how this story is likely to play out in practice, we need only go back a few years to the financial crisis of 2008-2009. At that time, most of the major banks, Bank of America, Citigroup, Goldman Sachs and Morgan Stanley, almost surely would have failed without government support.

In fact, some of the top economic advisors in the Obama administration wanted to let them fail and have the government take them over, as the FDIC does all the time with insolvent banks. However Larry Summers managed to carry the day by arguing that such a move would be far too risky at a time when the financial markets were so unsettled. As a result, the big banks got their government money and were allowed to consolidate so that they are now bigger than ever.

This was primarily a problem of banks that are too big and too interconnected to fail, not just a problem of commercial banks merging with investment banks. But these mergers certainly help banks to reach too-big-to-fail status.

Some may argue that the crisis of 2008-2009 involved extraordinary circumstances. However when banks fail it is generally because the economy faces a crisis. They do not typically fail in good times. And it is a safe bet that there will always be a smart and belligerent Larry Summers on the scene aggressively arguing the case against anyone who wants to subject the banks to market discipline.

What is striking about the argument on re-instating Glass-Steagall is that there really is no downside. The banks argue that it will be inconvenient to separate their divisions, but companies sell off divisions all the time.

They also argue that foreign banks are not generally required to adhere to this sort of separation. This is in part true, but irrelevant.

Stronger regulations might lead us to do more business with foreign-owned banks since weaker regulations could give them some competitive edge. That should bother us as much as it does that we buy clothes and toys from Bangladesh and China.

If foreign governments want to subject themselves and their economies to greater risk as a result of bad financial regulation, that is not an argument for us to do the same. Are we anxious to be the next Iceland or Cyprus?

In short, the senators are on the right track pushing for a new Glass-Steagall. The public should hope that bankers' lobby doesn't derail their efforts. ❑

Article 6.9

THE FINANCIAL CRISIS AND THE SECOND GREAT DEPRESSION MYTH

BY DEAN BAKER
September 2013, Truthout

All knowledgeable D.C. types know that the TARP and Fed bailout of Wall Street banks five years ago saved us from a second Great Depression. Like most things known by knowledgeable Washington types, this is not true.

Just to remind folks, the Wall Street banks were on life support at that time. Bear Stearns, one of the five major investment banks, would have collapsed in March of 2008 if the Fed had not been able to arrange a rescue by offering guarantees on almost $30 billion in assets to J.P. Morgan. Fannie Mae and Freddie Mac both went belly up in September. The next week Lehman, another of the five major investment banks did go under. AIG, the country's largest insurer was about to follow suit when the Fed and Treasury jerry-rigged a rescue.

Without massive government assistance, it was a virtual certainty that the remaining three investment banks, Goldman Sachs, Morgan Stanley, and Merrill Lynch, were toast. Bank of America and Citigroup also were headed rapidly for the dustbin of history. It is certainly possible, if not likely, that the other two giant banks, Wells Fargo and J.P. Morgan, would have been sucked down in the maelstrom.

In short, if we allowed the magic of the market to do its work, we would have seen an end to Wall Street as we know it. The major banks would be in receivership. Instead of proffering economic advice to the president, the top executives of these banks would be left walking the streets and dodging indictments and lawsuits.

This was when they turned socialist on us. We got the TARP and infinite money and guarantees from the Fed, FDIC, and Treasury to keep the Wall Street crew in their expensive suits. All the politicians told us how painful it was for them to hand out this money to the wealthy, but the alternative was a Second Great Depression.

It's not clear what these people think they mean, but let's work it through. Suppose that we did see a full meltdown. The commercial banks that handle checking and saving accounts and are responsible for most personal and business transactions would then be under control of the FDIC.

The FDIC takes banks over all the time. This would be more roadkill than it was accustomed to, but there is little reason to think that after a few days most of us would not be able to get to most of the money in our accounts and carry through normal transactions.

Credit conditions would likely be uncertain for business loans for some time, as in fact was the case even with the bailouts. Mortgage credit would have been provided by Fannie Mae and Freddie Mac, as has been the case since September of 2008.

One item deserving special attention in this respect is the commercial paper market. This is the market that most major businesses rely upon to meet regular payments like payroll and electric bills. When he was lobbying Congress for the

TARP, Federal Reserve Board Chair Ben Bernanke said that this market was shutting down, which would in fact be disastrous for the economy.

What Bernanke neglected to mention was that he unilaterally had the ability to support the commercial paper market through the Fed. In fact he announced a special lending facility for exactly this purpose, the weekend after Congress approved the TARP.

It is also worth ridiculing people who say the government made a profit on its bailout loans. It's true that most loans were repaid with interest. However these loans were made to favored borrowers (Wall Street banks) at far-below-the-market interest rates at the time.

The Congressional Oversight Panel commissioned a study on the subsidies involved in just the first round of TARP loans. The study put the subsidies at a bit more than 30 percent of the money lent out, implying bank subsidies of almost $80 billion from just this small segment of the bailout. Adding in other loans and various implicit and explicit guarantees would certainly increase this number considerably.

But suppose we hadn't opened the government's wallet and instead let the banks drown in their own greed. Would we have faced a decade of double-digit unemployment?

From an economic standpoint there would be no reason for concern. We know from the last Great Depression, the key to recovery from a period of weak demand is to have the government spend lots of money. We eventually got out of the Great Depression by spending huge amounts of money on World War II. To get the economy jump-started this time we could have had massive spending on education, child care, rebuilding the infrastructure and making the economy more energy efficient. As Paul Krugman has repeatedly joked, if we need a political rationale for this spending we can say it is necessary to protect the United States from a Martian invasion.

Of course as a political matter, such massive spending could prove a tough sell given the present day politics. But that is a political argument, not an economic one.

Since we would be in uncharted water following this sort of collapse, no one can with a straight face claim they know how the politics would play out. We can separate out three camps.

First we have the folks who would like the government to spend enough to restore full employment, but argue the political opposition would be too great. These people have a coherent second Great Depression story, but based on politics, not economics. The bad guys would have forced us to endure a decade of double-digit unemployment if we didn't rescue Wall Street.

Then we have the people who don't like government spending and would oppose efforts to boost the economy back to full employment. These people are saying that we would have faced a second Great Depression if we didn't rescue Wall Street because they would have insisted upon it.

Finally, there are Washington Very Serious People types like the Washington Post editorial page, who would go along with restarting the economy but only if accompanied by sharp cuts to programs like Social Security and Medicare. These people are hostage takers who are saying that if the country didn't bailout Wall Street, they would force it to endure a second Great Depression, unless it eviscerated essential programs that working people need.

So the long and short is that we only need to have worried about a Second Great Depression if the bad guys got their way. And most of the people who warn about a Second Great Depression were on the list of bad guys. The prospect of a second Great Depression was not a warning, it was a threat. ❑

Article 6.10

SECURITIZATION, THE BUBBLE, AND THE CRISIS

BY ARTHUR MacEWAN
July/August 2009

Dear Dr. Dollar:
What is "securitization" and what role did it play in the emergence and, then, collapse of the housing bubble?
—Anonymous, Boston, Mass.

Fraud in the housing bubble of the early 2000s—which led into the financial crisis that became apparent in 2008—took place partly in the mortgage companies' and banks' use of deceit in getting people to take on mortgages when it was virtually certain that, at some point, the borrowers would not be able to make their payments. While this practice may not always have been fraud in the formal legal sense, it was certainly a deliberate deception. Here's one example, provided in a December 28, 2008, *New York Times* story on the failed Washington Mutual Bank:

> As a supervisor at a Washington Mutual mortgage processing center, John D. Parsons was accustomed to seeing baby sitters claiming salaries worthy of college presidents, and schoolteachers with incomes rivaling stockbrokers'. He rarely questioned them. A real estate frenzy was under way and WaMu, as his bank was known, was all about saying yes.
>
> Yet even by WaMu's relaxed standards, one mortgage four years ago raised eyebrows. The borrower was claiming a six-figure income and an unusual profession: mariachi singer.
>
> Mr. Parsons could not verify the singer's income, so he had him photographed in front of his home dressed in his mariachi outfit. The photo went into a WaMu file. Approved.

But why did WaMu and other financial firms issue loans—the mortgages—to people when the firms knew that many of those loans would never be paid back? The answer to this question lies in "securitization."

Securitization is the practice of putting together several mortgages (or other types of contractual debt) to create a package that is then sold as a single security. The payments on those mortgages go to the buyer(s) of this new security, which is called a collateralized debt obligation or CDO. Because a mortgage-based CDO is made up of many underlying mortgages, perhaps thousands, it is viewed as a diversified investment—and diversification is often a characteristic of safe investments.

So when a financial firm—a mortgage company or a bank—made a mortgage loan, it quickly sold that mortgage to be placed into a CDO. The firm itself, then, would not be hurt if the person who took on the mortgage failed to make payments. At the same time, the firm collected substantial fees for making the mortgage and passing it along in this manner.

The buyers of CDOs viewed them as good investments, partly because the securities contained a diverse set of assets, partly because the buyers failed to recognize the deceptive practices that were widespread in the mortgage market, and partly because the CDOs received good ratings from the major securities rating agencies—Moody's, Standard & Poors, and Fitch. No one seemed to care that the rating agencies were being paid by the large financial firms that were handling the sales of the CDOs—a bit like food critics being paid by the restaurants they are rating.

Nonetheless, buyers of CDOs generally purchased insurance on them, just in case. The insurance policies were called credit default swaps, or simply "swaps" (and are purchased on a wide variety of assets). Unlike other forms of insurance, however, swaps were not regulated. The sellers of swaps did not have to hold funds in reserve in case a large amount of the CDOs failed at the same time. Moreover, as with the mortgages and CDOs, there was an extensive market in the credit default swaps; in fact, people could buy and sell swaps when they had no direct connection to the underlying security that was being insured.

Swaps, CDOs, and even the mortgages are forms of "derivatives." These are securities whose value is derived from the value of some other asset—the value of the swaps derived from the value of the CDOs, the value of the CDOs derived from the value of the mortgages, the value of the mortgages derived from the value of the real properties. So if something happens to the value of the real properties (houses), the whole chain of derivative assets is affected.

When the housing bubble did burst, as all bubbles eventually do, the market for CDOs and swaps fell apart. People and financial institutions stopped buying these assets. The financial markets "froze up" or "melted down" (whichever of these two seemingly contradictory metaphors you like). And there we were, at the financial crisis of 2008, the recession of 2009, and the economic malaise that is still with us. ❑

Chapter 7

UNEMPLOYMENT AND INFLATION

INTRODUCTION

In June 2009, with the economy still in the throes of its worst crisis since the Great Depression, supply-side economist Arthur Laffer warned of the threat of inflation. In an op-ed piece in the *Wall Street Journal*, Laffer wrote that "we can expect rapidly rising prices over the next four or five years." He argued that the Fed's unprecedented expansion of the money supply during the crisis has the potential to unleash an inflation spiral more virulent than that of the 1970s.

There might be something to Laffer's concerns about price stability over the longer term, although we have seen precious few signs of a pick-up in inflation in the last four years. But why voice those concerns just three days after the economy had registered its highest unemployment rate in 26 years? Do conservative economists think it is more important to address a threat of inflation that may not manifest itself for years (if at all) than to deal with record-setting unemployment today?

The short answer is yes. This is hardly a surprise when considering that investors and stockholders feel precisely the same way. Why is that?

To start, it is necessary to understand the trade-off between inflation and unemployment described by the "Phillips curve." Economist Ramaa Vasudevan takes a careful look at the relationship between inflation and unemployment and how that trade-off changed during two historical periods: the stagflation of the 1970s and the productivity boom of the 1990s. She attributes the sustained low inflation during the 1990s, despite low unemployment, to the relatively weak bargaining position of workers (Article 7.1).

Economist Robert Pollin delves more deeply into why the textbook trade-off between inflation and unemployment affects the returns of stockholders and other investors. The answer, Pollin points out, is "all about class conflict." Wall Street investors, out to protect the value of their assets and their investment profits, are hyper-concerned with price stability. This pits them against workers on Main Street, who care about employment and wage growth. Higher unemployment rates and fewer jobs eat away at the bargaining power of workers, keeping wage growth and inflation in check and corporate profit margins wide. Pollin captures that dynamic in Article 7.2, "The 'Natural Rate' of Unemployment." As he sees it, the unemployment rate consistent with price stability—the so-called "natural rate"—declined dramatically in the 1990s because workers' economic power eroded during the decade.

The next two articles consider controversies about the causes of unemployment. John Miller and Jeannette Wicks-Lim take on the claim that the persistently high unemployment in the U.S. economy is due to a "skills deficit" among those looking for work. They examine the data on job openings, hires, and unemployment, and find that there are plenty of experienced workers still looking for work even in the industries doing most of the hiring. For them, a jobs deficit, not a skills deficit, is the cause of today's unemployment problems (Article 7.3). Meanwhile, Dean Baker tackles arguments that excessive regulation is stifling job growth. Baker argues that these claims have clear implications about what industries will be affected and how they will respond. The data, he argues, simply do not bear out the regulation-bashing story (Article 7.4).

The chapter's next two articles look at the distribution of unemployment during the Great Recession. Economist Sylvia Allegretto and labor analyst Steven Pitts examine how black workers fared in the Great Recession and the current "jobless" economic recovery. Despite starting from a higher level, black unemployment rates increased more quickly than white unemployment rates during the downturn. And after white unemployment rates eventually stopped rising and began to come down, black unemployment rates continued to rise (Article 7.5). Next, economist Heather Boushey documents how job losses in the Great Recession hit male-dominated jobs especially hard. While the economic recovery has put men back to work more quickly than women, her call for more support for female workers who increasingly find themselves in the role of family breadwinners remains timely (Article 7.6).

Alejandro Reuss writes that we do not have one "jobs problem" in the United States—we have three (Article 7.7). The rate of job creation has had trouble keeping up with population growth; insecure and insufficient employment puts workers in a weak bargaining position, which keeps wages down; and most other factors affecting bargaining power have swung in favor of employers and against workers. In this context, we have seen the loss of "good jobs" and creation of "bad jobs." But the triple jobs problem is not simply an unfortunate market phenomenon. It is an outcome of deliberate political choices.

Lastly, John Miller delves into the very real consequences of seemingly arcane, technical decisions about the construction of the consumer price index and calculation of the inflation rate (Article 7.8). Depending on the choices made, people will get greater or lesser benefits from programs like Social Security.

Discussion Questions

1. (Article 7.1) What are the costs of higher inflation and who bears those costs? According to Vasudevan's evidence, what is the relationship between inflation and growth?

2. (Articles 7.1 and 7.2) What forces led to sustained low inflation and low unemployment during the 1990s? How are those conditions changing today?

3. (Article 7.2) What is the concept of the non-accelerating inflation rate of unemployment (the NAIRU, or natural rate of unemployment)? Is there a natural rate? What kinds of factors determine the level of the NAIRU?

4. (Article 7.2) Given the class conflict inherent in the trade-off between inflation and unemployment, what policies might lead to improved standards of living for workers in today's economy?

5. (Article 7.3) What data support the case that today's high unemployment rates can be attributed to a mismatch between job openings and workers' skills? How do Miller and Wicks-Lim respond to these arguments?

6. (Article 7.4) What are the five implications of the view that regulation is to blame for weak job creation? Do the data show what we would expect if this hypothesis were correct? What conclusions does Baker reach?

7. (Articles 7.5 and 7.6) Is the overall unemployment rate a deceptive measure of economic hardship? Consider who is more likely to be unemployed (relative to the overall rate) and who is less likely.

8 (Article 7.5) How do unemployment figures for black workers differ from those for other groups of workers? What are the likely implications of historical unemployment experience for black workers during a "jobless" (very slow job growth) economic recovery?

9. (Article 7.6) Why did some commentators term the recent recession the "man-cession" or "he-cession"? How did unemployment in predominantly male occupations affect women? How has the unemployment picture changed more recently?

10. (Article 7.7) Over the past few decades ago, the U.S. economy has shed many "good jobs"—those that provided secure, middle-class incomes—while adding "bad jobs" —those that offer insecure and poorly paid employment. Why does Reuss consider the (triple) jobs problem to be, at its root, a political problem?

11. (Article 7.8) How does the cost of living adjustment (COLA) of the CPI-U (chained CPI) differ from that of the CPI-W? Why does the CPI-W rise faster than the CPI-U? What does Miller propose as a more accurate way to capture changes in the cost of living for retirees?

Article 7.1

THE RELATIONSHIP OF UNEMPLOYMENT AND INFLATION

BY RAMAA VASUDEVAN
September/October 2006

> Dear Dr. Dollar:
> *Back in first-year economics we learned that there is a tradeoff between un-*
> *employment and inflation, so you can't really have both low inflation and low*
> *unemployment at the same time. Do economists still consider that to be true?*
> —Edith Bross, Cambridge, Mass.

The trade-off between inflation and unemployment was first reported by A. W. Phillips in 1958—and so has been christened the Phillips curve. The simple intuition behind this trade-off is that as unemployment falls, workers are empowered to push for higher wages. Firms try to pass these higher wage costs on to consumers, resulting in higher prices and an inflationary buildup in the economy. The trade-off suggested by the Phillips curve implies that policymakers can target low inflation rates or low unemployment, but not both. During the 1960s, monetarists emphasized price stability (low inflation), while Keynesians more often emphasized job creation.

The experience of so-called stagflation in the 1970s, with simultaneously high rates of both inflation and unemployment, began to discredit the idea of a stable trade-off between the two. In place of the Phillips curve, many economists began to posit a "natural rate of unemployment." If unemployment were to fall below this "natural" rate, however slightly, inflation would begin to accelerate. Under the "natural rate of unemployment" theory (also called the Non-Accelerating Inflation Rate of Unemployment, or NAIRU), instead of choosing between higher unemployment and higher inflation, policymakers were told to focus on ensuring that the economy remained at its "natural" rate: the challenge was to accurately estimate its level and to steer the economy toward growth rates that maintain price stability, no matter what the corresponding level of unemployment.

The NAIRU has been extremely difficult to pin down in practice. Not only are estimates of it notoriously imprecise, the rate itself evidently changes over time. In the United States, estimates of the NAIRU rose from about 4.4% in the 1960s, to 6.2% in the 1970s, and further to 7.2% in the 1980s. This trend reversed itself in the 1990s, as officially reported unemployment fell. In the latter half of the 1990s, U.S. inflation remained nearly dormant at around 3%, while unemployment fell to around 4.6%. In the later Clinton years many economists warned that if unemployment was brought any lower, inflationary pressures might spin out of control. But growth in these years did not spill over into accelerating inflation. The United States, apparently, had achieved the Goldilocks state—everything just right!

What sustained this combination of low inflation and low unemployment? Explanations abound: a productivity boom, the high rates of incarceration of those who would otherwise fall within the ranks of the unemployed, the openness of the US economy to world trade and competition, among others.

The full story, however, has to do with class conflict and the relatively weak position of workers in the 1990s. Both the breakdown of the Phillips curve in the 1970s and the recent "disappearance" of the natural rate of unemployment are in essence a reflection of institutional and political changes that affect the bargaining strength of working people—in other words, their ability to organize effective unions and establish a decent living wage.

Following the Reagan offensive against trade unions, workers' power fell dramatically. Consequently, unionization rates and the real value of the minimum wage each fell precipitously between the late 1970s and the 1990s. The period of stagflation, in contrast, had been one of labor militancy and rising wages. (Although "stagflation" has a negative ring, by many measures nonsupervisory workers—i.e., the vast majority of the U.S. labor force—fared better in the economy of the early-to mid-1970s than they do today, even after the long 1990s economic expansion.) Labor's weaker position in the 1990s meant that despite low unemployment, workers were not able to win higher wages that would have spurred inflation.

The long period of stable prices and low interest rates in the United States now seems to be coming to a close. The cost of the Iraq War and rising oil prices, among other factors, have fueled expectations of a resurgence of inflation. At the same time, the near jobless recovery from the last recession might suggest that the "natural rate" of unemployment is on the rise again—and that we are witnessing yet another twist in the strange history of the Phillips curve!

With inflation rising (albeit slowly, and still relatively mild at around 4.2%), some business sectors will no doubt begin clamoring for tighter monetary policies that sacrifice job-creation and wage growth by slowing the economy growth. But these fears of inflation are probably misplaced. A moderate rate of inflation is conducive to the growth of real investment, and in the context of a decades-long squeeze on workers' wage share, there is room to expand employment without setting off a wage-price spiral. What workers need is not greater fiscal and monetary austerity, but rather a revival of a Keynesian program of "employment targeting" that would sustain full employment and empower workers to push for higher wages. It's not likely, however, that the owners of capital and their political allies would sit idly by were such a program to be enacted. ❑

Article 7.2

THE "NATURAL RATE" OF UNEMPLOYMENT
It's all about class conflict.

BY ROBERT POLLIN
September/October 1998

In 1997, the official U.S. unemployment rate fell to a 27-year low of 4.9%. Most orthodox economists had long predicted that a rate this low would lead to uncontrollable inflation. So they argued that maintaining a higher unemployment rate— perhaps as high as 6%—was crucial for keeping the economy stable. But there is a hitch: last year the inflation rate was 2.3%, the lowest figure in a decade and the second lowest in 32 years. What then are we to make of these economists' theories, much less their policy proposals?

Nobel prize-winning economist Milton Friedman gets credit for originating the argument that low rates of unemployment would lead to accelerating inflation. His 1968 theory of the so-called "natural rate of unemployment" was subsequently developed by many mainstream economists under the term "Non-Accelerating Inflation Rate of Unemployment," or NAIRU, a remarkably clumsy term for expressing the simple concept of a threshold unemployment rate below which inflation begins to rise.

According to both Friedman and expositors of NAIRU, inflation should accelerate at low rates of unemployment because low unemployment gives workers excessive bargaining power. This allows the workers to demand higher wages. Capitalists then try to pass along these increased wage costs by raising prices on the products they sell. An inflationary spiral thus ensues as long as unemployment remains below its "natural rate."

Based on this theory, Friedman and others have long argued that governments should never actively intervene in the economy to promote full employment or better jobs for workers, since it will be a futile exercise, whose end result will only be higher inflation and no improvement in job opportunities. Over the past generation, this conclusion has had far-reaching influence throughout the world. In the United States and Western Europe, it has provided a stamp of scientific respectability to a whole range of policies through which governments abandoned even modest commitments to full employment and workers' rights.

This emerged most sharply through the Reaganite and Thatcherite programs in the United States and United Kingdom in the 1980s. But even into the 1990s, as the Democrats took power in the United States, the Labour Party won office in Britain, and Social Democrats won elections throughout Europe, governments remained committed to stringent fiscal and monetary policies, whose primary goal is to prevent inflation. In Western Europe this produced an average unemployment rate of over 10% from 1990-97. In the United States, unemployment rates have fallen sharply in the 1990s, but as an alternative symptom of stringent fiscal and monetary policies, real wages for U.S. workers also declined dramatically over the past generation. As of 1997, the average real wage for nonsupervisory workers in the United States was 14% below its peak in 1973, even though average worker productivity rose between 1973 and 1997 by 34%.

Why have governments in the United States and Europe remained committed to the idea of fiscal and monetary stringency, if the natural rate theory on which such policies are based is so obviously flawed? The explanation is that the natural rate theory is really not just about predicting a precise unemployment rate figure below which inflation must inexorably accelerate, even though many mainstream economists have presented the natural rate theory in this way. At a deeper level, the natural rate theory is bound up with the inherent conflicts between workers and capitalists over jobs, wages, and working conditions. As such, the natural rate theory actually contains a legitimate foundation in truth amid a welter of sloppy and even silly predictions.

The "Natural Rate" Theory Is About Class Conflict

In his 1967 American Economic Association presidential address in which he introduced the natural rate theory, Milton Friedman made clear that there was really nothing "natural" about the theory. Friedman rather emphasized that: "by using the term 'natural' rate of unemployment, I do not mean to suggest that it is immutable and unchangeable. On the contrary, many of the market characteristics that determine its level are man-made and policy-made. In the United States, for example, legal minimum wage rates ... and the strength of labor unions all make the natural rate of unemployment higher than it would otherwise be."

In other words, according to Friedman, what he terms the "natural rate" is really a social phenomenon measuring the class strength of working people, as indicated by their ability to organize effective unions and establish a livable minimum wage.

Friedman's perspective is supported in a widely-read 1997 paper by Robert Gordon of Northwestern University on what he terms the "time-varying NAIRU." What makes the NAIRU vary over time? Gordon explains that, since the early 1960s, "The two especially large changes in the NAIRU... are the increase between the early and late 1960s and the decrease in the 1990s. The late 1960s were a time of labor militancy, relatively strong unions, a relatively high minimum wage and a marked increase in labor's share in national income. The 1990s have been a time of labor peace, relatively weak unions, a relatively low minimum wage and a slight decline in labor's income share."

In short, class conflict is the spectre haunting the analysis of the natural rate and NAIRU: this is the consistent message stretching from Milton Friedman in the 1960s to Robert Gordon in the 1990s.

Stated in this way, the "Natural Rate" idea does, ironically, bear a close family resemblance to the ideas of two of the greatest economic thinkers of the left, Karl Marx and Michal Kalecki, on a parallel concept—the so-called "Reserve Army of Unemployed." In his justly famous Chapter 25 of Volume I of *Capital,* "The General Law of Capitalist Accumulation," Marx argued forcefully that unemployment serves an important function in capitalist economies. That is, when a capitalist economy is growing rapidly enough so that the reserve army of unemployed is depleted, workers will then utilize their increased bargaining power to raise wages. Profits are correspondingly squeezed as workers get a larger share of the country's total income. As a result, capitalists anticipate further declines in profitability and they therefore reduce their investment spending. This then leads to a fall in job creation, higher unemployment, and a replenishment of the reserve army. In other words, the reserve army of the unemployed is the instrument capitalists use to prevent significant wage increases and thereby maintain profitability.

Kalecki, a Polish economist of the Great Depression era, makes parallel though distinct arguments in his also justly famous essay, "The Political Aspects of Full Employment." Kalecki wrote in 1943, shortly after the 1930s Depression had ended and governments had begun planning a postwar world in which they would deploy aggressive policies to avoid another calamity of mass unemployment. Kalecki held, contrary to Marx, that full employment can be beneficial to the profitability of businesses. True, capitalists may get a smaller share of the total economic pie as workers gain bargaining power to win higher wages. But capitalists can still benefit because the size of the pie is growing far more rapidly, since more goods and services can be produced when everyone is working, as opposed to some significant share of workers being left idle.

But capitalists still won't support full employment, in Kalecki's view, because it will threaten their control over the workplace, the pace and direction of economic activity, and even political institutions. Kalecki thus concluded that full employment could be sustainable under capitalism, but only if these challenges to capitalists' social and political power could be contained. This is why he held that fascist social and political institutions, such as those that existed in Nazi Germany when he was writing, could well provide one "solution" to capitalism's unemployment problem, precisely because they were so brutal. Workers would have jobs, but they would never be permitted to exercise the political and economic power that would otherwise accrue to them in a full-employment economy.

Broadly speaking, Marx and Kalecki do then share a common conclusion with natural rate proponents, in that they would all agree that positive unemployment rates are the outgrowth of class conflict over the distribution of income and political power. Of course, Friedman and other mainstream economists reach this conclusion via analytic and political perspectives that are diametrically opposite to those of Marx and Kalecki. To put it in a nutshell, in the Friedmanite view mass unemployment results when workers demand more than they deserve, while for Marx and Kalecki, capitalists use the weapon of unemployment to prevent workers from getting their just due.

From Natural Rate to Egalitarian Policy

Once the analysis of unemployment in capitalist economies is properly understood within the framework of class conflict, several important issues in our contemporary economic situation become much more clear. Let me raise just a few:

1. Mainstream economists have long studied how workers' wage demands cause inflation as unemployment falls. However, such wage demands never directly cause inflation, since inflation refers to a general rise in prices of goods and services sold in the market, not a rise in wages. Workers, by definition, do not have the power to raise prices. Capitalists raise prices on the products they sell. At low unemployment, inflation occurs when capitalists respond to workers' increasingly successful wage demands by raising prices so that they can maintain profitability. If workers were simply to receive a higher share of national income, then lower unemployment and higher wages need not cause inflation at all.

2. There is little mystery as to why, at present, the so-called "time-varying" NAIRU has diminished to a near vanishing point, with unemployment at a 25-year low while inflation remains dormant. The main explanation is the one stated by Robert Gordon—that workers' economic power has been eroding dramatically through the 1990s. Workers have been almost completely unable to win wage increases over the course of the economic expansion that by now is seven years old.

3. This experience over the past seven years, with unemployment falling but workers showing almost no income gains, demonstrates dramatically the crucial point that full employment can never stand alone as an adequate measure of workers' well-being. This was conveyed vividly to me when I was working in Bolivia in 1990 as part of an economic advising team led by Keith Griffin of the University of California-Riverside. Professor Griffin asked me to examine employment policies.

I began by paying a visit to the economists at the Ministry of Planning. When I requested that we discuss the country's employment problems, they explained, to my surprise, that the country *had no employment problems.* When I suggested we consider the situation of the people begging, shining shoes, or hawking batteries and Chiclets in the street just below the window where we stood, their response was that these people *were* employed. And of course they were, in that they were actively trying to scratch out a living. It was clear that I had to specify the problem at hand far more precisely. Similarly, in the United States today, we have to be much more specific as to what workers should be getting in a fair economy: jobs, of course, but also living wages, benefits, reasonable job security, and a healthy work environment.

4. In our current low-unemployment economy, should workers, at long last, succeed in winning higher wages and better benefits, some inflationary pressures are likely to emerge. But if inflation does not accelerate after wage increases are won, this would mean that businesses are not able to pass along their higher wage costs to their customers. Profits would therefore be squeezed. In any case, in response to *either* inflationary pressures or a squeeze in profitability, we should expect that many, if not most, segments of the business community will welcome a Federal Reserve policy that would slow the economy and raise the unemployment rate.

Does this mean that, as long as we live in a capitalist society, the control by capitalists over the reserve army of labor must remain the dominant force establishing the limits of workers' strivings for jobs, security, and living wages? The challenge for the progressive movement in the United States today is to think through a set of policy ideas through which full employment at living wages can be achieved and sustained.

Especially given the dismal trajectory of real wage decline over the past generation, workers should of course continue to push for wage increases. But it will also be crucial to advance these demands within a broader framework of proposals. One important component of a broader package would be policies through which labor and capital bargain openly over growth of wages and profits after full employment is achieved. Without such an open bargaining environment, workers, with reason, will push for higher wages once full employment is achieved, but capitalists will then respond by either raising prices or favoring high unemployment. Such open bargaining policies were conducted with considerable success in Sweden and other Nordic countries from the 1950s to the 1980s, and as a result, wages there continued to rise at full employment, while both accelerating inflation and a return to high unemployment were prevented.

Such policies obviously represent a form of class compromise. This is intrinsically neither good nor bad. The question is the terms under which the compromise is achieved. Wages have fallen dramatically over the past generation, so workers deserve substantial raises as a matter of simple fairness. But workers should also be willing to link their wage increases to improvements in productivity growth, i.e., the rate at which workers produce new goods and services. After all, if the average wage had just risen at exactly the rate of productivity growth since 1973 and not a penny more, the average hourly wage today for nonsupervisory workers would be $19.07 rather than $12.24.

But linking wages to improvements in productivity then also raises the question of who controls the decisions that determine the rate of productivity growth. In fact, substantial productivity gains are attainable through operating a less hierarchical workplace and building strong democratic unions through which workers can defend their rights on the job. Less hierarchy and increased workplace democracy creates higher morale on the job, which in turn increases workers' effort and opportunities to be inventive, while decreasing turnover and absenteeism. The late David Gordon of the New School for Social Research was among the leading analysts demonstrating how economies could operate more productively through greater workplace democracy.

But improvements in productivity also result from both the public and private sector investing in new and better machines that workers put to use every day, with the additional benefit that it means more jobs for people who produce those machines. A pro-worker economic policy will therefore also have to be concerned with increasing investments to improve the stock of machines that workers have at their disposal on the job.

In proposing such a policy approach, have I forgotten the lesson that Marx and Kalecki taught us, that unemployment serves a purpose in capitalism? Given that this lesson has become part of the standard mode of thinking among mainstream economists ranging from Milton Friedman to Robert Gordon, I would hope that I haven't let it slip from view. My point nevertheless is that through changing power relationships at the workplace and the decision-making process through which investment decisions get made, labor and the left can then also achieve a more egalitarian economy, one in which capitalists' power to brandish the weapon of unemployment is greatly circumscribed. If the labor movement and the left neglect issues of control over investment and the workplace, we will continue to live amid a Bolivian solution to the unemployment problem, where full employment is the by-product of workers' vulnerability, not their strength. ❑

Sources: A longer version of this article appears as "The 'Reserve Army of Labor' and the 'Natural Rate of Unemployment': Can Marx, Kalecki, Friedman, and Wall Street All Be Wrong?," *Review of Radical Political Economics,* Fall 1998. Both articles derive from a paper originally presented as the David Gordon Memorial Lecture at the 1997 Summer Conference of the Union for Radical Political Economics. See also Robert Pollin and Stephanie Luce, *The Living Wage: Building a Fair Economy,* 1998; David Gordon, *Fat and Mean,* 1997; David Gordon, "Generating Affluence: Productivity Gains Require Worker Support," *Real World Macro,* 15th ed., 1998.

Article 7.3

UNEMPLOYMENT: A JOBS DEFICIT OR A SKILLS DEFICIT?

BY JOHN MILLER AND JEANNETTE WICKS-LIM

January/February 2011

Millions of Americans remain unemployed nearly a year and a half after the official end-date of the Great Recession, and the nation's official unemployment rate continues at nearly 10%.

Why? We are being told that it is because—wait for it—workers are not qualified for the jobs that employers are offering.

Yes, it's true. In the aftermath of the deepest downturn since the Great Depression, some pundits and policymakers—and economists—have begun to pin persistently high unemployment on workers' inadequate skills.

The problem, in this view, is a mismatch between job openings and the skills of those looking for work. In economics jargon, this is termed a problem of "structural unemployment," in contrast to the "cyclical unemployment" caused by a downturn in the business cycle.

The skills-gap message is coming from many quarters. Policymaker-in-chief Obama told Congress in February 2009: "Right now, three-quarters of the fastest-growing occupations require more than a high school diploma. And yet, just over half of our citizens have that level of education." His message: workers need to go back to school if they want a place in tomorrow's job market.

The last Democrat in the White House has caught the bug too. Bill Clinton explained in a September 2010 interview, "The last unemployment report said that for the first time in my lifetime, and I'm not young … we are coming out of a recession but job openings are going up twice as fast as new hires. And yet we can all cite cases that we know about where somebody opened a job and 400 people showed up. How could this be? Because people don't have the job skills for the jobs that are open."

Economists and other "experts" are most likely the source of the skills-gap story. Last August, for instance, Narayana Kocherlakota, president of the Federal Reserve Bank of Minneapolis, wrote in a Fed newsletter: "How much of the current unemployment rate is really due to mismatch, as opposed to conditions that the Fed can readily ameliorate? The answer seems to be a lot." Kocherlakota's point was that the Fed's monetary policy tools may be able to spur economic growth, but that won't help if workers have few or the wrong skills. "The Fed does not have a means to transform construction workers into manufacturing workers," he explained.

The skills-mismatch explanation has a lot to recommend it if you're a federal or Fed policymaker: it puts the blame for the economic suffering experienced by the 17% of the U.S. workforce that is unemployed or underemployed on the workers themselves. Even if the Fed or the government did its darndest to boost overall spending, unemployment would be unlikely to subside unless workers upgraded their own skills.

The only problem is that this explanation is basically wrong. The weight of the evidence shows that it is not a mismatch of skills but a lack of demand that lies at the heart of today's severe unemployment problem.

High-Skill Jobs?

President Obama's claim that new jobs are requiring higher and higher skill levels would tend to support the skills-gap thesis. His interpretation of job-market trends, however, misses the mark. The figure that Obama cited comes from the U.S. Department of Labor's employment projections for 2006 to 2016. Specifically, the DOL reports that among the 30 fastest growing occupations, 22 of them (75%) will typically require more than a high school degree. These occupations include network systems and data communications analysts, computer software engineers, and financial advisors. What he fails to say, however, is that these 22 occupations are projected to represent less than 3% of all U.S. jobs.

What would seem more relevant to the 27 million unemployed and underemployed workers are the occupations with the *largest* growth. These are the occupations that will offer workers the greatest number of new job opportunities. Among the 30 occupations with the largest growth, 70%—21 out of 30—typically do not require more than a high school degree. To become fully qualified for these jobs, workers will only need on-the-job training. The DOL projects that one-quarter of all jobs in 2016 will be in these 21 occupations, which include retail salespeople, food-preparation and food-service workers, and personal and home care aides.

In fact, the DOL employment projections estimate that more than two-thirds (68%) of the jobs in 2016 will be accessible to workers with a high school degree

---

LABOR MARKET MUSICAL CHAIRS

To understand the data discussed here, try picturing the U.S. labor market as a game of musical chairs, with a few twists. At any time, chairs (job openings) can be added to the circle and players can sit down (get hired). When the music stops at the end of the month, not all the chairs are filled. Still, many people—far more people than the number of empty chairs—are left standing.

Each month, the Bureau of Labor Statistics reports on what happened in that month's game of labor market musical chairs in its various measures of unemployment and in the Job Openings and Labor Turnover Survey (JOLTS). Here's how the BLS scorecard for labor market musical chairs works.

- **Job openings** is a snapshot of the number of jobs available on the last day of the month—the number of empty chairs when the music stops.
- **Hires** are all the new additions to payroll during the month—the number of people who found a chair to sit in while the music was playing. Because many chairs are added to the circle and filled within the same month, the number of hires over a month is typically greater than the number of openings available on the last day of that month.
- **Unemployed person**s are those who looked for a job that month but couldn't find one—the number of people who played the game but were left standing when the music stopped at the end of the month.

or less. Couple this with the fact that today, nearly two-thirds (62%) of the adult labor force has at least some college experience, and an alleged skills gap fails to be convincing as a driving force behind persistent high unemployment.

Low-Skill Workers?

If employers were having a hard time finding qualified workers to fill job openings, you'd think that any workers who are qualified would be snapped right up. But what the unemployment data show is that there remains a substantial backlog of experienced workers looking for jobs or for more hours in their existing part-time jobs in those major industries that have begun hiring—including education, healthcare, durable goods manufacturing, and mining.

Most telling are the *underemployed*—those with part-time jobs who want to work full-time. Today there are more underemployed workers in each of the major industries of the private economy than during the period from 2000 to 2007, as Arjun Jayadev and Mike Konczal document in a recent paper published by the Roosevelt Institute. Even in the major industries with the highest number of job openings—education and health services, professional and business services, transportation and utilities, leisure and hospitality, and manufacturing—underemployment in 2010 remains at levels twice as high or nearly twice as high as during the earlier period (measured as a percentage of employed workers).

Purveyors of the mismatch theory would have a hard time explaining how it is that underemployed workers who want full-time work do not possess the skills to do the jobs full time that they are already doing, say, 20 hours a week.

More broadly, workers with a diverse set of skills—not just construction workers—lost jobs during the Great Recession. Workers in manufacturing, professional and business services, leisure and hospitality, transportation and utilities, and a host of other industries were turned out of their jobs. And many of these experienced workers are still looking for work. In each of the 16 major industries of the economy unemployment rates in September 2010 were still far higher than they had been at the onset of the Great Recession in December 2007. In the industries with a large number of (cumulative) job openings during the recovery—education and health services, professional and business services, and manufacturing—experienced workers face unemployment rates twice what they were back in December 2007.

There are plenty of experienced workers still looking for work in the industries with job openings. To be faithful to the data, Kocherlakota and the other mismatch proponents would need to show that experienced workers no longer possess the skills to work in their industry, even though that industry employed them no more than three years ago. That seems implausible.

Statistical Errors

Still, the statistical oddity that Bill Clinton and many economists have pointed to does seem to complicate the picture. If the number of job openings is rising at a good clip yet the number of new hires is growing more slowly and the unemployment rate is stagnant, then maybe employers *are* having trouble finding qualified folks to hire.

Once you take a closer looks at the numbers, though, there is less here than meets the eye.

First, the *rate* at which job openings and new hires numbers change over time is not the right place to look. What we really need to know is how the number of unfilled job posts compares to the number of qualified workers employers hire over the same month. If employers in today's recovery are having a hard time finding workers, then the job openings left unfilled at the end of the month should be relatively high compared to the number of newly hired workers that month. In other words, if the number of positions left unfilled at the end of the month relative to the number of new hires rises *above* what we've seen during past recoveries, this would mean that employers are finding it harder to fill their positions with the right workers this time around.

But it turns out that the ratio of unfilled job openings to new hires is approximately the same during this recovery as in the recovery from the 2001 recession. In September 2010, fifteen months into the current economic recovery, the ratio of job posts left unoccupied at the end of the month to the number of monthly new hires stood at 69%—very close to its 67% level in February 2003, fifteen months into the

---

WHERE MISMATCHES MAY MATTER

The skills-mismatch theory does not go very far toward explaining stubbornly high U.S. unemployment. Still, there are unquestionably some unemployed and underemployed workers whose job prospects are limited by "structural" factors.

One kind of structural unemployment that does seem to fit the contours of the Great Recession to at least some degree is that caused by a mismatch of geography: the workers are in one part of the country while the jobs they could get are in another. The housing crisis surely has compromised the ability of unemployed workers to unload their single largest asset, a house, and move to another part of the country. Plus, job losses have been particularly heavy in regions where the housing crisis hit hardest.

But at the same time, lost jobs have been widespread across industries and there is little real evidence of geographic mismatch between job openings and unemployed workers. As labor economist Michael Reich reports, "economic decline and the growth of unemployment have been more widespread than ever before, making it unclear where the unemployed should migrate for greater job opportunities."

Even where there is a skills mismatch, that doesn't mean the government shouldn't get involved. On the contrary, government policies to boost economic demand can help significantly. When demand is high, labor markets become very tight and there are few available workers to hire. Workers previously viewed as "unemployable" get hired, get experience and on-the-job training, and see their overall career prospects brighten.

And, of course, government can fund expanded job-training programs. If the economy continues to slog along with low growth rates and persistent unemployment, the ranks of the long-term unemployed will rise. As they go longer and longer without work, their skills will atrophy or become obsolete and they will face a genuine skills-mismatch problem that will make job-training programs more and more necessary.

last recovery. In other words, today's employers are filling their job openings with the same rate of success as yesterday's employers.

Comparisons that focus on the unemployment rate rather than on the number of new hires are even less meaningful. As hiring picks up at the beginning of an economic recovery, workers who had given up the job search start looking again. This brings them back into the official count of the unemployed, keeping the unemployment rate from dropping even as both job openings and new hires rise.

Not Enough Jobs

The reality of the situation—the widespread job losses and the long, fruitless job searches of experienced workers—make it clear that today's employment problem is a jobs deficit across the economy, not a skills deficit among those looking for work.

While it's true that any given month ends with some number of unfilled job openings, the total number of jobs added to the economy during this recovery has simply been inadequate to put the unemployed back to work. In fact, if every job that stood open at the end of September 2010 had been filled, 11.7 million officially unemployed workers would still have been jobless.

This recovery has seen far fewer job openings than even the so-called "jobless" recovery following the 2001 recession. Economists Lawrence Mishel, Heidi Shierholz, and Kathryn Edwards of the Economic Policy Institute report that cumulative job openings during the first year of this recovery were roughly 25% lower than during the first year of the recovery following the 2001 recession—that's 10 million fewer jobs. Even in the industries generating the most job openings in the current recovery—education and health services, professional and business services, leisure and hospitality, and manufacturing—the cumulative number of job openings has lagged well behind the figure for those industries during the first year of the recovery from the 2001 recession. (Only the mining and logging category, which accounted for just 0.5% of employment in 2007, has had more job openings during the first year of this recovery than during the first year of the 2001 recovery.)

Why has the pick-up in jobs following the Great Recession been worse than usual? The simple answer is that the recession was worse than usual. The sharp and extreme decline of output and employment in the Great Recession has severely dampened demand—that is, people have not had money to buy things. With the resulting lack of sales, businesses were not willing to either invest or hire; and this in turn has meant a continuing lack of demand.

If businesses have barely resumed hiring, it has not been for lack of profits. By the middle of 2010, corporate profits (adjusted for inflation) were about 60% above their low point at the end of 2008, well on their way back to the peak level of mid-2006. Also, in early 2010 non-financial firms were sitting on almost $2 trillion in cash. There was no lack of ability to invest and hire, but there was a lack of incentive to invest and hire, that is, a lack of an expectation that demand (sales) would rise. As is well known, small businesses have generally accounted for a disproportionately large share of job growth. Yet, since the onset of the Great Recession, small business owners have consistently identified poor sales as their single most important problem—and thus, presumably, what has prevented them from expanding employment.

LONG-TERM UNEMPLOYMENT RISES EVEN AFTER RECESSION

Record job losses and persistent unemployment have left the U.S. economy out of order and forced those looking for a job to longer and longer without work.

When the Great Recession hit at the end of 2007 jobs disappeared, unemployment rose, and its duration lengthened. By the official end of the recession in midyear 2009 the unemployed who had gone 27 weeks or longer without work, what economists call long-term unemployment, had nearly doubled to 29% of those job seekers.

But as the anemic economic recovery that followed did little to put people back to work, long term unemployment rate continued to climb reaching a peak of 45% of the unemployed in April 2010. In February 2012, more than two and half years into this "97 pound weakling of a recovery," as Time Magazine called it, more than 5.4 million job-seekers had gone more than a half of year without work and the long term unemployment rate still stood at 42.6% of the unemployed.

Long-term unemployment in the current period is more pervasive than any time on record, with data available in 1948. During the typical downturn of the last 60 years less than one fifth of the unemployed went more than 27 weeks without a job.

As long-term unemployment increases so too does the economic suffering inflicted on those without work and their families. At the beginning of 2012, more than 2 million of the unemployed had gone 99 weeks or more without work, exhausting their unemployment benefits. Also, as the Congressional Research Service confirms, when unemployment spells lengthen the prospects for finding employment diminishes. Finally the long-term unemployed are at increasing risk of drop out the labor force (by not actively searching for a job) and joining those without work who go uncounted in this data even though they want a job.

Long-term unemployment hits older workers and black workers especially hard. While the official unemployment rates for older workers are lower than those of younger workers, older workers who lose their jobs find it particularly difficult to find another. In February 2012, more than half (52.4%) of the unemployed 55 to 64 year olds had gone more than 27 weeks without a job. For black workers conditions are considerably worse. Nearly the same share of the black unemployed had been out of work for 27 months or more as for older workers. (In February 2012 the long-term unemployment stood at 46.7% for unemployed black men and 51.8% for unemployed black women.) But the official unemployment rate for blacks was 14.1% in February 2012, while the rate for workers 55 and older was 5.9%.
—*John Miller*

Sources: Bureau of Labor Statistics, "The Employment Situation – February 2012," Table A-2, Table A-12, Table A-36; The 97-lb. Recovery," by Rana Foroohar and Bill Saporito. Time Magazine, April 12, 2012; "The Trend in Long-Term Unemployment and Characteristics of Workers Unemployed for More than 99 Weeks," by Gerald Mayer, Congressional Research Service, December 20, 2010; and, "Long-Term Hardship in the Labor Market," by John Schmitt and Janelle Jones, Center for Economic and Policy Research, March 2012.

The Role of Demand

Regardless of the lack of evidence to support it, the skills-mismatch story has seeped into media coverage of the economy. Take, for example, National Public Radio's recent Morning Edition series titled "Skills gap: holding back the labor market." In one segment, reporter Wendy Kaufman presents anecdotes about employers turning down record numbers of applicants and leaving job openings unfilled. Economist Peter Capelli then comes on and remarks, "You know, a generation ago you'd never expect that somebody could come into a reasonably skilled, sophisticated position in your organization and immediately make a contribution. That's a brand new demand." Now, that comment does not point to today's workers possessing fewer skills or qualifications. Rather, it suggests that employers have raised the bar: they are pickier than in the past.

That makes sense. We've seen that employers are successfully filling positions at about the same rate as in the recent past. What's different this time around is that employers have had up to six unemployed workers competing for every job opening left vacant at the close of the month. This is by far the highest ratio on record with data back to 2000. During the 2001 recession, that ratio rose to just over two unemployed workers for each opening. (In the first years of the "jobless recovery" following the 2001 recession, the ratio continued to rise, but it remained below three to one.) Clearly, these numbers favor the alternative explanation. Unfortunately, Kaufman doesn't even consider it.

That's too bad. Recognizing that a lack of demand for goods and services is to blame for the severe crisis of unemployment puts the focus squarely back on the federal government and on the Fed, which could help to remedy the problem —*if* they had the political will to do so. Millions of unemployed workers, organized and armed with an accurate diagnosis of the problem, could create that political will— unless they are distracted by a wrong-headed diagnosis that tries to blame them for the problem. ❑

Sources: Bureau of Labor Statistics Table A-14, Unemployed persons by industry and class of workers, not seasonally adjusted, historical data (bls.gov); Lawrence Mishel, Heidi Shierholz, and Kathryn Anne Edwards, "Reasons for Skepticism About Structural Unemployment," Economic Policy Institute, Briefing Paper #279, September 22, 2010 (epi.org); Arjun Jayadev and Mike Konczal, "The Stagnating Labor Market," The Roosevelt Institute, September 19, 2010 (rooseveltinstitute. org); Bureau of Labor Statistics, Job Openings and Labor Turnover (JOLTS) Highlights, September 2010 (bls.gov); Michael Reich, "High Unemployment after the Great Recession: Why? What Can We Do?," Policy Brief from the Center on Wage and Employment Dynamics, Institute for Research on Labor and Employment, University of California, Berkeley, June 2010 (irle.berkeley.edu/cwed); Narayana Kocherlakota, President Federal Reserve Bank of Minneapolis, "Inside the FOMC," Marquette, Michigan, August 17, 2010 (minneapolisfed.org); Lawrence Mishel and Katherine Anne Edwards, "Bill Clinton Gets It Wrong," Economic Policy Institute, Economic Snapshot, September 27, 2010 (epi.org); "Remarks of President Barack Obama—Address to Joint Session of Congress," February 24, 2009 (whitehouse.gov); "The Skills Gap: Holding Back the Labor Market," Morning Edition, National Public Radio, November 15, 2010 (npr.org).

Article 7.4

BADGE OF IGNORANCE: THE NOTION THAT REGULATION IS THE CAUSE OF UNEMPLOYMENT

BY DEAN BAKER
October 2011; Al Jazeera English

Politicians pushing right-wing positions in public debate now operate with the assumption that they can get away with saying anything without getting serious scrutiny from the media. That is why right-wing politicians repeatedly blame government regulation for the failure of the economy to generate jobs. Even though there is no truth whatsoever to the claim, right-wing politicians know that the media will treat their nonsense respectfully in news coverage.

If political reporters did their job, they would make an effort to determine the validity of the regulation-killing-jobs story and expose the politicians making the claim as either ignorant or dishonest, just as if a politician were going around claiming that September 11 was an inside job. However, today's reporters are either too lazy or incompetent to do their homework. What follows is a bit of a how-to manual to make reporters' jobs easier.

The first step in assessing the right-wingers' claim about regulation killing jobs is to figure out what it is. The argument is usually that companies have enough demand for labor that they would be hiring now, but because of existing or expected regulations, such as President Obama's health care plan that mostly takes effect in January of 2014, they are declining to hire more workers.

Governor Romney was kind enough to spell this argument out explicitly in the presidential debate on the economy. He told the audience that businesses have to look two or three years ahead when they make hiring decisions, not just a few months.

With this in mind, there are some clear implications of the regulations-cost-jobs story. First, we would expect that firms would be looking to increase hours per workers as an alternative to hiring. If employers can't hire more workers due to regulations, then they would look to get more labor out of each of the workers that they already have.

Second, employers would hire temporary workers as an alternative to hiring permanent employees. Temporary workers can be easily dismissed if regulations make it unprofitable to keep employees on staff.

Third, the companies that are most affected by the regulations should see the largest impact on their hiring. If costly regulations are keeping companies from hiring, then we should see that expect that the companies that are most affected by these regulations will have the sharpest reduction in employment.

Fourth, industries with longer-term employment should have the greatest reduction in employment. It may make sense for a company to not hire today because of a regulation that only kicks in two years from now if they expect the new hires to still be with them in two years. However, if a company has frequent turnover, then hiring workers today will not increase their employment in two years, unless they decide to replace workers as they leave.

Finally, if regulations are preventing firms from hiring, then we would expect them to complain about regulation when asked in employer surveys.

If we look at the data, we find that none of these conditions hold. The length of the average workweek was 34.3 hours in September. This is up from 33.7 hours at the low-point of the downturn in 2009, but it is still down by 0.4 hours from its pre-recession peaks. With average workweeks still shorter than before the downturn, there is no evidence that employers are requiring each worker to put in longer hours as an alternative to hiring new workers.

The same story applies to temp workers. Temp employment is up by 550,000 from the trough of the downturn, but it is still down by almost 400,000 from its pre-recession peak. If employers are hesitant to hire because of regulations, they clearly are not turning to temps as alternative. They hired far more temp workers before the big bad Obama let the regulators run wild.

The third point is that we should see more of an impact on hiring in the firms that are most affected by the regulation. The right's biggest villain here is Obamacare. This would have the greatest impact on hiring at mid-size firms. There is little in the legislation that affects firms of less than 50 and most of the biggest firms already provide care that exceeds what is required under the bill. So, we should see the largest falloff in hiring in firms that exceed the 50-employee limit but don't already provide health care.

In fact it is impossible to find any clear pattern in hiring by firm size. In 2010, hiring by firms that employ 50-100 workers was down by 14.5 percent from pre-recession levels, while hiring by firms that employ 100-250 workers was down by 13.3 percent. By comparison, hiring by the largest firms (over 1,000 workers) was down by only 11.4 percent, but hiring by firms that employ 10-19 workers was down by 15.8 percent.

There is a similar story when we look at industry groups. Manufacturing and health care, where industries workers often hold jobs for long periods of time, are both adding jobs more rapidly than before the downturn. By contrast, restaurants, where turnover is frequent, are adding jobs at just over half of their pre-recession pace.

Finally, employers themselves don't list regulation as major factor when asked in surveys. The National Federation of Independent Businesses, an association of small businesses, has fielded a survey for close to three decades that asks its members what are the biggest obstacles they face. Only around 14 percent list regulation, not much different than in the years before President Obama was elected.

In short, there is no evidence that is consistent with the regulation-impeding-job-growth story. When politicians repeat this line, they are just making things up and reporters should call them on it. ❑

Article 7.5

HOW BLACKS MIGHT FARE IN THE JOBLESS RECOVERY

BY SYLVIA ALLEGRETTO AND STEVEN PITTS
October 2010

There have been seemingly contradictory announcements recently concerning the economy. In September another 95,000 jobs were shed as the official unemployment rate remained at 9.6%. Unemployment has been at 9.5% or higher for well over a year now. About the same time this bad news about employment came out, it was announced that the recession, which began in December 2007, had actually ended in June of 2009—thus we are several months into the second year of recovery.

How could the recession be over, even amidst continued job losses and stubbornly high unemployment? And how might black workers, whose levels of unemployment have (as usual) been much higher than white workers' in this recession, fare in a "jobless recovery"?

The Dating of the Business Cycle

The task of officially declaring the start and end dates of recessions is performed by the Business Cycle Dating Committee of the National Bureau of Economic Research. The Committee is currently comprised of seven economists (an eighth is on leave) from prominent universities. The Committee examines the data trends of several economic indicators, including measures of:

- Overall output
- Overall national income
- Total employment
- Aggregate hours worked

The Committee did not say that the economy had returned to its pre-recession level of activity or that the economy was strong; it just stated that the decline in several economic measures that began in December 2007 had ended and any new decline in economic activity would represent a new recession. That the economy is not officially in recession does not mean that it doesn't feel as if it is for many workers and their families. There is often not a palpable difference between a recessionary economy and a weak recovery—this is especially true with what are called "jobless recoveries."

What Is Meant by a "Jobless Recovery"?

An economy officially in recovery that continues to shed jobs as if in recession, or experiences prolonged tepid job growth, is deemed a "jobless recovery." In a jobless recovery it takes an inordinate amount of time to recoup the jobs lost during the downturn. While the recession officially ended in June 2009, the employment picture remains quite dismal. At the lowest point for jobs, in December 2009, 8.4 million jobs were lost, which represented 6.1% of all jobs. To date job losses are still at 7.7 million, which represents 5.6% of all jobs. Since the onset of recovery, the monthly employment reports have been mixed, but the net employment level has fallen by an additional 439,000.

Figure 1 depicts the dynamics of recessionary job losses and jobless recoveries. Each line represents the trajectory of job growth from the onset of recession until jobs were finally recouped (when the line crosses the horizontal axis—which represents months since the onset of recession). The solid black line represents average job losses for recessions prior to 1990. (On average the pre-1990 recessions were about eleven months long and it took about 21 months to recoup pre-recessionary job level.)

Job losses due to the 1990 recession (the solid gray line) were just about 1.5%—quite shallow comparatively and the recession was officially just eight months long. But employment lingered at the trough for a long time and it took about 31 months to recoup those lost jobs. The downturn in 2001 (dotted black line) was also eight months long and about 2% of jobs were lost—again relatively mild—but it took 46 months to recoup those lost jobs.

It is clear from the figure that the recession that started in December 2007 (dotted gray line) led to a reduction in employment that far exceeded that of the previous recessions. This recession was 18 months long and ended in June 2009. Job losses were catastrophic. At its worst point jobs were down 8.4 million. Job growth turned positive in the spring of 2010—mostly due to the temporary hiring of Census workers. But shortly after Census workers were hired they were let go, and job growth once again turned negative. At this point it is clear that the labor market is in the realm of a jobless recovery—a prolonged period of negative or weak job growth. It will be a very long time before this economy recoups the enormous amount of jobs lost over this recession.

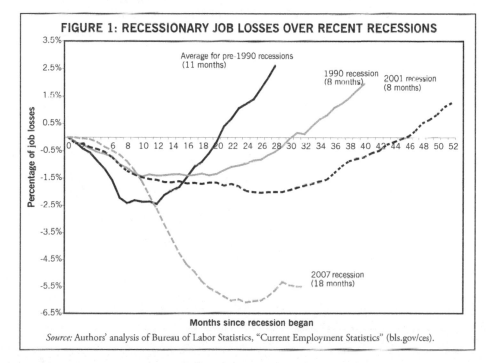

FIGURE 1: RECESSIONARY JOB LOSSES OVER RECENT RECESSIONS

Source: Authors' analysis of Bureau of Labor Statistics, "Current Employment Statistics" (bls.gov/ces).

How Might Blacks Fare?

While it is difficult to predict exactly what might happen to black workers during this jobless recovery, it is instructive to examine what happened to black unemployment during the last jobless recovery, which followed the 2001 recession. Chart 2 provides key information.

The gray bars in the chart mark key dates of the last two recessions and recoveries. In examining the trend in black unemployment since the 2001 recession, there are six key dates:

- The beginning of the recession (March 2001)
- The official end of the recession (November 2001)
- When job creation turned positive (September 2003)
- When the employment levels returned to pre-recession level (January 2005)
- The beginning of recession (December 2007)
- The official end of the recession (June 2009)

As Figure 2 indicates, unemployment rates continued to rise after the official end of the recession in November 2001. Over the jobless recovery—from November 2001 to September 2003—unemployment increased from 9.8% to 11% for blacks and 4.9% to 5.4% for whites. Black unemployment rates did not begin to steadily fall until the total number of jobs had reached the pre-recession level (January

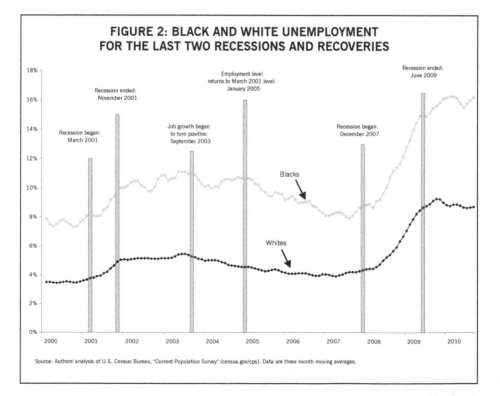

FIGURE 2: BLACK AND WHITE UNEMPLOYMENT FOR THE LAST TWO RECESSIONS AND RECOVERIES

Source: Authors' analysis of U.S. Census Bureau, "Current Population Survey" (census.gov/cps). Data are three month moving averages.

2005). The unemployment rates for whites started to fall just prior to September 2003—near the end of the jobless recovery.

Starting with the onset of the 2007 recession, again the black unemployment rate increased at a faster rate than did that of whites. Since the onset of recovery—in June 2009—the unemployment rate of blacks has increased by 1.4 percentage points, from 14.8% to 16.2%. The rate for whites at the start of recovery was 8.7%, and after an initial increase it is back to that same rate today.

If the 2001 pattern holds, it may well be that the current black unemployment rates will not begin to significantly abate until the employment level returns to its pre-recessionary level of December 2007. This will almost certainly take several years as the shortfall in jobs is currently at 7.7 million. In order to return the national unemployment rate to its December 2007 rate, the economy would need to create 290,000 jobs per month for five years; so far this year job creation has averaged 68,000 per month, even as the last four months have averaged -98,000.

In other words, for many black workers and their families, the recovery will continue to feel like a deep recession for many years to come. ❑

Resources: Bureau of Labor Statistics, "Current Employment Statistics" (bls.gov/ces); National Bureau of Economic Research, "The NBER's Business Cycle Dating Committee" (nber.org/cycles/recessions.html and nber.org/cycles/sept2010.html).

Article 7.6

WOMEN BREADWINNERS, MEN UNEMPLOYED

BY HEATHER BOUSHEY
July 2009; updated, March 2012

The employment situation over the past 19 months has dramatically changed for millions of American families. Since the Great Recession began in December 2007, there has been a sharp rise in the number of married couples where a woman is left to bring home the bacon because her husband is unemployed. What is striking is not only how many more families are experiencing unemployment among husbands, but also how this loss of the traditional breadwinner has occurred across a variety of demographic groups.

The reason that more married couples now boast women as the primary breadwinners is because men have experienced greater job losses than women over the course of this recession, losing three out of every four jobs lost. This puts a real strain on family budgets since women typically earn only 78 cents for every dollar men earn. In the typical married-couple family where both spouses work, the wife brings home just over a third—35.6%—of the family's income.

What's equally worrisome is that most families receive health insurance through the employers of their husbands. So when husbands lose their jobs, families are left struggling to find ways to pay for health insurance at the same time they are living on just a third of their prior income. These new health insurance costs can be crushing if families have to turn to the individual insurance market, where coverage is limited and expensive, or pay for continued coverage through their husbands' old insurance policies, which is possible because of federal law but is also expensive— though the American Recovery and Reinvestment Act subsidized that cost for many workers. Still, many families with an unemployed worker simply have to go without health insurance.

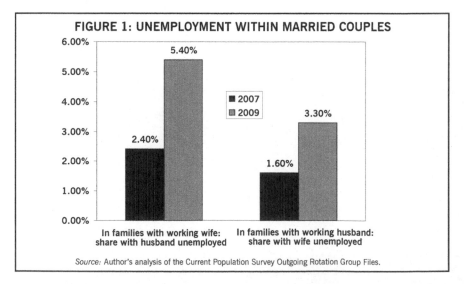

FIGURE 1: UNEMPLOYMENT WITHIN MARRIED COUPLES

- 2007
- 2009

In families with working wife: share with husband unemployed — 2.40%, 5.40%

In families with working husband: share with wife unemployed — 1.60%, 3.30%

Source: Author's analysis of the Current Population Survey Outgoing Rotation Group Files.

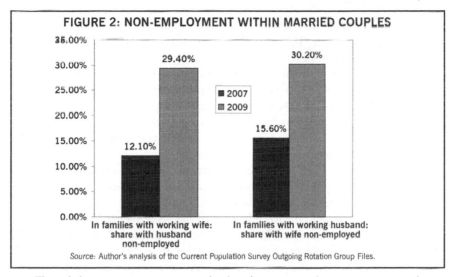

FIGURE 2: NON-EMPLOYMENT WITHIN MARRIED COUPLES

Source: Author's analysis of the Current Population Survey Outgoing Rotation Group Files.

The job losses mounting among husbands are acute this year. Figure 1 shows that the share of families where women hold down a job while men are unemployed jumped sharply in 2009 compared to 2007 at the peak of the last economic cycle. In the first five months of 2009, 5.4% of working wives had an unemployed husband at home—that is, a husband who was actively searching for work, but could not find a job—compared to an average of 2.4% over the first five months of 2007. This means that there are about 2 million working wives today with an unemployed husband.

In contrast, working husbands continue to be less likely to have an unemployed wife. In the first five months of 2009, an average of only 3.3% of husbands had an unemployed wife at home, up from 1.6%. Importantly, the difference in the shares of unemployed husbands and wives is not due to women telling the surveyor that they are "out of the labor force" rather than report they are out of a job, willing to work, and actively seeking employment. Figure 2 examines non-working spouses and shows not only a sharp rise in the share of working wives who have a non-working husband but also the share of both husbands and wives who are either unavailable to work or are not looking for a job.

So far this year, 15.6% of working wives have a husband who is not working, up a stunning 3.5 percentage points from early 2007, when 12.1% of working wives had a husband who did not work. But working husbands did not see a similarly large increase in their chances of having a non-working wife. In 2007, 29.4% of husbands had a non-working wife, up only 0.8 percentage points to 30.2% in 2009.

Families with children have been hit especially hard hit by unemployment. Among working wives in families with a small child—under age six—at home, 5.9% have an unemployed husband. This is higher than among families with a working wife but with no child under age six at home, where 5.3% have an unemployed husband.

Among families with a working wife and a child under age 18, the share with an unemployed husband is 5.7%, compared to 5.0% among those with no children. This means that there are 1 million working wives with children at home, but an unemployed husband. The numbers are smaller for families with a working husband and an unemployed wife. The share with a child under age 18 is 3.2%—compared to 3.4% among those with no children.

The share of workers with an unemployed spouse is lower than the overall unemployment rate of 9.5%. Typically, married workers have lower unemployment rates compared to single workers and they stay unemployed for shorter periods of time. There are many reasons why this is the case, but one is that married workers may have more of an incentive to find work as quickly as possible—if possible—because there are more people relying on their earnings, compared to single workers—at least single workers without children. Of course, single mothers, who typically have higher unemployment than other workers, do have children relying on their earnings and are under similar pressures to find employment.

Especially striking in the recently released data is the sharp increase in breadwinner wives and unemployed husbands across demographic groups. The table below shows, for example, that among young (ages 18 to 24) families with a working wife, one in ten married women (9.9%) has an unemployed husband, up 5.5

UNEMPLOYMENT AMONG FAMILIES WITH A WORKING SPOUSE

	In families with working wife: Share with husband unemployed			In families with working husband: Share with wife unemployed		
	January - May 2007	January - May 2009	Percentage point change	January - May 2007	January - May 2009	Percentage point change
All families	2.4	5.4	3	1.6	3.3	1.7
Ages 18 to 24	4.4	9.9	5.5	4.8	6	1.2
Ages 25 to 54	2.4	5.5	3.1	1.6	3.3	1.7
Ages 55 to 64	1.9	4.1	2.2	1.4	3	1.6
Less than highschool	4.3	8.3	4	2.7	5.8	3.1
High school	2.7	6.8	4.1	2	3.9	1.9
Some college	2.6	5.5	2.9	1.4	2.8	1.4
College	1.7	3.9	2.2	1.2	2.4	1.2
White, non-Hispanic	2.1	4.7	2.6	1.4	2.8	1.4
Black, non-Hispanic	4.1	7.8	3.7	2.9	3.9	1
Hispanic, any race	3.4	7.7	4.3	2.2	5.1	2.9
Other race, non-Hispanic	2.5	6.3	3.8	1.9	3.2	1.3
No children under age 18	2.3	5	2.7	1.6	3.4	1.8
Children under age 18	2.4	5.7	3.3	1.7	3.2	1.5
No children under age six	2.3	5.3	3	1.6	3.4	1.8
Children under age six	2.5	5.9	3.4	1.7	3	1.3

Source: Author's analysis of the Current Population Survey Outgoing Rotation Group Files.

percentage points from early 2007. Among working women without a high school degree, slightly less than one in ten (8.3%) have an unemployed husband, up four percentage points since 2007. This share of women with unemployed husbands has increased 2.2 percentage points among wives with a college degree.

There has also been a sharp rise in the share of families where both the husband and wife are unemployed. Between the first five months of 2007 and of 2009, the share of married-couple families with both spouses unemployed rose to 0.5% from 0.1%, meaning that one in 500 families is struggling with dual unemployment. The share of families with a child under age 18 with both parents unemployed is 0.6%, meaning that one in 165 families with children have both parents looking for work.

Among some demographic groups dual unemployment rises to one in 100: young couples (with a spouse between 18 and 24), less-educated couples (where either spouse has no more than a high-school degree), and African-American families (0.9% of African-American wives in the labor force are unemployed and have an unemployed husband, while 0.8% of African-American husbands in the labor force are unemployed with an unemployed wife).

The Great Recession that began in December 2007 has now lasted 19 months. The unemployment picture remains tough: Unemployment rose to 9.5% in June and 29.0% of unemployed workers have been out of work for at least six months— a shocking fact given that 3.4 million of the 6.5 million people who have lost their jobs since the recession began were laid off only within the past six months. There are now more than five unemployed workers available for every job opening and the employment prospects for men seem especially challenging given the continued lay-offs in manufacturing and construction. Families will continue to rely on the earnings of a working woman for a long time to come.

As families need the earnings of wives more than ever, policymakers should focus their attention on ensuring that women—including mothers—have access to good jobs with benefits that will support their families. There could not be a more important moment to pass legislation ensuring pay equity for all workers. Nor could there be a more important time to ensure that caregivers are not discriminated against by employers.

The Paycheck Fairness Act, which passed the House in January, would go a long way toward eradicating pay inequalities, but it is languishing in the Senate. The Equal Employment Opportunity Commission issued new guidelines in 2007 to help employers avoid caregiver discrimination, but more could be done to use develop this guidance to ensure that every caregiver has the same access to good jobs as other workers. These and other policy solutions to the crisis facing women breadwinners need to be acted upon swiftly. ❑

Source: Bureau of Labor Statistics, "Women in the Labor Force: A Databook," (Washington, DC: U.S. Department of Labor, 2008), Table 24.

The data analysis for this report was conducted by Jeff Chapman. The analysis compares the experiences of married couples from the first five months of 2007 to the first five months of 2009. Note that data are only for married heterosexual couples and do not include cohabiting heterosexual couples or lesbian or gay couples, married or otherwise.

Update, March 2012

The Great Recession had just come to an end when Heather Boushey published her article "Women Breadwinners, Men Unemployed. " Nearly three years into the anemic recovery that followed, fewer men are unemployed. The "man-covery," as it has been called, has done more to put men to work than to put women to work, bringing the adult (20 and older) men's unemployment rate down to that of adult women. Still, as of February 2012, both rates remain quite elevated at 7.7%. The "man-covery" was the sequel to the "man-cession," the moniker the press gave the Great Recession because twice as many men as women lost their jobs. But as the economy recovered fitfully, women continued to lose jobs well into 2011, largely because the public sector, especially state and local government, which disproportionately employs women, cut jobs instead of adding them.

Still, there is little reason to believe that women breadwinners are any less important for families. According to the latest data, wives' earning accounted for 37% of family earnings in 2009, and nearly 4 out 10 (38%) of working wives earned more than their husbands.   —*John Miller*

Sources: Heather Boushey, "The 'Man-covery': Women Gaining Jobs Recovery at a Slower Pace than Men," Center for American Progress, March 9, 2012; "Women in the Labor Force: A Data Book" (2011 Edition), Bureau of Labor Statistics, Tables 24 and 25.

Article 7.7

OUR TRIPLE JOBS PROBLEM

BY ALEJANDRO REUSS
September/October 2013

If you hear somebody talking about the U.S. "jobs problem," ask them which one they mean. Let's talk about three: First, even as unemployment has inched down, the economy has created barely enough jobs to match population growth. Second, this enormous labor-market "slack" has stifled workers' bargaining power and kept wages low. Third, even with a "tighter" labor market, workers would still be in a weak bargaining position due to the policies of the last thirty-some years, which have undermined unions, the welfare state, and labor-market regulation.

First, the Great Recession has left the United States with an enormous jobs hole. The silver lining of declining unemployment—down from 10% to about 7.5% over the last few years—surrounds a gigantic dark cloud: The employment-to-population ratio fell dramatically during the recession and has hardly budged since. That's because labor-force participation, the percentage of working-age individuals who are employed or looking for work, has plummeted. A stimulus too small to make up for the collapse in private spending and a premature turn toward deficit reduction have helped keep us in this jobs hole.

Next, high unemployment makes it hard for workers to bargain higher wages or better working conditions. Recoveries and booms bring lower unemployment and "tighter" labor markets, which increase workers' bargaining power and should make it easier for them to demand (and win) improvements in pay and conditions. This effect typically kicks in, however, only when the unemployment rate gets quite low—below 5%—and the lethargic employment growth during the last four years means we're a long way from there. With economic growth resuming but wages stagnant, corporate profits now account for a near-record percentage of total income. This helps explain why corporations have been content with policies allowing the crisis to drag on through years of lethargic "recovery."

Finally, the lack of high-quality jobs is no mere cyclical problem. It has been a central problem for three decades. Mainstream economists tend to emphasize the ostensibly inexorable forces of globalization and technological change, insinuating that the lack of good jobs is an unavoidable fact of life.

As economist Dean Baker of the Center for Economic and Policy Research (CEPR) notes, however, there's not much evidence that technological change is faster now than in earlier eras, nor particularly damaging to ordinary workers (as opposed to technical, professional, or managerial employees). Meanwhile, the current form of economic globalization is not some inevitable course of nature, but a result of the distribution of political power in our society. Elites designed laws and treaties to make capital more mobile across international borders—that is, to make it easier for companies to move (or threaten to move) operations to places where wages are lower and regulations weaker.

The current form of globalization, in turn, is only one of several changes undermining workers' bargaining power—along with government and employer attacks on labor unions, the weakening of the welfare state, and the rollback of labor regulations. These factors are missing from the mantra that workers should just resign themselves to the new reality, that the "good jobs" are gone and never coming back. But they're also missing from some well-meaning suggestions for getting those jobs back—whether a more favorable exchange rate, increased education and skills, or industrial policies to create new "blue collar" or "green collar" employment.

Whether a job is good or bad, for the most part, is not an inherent fact of industry or occupation. Manufacturing jobs became "good jobs"—in particular times and places—due to unionization, full-employment policies, labor-market regulations, etc. So-called good jobs in transportation and construction have not "gone" anywhere, but job quality in those sectors has declined due to deunionization, deregulation, and employers' increasing use of contingent labor.

Meanwhile, so-called "bad jobs" in hospitality, maintenance, and other service occupations are not uniformly bad. As Paul Osterman and Beth Shulman note in *Good Jobs America* (2011), food-service workers in Las Vegas, where unions are relatively strong, make about $2 more per hour than in largely non-union Orlando. Hotel room cleaners in Vegas, meanwhile, make about $4 more per hour than in Orlando.

There is nothing that makes food service an intrinsically bad job, any more than something makes factory work or trucking intrinsically good.

The fault, in other words, lies not in our jobs, but in our politics. ❑

Sources: Dean Baker, "Inequality: The Silly Tales Economists Like to Tell," Al Jazeera English, Oct. 30, 2012; Dean Baker, "Technology and Inequality: The Happy Myth," *The Guardian* Unlimited, July 16, 2012; Paul Osterman and Beth Shulman, *Good Jobs America: Making Work Better for Everyone* (Russell Sage Foundation, 2011).

Article 7.8

THE CHAINED CPI IS BAD FOR SENIORS AND FOR ACCURACY

BY JOHN MILLER
May/June 2013

> The word "thuggish" comes to mind. "I'm not a number," says the older man in a television ad funded by the seniors' lobby AARP. ... "But I am a voter. So Washington, before you even think about cutting my Medicare and Social Security benefits, here's a number you should remember: 50 million."
>
> This unyielding position, undergirded by a multimillion-dollar ad campaign, is as wrongheaded as the equivalent line-drawing of Grover Norquist and the no-new-taxes crowd. ...
>
> [T]he brutal fact is that Social Security cannot pay all promised benefits, and a debt discussion is a useful place to make reasonable tradeoffs.
>
> —*Washington Post*, "Congress should reject AARP's self-centered appeals on Social Security," Nov. 4, 2011.

That AARP television ad sure raised the hackles of the *Washington Post* editors back in 2011. The editors called AARP's threat—to vote out any politician who supported a reduction in the cost-of-living adjustment (COLA) for Social Security benefits—"thuggish," "self-centered," in denial about the crisis of Social Security, and as "wrongheaded" as conservative power-broker Grover Norquist. That last one had to hurt.

Back then, the proposal to reduce the Social Security COLA by switching to the "chained" Consumer Price Index (CPI) didn't come to pass. But now it's back, this time as part of the 2014 Obama budget proposal and going by its technical economic name—the "superlative CPI." Make no mistake, though. It's the same idea now as then, and would reduce the COLAs for Social Security and veterans' benefits, as well as the inflation adjustment for income-tax brackets.

What's all the fuss about? The Social Security Administration currently uses the CPI-W, a measure of the price of a basket of goods and services typically purchased by urban wage-earners and clerical workers, to calculate COLAs for Social Security recipients. The "chained CPI-U," as it is officially designated by the Bureau of Labor Statistics (BLS), grows at a slower rate than the CPI-W. Therefore, calculating the COLAs using the chained CPI will reduce future Social Security benefits by more and more each year. If that sounds to you like a roundabout way to hold down spending on Social Security, you've got it right.

The proposal is meant to establish Obama's deficit-reduction bona fides and to lure Republicans and conservative Democrats into a "grand bargain" boosting tax revenues and cutting entitlements spending. For good measure, the Obama administration is selling the superlative CPI as just that—"a more accurate measure of the average change in the cost of living than the standard CPI." And the Washington Post is once again on board, endorsing the Obama proposal for "Social Security spending restraint" as part of the "worthy end" of entitlement reform.

Using the chained CPI to reduce future Social Security spending, however, is far from the even-handed proposal the *Post* editors suggest. In truth, it is neither fair nor accurate. Worse yet, it would fall most heavily on some of the most vulnerable in our society—older women, veterans, and the disabled.

The CPI in Chains

To understand why, we need to look at just how the COLA for Social Security benefits is calculated. In 2013, the COLA was 1.7%, equal to the increase in the CPI-W from the third quarter of 2011 to the third quarter of 2012. For the typical Social Security retiree, this translated into about $250, boosting the average retirement benefit to just over $15,000 a year in 2013.

The CPI-W is what economists call a "fixed-weight" index. It measures the price of a fixed "basket" of 211 different items. (The basket of goods is updated every two years to keep up with changes in consumers' buying patterns.)

According to the persistent complaints of conservative politicians and economists, however, that fixed basket results in the CPI-W overstating the rate of inflation. They argue that consumers typically purchase less of those goods whose prices are rising compared to those of other goods. Take the example provided by BLS: If the price of pork rises while the price of beef falls, consumers are likely to purchase less pork and more beef.

That's the supposed problem the chained CPI is intended to correct. The "U" in "CPI-U," by the way, stands for all urban consumers, a broader group than urban workers. The basket used for the chained CPI, therefore, differs from that for the CPI-W. More importantly, however, the chained CPI uses a flexible basket of goods that captures how consumers adjust their purchases in reaction to rising prices. The basket used for the final chained CPI is updated monthly. In the example of rising pork prices and declining beef prices, then, declining pork consumption means that pork prices will have less weight in the calculation of the index. By the same token, rising beef consumption means that beef will have greater weight inthe index.

The long and the short of it is that the chained CPI reports a lower rate of inflation than the fixed-basket CPI-W. The Social Security Administration estimates that using the chained CPI instead of the CPI-W would reduce annual Social Security COLAs by about 0.3 percentage points per year. If the chained CPI had been used to calculate the Social Security COLA, the average retiree would have gotten $45 less in benefits this year.

Perhaps it is these small figures that have the *Post* editors convinced that AARP is "wrongheaded" about the switch. The loss of benefits, however, gets larger each year, and the cumulative effect is substantial. The average 65-year-old is now expected to live about 19 additional years. According to AARP projections, a chained-CPI

COLA would cost the average Social Security retiree more than $5,000 over the first 15 years of retirement and more than $9,000 over the first 20.

Nor is the chained CPI an accurate measure of the cost of living for most seniors. The typical senior spends a larger share of her income on medical care and housing than other consumers. The cost of both items has risen more quickly than other costs and it is hard to substitute for either item with other purchases. In addition, because seniors are less mobile than other consumers, it is harder for them to change their consumption patterns. This makes the chained CPI, whether or not it is valid for other individuals, inappropriate for calculating COLAs affecting seniors' retirement incomes.

Double and Triple Whammies

The reduction of the COLA would hit hardest on some of the most vulnerable in our society.

Older women would suffer, as the National Women's Law Center puts it, a "triple-whammy." First, the effects of the change would increase over time, and women tend to live longer than men. (A 65-year-old woman is more than 1.5 times as likely to live into her 90s as a 65-year-old man.) By age 90, a typical single woman who retired at age 65 would have lost $15,000 of benefits from the switch to a chained-CPI COLA.

Second, women rely more heavily on their Social Security benefits than men do. Among beneficiaries 80 or older, Social Security accounts for two-thirds of women's income, compared to three-fifths of men's. So any reduction in benefits will cost women a larger share of their total income than it will men.

Third, older women are more economically vulnerable than older men. Among women receiving Social Security benefits, almost 10% remain in poverty, nearly twice the rate as for men. Shifting to the chained CPI would heighten the risk of poverty for these women.

Veterans would also be hit by the switch to the chained CPI. Because veterans with twenty years of service are eligible for their pensions as early as age 50, the cumulative effect of a reduced COLA would be particularly large. Disabled veterans would face a double whammy. With a chained-CPI COLA, they would collect lower Social Security benefits and lower veterans' benefits.

The story is similar for those receiving disability benefits. The disabled typically start receiving Social Security benefits before retirement age, so their cumulative loss of future income will be much greater than retirees'. For instance, someone who began collecting disability benefits at age 30 would collect nearly 10% less in benefits at age 65 under the chained CPI, and the annual loss would get larger each year after that.

The switch to the chained CPI would also lower the inflation adjustment for income-tax brackets. While income taxes would go up across the board, more than three-quarters of the additional taxes would be paid by those with adjusted gross incomes under $200,000. Those with incomes between $30,000 and $40,000 would suffer the largest declines in their after-tax incomes, according to the Tax Policy Center.

Fair and Accurate

If accuracy were the goal of reforming the COLA, it would be far better to adopt the BLS's new CPI-E (for "elderly"). This fixed-weight experimental index is derived specifically from seniors' spending patterns, placing higher weights on housing and medical care than other indices, including the CPI-W. The BLS reports that between December 1982 and December 2011, the CPI-E added 0.2 percentage points to the annual inflation rate, compared to the CPI-W. (The difference between the two rates has shrunk recently as the rise in health-care costs has slowed.) Using the CPI-E would make it clear that the honest way to lower the COLA for seniors would be to rein in health costs and therefore slow the growth in their actual cost of living.

Finally, reducing benefits is neither right nor necessary to avoid the projected shortfall in Social Security payments starting in 2033. Currently, wage income above $113,700 is not subject to the payroll tax. Lifting this cap would eliminate the entire projected shortfall in one easy step. And unlike a reduction in the COLA, which would hurt the most vulnerable, lifting the cap would put the burden on some of those who benefited most from the lopsided economic growth of the last three decades. ❏

Sources: "Obama's 2014 budget is an offer to negotiate," *Washington Post*, April 10, 2013; Joan Entmacher and Katherine Gallagher Robbins, "Cutting the Social Security COLA by Changing the Way Inflation Is Calculated Would Especially Hurt Women," National Women's Law Center, June 2011 (nwlc.org); Tax Policy Center, "Distributional Effects of Using Chained CPI" (taxpolicycenter.org); Clark Burdick and Lynn Fisher, "Social Security Cost-of-Living Adjustments and the Consumer Price Index," *Social Security Bulletin*, Vol. 67, No. 3, 2007 (socialsecurity.gov); Alison Shelton, "Inflation Indexation in Major Federal Benefit Programs: Impact of the Chained CPI," AARP Public Policy Institute, March 2013.\

Chapter 8

INTERNATIONAL TRADE AND FINANCE

INTRODUCTION

When it comes to the global economy, most textbooks line up behind the "Washington Consensus"—a package of free-trade and financial-liberalization policies that the U.S. Treasury Department, the International Monetary Fund (IMF), and the World Bank have spun into the prevailing prescriptions for the world's developing economies. Mainstream textbook discussions of exchange rates, international trade, and economic-development policies almost always promote a market-dictated integration into the world economy. Outside the classroom, however, popular discontent with the Washington Consensus has spawned a worldwide movement calling into question the myth of self-regulating markets on which these policies rest.

While the doctrines of free trade and international financial deregulation are seldom questioned in mainstream economics textbooks, both are scrutinized here. Economist Arthur MacEwan shows how industrialized economies developed by protecting their own manufacturing sectors—never preaching the "gospel of free trade" until they were highly developed. Today, he argues, the United States government prescribes free trade not because it's the best way for others to develop, but because it gives U.S. corporations free access to the world's markets and resources, which in turn strengthens the power of businesses against workers (Article 8.1).

Ramaa Vasudevan takes a critical look at the doctrine of comparative advantage, the backbone of free-trade theory, and shows that it comes up short as a guide for economic development (Article 8.2).

The relationship between two economic giants, the United States and China, powerfully shapes the global economy. Exports are the engine of China's recent rapid growth, and the United States is China's main customer. The Chinese government has pursued a policy of actively pushing down the value of its currency, the yuan, to keep its exports cheaper. By examining why the United States, which has lost manufacturing jobs, does not protest more strenuously against this policy, Arthur MacEwan exposes the mutual dependence of the Chinese and U.S. economies (Article 8.3).

U.S. labor markets have been haunted by offshore outsourcing, which began with manufacturing and has now spread to back-office work and a wide swath of service-sector jobs. Economist John Miller notes that the alarming estimates of

235

the scope of offshore outsourcing have given even some inveterate free-traders second thoughts (Article 8.4).

Miller also replies to *Forbes* columnist Tim Worstall's contention that Bangladesh cannot afford the kind of worker-safety practices that we demand here in the United States—an argument Worstall made as the Rana Plaza disaster focused global attention on the sweatshops issue. Miller calculates just how economically feasible it is to replace sweatshop deathtraps with far safer factories and then looks at the political forces that could bring about the change (Article 8.5).

Kevin Gallagher looks at China's expanding role in international economic development through its development banks (Article 8.6). Chinese development banks could make significant improvements over the social and environmental records of the dominant international lending agencies—the International Monetary Fund (IMF) and World Bank—as well as over their own past conduct. It will be a great win for the world if they do (and a lost opportunity if they do not).

The next three articles look at international trade-and-investment agreements. Twenty years after the passage of the North American Free Trade Agreement (NAFTA), Dean Baker looks at its consequences for wage growth in the United States (Article 8.7) Timothy Wise, meanwhile, looks at the consequences of NAFTA for Mexico through the case study of the country's growing beer exports (Article 8.8). Roger Bybee looks at what the next big trade deal in the works, the Trans-Pacific Partnership, holds in store for us if passed (Article 8.9). Still greater inequality, he argues.

Lastly, Philip Arestis and Malcolm Sawyer look at the "fiscal compact" constraining the range of policy responses eurozone governments can use to combat recessions (Article 8.10). The compact's balanced-budget clause forces governments to undertake contractionary policy exactly when it is most devastating.

Discussion Questions

1. (Article 8.1) MacEwan claims that the "infant industry" argument for trade protection is much more widely applicable than standard theory suggests. To what countries and industries might it apply in today's world economy? Explain your answer.

2. (Article 8.1) Free trade, MacEwan argues, gives business greater power relative to labor. Why is this so? Is this a good reason to oppose free trade?

3. (Article 8.2) What is the theory of comparative advantage? Why, according to Vasudevan, is it not a good guide to successful economic development?

4. (Article 8.3) How does China's government keep down the prices of its exports? What are the reasons the U.S. government does not protest more strenuously against this policy?

5. (Article 8.4) What policies would best address the negative impacts of offshore outsourcing?

6. (Article 8.5) What is the basis of journalist Tim Worstall's claim that Bangladesh cannot afford to improve working conditions in sweatshops? Why does Miller find Worstall's claim unconvincing? Who do you think is right? Why?

7. (Article 8.6) What roles do development banks play in developing nations? Why does Gallagher believe better social and environmental safeguards would be in the development banks' own interest?

8. (Article 8.7) Baker reports that NAFTA has contributed to wage suppression and to lower prices on many goods. What is the net effect on distribution within the United States? Could a trade agreement result in different distributional outcomes?

9. (Article 8.8) Wise's look at the agricultural sector shows that, since NAFTA took effect, agricultural production has fallen in Mexico and the country has become more reliant on imports from the United States. Why is this the case?

10. (Article 8.9) What distributional consequences does Bybee predict will result the Trans-Pacific Partnership, if it passes? Why does he draw the conclusions he does?

11. (Article 8.10) Arestis and Sawyer provide two possible reasons for promoting a fiscal compact. One of these reasons—the most commonly voiced rationale—they consider to be misguided. The other they consider to be purposeful and harmful for the majority of the population. What are the two reasons? What empirical evidence do they use in arguing that the more common rationale is flawed?

Article 8.1

THE GOSPEL OF FREE TRADE: THE NEW EVANGELISTS

BY ARTHUR MacEWAN
November 1991; updated July 2009

Free trade! With the zeal of Christian missionaries, for decades the U.S. government has been preaching, advocating, pushing, and coercing around the globe for "free trade."

As the economic crisis emerged in 2007 and 2008 and rapidly became a global crisis, it was apparent that something was very wrong with the way the world economy was organized. Not surprisingly, as unemployment rose sharply in the United States, there were calls for protecting jobs by limiting imports and for the government to "buy American" in its economic stimulus program. Similarly, in many other countries, as unemployment jumped upwards, pressure emerged for protection— and some actual steps were taken. Yet, free trade missionaries did not retreat; they continued to preach the same gospel.

The free-traders were probably correct in claiming that protectionist policies would do more harm than good as a means to stem the rising unemployment generated by the economic crisis. Significant acts of protectionism in one country would lead to retaliation—or at least copying—by other countries, reducing world trade. The resulting loss of jobs from reduced trade would most likely outweigh any gains from protection.

Yet the argument over international economic policies should not be confined simply to what should be done in a crisis. Nor should it simply deal with trade in goods and services. The free-traders have advocated their program as one for long-run economic growth and development, yet the evidence suggests that free trade is not a good economic development strategy. Furthermore, the free-traders preach the virtue of unrestricted global movement of finance as well as of goods and services. As it turns out, the free flow of finance has been a major factor in bringing about and spreading the economic crisis that began to appear in 2007—as well as earlier crises.

The Push

While the U.S. push for free trade goes back several decades, it has become more intense in recent years. In the 1990s, the U.S. government signed on to the North American Free Trade Agreement (NAFTA) and in 2005 established the Central American Free Trade Agreement (CAFTA). Both Republican and Democratic presidents, however, have pushed hard for a *global* free trade agenda. After the demise of the Soviet Union, U.S. advisers prescribed unfettered capitalism for Eastern and Central Europe, and ridiculed as unworkable any move toward a "third way." In low-income countries from Mexico to Malaysia, the prescription has been the same: open markets, deregulate business, don't restrict international investment, and let the free market flourish.

In the push for worldwide free trade, the World Trade Organization (WTO) has been the principal vehicle of change, establishing rules for commerce that assure markets are open and resources are available to those who can pay. And the International Monetary Fund (IMF) and World Bank, which provide loans to many governments, use their financial power to pressure countries around the world to accept the gospel and open their markets. In each of these international organizations, the United States—generally through the U.S. Treasury—plays a dominant role.

Of course, as with any gospel, the preachers often ignore their own sermons. While telling other countries to open their markets, the U.S. government continued, for instance, to limit imports of steel, cotton, sugar, textiles, and many other goods. But publicly at least, free-trade boosters insist that the path to true salvation—or economic expansion, which, in this day and age, seems to be the same thing—lies in opening our market to foreign goods. Get rid of trade barriers at home and abroad, allow business to go where it wants and do what it wants. We will all get rich.

Yet the history of the United States and other rich countries does not fit well with the free-trade gospel. Virtually all advanced capitalist countries found economic success through heavy government regulation of their international commerce, not in free trade. Likewise, a large role for government intervention has characterized those cases of rapid and sustained economic growth in recent decades—for example, Japan after World War II, South Korea in the 1970s through the 1990s, and China most recently.

Free trade does, however, have its uses. Highly developed nations can use free trade to extend their power and control of the world's wealth, and business can use it as a weapon against labor. Most important, free trade can limit efforts to redistribute income more equally, undermine social programs, and keep people from democratically controlling their economic lives.

A Day in the Park

At the beginning of the 19th century, Lowell, Massachusetts, became the premier site of the U.S. textile industry. Today, thanks to the Lowell National Historical Park, you can tour the huge mills, ride through the canals that redirected the Merrimack River's power to those mills, and learn the story of the textile workers, from the Yankee "mill girls" of the 1820s through the various waves of immigrant laborers who poured into the city over the next century.

During a day in the park, visitors get a graphic picture of the importance of 19th-century industry to the economic growth and prosperity of the United States. Lowell and the other mill towns of the era were centers of growth. They not only created a demand for Southern cotton, they also created a demand for new machinery, maintenance of old machinery, parts, dyes, *skills*, construction materials, construction machinery, *more skills*, equipment to move the raw materials and products, parts maintenance for that equipment, *and still more skills*. The mill towns also created markets—concentrated groups of wage earners who needed to buy products to sustain themselves. As centers of economic activity, Lowell and similar mill towns contributed to U.S. economic growth far beyond the value of the textiles they produced.

The U.S. textile industry emerged decades after the industrial revolution had spawned Britain's powerful textile industry. Nonetheless, it survived and prospered. British linens inundated markets throughout the world in the early 19th century, as the British navy nurtured free trade and kept ports open for commerce. In the United States, however, hostilities leading up to the War of 1812 and then a substantial tariff made British textiles relatively expensive. These limitations on trade allowed the Lowell mills to prosper, acting as a catalyst for other industries and helping to create the skilled work force at the center of U.S. economic expansion.

Beyond textiles, however, tariffs did not play a great role in the United States during the early 19th century. Southern planters had considerable power, and while they were willing to make some compromises, they opposed protecting manufacturing in general because that protection forced up the prices of the goods they purchased with their cotton revenues. The Civil War wiped out the planters' power to oppose protectionism, and from the 1860s through World War I, U.S. industry prospered behind considerable tariff barriers.

Different Countries, Similar Experiences

The story of the importance of protectionism in bringing economic growth has been repeated, with local variations, in other advanced capitalist countries. During the late 19th century, Germany entered the major league of international economic powers with substantial protection and government support for its industries. Likewise, in 19th-century France and Italy, national consolidation behind protectionist barriers was a key to economic development.

Britain—which entered the industrial era first—is often touted as the prime example of successful development without tariff protection. Yet, Britain embraced free trade only after its industrial base was well established; as in the U.S., the early and important textile industry was erected on a foundation of protectionism. In addition, Britain built its industry through the British navy and the expansion of empire, hardly prime ingredients in any recipe for free trade.

Japan provides an especially important case of successful government protection and support for industrial development. In the post-World War II era, when the Japanese established the foundations for their economic "miracle," the government rejected free trade and extensive foreign investment and instead promoted its national firms.

In the 1950s, for example, the government protected the country's fledgling auto firms from foreign competition. At first, quotas limited imports to $500,000 (in current dollars) each year; in the 1960s, prohibitively high tariffs replaced the quotas. Furthermore, the Japanese allowed foreign investment only insofar as it contributed to developing domestic industry. The government encouraged Japanese companies to import foreign technology, but required them to produce 90% of parts domestically within five years.

The Japanese also protected their computer industry. In the early 1970s, as the industry was developing, companies and individuals could only purchase a foreign machine if a suitable Japanese model was not available. IBM was allowed to produce within the country, but only when it licensed basic patents to Japanese firms. And IBM computers produced in Japan were treated as foreign-made machines.

In the 20th century, no other country matched Japan's economic success, as it moved in a few decades from a relative low-income country, through the devastation of war, to emerge as one of the world's economic leaders. Yet one looks back in vain to find a role for free trade in this success. The Japanese government provided an effective framework, support, and protection for the country's capitalist development.

Likewise, in many countries that have been late-comers to economic development, capitalism has generated high rates of economic growth where government involvement, and not free trade, played the central role. South Korea is a striking case. "Korea is an example of a country that grew very fast and yet violated the canons of conventional economic wisdom," writes Alice Amsden in *Asia's Next Giant: South Korea and Late Industrialization,* widely acclaimed as perhaps the most important analysis of the South Korean economic success. "In Korea, instead of the market mechanism allocating resources and guiding private entrepreneurship, the government made most of the pivotal investment decisions. Instead of firms operating in a competitive market structure, they each operated with an extraordinary degree of market control, protected from foreign competition."

Free trade, however, has had its impact in South Korea. In the 1990s, South Korea and other East Asian governments came under pressure from the U.S. government and the IMF to open their markets, including their financial markets. When they did so, the results were a veritable disaster. The East Asian financial crisis that began in 1997 was a major setback for the whole region, a major disruption of economic growth. After extremely rapid economic growth for three decades, with output expanding at 7% to 10% a year, South Korea's economy plummeted by 6.3% between 1997 and 1998.

Mexico and Its NAFTA Experience

While free trade in goods and services has its problems, which can be very serious, it is the free movement of capital, the opening of financial markets that has sharp, sudden impacts, sometimes wrecking havoc on national economies. Thus, virtually as soon as Mexico, the United States and Canada formed NAFTA at the beginning of 1994, Mexico was hit with a severe financial crisis. As the economy turned downward at the beginning of that year, capital rapidly left the country, greatly reducing the value of the Mexican peso. With this diminished value of the peso, the cost of servicing international debts and the costs of imports skyrocketed—and the downturn worsened.

Still, during the 1990s, before and after the financial crisis, free-traders extolled short periods of moderate economic growth in Mexico —3% to 4% per year—as evidence of success. Yet, compared to earlier years, Mexico's growth under free trade has been poor. From 1940 to 1990 (including the no-growth decade of the 1980s), when Mexico's market was highly protected and the state actively regulated economic affairs, output grew at an average annual rate of 5%.

Most important, Mexico's experience discredits the notion that free-market policies will improve living conditions for the masses of people in low-income countries. The Mexican government paved the way for free trade policies by reducing or eliminating social welfare programs, and for many Mexican workers wages declined sharply during the free trade era. The number of households living in poverty rose dramatically, with some 75% of Mexico's population below the poverty line at the beginning of the 21st century.

China and Its Impact

Part of Mexico's problem and its economy's relatively weak performance from the 1990s onward has been the full-scale entrance of China into the international economy. While the Mexican authorities thought they saw great possibilities in NAFTA with the full opening of the U.S. market to goods produced with low-wage Mexican labor, China (and other Asian countries) had even cheaper labor. As China also gained access to the U.S. market, Mexican expectations were dashed.

The Chinese economy has surely gained in terms of economic growth as it has engaged more and more with the world market, and the absolute levels of incomes of millions of people have risen a great deal. However, China's rapid economic growth has come with a high degree of income inequality. Before its era of rapid growth, China was viewed as a country with a relatively equal distribution of income. By the beginning of the new millennium, however, it was much more unequal than any of the other most populace Asian countries (India, Indonesia, Bangladesh, Pakistan), and more in line with the high-inequality countries of Latin America. Furthermore, with the inequality has come a great deal of social conflict. Tens of thousands of "incidents" of conflict involving violence are reported each year, and most recently there have been the major conflicts involving Tibetans and Ouigers.

In any case, the Chinese trade and growth success should not be confused with "free trade." Foundations for China's surge of economic growth were established through state-sponsored infrastructure development and the vast expansion of the country's educational system. Even today, while private business, including foreign business, appears to have been given free rein in China, the government still plays a controlling role—including a central role in affecting foreign economic relations.

A central aspect of the government's role in the county's foreign commerce has been in the realm of finance. As Chinese-produced goods have virtually flooded international markets, the government has controlled the uses of the earnings from these exports. Instead of simply allowing those earnings to be used by Chinese firms and citizens to buy imports, the government has to a large extent held those earnings as reserves. Using those reserves, China's central bank has been the largest purchaser of U.S. government bonds, in effect becoming a major financer of the U.S. government's budget deficit of recent years.

China's reserves have been one large element in creating a giant pool of financial assets in the world economy. This "pool" has also been built up as the doubling of oil prices following the U.S. invasion of Iraq put huge amounts of funds in the pockets of oil-exporting countries and firms and individuals connected to the oil industry. Yet slow growth of the U.S. economy and extremely low interest rates, resulting from the Federal Reserve Bank's efforts to encourage more growth, limited the returns that could be obtained on these funds. One of the consequences—through a complex set of connections—was the development of the U.S. housing bubble, as financial firms, searching for higher returns, pushed funds into more and more risky mortgage loans.

It was not simply free trade and the unrestricted flow of international finance that generated the housing bubble and subsequent crisis in the U.S. economy. However, the generally unstable global economy—both in terms of trade and finance—

that has emerged in the free trade era was certainly a factor bringing about the crisis. Moreover, as is widely recognized, it was not only the U.S. economy and U.S. financial institutions that were affected. The free international flow of finance has meant that banking has become more and more a global industry. So as the U.S. banks got in trouble in 2007 and 2008, their maladies spread to many other parts of the world.

The Uses of Free Trade

While free trade is not the best economic growth or development policy and, especially through the free flow of finance, can precipitate financial crises, the largest and most powerful firms in many countries find it highly profitable. As Britain preached the loudest sermons for free trade in the early 19th century, when its own industry was already firmly established, so the United States—or at least many firms based in the United States—find it a profitable policy at the beginning of the 21st century. The Mexican experience provides an instructive illustration.

For U.S. firms, access to foreign markets is a high priority. Mexico may be relatively poor, but with a population of 105 million it provides a substantial market. Furthermore, Mexican labor is cheap relative to U.S. labor; and using modern production techniques, Mexican workers can be as productive as workers in the United States. For U.S. firms to obtain full access to the Mexican market, the United States has to open its borders to Mexican goods. Also, if U.S. firms are to take full advantage of cheap foreign labor and sell the goods produced abroad to U.S. consumers, the United States has to be open to imports.

On the other side of the border, wealthy Mexicans face a choice between advancing their interests through national development or advancing their interests through ties to U.S. firms and access to U.S. markets. For many years, they chose the former route. This led to some development of the Mexican economy but also—due to corruption and the massive power of the ruling party, the PRI—huge concentrations of wealth in the hands of a few small groups of firms and individuals. Eventually, these groups came into conflict with their own government over regulation and taxation. Having benefited from government largesse, they came to see their fortunes in greater freedom from government control and, particularly, in greater access to foreign markets and partnerships with large foreign companies. National development was a secondary concern when more involvement with international commerce would produce greater riches more quickly.

In addition, the old program of state-led development in Mexico ran into severe problems. These problems came to the surface in the 1980s with the international debt crisis. Owing huge amounts of money to foreign banks, the Mexican government was forced to respond to pressure from the IMF, the U.S. government, and large international banks which sought to deregulate Mexico's trade and investment. That pressure meshed with the pressure from Mexico's own richest elites, and the result was the move toward free trade and a greater opening of the Mexican economy to foreign investment.

Since the early 1990s, these changes for Mexico and the United States (as well as Canada) have been institutionalized in NAFTA. The U.S. government's agenda since then has been to spread free trade policies to all of the Americas through more regional agreements like CAFTA and ultimately through a Free Trade Area of the Americas. On a broader scale, the U.S. government works through the WTO, the IMF, and the World Bank to open markets and gain access to resources beyond the Western Hemisphere. In fact, while markets remain important everywhere, low-wage manufacturing is increasingly concentrated in Asia—especially China—instead of Mexico or Latin America.

The Chinese experience involves many of the same advantages for U.S. business as does the Mexican—a vast market, low wages, and an increasingly productive labor force. However, the Chinese government, although it has liberalized the economy a great deal compared to the pre-1985 era, has not abdicated its major role in the economy. For better (growth) and for worse (inequality and repression), the Chinese government has not embraced free trade.

Who Gains, Who Loses?

Of course, in the United States, Mexico, China and elsewhere, advocates of free trade claim that their policies are in everyone's interest. Free trade, they point out, will mean cheaper products for all. Consumers in the United States, who are mostly workers, will be richer because their wages will buy more. In Mexico and China, on the one hand, and in the United States, on the other hand, they argue that rising trade will create more jobs. If some workers lose their jobs because cheaper imported goods are available, export industries will produce new jobs.

In recent years this argument has taken on a new dimension with the larger entrance of India into the world economy and with the burgeoning there of jobs based in information technology—programming and call centers, for example. This "outsourcing" of service jobs has received a great deal of attention and concern in the United States. Yet free-traders have defended this development as good for the U.S. economy as well as for the Indian economy.

Such arguments obscure many of the most important issues in the free trade debate. Stated, as they usually are, as universal truths, these arguments are just plain silly. No one, for example, touring the Lowell National Historical Park could seriously argue that people in the United States would have been better off had there been no tariff on textiles. Yes, in 1820, they could have purchased textile goods more cheaply, but in the long run the result would have been less industrial advancement and a less wealthy nation. One could make the same point with the Japanese auto and computer industries, or indeed with numerous other examples from the last two centuries of capitalist development.

In the modern era, even though the United States already has a relatively developed economy with highly skilled workers, a freely open international economy does not serve the interests of most U.S. workers, though it will benefit large firms. U.S. workers today are in competition with workers around the globe. Many different workers in many different places can produce the same goods and services. Thus, an international economy governed by the free trade agenda will tend to bring down wages for many U.S. workers. This phenomenon has certainly been one of the factors leading to the substantial rise of income inequality in the United States during recent decades.

The problem is not simply that of workers in a few industries—such as auto and steel, or call-centers and computer programming—where import competition is an obvious and immediate issue. A country's openness to the international economy affects the entire structure of earnings in that country. Free trade forces down the general level of wages across the board, even of those workers not directly affected by imports. The simple fact is that when companies can produce the same products in several different places, it is owners who gain because they can move their factories and funds around much more easily than workers can move themselves around. Capital is mobile; labor is much less mobile. Businesses, more than workers, gain from having a larger territory in which to roam.

Control Over Our Economic Lives

But the difficulties with free trade do not end with wages. In both low-income and high-income parts of the world, free trade is a weapon in the hands of business when it opposes any progressive social programs. Efforts to place environmental restrictions on firms are met with the threat of moving production abroad. Higher taxes to improve the schools? Business threatens to go elsewhere. Better health and safety regulations? The same response.

Some might argue that the losses from free trade for people in the United States will be balanced by gains for most people in poor countries—lower wages in the United States, but higher wages in Mexico and China. Free trade, then, would bring about international equality. Not likely. In fact, as pointed out above, free trade reforms in Mexico have helped force down wages and reduce social welfare programs, processes rationalized by efforts to make Mexican goods competitive on international markets. China, while not embracing free trade, has seen its full-scale entrance into global commerce accompanied by increasing inequality.

Gains for Mexican or Chinese workers, like those for U.S. workers, depend on their power in relation to business. Free trade or simply the imperative of international "competitiveness" are just as much weapons in the hands of firms operating in Mexico and China as they are for firms operating in the United States. The great mobility of capital is business's best trump card in dealing with labor and popular demands for social change—in the United States, Mexico, China and elsewhere.

None of this means that people should demand that their economies operate as fortresses, protected from all foreign economic incursions. There are great gains that can be obtained from international economic relations—when a nation manages those relations in the interests of the great majority of the people. Protectionism often simply supports narrow vested interests, corrupt officials, and wealthy industrialists. In rejecting free trade, we should move beyond traditional protectionism.

Yet, at this time, rejecting free trade is an essential first step. Free trade places the cards in the hands of business. More than ever, free trade would subject us to the "bottom line," or at least the bottom line as calculated by those who own and run large companies. ❑

Article 8.2

COMPARATIVE ADVANTAGE

BY RAMAA VASUDEVAN
July/August 2007

> Dear Dr. Dollar:
> *When economists argue that the outsourcing of jobs might be a plus for the U.S. economy, they often mention the idea of comparative advantage. So free trade would allow the United States to specialize in higher-end service-sector business-es, creating higher-paying jobs than the ones that would be outsourced. But is it really true that free trade leads to universal benefits?*
> —David Goodman, Boston, Mass.

You're right: The purveyors of the free trade gospel do invoke the doctrine of comparative advantage to dismiss widespread concerns about the export of jobs. Attributed to 19th-century British political economist David Ricardo, the doctrine says that a nation always stands to gain if it exports the goods it produces *relatively* more cheaply in exchange for goods that it can get *comparatively* more cheaply from abroad. Free trade would lead to each country specializing in the products it can produce at *relatively* lower costs. Such specialization allows both trading partners to gain from trade, the theory goes, even if in one of the countries production of *both* goods costs more in absolute terms.

For instance, suppose that in the United States the cost to produce one car equals the cost to produce 10 bags of cotton, while in the Philippines the cost to produce one car equals the cost to produce 100 bags of cotton. The Philippines would then have a comparative advantage in the production of cotton, producing one bag at a cost equal to the production cost of 1/100 of a car, versus 1/10 of a car in the United States; likewise, the United States would hold a comparative advantage in the production of cars. Whatever the prices of cars and cotton in the global market, the theory goes, the Philippines would be better off producing only cotton and importing all its cars from the United States, and the United States would be better off producing only cars and importing all of its cotton from the Philippines. If the international terms of trade—the relative price—is one car for 50 bags, then the United States will take in 50 bags of cotton for each car it exports, 40 more than the 10 bags it forgoes by putting its productive resources into making the car rather than growing cotton. The Philippines is also better off: it can import a car in exchange for the ex-port of 50 bags of cotton, whereas it would have had to forgo the production of 100 bags of cotton in order to produce that car domestically. If the price of cars goes up in the global marketplace, the Philippines will lose out in relative terms—but will still be better off than if it tried to produce its own cars.

The real world, unfortunately, does not always conform to the assumptions un-derlying comparative-advantage theory. One assumption is that trade is balanced. But many countries are running persistent deficits, notably the United States, whose trade deficit is now at nearly 7% of its GDP. A second premise, that there is full employment within the trading nations, is also patently unrealistic. As global trade intensifies, jobs created in the export sector do not necessarily compensate for the jobs lost in the sectors wiped out by foreign competition.

The comparative advantage story faces more direct empirical challenges as well. Nearly 70% of U.S. trade is trade in similar goods, known as *intra-industry trade*: for example, exporting Fords and importing BMWs. And about one third of U.S. trade as of the late 1990s was trade between branches of a single corporation located in different countries (*intra-firm trade*). Comparative advantage cannot explain these patterns.

Comparative advantage is a static concept that identifies immediate gains from trade but is a poor guide to economic development, a process of structural change over time which is by definition dynamic. Thus the comparative advantage tale is particularly pernicious when preached to developing countries, consigning many to "specialize" in agricultural goods or be forced into a race to the bottom where cheap sweatshop labor is their sole source of competitiveness.

The irony, of course, is that none of the rich countries got that way by following the maxim that they now preach. These countries historically relied on tariff walls and other forms of protectionism to build their industrial base. And even now, they continue to protect sectors like agriculture with subsidies. The countries now touted as new models of the benefits of free trade—South Korea and the other "Asian tigers," for instance—actually flouted this economic wisdom, nurturing their technological capabilities in specific manufacturing sectors and taking advantage of their lower wage costs to *gradually* become effective competitors of the United States and Europe in manufacturing.

The fundamental point is this: contrary to the comparative-advantage claim that trade is universally beneficial, nations as a whole do not prosper from free trade. Free trade creates winners and losers, both within and between countries. In today's context it is the global corporate giants that are propelling and profiting from "free trade": not only outsourcing white-collar jobs, but creating global commodity chains linking sweatshop labor in the developing countries of Latin America and Asia (Africa being largely left out of the game aside from the export of natural resources such as oil) with ever-more insecure consumers in the developed world. Promoting "free trade" as a political cause enables this process to continue.

It is a process with real human costs in terms of both wages and work. People in developing countries across the globe continue to face these costs as trade liberalization measures are enforced; and the working class in the United States is also being forced to bear the brunt of the relentless logic of competition. ❑

Sources: Arthur MacEwan, "The Gospel of Free Trade: The New Evangelists," *Dollars & Sense*, July/August 2002; Ha-Joon Chang, *Kicking away the Ladder: The Real History of Fair Trade*, Foreign Policy in Focus, 2003; Anwar Shaikh, "Globalization and the Myths of Free Trade," in *Globalization and the Myths of Free Trade: History, Theory, and Empirical Evidence*, ed. Anwar Shaikh, Routledge 2007.

Article 8.3

IS CHINA'S CURRENCY MANIPULATION HURTING THE U.S.?

BY ARTHUR MacEWAN
November/December 2010

> Dear Dr. Dollar:
> *Is it true that China has been harming the U.S. economy by keeping its currency "undervalued"? Shouldn't the U.S. government do something about this situation?*
> —Jenny Boyd, Edmond, W.Va.

The Chinese government, operating through the Chinese central bank, does keep its currency unit—the yuan—cheap relative to the dollar. This means that goods imported *from* China cost less (in terms of dollars) than they would otherwise, while U.S. exports *to* China cost more (in terms of yuan). So we in the United States buy a lot of Chinese-made goods and the Chinese don't buy much from us. In the 2007 to 2009 period, the United States purchased $253 billion more in goods annually from China than it sold to China.

This looks bad for U.S workers. For example, when money gets spent in the United States, much of it is spent on Chinese-made goods, and fewer jobs are then created in the United States. So the Chinese government's currency policy is at least partly to blame for our employment woes. Reacting to this situation, many people are calling for the U.S. government to do something to get the Chinese government to change its policy.

But things are not so simple.

First of all, there is an additional reason for the low cost of Chinese goods—low Chinese wages. The Chinese government's policy of repressing labor probably accounts for the low cost of Chinese goods at least as much as does its currency policy. Moreover, there is a lot more going on in the global economy. Both currency problems and job losses involve much more than Chinese government actions—though China provides a convenient target for ire.

And the currency story itself is complex. In order to keep the value of its currency low relative to the dollar, the Chinese government increases the supply of yuan, uses these yuan to buy dollars, then uses the dollars to buy U.S. securities, largely government bonds but also private securities. In early 2009, China held $764 billion in U.S. Treasury securities, making it the largest foreign holder of U.S. government debt. By buying U.S. government bonds, the Chinese have been financing the federal deficit. More generally, by supplying funds to the United States, the Chinese government has been keeping interest rates low in this country.

If the Chinese were to act differently, allowing the value of their currency to rise relative to the dollar, both the cost of capital and the prices of the many goods imported from China would rise. The rising cost of capital would probably not be a serious problem, as the Federal Reserve could take counteraction to keep interest rates low. So, an increase in the value of the yuan would net the United States some jobs, but also raise some prices for U.S. consumers.

It is pretty clear that right now what the United States needs is jobs. Moreover, low-cost Chinese goods have contributed to the declining role of manufacturing in the United States, a phenomenon that both weakens important segments of organized labor and threatens to inhibit technological progress, which has often been centered in manufacturing or based on applications in manufacturing (e.g., robotics).

So why doesn't the U.S. government place more pressure on China to raise the value of the yuan? Part of the reason may lie in concern about losing Chinese financing of the U.S. federal deficit. For several years the two governments have been co-dependent: The U.S. government gets financing for its deficits, and the Chinese government gains by maintaining an undervalued currency. Not an easy relationship to change.

Probably more important, however, many large and politically powerful U.S.-based firms depend directly on the low cost goods imported from China. Wal-mart and Target, as any shopper knows, are filled with Chinese-made goods. Then there are the less visible products from China, including a power device that goes into the Microsoft Xbox, computer keyboards for Dell, and many other goods for many other U.S. corporations. If the yuan's value rose and these firms had to pay more dollars to buy these items, they could probably not pass all the increase on to consumers and their profits would suffer.

Still, in spite of the interests of these firms, the U.S. government may take some action, either by pressing harder for China to let the value of the yuan rise relative to the dollar or by placing some restrictions on imports from China. But don't expect too big a change. ❏

Article 8.4

OUTSIZED OFFSHORE OUTSOURCING

The scope of offshore outsourcing gives some economists and the business press the heebie-jeebies.

BY JOHN MILLER
September/October 2007

A t a press conference introducing the 2004 *Economic Report of the President*, N. Gregory Mankiw, then head of President Bush's Council of Economic Advisors, assured the press that "Outsourcing is probably a plus for the economy in the long run [and] just a new way of doing international trade."

Mankiw's comments were nothing other than mainstream economics, as even Democratic Party-linked economists confirmed. For instance Janet Yellen, President Clinton's chief economist, told the *Wall Street Journal*, "In the long run, outsourcing is another form of trade that benefits the U.S. economy by giving us cheaper ways to do things." Nonetheless, Mankiw's assurances were met with derision from those uninitiated in the economics profession's free-market ideology. Sen. John Edwards (D-N.C.) asked, "What planet do they live on?" Even Republican House Speaker Dennis Hastert (Ill.) said that Mankiw's theory "fails a basic test of real economics."

Mankiw now jokes that "if the American Economic Association were to give an award for the Most Politically Inept Paraphrasing of Adam Smith, I would be a leading candidate." But he quickly adds, "the recent furor about outsourcing, and my injudiciously worded comments about the benefits of international trade, should not eclipse the basic lessons that economists have understood for more than two centuries."

In fact Adam Smith never said any such thing about international trade. In response to the way Mankiw and other economists distort Smith's writings, economist Michael Meeropol took a close look at what Smith actually said; he found that Smith used his invisible hand argument to favor domestic investment over far-flung, hard-to-supervise foreign investments. Here are Smith's words in his 1776 masterpiece, *The Wealth of Nations*:

> By preferring the support of domestic to that of foreign industry, he [the investor] intends only his own security; and by directing that industry in such a manner as its produce may be of the greatest value, he intends only his own gain, and he is in this, as in many other cases, led by an invisible hand to promote an end, which was no part of his intention.

Outsized offshore outsourcing, the shipping of jobs overseas to take advantage of low wages, has forced some mainstream economists and some elements of the business press to have second thoughts about "free trade." Many are convinced that the painful transition costs that hit before outsourcing produces any ultimate benefits may be the biggest political issue in economics for a generation. And some recognize, as Smith did, that there is no guarantee unfettered international trade will leave the participants better off even in the long run.

Keynes's Revenge

Writing during the Great Depression of the 1930s, John Maynard Keynes, the preeminent economist of the twentieth century, prescribed government spending as a means of compensating for the instability of private investment. The notion of a mixed private/government economy, Keynes's prosthesis for the invisible hand of the market, guided U.S. economic policy from the 1940s through the 1970s.

It is only fitting that Paul Samuelson, the first Nobel Laureate in economics, and whose textbook introduced U.S. readers to Keynes, would be among the first mainstream economist to question whether unfettered international trade, in the context of massive outsourcing, would necessarily leave a developed economy such as that of the United States better off—even in the long run. In an influential 2004 article, Samuelson characterized the common economics wisdom about outsourcing and international trade this way:

> Yes, good jobs may be lost here in the short run. But …the gains of the winners from free trade, properly measured, work out to exceed the losses of the losers. … Never forget to tally the real gains of consumers alongside admitted possible losses of some producers. … The gains of the American winners are big enough to more than compensate the losers.

Samuelson took on this view, arguing that this common wisdom is "dead wrong about [the] *necessary* surplus of winning over losing" [emphasis in the original]. In a rather technical paper, he demonstrated that free trade globalization can sometimes give rise to a situation in which "a productivity gain in one country can benefit that country alone, while permanently hurting the other country by reducing the gains from trade that are possible between the two countries."

OFFSHORED? OUTSOURCED? CONFUSED?

The terms "offshoring" and "outsourcing" are often used interchangeably, but they refer to distinct processes:

Outsourcing – When a company hires another company to carry out a business function that it no longer wants to carry on in-house. The company that is hired may be in the same city or across the globe; it may be a historically independent firm or a spinoff of the first company created specifically to outsource a particular function.

Offshoring or *Offshore Outsourcing* – When a company shifts a portion of its business operation abroad. An offshore operation may be carried out by the same company or, more typically, outsourced to a different one.

Many in the economics profession do admit that it is hard to gauge whether intensified offshoring of U.S. jobs in the context of free-trade globalization will give more in winnings to the winners than it takes in losses from the losers. "Nobody has a clue about what the numbers are," as Robert C. Feenstra, a prominent trade economist, told *BusinessWeek* at the time.

The empirical issues that will determine whether offshore outsourcing ultimately delivers, on balance, more benefits than costs, and to whom those benefits and costs will accrue, are myriad. First, how wide a swath of white-collar workers will see their wages reduced by competition from the cheap, highly skilled workers who are now becoming available around the world? Second, by how much will their wages drop? Third, will the U.S. workers thrown into the global labor pool end up losing more in lower wages than they gain in lower consumer prices? In that case, the benefits of increased trade would go overwhelmingly to employers. But even employers might lose out depending on the answer to a fourth question: Will cheap labor from abroad allow foreign employers to out-compete U.S. employers, driving down the prices of their products and lowering U.S. export earnings? In that case, not only workers, but the corporations that employ them as well, could end up worse off.

Bigger Than A Box

Another mainstream Keynesian economist, Alan Blinder, former Clinton economic advisor and vice-chair of the Federal Reserve Board, doubts that outsourcing will be "immiserating" in the long run and still calls himself "a free-trader down to his toes." But Blinder is convinced that the transition costs will be large, lengthy, and painful before the United States experiences a net gain from outsourcing. Here is why.

First, rapid improvements in information and communications technology have rendered obsolete the traditional notion that manufactured goods, which can generally be boxed and shipped, are tradable, while services, which cannot be boxed, are not. And the workers who perform the services that computers and satellites have now rendered tradable will increasingly be found offshore, especially when they are skilled and will work for lower wages.

Second, another 1.5 billion or so workers—many in China, India, and the former Soviet bloc—are now part of the world economy. While most are low-skilled workers, some are not; and as Blinder says, a small percentage of 1.5 billion is nonetheless "a lot of willing and able people available to do the jobs that technology will move offshore." And as China and India educate more workers, offshoring of high-skill work will accelerate.

ATTRIBUTES OF JOBS OUTSOURCED

- No Face-to-Face Customer Servicing Requirement
- High Information Content
- Work Process is Telecommutable and Internet Enabled
- High Wage Differential with Similar Occupation in Destination Country
- Low Setup Barriers
- Low Social Networking Requirement

Third, the transition will be particularly painful in the United States because the U.S. unemployment insurance program is stingy, at least by first-world standards, and because U.S. workers who lose their jobs often lose their health insurance and pension rights as well.

How large will the transition cost be? "Thirty million to 40 million U.S. jobs are potentially offshorable," according to Blinder's latest estimates. "These include scientists, mathematicians and editors on the high end and telephone operators, clerks and typists on the low end."

Blinder arrived at these figures by creating an index that identifies how easy or hard it will be for a job to be physically or electronically "offshored." He then used the index to assess the Bureau of Labor Statistics' 817 U.S. occupational categories. Not surprisingly, Blinder classifies almost all of the 14.3 million U.S. manufacturing jobs as offshorable. But he also classifies more than twice that many U.S. service sector jobs as offshorable, including most computer industry jobs as well as many others, for instance, the 12,470 U.S. economists and the 23,790 U.S. multimedia artists and animators. In total, Blinder's analysis suggests that 22% to 29% of the jobs held by U.S. workers in 2004 will be potentially offshorable within a decade or two, with nearly 8.2 million jobs in 59 occupations "highly offshorable." Table 2 (next page) provides a list of the broad occupational categories with 300,000 or more workers that Blinder considers potentially offshorable.

Mankiw dismissed Blinder's estimates of the number of jobs at risk to offshoring as "out of the mainstream." Indeed, Blinder's estimates are considerably larger than earlier ones. But these earlier studies either aim to measure the number of U.S. jobs that will be outsourced (as opposed to the number at risk of being outsourced), look at a shorter period of time, or have shortcomings that suggest they underestimate the number of U.S. jobs threatened by outsourcing. (See "Studying the Studies," p. 228.)

Global Arbitrage

Low wages are the reason U.S. corporations outsource labor. Computer programmers in the United States, for example, make wages nearly *ten times* those of their counterparts in India and the Philippines.

Today, more and more white-collar workers in the United States are finding themselves in direct competition with the low-cost, well-trained, highly educated workers in Bangalore, Shanghai, and Eastern and Central Europe. These workers often use the same capital and technology and are no less productive than the U.S. workers they replace. They just get paid less.

This global labor arbitrage, as Morgan Stanley's chief economist Stephen Roach calls it, has narrowed international wage disparities in manufacturing, and now in services too, by unrelentingly pushing U.S. wages down toward international norms. ("Arbitrage" refers to transactions that yield a profit by taking advantage of a price differential for the same asset in different locations. Here, of course, the "asset" is wage labor of a certain skill level.) A sign of that pressure: about 70% of laid-off workers in the United States earn less three years later than they did at the time of the layoff; on average, those reemployed earn 10% less than they did before.

And it's not only laid-off workers who are hurt. A study conducted by Harvard labor economists Lawrence F. Katz, Richard B. Freeman, and George J. Borjas finds that every other worker with skills similar to those who were displaced also loses out. Every 1% drop in employment due to imports or factories gone abroad shaves 0.5% off the wages of the remaining workers in that occupation, they conclude.

Global labor arbitrage also goes a long way toward explaining the poor quality and low pay of the jobs the U.S. economy has created this decade, according to Roach. By dampening wage increases for an ever wider swath of the U.S. workforce, he argues, outsourcing has helped to drive a wedge between productivity gains and wage gains and to widen inequality in the United States. In the first four years of this decade, nonfarm productivity in the United States has recorded a cumulative increase of 13.3%—more than double the 5.9% rise in real compensation per hour over the same period. ("Compensation" includes wages, which have been stagnant for the average worker, plus employer spending on fringe benefits such as health insurance, which has risen even as, in many instances, the actual benefits have been cut back.) Roach reports that the disconnect between pay and productivity growth during the current economic expansion has been much greater in services than in manufacturing, as that sector weathers the powerful forces of global labor arbitrage for the first time.

Doubts in the Business Press?!

Even in the business press, doubts that offshore outsourcing willy-nilly leads to economic improvement have become more acute. Earlier this summer, a *BusinessWeek* cover story, "The Real Cost of Offshoring," reported that government statistics have underestimated the damage to the U.S. economy from offshore outsourcing. The problem is that since offshoring took off, *import* growth, adjusted for inflation, has been faster than the official numbers show. That means improvements in living standards, as well as corporate profits, depend more on cheap imports, and less on improving domestic productivity, than analysts thought.

Growing angst about outsourcing's costs has also prompted the business press to report favorably on remedies for the dislocation brought on by offshoring that deviate substantially from the non-interventionist, free-market playbook. Even the most unfazed pro-globalization types want to beef up trade adjustment assistance for displaced workers and strengthen the U.S. educational system. But both proposals are inadequate.

More education, the usual U.S. prescription for any economic problem, is off the mark here. Cheaper labor is available abroad up and down the job-skill ladder, so even the most rigorous education is no inoculation against the threat of offshore outsourcing. As Blinder emphasizes, it is the need for face-to-face contact that stops jobs from being shipped overseas, not the level of education necessary to perform them. Twenty years from now, home health aide positions will no doubt be plentiful in the United States; jobs for highly trained IT professionals may be scarce.

Trade adjustment assistance has until now been narrowly targeted at workers hurt by imports. Most new proposals would replace traditional trade adjustment assistance and unemployment insurance with a program for displaced workers that offers wage insurance to ease the pain of taking a lower-paying job and provides for portable health insurance and retraining. The pro-globalization research group McKinsey Global Institute (MGI), for example, claims that for as little as 4% to 5% of the amount they've saved in lower wages, companies could cover the wage losses of all laid-off workers once they are reemployed, paying them 70% of the wage differential between their old and new jobs (in addition to health care subsidies) for up to two years.

While MGI confidently concludes that this proposal will "go a long way toward relieving the current anxieties," other globalization advocates are not so sure. They recognize that economic anxiety is pervasive and that millions of white-collar workers now fear losing their jobs. Moreover, even if fears of actual job loss are overblown, wage insurance schemes do little to compensate for the downward pressure offshoring is putting on the wages of workers who have not been laid off.

Other mainstream economists and business writers go even further, calling for not only wage insurance but also taxes on the winners from globalization. And globalization has produced big winners: on Wall Street, in the corporate boardroom, and among those workers in high demand in the global economy.

Economist Matthew Slaughter, who recently left President Bush's Council of Economic Advisers, told the *Wall Street Journal*, "Expanding the political support for open borders [for trade] requres making a radical change in fiscal policy." He proposes eliminating the Social Security-Medicare payroll tax on the bottom half of workers—roughly, those earning less than $33,000 a year—and making up the lost revenue by raising the payroll tax on higher earners.

The goal of these economists is to thwart a crippling political backlash against trade. As they see it, "using the tax code to slice the apple more evenly is far more palatable than trying to hold back globalization with policies that risk shrinking the economic apple."

Some even call for extending global labor arbitrage to CEOs. In a June 2006 *New York Times* op-ed, equity analyst Lawrence Orlowski and New York University assistant research director Florian Lengyel argued that offshoring the jobs of U.S. chief executives would reduce costs and release value to shareholders by bringing the compensation of U.S. CEOs (on average 170 times greater than the compensation of average U.S. workers in 2004) in line with CEO compensation in Britain (22 times greater) and in Japan (11 times greater).

Yet others focus on the stunning lack of labor mobility that distinguishes the current era of globalization from earlier ones. Labor markets are becoming increasingly free and flexible under globalization, but labor enjoys no similar freedom of movement. In a completely free market, the foreign workers would come here to do the work that is currently being outsourced. Why aren't more of those workers coming to the United States? Traditional economists Gary Becker and Richard Posner argue the answer is clear: an excessively restrictive immigration policy.

Onshore and Offshore Solidarity

Offshoring is one of the last steps in capitalism's conversion of the "physician, the lawyer, the priest, the poet, the man of science, into its paid wage laborers," as

Marx and Engels put it in the *Communist Manifesto* 160 years ago. It has already done much to increase economic insecurity in the workaday world and has become, Blinder suggests, the number one economic issue of our generation.

Offshoring has also underlined the interdependence of workers across the globe. To the extent that corporations now organize their business operations on a global scale, shifting work around the world in search of low wages, labor organizing must also be global in scope if it is to have any hope of building workers' negotiating strength.

Yet today's global labor arbitrage pits workers from different countries against each other as competitors, not allies. Writing about how to improve labor standards, economists Ajit Singh and Ann Zammit of the South Centre, an Indian non-governmental organization, ask the question, "On what could workers of the world unite" today? Their answer is that faster economic growth could indeed be a positive-sum game from which both the global North and the global South could gain. A pick-up in the long-term rate of growth of the world economy would generate higher employment, increasing wages and otherwise improving labor standards in both regions. It should also make offshoring less profitable and less painful.

The concerns of workers across the globe would also be served by curtailing the ability of multinational corporations to move their investment anywhere, which weakens the bargaining power of labor both in advanced countries and in the global South. Workers globally would also benefit if their own ability to move between countries was enhanced. The combination of a new set of rules to limit international capital movements and to expand labor mobility across borders, together with measures to ratchet up economic growth and thus increase worldwide demand for labor, would alter the current process of globalization and harness it to the needs of working people worldwide. ❑

Sources: Alan S. Blinder, "Fear of Offshoring," CEPS Working Paper #119, Dec. 2005; Alan S. Blinder, "How Many U.S. Jobs Might Be Offshorable?" CEPS Working Paper #142, March 2007; N. Gregory Mankiw and P. Swagel, "The Politics and Economics of Offshore Outsourcing," Am. Enterprise Inst. Working Paper #122, 12/7/05; "Offshoring: Is It a Win-Win Game?" McKinsey Global Institute, August 2003; Diane Farrell et al., "The Emerging Global Labor Market, Part 1: The Demand for Talent in Services," McKinsey Global Institute, June 2005; Ashok Bardhan and Cynthia Kroll, "The New Wave of Outsourcing," Research Report #113, Fisher Center for Real Estate and Urban Economics, Univ. of Calif., Berkeley, Fall 2003; Paul A. Samuelson, "Where Ricardo and Mill Rebut and Confirm Arguments of Mainstream Economists Supporting Globalization," *J Econ Perspectives* 18:3, Summer 2004; Alan S. Blinder, "Free Trade's Great, but Offshoring Rattles Me," *Wash. Post*, 5/6/07; Michael Mandel, "The Real Cost of Offshoring," *BusinessWeek*, 6/18/07; Aaron Bernstein, "Shaking Up Trade Theory," *BusinessWeek*, 12/6/04; David Wessel, "The Case for Taxing Globalization's Big Winners," *WSJ*, 6/14/07; Bob Davis, "Some Democratic Economists Echo Mankiw on Outsourcing," *WSJ*; N. Gregory Mankiw, "Outsourcing Redux," gregmankiw. blogspot.com/2006/05/outsourcing-redux; David Wessel and Bob Davis, "Pain From Free Trade Spurs Second Thoughts," *WSJ*, 3/30/07; Ajit Singh and Ann Zammit, "On What Could Workers of the World Unite? Economic Growth and a New Global Economic Order," from *The Global Labour Standards Controversy: Critical Issues For Developing Countries*, South Centre, 2000; Michael Meeropol, "Distorting Adam Smith on Trade," *Challenge*, July/Aug 2004.

Article 8.5

AFTER HORROR, APOLOGETICS

Sweatshop apologists cover for intransigent U.S. retail giants.

BY JOHN MILLER
September/October 2013

> Bangladesh just isn't rich enough to support the sort of worker safety
> laws that we have ourselves. ...
> [S]horter working hours ... , safer workplaces, unemployment protec-
> tions and the rest ... are the products of wealth. ...
> [A]ll of us who would like to see those conditions improve ... should be
> cheering on the export led growth of that Bangladeshi economy.
> —Tim Worstall, "Sadly, Bangladesh Simply Cannot Afford Rich World
> Safety And Working Standards," *Forbes*, April 28, 2013.

The April 24 collapse of the Rana Plaza building, just outside of Dhaka, Bangladesh's capital city, killed over 1,100 garment workers toiling in the country's
growing export sector.

The horrors of the Rana Plaza disaster, the worst ever in the garment industry,
sent shockwaves across the globe. In the United States, the largest single destination
for clothes made in Bangladesh, newspaper editors called on retailers whose wares are
made in the country's export factories to sign the legally binding fire-and-safety accord already negotiated by mostly European major retailers. Even some of the business
press chimed in. The editors of Bloomberg Businessweek admonished global brand-
name retailers that safe factories are "not only right but also smart." But just two U.S.
retailers signed on, while most opted to sign a non-legally binding ersatz accord.

The business press, however, also turned their pages over to sweatshop defenders, contrarians who refuse

to let the catastrophic loss of life in Bangladesh's export factories shake their
faith in neoliberal globalization. Tim Worstall, a fellow at London's free-market
Adam Smith Institute, told Forbes readers that "Bangladesh simply cannot afford
rich world safety and working standards." Economist Benjamin Powell, meanwhile,
took the argument that sweatshops "improve the lives of their workers and boost
growth" out for a spin on the Forbes op-ed pages.

The sweatshop defenders are twisting Bangladesh workers' need for more and
better jobs into a case for low wages and bad working conditions. Their misleading
arguments, moreover, are no excuse for major U.S. retailers to refuse to sign onto
the European-initiated safety agreement, a truly positive development in the fight
against sweatshops.

More Jobs, Not More Sweatshops

Bangladesh is "dirt poor," as Worstall puts it. The country is on the United Nations'
list of 46 Least Developed Countries. Its gross domestic product (GDP) per capita,

the most common measure of economic development, is about one-fiftieth that of the United States.

The garment industry is the leading sector of the Bangladeshi economy, responsible for some 80% of total exports by value. Bangladesh's garment exports tripled between 2005 and 2010, boosting the nation's growth rate. By 2011, Bangladesh was the third-largest exporter of clothes in the world, after China and Italy.

On top of that, the garment industry has provided much-needed jobs. Bangladesh has about 5,000 garment factories that employ 3.6 million workers, the vast majority of them women. Wages for women in the garment industry were 13.7% higher than wages for women with similar years of education and experience in other industries in Bangladesh, according to a 2012 study. And the most common alternative employments for women, such as domestic service and agriculture labor, pay far less than factory jobs.

Still, none of that is a good reason to endorse sweatshops.

While Bangladesh's garment industry boosted economic growth and added to employment, neither its horrific working conditions nor its dismally low wages improved without government intervention.

Rana Plaza was a deathtrap. But it was only the latest tragedy to have struck Bangladeshi workers sewing garments for major U.S. and European retailers. Less than five months earlier, a devastating fire at Tazreen Fashions, a garment factory not far from Rana Plaza, killed 117 workers. In addition to the 1,129 workers killed at Rana Plaza, more than 600 garment workers have died in factory fires in Bangladesh since 2005, according to Fatal Fashion, a 2013 report published by SOMO Centre for Research on Multinational Corporations. From 2000 to 2010, wages in the garment industry remained flat, according to a survey conducted by War on Want, a British nonprofit. Even after the minimum wage in the garment industry nearly doubled in 2010, itself part of the fight against sweatshop conditions, wages remained among the lowest in the world. A seamstress in Bangladesh earns less than $50 a month, versus $100 in Vietnam and $235 in China, according to World Bank data. The bottom line, as Businessweek puts it, is that "Bangladesh's $18 billion garment industry relies on super-low wages and women desperate for work."

This does not mean that trying to improve these conditions is a futile undertaking. Safer working conditions and higher wages are unlikely to stand in the way of investment in Bangladesh's garment industry and job creation.

Factory costs, including wages, make up only a small portion of the overall cost of most garments. Leading Bangladesh garment makers told Businessweek that their total factory costs for a $22 pair of jeans was just 90 cents. That's just 4% of the price paid by consumers. On the other hand, a 2009 study of the sales in a major New York retail store found that the company could use "social labeling" to charge up to 20% more and still expect sales revenues to rise. In other words, doubling the wages paid to Bangladeshi garment workers and at the same time improving working conditions would not have to diminish retailer revenues.

Nor does improving worker safety have to be that expensive. The Worker Rights Consortium, an independent labor-rights monitoring group, estimates that it would cost an average of $600,000 to elevate each of Bangladesh's 5,000 factories to Western safety standards, for a total of $3 billion. If the $3 billion were spread over five years, it would add an average of less than 10 cents to the price paid by retail companies for each of the 7 billion garments that Bangladesh sells each year to Western brands.

How to Stop Sweatshop Abuse

For sweatshop apologists like Worstall and Powell, yet more export-led growth is the key to improving working and safety conditions in Bangladesh. "Economic development, rather than legal mandates," Powell argues, "drives safety improvements." Along the same lines, Worstall claims that rapid economic growth and increasing wealth are what improved working conditions in the United States a century ago and that those same forces, if given a chance, will do the same in Bangladesh.

But their arguments distort the historical record and misrepresent the role of economic development in bringing about social improvement. Working conditions have not improved because of market-led forces alone, but due to economic growth combined with the very kind of social action that sweatshops defenders find objectionable.

U.S. economic history makes that much clear. It was the 1911 Triangle Shirtwaist fire, which cost 146 garment workers their lives, along with the hardships of the Great Depression, that inspired the unionization of garment workers and led to the imposition of government regulations to improve workplace safety. Those reforms, combined with the post-World War II economic boom, nearly eliminated U.S. sweatshops.

Since then, declining economic opportunity, severe cutbacks in inspectors, and declining union representation have paved the way for the return of sweatshops to the United States. This trend further confirms that economic development, by itself, will not eliminate inhuman working conditions.

In contrast, a combination of forces that could eliminate sweatshops is forming in Bangladesh today. Despite the government's record of repressing labor protest and detaining labor leaders, the horror of the Rana Plaza collapse has sparked massive protests and calls for unionization in Bangladesh. In reaction, the government has amended its labor laws to remove some of the obstacles to workers forming unions, although formidible obstacles remain (including the requirement that at least 30% of the workers at an entire company—not at a single workplace as in the United States—be members of a union before the government will grant recognition).

Meanwhile, 80 mostly European retail chains that sell Bangladesh-made garments have signed the legally binding Accord on Fire and Building Safety in Bangladesh. For the first time, apparel manufacturers and retailers will be held accountable for the conditions in the factories that make their clothes. This "joint liability" aspect, a long-held goal of labor-rights advocates, is precisely what makes this international accord so important.

Negotiated with worker-safety groups and labor unions, the five-year accord sets up a governing board with equal numbers of labor and retail representatives, and a chair chosen by the International Labor Organization (ILO) An independent inspector will conduct audits of factory hazards and make the results public. Corrective actions recommended by the inspector will be mandatory and retailers will be forbidden from doing business with noncompliant facilities. Each retailer will contribute to the cost of implementing the accord based on how much they produce in Bangladesh, up to a maximum of $2.5 million over five years to pay for administering the safety plan and pick up the tab for factory repairs and renovations. The accord subjects disputes between retailers and union representatives to arbitration, with decisions enforceable by a court of law in the retailer's home country.

The signatories include Swedish retailer Hennes and Mauritz, which has more of its clothes made in Bangladesh than any other company; Benetton Group S.p.A., the Italian retailer whose order forms were famously found in the rubble of the collapsed Rana Plaza factory; and Canada's Loblow Companies, whose Joe Fresh clothing was also found at Rana Plaza. Together, their clothes are made in over 1,000 of Bangladesh's 5,000 factories.

However, only two U.S. companies, Abercrombie & Fitch and PVH (parent of Tommy Hilfiger and Calvin Klein), have signed the accord. Walmart, The Gap, J.C. Penney, Sears, and the rest of the major U.S. retailers doing business in Bangladesh have refused. The industry trade group, the National Retail Federation, objected to the accord's "one-size-fits-all approach" and its "legally questionable binding arbitration provision" that could bring disputes to court in the highly litigious United States. Several of those retailers cobbled together an alternative agreement signed so far by 17 mostly U.S. retailers.

But their "company-developed and company-controlled" plan, as a coalition of labor-rights groups described it, falls well short of the European-initiated plan. It is not legally binding and lacks labor organization representatives. Moreover, while retailers contribute to the implementation of their safety plan, they will face no binding commitment to pay for improving conditions. An AFL-CIO spokesperson put it most succinctly, "This is a matter of life or death. Quite simply, non-binding is just not good enough." ❑

Sources: Benjamin Powell, "Sweatshops in Bangladesh Improve the Lives of Their Workers, and Boost Growth," Forbes, May 2, 2013; JSOMO Centre for Research on Multinational Corporations and Clean Clothes Campaign, *Fatal Fashion*, March 2013; International Labor Rights Forum, "Accord on Fire and Building and Safety in Bangladesh," May 13, 2012; Michael Hiscox and Nicholas Smyth,"Is There Consumer Demand for Improved Labor Standards: Evidence from Field Experiments in Social Labeling," Department of Government, Harvard University, 2012; Rachel Heath and Mushfig Mubarak, "Does Demand or Supply Constrain Investments in Education? Evidence from Garment Sector Jobs in Bangladesh," Aug. 15, 2012; Rubana Huq, "The Economics of a $6.75 Shirt," *Wall Street Journal*, May 16, 2003; "Halfhearted Labor Reform in Bangladesh," *New York Times*, July 17, 2013; International Labour Organization, "A Handbook on the Bangladesh Labour Act, 2006"; Renee Dudley, "Bangladesh Fire Safety to Cost Retailers $3 Billion, Group Says," *Bloomberg Businessweek*, Dec. 10, 2012; Mehul Srivastava and Arun Deynath, "Bangladesh's Paradox for Poor Women Workers," *Bloomberg Businessweek*, May 9, 2013; Mehul Srivastava and Sarah Shannon, "Ninety Cents Buys Safety on $22 Jeans in Bangladesh," *Bloomberg Businessweek*, June 6, 2013; "Bloomberg View: How to Fix Bangladesh's Factories," *Bloomberg Businessweek*, May 2, 2013; Steven Greenhouse and Stephanie Clifford, "U.S. Retailers Offer Plan For Safety at Factories," *New York Times*, July 10, 2013; Alliance for Bangladesh Worker Safety, "Alliance of Leading Retailers in North America Join Forces in Comprehensive, Five-Year Commitment to Improve Factory Safety Conditions For Workers in Bangladesh," press release, July 10, 2013.

Article 8.6

CHINA'S DEVELOPMENT BANKS GO GLOBAL: THE GOOD AND THE BAD

BY KEVIN GALLAGHER
November/December 2013

China is redefining the global development agenda. While the West preaches trade liberalization and financial deregulation, China orchestrates massive infrastructure and industrial policies under regulated trade and financial markets. China transformed its economy and brought more than 600 million people out of poverty. Western policies led to financial crises, slow growth and relatively less poverty alleviation across the globe.

China is now exporting its model across the world. The China Development Bank (CDB) and the Export-Import Bank of China (EIBC) now provide more financing to developing countries than the World Bank does. What is more, China's finance doesn't come with the harsh conditions—such as trade liberalization and fiscal austerity—that western-backed finance has historically. China's development banks are not only helping to spur infrastructure development across the world, they are also helping China's bottom line as they make a strong profit and often provide opportunities for Chinese firms.

It is well known that China is taking the lead in developing and deploying clean energy technologies, as it has become the world's leading producer of solar panels. China is pumping finance into cleaner energy abroad as well. According to a new study by the World Resources Institute, since 2002 Chinese firms have put an additional $40 billion into solar and wind projects across the globe.

However, China's global stride may be jeopardized unless it begins to incorporate environmental and social safeguards into its overseas operations. In a policy memorandum for the Paulson Institute, I note how there is a growing backlash against China's development banks on these grounds. By remedying these concerns, China can become the global leader in development finance.

There is a growing number of cases where Chinese financial institutions may be losing ground over social and environmental concerns.

One example is CDB's multibillion-dollar China-Burma oil and gas pipeline projects. The Shwe gas project is coordinated by China National Petroleum Corporation, which has contracted out some operations to Sinohydro (the state-owned hydro-electric company). Local civil society organizations have mounted campaigns against land confiscation with limited compensation, loss of livelihoods, the role of Burmese security forces in protecting the project, and environmental degradation (deforestation, river dredging and chemical pollution).

Another example is the Patuca hydroelectric project in Honduras, supported by EIBC and operated by Sinohydro. Approved by the Honduran government in 2011, one of the projects is said to entail flooding 42 km of rainforest slated to be part of Patuca national park and the Tawahka Asangni biosphere reserve. The project was denounced by local civil society organizations, which cited the shaky foundations of the project's environmental impact assessment. NGOs including International Rivers and The Nature Conservancy have also sought to reevaluate the project. Such campaigns, uniting locally affected communities with globally recognized NGOs that have access to media worldwide, have slowed projects and tainted investors' images.

Extraction from the Belinga iron ore deposit in Gabon was contracted in 2007 between the government in Libreville and the China Machinery Energy Corporation, with financing from EIBC. The project sparked significant local protest over its environmental impact, and, as a result, has been perpetually renegotiated and delayed, and may ultimately be denied.

Environment-related political risk can severely affect the bottom line of the major Chinese development banks to the extent that local skepticism and protests result in delays or even loss of projects. Doing the right thing on the environment and human rights would help maintain China's market access and help mitigate risks to China's development banks.

Adopting established international norms may help China's banks to secure markets in more developed countries. Chinese banks clearly seek to further penetrate markets such as the United States and Europe, where even higher environmental and social standards exist. Establishing a track record of good practice in emerging markets and developing countries could help Chinese banks assimilate, adapt, and ultimately incorporate such practices into their daily operations, an experience that could prove essential as they also seek to navigate markets in Organisation for Economic Co-operation and Development (OECD) countries.

For decades, developing countries have pined for a development bank that provides finance for inclusive growth and sustainable development—without the draconian conditions that the IMF and World Bank have often imposed as a condition of their lending. That conditionality, and the egregious environmental record of early World Bank and other international-financial-institution projects, spurred a global backlash against these institutions. If China's development banks can add substantial social and environmental safeguards, they can become a beacon of 21st century development finance. ❑

Article 8.7

IT LOWERED WAGES, AS IT WAS SUPPOSED TO DO

BY DEAN BAKER
The New York Times, November 2013

Given the trends in U.S. trade with Mexico over the last two decades, it is strange that there is much of a debate over Nafta's impact on wages. At the time Nafta was passed in 1993 the United States had a modest trade surplus with Mexico. In 2013 we are on a path to have a trade deficit of more than $50 billion. The $50 billion in lost output corresponds to roughly 0.3 percent of gross domestic product, assuming the same impact on employment, this would translate into more than 400,000 jobs. If each lost job would have led to half a job being created as a result of workers spending their wages, this would bring the total impact to 600,000 jobs.

Of course some of the shift from surplus to deficit might have occurred even without Nafta, but it would be difficult to argue that Nafta was not a major contributing factor. After all, one of the main purposes of the agreement was to make U.S. firms feel confident that they could locate operations in Mexico without having to fear that their factories could be nationalized or that Mexico would impose restrictions on repatriating profits. This encouraged firms to take advantage of lower cost labor in Mexico, and many did.

This can produce economic gains; they just don't go to ordinary workers. The lower cost of labor translates to some extent into lower prices and to some extent into higher corporate profits. The latter might be good news for shareholders and top management, but is not beneficial to most workers.

Lower prices are helpful to workers as consumers, but are not likely to offset the impact on wages. To see this point, imagine that Nafta was about reducing the wages of doctors by eliminating the barriers that made it difficult for Mexican school children to train to U.S. standards and practice medicine in the United States.

If we got an additional 200,000 doctors from Mexico over the last 20 years then it would likely go far toward bringing the pay of doctors in the United States more in line with the pay of doctors in other wealthy countries. This would lead to tens of billions of years in savings in health care costs to patients and the government.

Even doctors would share in these savings, since they too would have to pay less for their health care. However no one would try to tell doctors that they were better off from this trade deal because of their reduced health care costs. The hit to their wages would have swamped the savings on their health care bill. This is the same story with ordinary workers and the impact of Nafta.

Nafta could have been structured to bring the pay of doctors and other highly paid professionals more in line with their pay in other wealthy countries by removing barriers. This would have produced substantial economic gains to the economy as a whole (it's the exact same model as economists use to show gains from the Nafta we have), except these gains would be associated with a downward rather than an upward redistribution of income.

The doctors and their allies among the elite have been able to prevent such a deal from being considered by the politicians in Washington, American workers don't have that power. ❑

Article 8.8

HOW BEER EXPLAINS 20 YEARS OF NAFTA'S DEVASTATING EFFECTS ON MEXICO

BY TIMOTHY A. WISE
January 2014, Global Post

Mexico's largest agribusiness associated invited me to Aguascalientes to partici-pate in its annual forum in October. The theme for this year's gathering was "New Perspectives on the Challenge of Feeding the World."

But it was unclear why Mexico, which now imports 42 percent of its food, would be worried about feeding the world. It wasn't doing so well feeding its own people.

In part, you can thank the North American Free Trade Agreement (NAFTA) for that. Twenty years ago, on January 1, 1994, NAFTA took effect, and Mexico was the poster child for the wonders of free trade. The promises seemed endless.

Mexico would enter the "First World" of developed countries on the crest of rising trade and foreign investment. Its dynamic manufacturing sector would create so many jobs it would not only end the U.S. immigration problem but absorb millions of peasant farmers freed from their unproductive toil in the fields. Mexico could import cheap corn and export electronics.

So much for promises.

NAFTA produced a devastating one-two punch. For the first 10 years, the flood of U.S. exports of corn, wheat, meat and other staples drove Mexican producer prices well below the costs of production.

Mexico's three million small-scale corn farmers saw prices for their crops fall 66 percent, largely because the United States increased corn exports by 400 percent, exporting at prices 19 percent below even U.S. farmers' costs of production. (See my earlier study.) Call it the Age of Agricultural Dumping.

Soybeans, wheat, cotton and rice saw similar export surges under NAFTA, with similar drops in producer prices. Mexico's agricultural exports to the United States increased as well, but it takes a lot of tomatoes and strawberries to make up for the surge in staple-food imports.

By the mid-2000s, Mexico was importing 42 percent of its food, mostly from the United States. Corn import dependence had grown from 8 percent before NAFTA to 32 percent. Mexico was importing nearly 60 percent of its wheat where before it had imported less than 20 percent.

Import dependence was more than 70 percent for soybeans, rice and cotton.

Then came the sucker punch. In 2007, international prices for many staple crops doubled or tripled, and so did the cost of importing them. Countries like Mexico that had gotten hooked on cheap imports paid a heavy price. Call it the Age of Dependency.

U.S. policies had as much to do with these high and volatile prices as they had with the Age of Dumping. Now, instead of price-depressing surpluses caused by

U.S. agricultural policies, U.S. subsidies and incentives were diverting 40 percent of U.S. corn — 15 percent of the global supply — into ethanol production.

This drove up the price of corn, but also prices for related crops, like soybeans and wheat, and the livestock products that had relied for so long on cheap feed.

Compounding the price volatility, U.S. deregulation of financial markets in the early 2000s had brought agricultural commodity markets into the global casino. Financial speculators, fleeing the collapsing U.S. housing and stock markets in 2007, went "all in" on commodities, driving prices to disruptive highs, then lows, then highs again.

This was devastating for countries dependent on imported food. The world's Least Developed Countries, which had exported more than they imported in the early 1980s, saw their food import bills skyrocket to more than $25 billion, driving their collective agricultural trade deficit to more than $19 billion. (See my earlier report.)

Mexico's agricultural imports topped $20 billion following the price spikes, with its agricultural trade deficit jumping to more than $4 billion. Corn imports accounted for more than half the bill.

And most telling: twenty years into NAFTA, 55 million Mexicans — about half the population — are estimated to be in poverty, many without secure access to food.

The night before my talk in Aguascalientes, in which I would gently call attention to the high cost of Mexico's failed cheap-food experiment under NAFTA, I ended up at a lush cocktail reception talking to the U.S. Embassy's agricultural attaché. I must have said something about Mexico's agricultural trade deficit, and he immediately took offense.

"This year," he proclaimed, "Mexico may actually run a surplus."

I knew better; I'd seen this statistical sleight-of-hand many times.

"Do you mean the 'agri-food' trade balance?" I asked.

He nodded.

The one that has beer as one of Mexico's biggest agricultural exports?"

He nodded again, and not sheepishly. Beer has undoubtedly been a NAFTA success story for Mexico.

"Beer is a product of agriculture," he said, with conviction.

I took a sip of my margarita.

"Don't you think including beer distorts how Mexican agriculture is really doing under NAFTA?" I asked.

Not at all, he replied, the beer sector is a perfect example of the kind of integration NAFTA can achieve.

"Look, Mexico's even importing the barley malt from us to make its beer!" I said.

I took another sip.

"So Mexico's agricultural contribution to its beer exports is … what?" I asked.

Nervous laughter.

Here is a case where NAFTA has gotten the United States to open its market to something of value that Mexico can export, and Mexico can't even capture the value from it. The industry's growth benefits U.S. barley growers and U.S. malt makers.

Mexico can't even import the barley and make the malt themselves.

So the country is basically a maquiladora for beer bottling. I guess Mexico contributes the water. Which it doesn't have enough of.

This has been Mexico under NAFTA in a nutshell. Giving away everything of value, then deluding yourself that your farm sector is doing fine because your Corona beer, bottled from U.S. ingredients, is a big hit in the States.

Meanwhile, hungry corn farmers wait for their government to invest in producing more of its own food. ❑

Article 8.9

TPP: TRUMPING PUBLIC PRIORITIES

Obama's Pacific deal would deepen the income divide.

BY ROGER BYBEE
March/April 2014

"Those at the top have never done better," President Obama ruefully acknowledged in his January 28 State of the Union speech. "But average wages have barely budged. Inequality has deepened."

Yet, moments later, Obama heartily endorsed the Trans-Pacific Partnership (TPP), which as drafted directly reflects the demands of "those at the top" and would, if passed, severely intensify the very inequality spotlighted by the president. The TPP would provide transnational corporations with easier access to cheap labor in Pacific Rim nations and give them new power to trump public-interest protections—on labor, food safety, drug prices, financial regulation, domestic procurement laws, and a host of other matters—established over the last century by democratic governments. The nations currently negotiating the TPP, which taken together comprise nearly 40% of the world economy, are: the United States, Australia, Brunei, Canada, Chile, Japan, Malaysia, Mexico, New Zealand, Peru, Singapore, and Vietnam. Among them, Brunei, Malaysia, Mexico, Singapore, and Vietnam are all notorious violators of labor rights. The TPP's labor provisions are far too weak to begin uplifting wages, conditions, and rights for workers in these nations.

As with NAFTA, the TPP will benefit U.S. companies relocating jobs to low-wage, high-repression nations, argues economist Mark Weisbrot, co-director of the Center for Economic and Policy Research (CEPR). This would also exert strong downward pressures on the pay of U.S. workers, "Most U.S. workers are likely to lose out from the TPP," Weisbrot says. "This may come as no surprise after 20 years of NAFTA and an even-longer period of trade policy designed to put lower- and middle-class workers in direct competition with low-paid workers in the developing world."

Obama has billed the TPP as a "trade agreement" that will create U.S. jobs. The pact, however, actually has little to do with reducing trade restrictions. Tariffs are now a minimal factor for most global trade. Lori Wallach, director of Public Citizen's Global Trade Watch, points out that only five of the TPP's twenty-nine chapters are about trade at all. But the remaining provisions cover such immensely important measures as the creation of a kind of corporate supremacy over the democratically established regulations enacted by member nations. If an existing law threats to diminish profits, corporations in the TPP nations would be entitled to bring their complaint to an international dispute panel of anonymous corporate members, who could impose major financial penalties on the "offending" countries. "The Trans-Pacific Partnership," Wallach concludes, "is a Trojan horse for a host of awful measures that have nothing to do with trade and would never get through Congress in the light of day."

Some of the most controversial TPP features have become public only thanks to Wikileaks. American participation in the TPP negotiations has been limited to a tiny circle of just 600 top corporate executives. Numerous members of Congress have complained about the secrecy surrounding the negotiations, charging that it exceeds even that practiced by the Bush-Cheney administration. The public's understanding of the massive stakes involved in the TPP has been further hampered by the failure of major media to offer even minimal analysis. The major-network news shows, according to a new study by Media Matters, made no mention at all of the TPP from August 2013 through January 2014.

Despite remaining in the shadows, the TPP has met fierce opposition from both elected representatives and hundreds of labor, consumer, small-farmer, health-reform, and other civic organizations. TPP's only foreseeable path to passage in the near future had been the use of a "fast-track" procedure, under which NAFTA and subsequent international agreements have been negotiated. Instead of the normal process of deliberation and debate by Congress, the fast-track process (which requires separate congressional approval) substitutes minimal debate and permits no amendments. Senate Majority Leader Harry Reid, acutely aware of public resentment against NAFTA's 20-year legacy of job loss and wage decline, has firmly ruled out the fast-track route for the TPP.

Influential Democratic senators like Elizabeth Warren (D-MA) and Sherrod Brown (D-OH) have already directed their fire at the TPP, with Warren demonstrating her seriousness by voting against Obama's nominee for U.S. Trade Representative, former Citigroup managing director Michael Froman. Meanwhile, 150 House Democrats and several dozen Republicans signed a November letter opposing the fast-track process.

"We're seeing 'trans-partisan' opposition to the Partnership," said Michael Dolan, the International Brotherhood of Teamsters (IBT) legislative representative on trade issues. As with NAFTA, where some conservative Pat Buchanan-style nationalists saw a transnational corporate threat to U.S. sovereignty, some normally pro-corporate members of Congress are adopting an oppositional stance. The Republican opposition to the TPP includes Tea Partiers Michele Bachmann (R-MN) and Louie Gohmert (R-TX) and over 20 others. According to Arthur Stamoulis, executive director of the Citizens Trade Campaign which is leading opposition to the TPP, the stance of these Republicans goes beyond their seemingly reflexive opposition to any Obama initiative.

While a number of Tea Party Republicans voted in favor of the three Obama-promoted free-trade agreements in 2011, they are viewing the TPP differently because of its magnitude and due to pressure from the Republican base. "Because of its massive size, the TPP has captured a lot more attention from the Right than the Korea pact ever did," Stamoulis says. "With Republicans' base much more engaged on the TPP—the Tea Party Nation and others opposing it—I expect to see a lot more Republican opposition this time around, and indeed, we already are seeing that." The visceral dislike of Obama by many on the Right may add fuel to rightist opposition to the TPP and the fast-track procedure, Stamoulis concedes, but he points out that opposition to corporate-style globalization has been mounting among Republican voters for some time. "Polls showed that Republican voters' opposition to free-trade agreements existed back during the Bush administration as well," he notes.

On the Democratic side, only a relative handful of remaining "free-traders" (their ranks having been thinned in recent elections that have unseated pro-globalization Dems) like Rep. Ron Kind (Wisc.), stand with Obama at this point. Unlike the NAFTA vote in 1993, where almost half of House Democrats and over 3/4 of Senate Republicans voted for the measure, Democrats in both Houses have become notably disenchanted with the results of "free trade" and the resultant offshoring of jobs. "Democratic opposition to job-killing Free Trade Agreements has hardened in recent years," says CTC's Stamoulis.

"Not only do more members of Congress understand the disastrous effects of pacts like NAFTA, but they also see that two years into President Obama's biggest trade agreement to date—the Korea Free Trade Agreement—not only is our deficit with South Korea up, but the promised exports are actually down." The Democratic base, as reflected in polling data, also seems more actively opposed to any massive new free trade agreement, based on the 20 years of job loss and community devastation that they see as products of NAFTA.

A wide array of mostly progressive organizations, including 564 labor, environmental, family farm, human rights, and other groups, signed on to a letter opposing the fast-track route to passing the TPP. With this pressure from the grassroots, "Democrats in Congress are beginning to understand not only the policy folly of TPP, but the political folly associated with it as well," Stamoulis states.

With implacable opposition to the TPP among both the president's strongest allies and most ardent enemies, the TPP has little chance of passage before the November mid-term elections, the Teamsters' Dolan told *Dollars & Sense*. But there is still a danger that Obama might seek to gain passage of the Trans-Pacific Partnership, using the fast-track procedure, in the "lame-duck" session after the elections, when defeated and retiring members of Congress are no longer accountable to voters.

However, such a ploy would leave Obama with a legacy of making little headway for workers against rising inequality, while succeeding only in promoting the TPP and other trade agreements that will worsen America's glaring economic fault lines. ❑

Sources: "Most U.S. Workers Likely to Lose Out from Proposed Trans-Pacific Trade Agreement, Report Finds", news release, Center on Economic and Policy Research, September 10, 2014 (cepr. net); Dean Baker, "TPP: A Trade Deal for Protectionists, Truthout, October 29, 2013 (truthout. org); Roger Bybee, "Obama's Double Game on Outsourcing," *Dollars & Sense*, Sept/Oct 2012; Roger Bybee, "Offshoring and Obama," *Z Magazine*, July 2011; Roger Bybee, "Corporations Secede from US for Cheap Labor," *Progressive Populist*, November 15, 2011; Gordon Lafer, "Partnership or Putsch?" Democratic Underground, January, 15, 2014 (democraticunderground.com); Craig Harrington and Brian Powell ,"Media Leave Viewers in the Dark About Trans-Pacific Partnership," Media Matters, February 5, 2014 (mediamatters.org); Dave Johnson, "TPP/Fast Track Trade Fight Is On," Common Dreams, October 30, 2013 (commondreams.org); Don Lee, "The Trans-Pacific Partnership: Who wins, who loses, why it matters," *LA Times*, February 19, 2014; John Nichols, "State of the Union: Right on Wages, Wrong on Trade," *The Nation* Jan. 28, 2014; John Nichols, "Harry Reid Knows Opposing Fast Track is Smart Policy and Smart Politics," *The Nation*, February 4, 2014; Gretchen Morgenson, "Barriers to Change, From Wall St. and Geneva," *New York Times*, March 17, 2012; John Queally, "As TPP Opposition Soars, Corporate Media Blackout Deafening" Common Dreams, February 6, 2014 (commondreams.org); David Rosnick, "Gains from Trade? The Net Effect of the Trans-Pacific Partnership Agreement on U.S. Wages," Center on Economic and Policy Research, September 1, 2013 (cepr.net); James Shcoch, "Organized Labor vs. Globalization," in Lowell Turner, et al., *Rekindling the Movement: Labor's Quest for Relevance in the 21st Century* (Ithaca: ILR/Cornell Books, 2001); Yves Smith, "TPP Disclosures Shows it Will Kill People and Internet," Naked Capitalism (nakedcapitalism.com), November 15, 2013; Lori Wallach and Ben Beachy, "Obama's Covert Trade Deal," *New York Times*, June 13, 2013.

Article 8.10

THE EUROZONE BALANCED-BUDGET DISASTER

BY PHILIP ARESTIS AND MALCOLM SAWYER
January/February 2014

In the immediate aftermath of the financial crisis, most European governments allowed the automatic stabilizers to kick in—let tax revenues fall and expenditures such as unemployment benefits rise, creating budget deficits—and implemented some mild discretionary fiscal-stimulus measures. All that amounts to a mildly Keynesian stance of fiscal expansion by deficit spending during a business-cycle downturn. But it was not long before the siren calls for "fiscal consolidation," that is, slashing government spending, arose, spurred on by spurious promises of "expansionary fiscal consolidation" and now-discredited claims that high debt-to-GDP ratios threatened economic disaster. These calls came from conservative politicians, economists, the Troika (European Commission, European Central Bank, and International Monetary Fund), and countries (like Germany) that were not as deeply in trouble. Proponents of consolidation claimed that the failure to constrain budget deficits in the mid 2000s was to blame for the debt crisis and had limited the ability of governments to respond to the Great Recession.

Within the eurozone, fingers were pointed at the failures of the Stability and Growth Pact (SGP), which is intended to govern the macroeconomic operations of the Economic and Monetary Union. The SGP had been intended to keep national budget deficits below 3% of GDP at all times, to have budgets balance over the business cycle, and to keep debt-to-GDP ratios below 60%. From 2002 to 2007, budget deficits averaged around 2% of GDP, the 3% limit was breached on numerous occasions, and, even in 2007 (before the crisis hit), seven of the then-twelve eurozone members had debt ratios of over 60%.

The SGP was modified slightly in 2005 to take some account of capital spending, but the essence of the pact remained. The budget deficit conditions had been broken in 2004, when France and Germany breached the 3% limit without penalty and then Portugal breached the limit and was punished; that meant becoming subjected to the Excessive Deficit Procedure (EDP). But countries kept on breaking the SGP deficit limits (and the debt ratio was persistently breached). In light of these experiences, the rise in budget deficits during the Great Recession and the perception that balanced budgets were needed, the European leaders decided, in December 2011, to adopt tighter rules on budget deficits and stricter enforcement of those rules.

The "fiscal compact" rules are now embedded in the inter-government Treaty on Stability, Coordination and Governance, with the budget rules written into national constitutions or their equivalents. The deficit rule becomes the requirement of a "balanced structural budget," that is, a budget which is balanced (or close, with a deficit of less than 0.5% of GDP) when the economy is operating at potential output (or a zero "output gap"). There is a further deflationary twist, with the addition of an "excess deficit procedure" to force governments with debt ratios of over 60% to run budget surpluses. There is also a requirement for the submission of national budgets to the European Commission, which will have the power to require that they be revised.

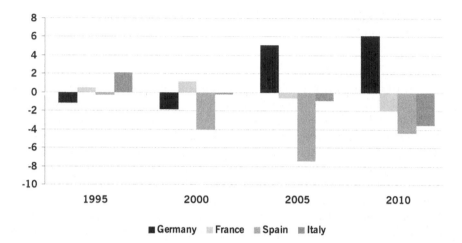

1995   2000   2005   2010

■ Germany   ■ France   ■ Spain   ■ Italy

This figure illustrates the major differences among these four major countries in terms of the degree to which private savings and private investment differ. There is a tendency for investment to be less than savings. Spain is the exception here where the (unsustainable) construction boom of the mid-2000s led to high levels of investment, largely funded by borrowing from outside the country. Note the position of Germany, where savings greatly exceed investment.

The underlying rationale appears to be that governments are profligate, running deficits for the hell of it, and have to be contained. In this account, the euro crisis was due to fiscal indiscipline; consequently, more discipline is the only solution. This is the rationale given, though it is also a mechanism for austerity, which ruling elites have independent reasons for wanting (e.g., dismantling the welfare state). So the treaty need not be viewed as merely misguided, but as reflecting ruling elites' interests. If budget deficits were due to government profligacy, however, we would observe that the private sector was being "crowded out" and the economy overheating. There was precious little evidence of that.

There is, in fact, a quite different reason for governments to run budget deficits—to secure a reasonable level of demand. This is not the case for all government deficits, but it is for the majority. There is no good reason for a balanced-budget requirement that places restrictions on the use of fiscal policy in the face of economic crises. There are already signs that countries are not able to meet the targets set by the "fiscal compact," with failures to meet the budget deficit reductions demanded. In other words, the intermediate targets set by the treaty as steps towards the compact coming fully into force.

Our Critique

Countries differ substantially in terms of their balance between private savings and private investment (see Figure 1) and their current account position (see Figure 2). Figure 1 highlights the huge investment boom in Spain that came crashing down when the crisis hit. It also shows how Germany had a larger and larger excess of savings over investment, which raises the question of how it could sustain economic growth and low unemployment with this big "leakage" from aggregate demand. Figure 2 shows how "peripheral" countries, like Spain, had little or no trade deficit—or, as in the case of Italy, a modest trade surplus—until the recent boom. Meanwhile, Germany's recent enormous trade surpluses gave it the ability to avoid large fiscal deficits despite its excess savings. By definition, for all countries, the budget position (government spending minus taxes) plus the balance between private investment and savings (investment minus savings) plus the current account balance (primarily the trade balance, i.e. exports minus imports) must add up to zero. If the second and third components differ across countries, then necessarily those countries' budget positions must differ. It does not make much sense to impose the same budget deficit requirements on each country when there are these other differences.

Imposing a balanced budget requirement means that the other two components, 1) private investment minus private savings and 2) the current account balance, must sum to zero. There is little reason to think that such a relationship is compatible with economy operating at potential output, let alone at full employment. Attempts to achieve a balanced structural budget—without actions that will raise investment, lower savings, or promote net exports—are doomed. The pursuit of balanced budgets will involve cutting public expenditures and raising taxes; it will not achieve the bud-

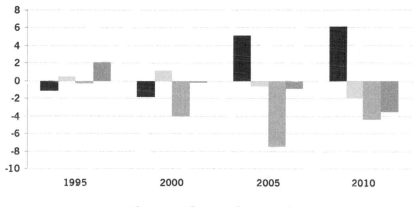

get targets and will inflict a great deal of misery along the way.

How long will it take until the eurozone authorities and countries recognize that the conditions of the "fiscal compact" are unattainable in the sense that, while some countries are able to have a budget balanced at "potential output," most cannot? Continuing to insist that fiscal austerity be pursued to balance budgets will bring misery. This is both a misguided policy that unwittingly inflicts misery in a futile pursuit, and it is a purposeful policy that policymakers are willing to impose with little thought to how much misery it causes. But now that the structural balanced-budget requirement is written into national constitutions, with penalties for failure to do, how will the countries that have signed the Treaty escape that straight jacket when it becomes apparent that such balanced budgets cannot be achieved?

Sources: European Commission, Economic and Financial Affairs, Annual macro-economic database (AMECO), series on balance on current transactions, private savings, private gross fixed capital formation, and gross domestic production (ec.europa.eu), accessed September 2013.\

Chapter 9

RESISTANCE AND ALTERNATIVES

INTRODUCTION

Many of the articles in this book are about problems in the U.S. and global economies. Both the dominant economic ideologies and the ruling institutions, many authors argue, favor the wealthy and powerful and are stacked against workers, poor people, developing countries, and other less-powerful actors in the domestic and intenational economies. That is not, however, the whole story. Those who are getting a raw deal under existing arrangements are not merely passive victims. Some are standing up and resisting poverty, inequality, and enforced powerlessness. Some are fighting for changes in policies and institutions that would help shift the existing balance of power, and improve conditions of life for those at the "bottom," for a change. This chapter describes both resistance and alternatives to the current "neoliberal" economic orthodoxy, on the domestic U.S. and international scenes.

The first three articles in this chapter focus on the U.S. economy and its institutions. For starters, economist Jeannette Wicks-Lim argues that a clean-energy program would produce more jobs, dollar for dollar, than fossil-fuel related activities. She adds that while a clean-energy program would generate jobs for workers at all levels of education, many of those jobs would be accessible to workers without a college education, who have been the hardest hit in the Great Recession (Article 9.1).

Next, economist Gerald Friedman makes the case that a single-payer health-care system can not only solve the health-care mess in the United States but also reduce the strain on government budgets that comes from continuously rising health costs (Article 9.2).

Rounding out the domestic section of this chapter, economist Robert Pollin makes the case for transforming the Fed into a democratically controlled investment bank that serves the interests of all of us (Article 9.3).

The rest of the chapter turns toward the international economy. Economist Armagan Gezici examines the return of "capital controls"—regulations on international financial flows—to world prominence (Article 9.4). She notes how some developing countries bucked the "free market" orthodoxy and embraced capital controls in the wake of the global economic crisis. Far from being just emergency measures, however, she argues for them as part of the permanent toolkit of economic policy.

Marjolein van der Veen explores the competing ways out of the economic crisis, focusing on Greece but with broader implications for Europe and the world (Article 9.5). She describes not only the neoliberal "austerity" path that has dominated to date, but also Keynesian and socialist alternatives.

Robin Broad explains the corporate "rights" embedded in many trade agreements, rights that limit the ability of citizens and democratic governments to pass and enforce laws to protect consumers, workers, public health, and the environment (Article 9.6). But the expansion of corporate power is contested and Broad summarizes some of the ongoing activism seeking to reassert local democratic governance.

Lastly, Dean Baker observes that the U.S. workforce is split between the overworked and the unemployed and suggests a more equitable distribution of work hours to address both problems (Article 9.7). Reducing average work hours could bring more people into paid employment and allow us to convert productivity gains into more leisure time. With lower unemployment rates, workers would also have a better shot at capturing a healthy share of those productivity gains in their wages.

Discussion Questions

1. (Article 9.1) What factors make government spending on clean energy an effective economic stimulus and jobs program?

2. (Article 9.2) What are the different cost savings that Friedman argues a single-payer, universal health-care system would provide while improving heath-care results? In your estimation, how does the single-payer proposal Friedman discusses measure up against our current health-care policies?

3. (Article 9.3) What are the chief elements of Pollin's proposal to transform the Fed? How would the Fed's focus and decision-making change? Do you think Pollin's proposal would be effective?

4. (Article 9.4) What are "capital controls"? What are some possible negative consequences of uncontrolled capital inflows on developing countries' economies? Why does Gezici argue that capital controls are an essential part of developing countries' normal economic-policy repertoire, not only temporary emergency measures?

5. (Article 9.5) Describe each of the three main "ways out" of the Greek economic crisis. What factors do you think will determine what kind of solution is eventually implemented?

6. (Article 9.6) Why does Broad argue that investor rights are in conflict with citizens' right to democratic self-governance?

7. (Article 9.7) Baker's article includes some thought exercises to illustrate the connection between average work hours for those employed and the unemployment rate. If our goal is to redistribute work hours to increase leisure time and decrease the unemployment rate, how do you think we could accomplish this change in real time in the real world?

Article 9.1

WE NEED A (GREEN) JOBS PROGRAM

Clean-energy investment would promote job growth for a wide swath of the U.S. workforce.

BY JEANNETTE WICKS-LIM
September/October 2010

Fourteen months of an unemployment rate at or near 10% clearly calls for the federal government to take a lead role in job creation. The White House should push its clean-energy agenda as a jobs program but steer clear of all the hype about "green-collar" jobs. Green-collar jobs are widely perceived as job opportunities accessible only to an elite segment of the U.S. workforce—those with advanced degrees, such as environmental engineers, lab technicians, and research scientists. Such jobs are inaccessible to the 52% of unemployed workers with no college experience. The truth is, however, that clean-energy investments could serve as a powerful engine for job growth for a wide swath of the U.S. workforce.

My colleagues at the Political Economy Research Institute and I examined a clean-energy program that includes making buildings more energy efficient, expanding and improving mass transit, updating the national electric grid, and developing each of three types of renewable energy sources: wind, solar, and biomass fuels. Here's what we found.

First, clean-energy activities produce more jobs, dollar for dollar, than fossil fuel-related activities. This is because clean-energy activities tend to be more labor intensive (i.e., more investment dollars go to hiring workers than buying machines), have a higher domestic content (i.e., more dollars are spent on goods and services produced within the United States) and have lower average wages than fossil fuel-related activities. The figures in the table below show how a $1 million investment in clean-energy activities would create more than three times the number of jobs that would be created by investing the same amount in fossil fuels.

Second, many clean energy sector jobs would be accessible to workers with no college experience. The table also shows how the jobs created by a $1 million investment in clean energy would be spread across three levels of education: high school degree or less, some college, and B.A. or more. Nearly half of the clean energy jobs would be held by workers with a high school degree or less. These include jobs for construction laborers, carpenters, and bus drivers. Fewer than one-quarter of clean-energy jobs would require a B.A. or more. The figures for the fossil fuels sector (second column) show that they are more heavily weighted toward jobs requiring college degrees.

Does this mean green investments will just create lots of low-paying jobs? No. The figures in the table on the next page show that investing $1 million in green activities rather than fossil fuel-related activities would generate many more jobs for workers at *all three levels* of formal education credentials. Compared to the fossil fuels sector, the clean energy sector would produce nearly four times the number

JOB CREATION: CLEAN ENERGY VS. FOSSIL FUELS

Number of jobs created by investing $1 million dollars in clean energy versus fossil-fuels activities, by education credentials

Education Credentials	Clean Energy	Fossil Fuels
Total	16.7 jobs (100%)	5.3 jobs (100%)
High school diploma or less	8.0 jobs (47.9%)	2.2 jobs (41.5%)
Some college, no B.A.	4.8 jobs (28.7%)	1.6 jobs (30.2%)
B.A. or more	3.9 jobs (23.3%)	1.5 jobs (28.3%)

of jobs that require a high school degree or less, three times the number of jobs that require some college experience, and 2.5 times the number of jobs that require a B.A. or more. Green investments would produce more jobs at all education and wage levels, even while generating proportionately *more* jobs that are accessible to workers with a high school degree or less.

Workers are right to worry about whether these high school degree jobs would offer family-supporting wages. Construction laborers, for example, average at $29,000 annually—awfully close to the $22,000 official poverty line. In addition, women and workers of color have historically faced discrimination in the construction industry, which would be the source of a lot of the lower-credentialed jobs in the clean energy sector. Workers will need to do some serious organizing to put in place labor protections such as living-wage laws, strong collective bargaining rights, and affirmative action policies to insure that these jobs pay decent wages and are equally accessible to all qualified workers. ❑

Sources: Robert Pollin, Jeannette Wicks-Lim, and Heidi Garrett-Peltier, *Green Prosperity: How Clean-Energy Policies Can Fight Poverty and Raise Living Standards in the United States,* Political Economy Research Institute, 2009, www.peri.umass.edu/green_prosperity.

Article 9.2

UNIVERSAL HEALTH CARE:
CAN WE AFFORD ANYTHING LESS?

Why only a single-payer system can solve America's health-care mess.

BY GERALD FRIEDMAN
July/August 2011

America's broken health-care system suffers from what appear to be two separate problems. From the right, a chorus warns of the dangers of rising costs; we on the left focus on the growing number of people going without health care because they lack adequate insurance. This division of labor allows the right to dismiss attempts to extend coverage while crying crocodile tears for the 40 million uninsured. But the division between problem of cost and the problem of coverage is misguided. It is founded on the assumption, common among neoclassical economists, that the current market system is efficient. Instead, however, the current system is inherently inefficient; it is the very source of the rising cost pressures. In fact, the only way we can control health-care costs and avoid fiscal and economic catastrophe is to establish a single-payer system with universal coverage.

The rising cost of health care threatens the U.S. economy. For decades, the cost of health insurance has been rising at over twice the general rate of inflation; the share of American income going to pay for health care has more than doubled since 1970 from 7% to 17%. By driving up costs for employees, retirees, the needy, the young, and the old, rising health-care costs have become a major problem for governments at every level. Health costs are squeezing public spending needed for education and infrastructure. Rising costs threaten all Americans by squeezing the income available for other activities. Indeed, if current trends continued, the entire economy would be absorbed by health care by the 2050s.

Conservatives argue that providing universal coverage would bring this fiscal Armageddon on even sooner by increasing the number of people receiving care. Following this logic, their policy has been to restrict access to health care by raising insurance deductibles, copayments, and cost sharing and by reducing access to insurance. Even before the Great Recession, growing numbers of American adults were uninsured or underinsured. Between 2003 and 2007, the share of non-elderly adults without adequate health insurance rose from 35% to 42%, reaching 75 million. This number has grown substantially since then, with the recession reducing employment and with the continued decline in employer-provided health insurance. Content to believe that our current health-care system is efficient, conservatives assume that costs would have risen more had these millions not lost access, and likewise believe that extending health-insurance coverage to tens of millions using a plan like the Affordable Care Act would drive up costs even further. Attacks on employee health insurance and on Medicare and Medicaid come from this same logic—the idea that the only way to control health-care costs is to reduce the number of people with access to health care. If we do not find a way to control costs by increasing access, there will be more proposals like that of Rep. Paul Ryan (R-Wisc.) and the Republicans in the House of Representatives to slash Medicaid and abolish Medicare.

The Problem of Cost in a Private, For-Profit Health Insurance System

If health insurance were like other commodities, like shoes or bow ties, then reducing access might lower costs by reducing demands on suppliers for time and materials. But health care is different because so much of the cost of providing it is in the administration of the payment system rather than in the actual work of doctors, nurses, and other providers, and because coordination and cooperation among different providers is essential for effective and efficient health care. It is not cost pressures on providers that are driving up health-care costs; instead, costs are rising because of what economists call transaction costs, the rising cost of administering and coordinating a system that is designed to reduce access.

The health-insurance and health-care markets are different from most other markets because private companies selling insurance do not want to sell to everyone, but only to those unlikely to need care (and, therefore, most likely to drop coverage if prices rise). As much as 70% of the "losses" suffered by health-insurance providers—that is, the money they pay out in claims—goes to as few as 10% of their subscribers. This creates a powerful incentive for companies to screen subscribers, to identify those likely to submit claims, and to harass them so that they will drop their coverage and go elsewhere. The collection of insurance-related information has become a major source of waste in the American economy because it is not organized to improve patient care but to harass and to drive away needy subscribers and their health-care providers. Because driving away the sick is so profitable for health insurers, they are doing it more and more, creating the enormous bureaucratic waste that characterizes the process of billing and insurance handling. Rising by over 10% a year for the past 25 years, health insurers' administrative costs are among the fastest-growing in the U.S. health-care sector. Doctors in private practice now spend as much as 25% of their revenue on administration, nearly $70,000 per physician for billing and insurance costs.

For-profit health insurance also creates waste by discouraging people from receiving preventive care and by driving the sick into more expensive care settings. Almost a third of Americans with "adequate" health insurance go without care every year due to costs, and the proportion going without care rises to over half of those with "inadequate" insurance and over two-thirds for those without insurance. Nearly half of the uninsured have no regular source of care, and a third did not fill a prescription in the past year because of cost. All of this unutilized care might appear to save the system money. But it doesn't. Reducing access does not reduce health-care expenditures when it makes people sicker and pushes them into hospitals and emergency rooms, which are the most expensive settings for health care and are often the least efficient because care provided in these settings rarely has continuity or follow-up.

The great waste in our current private insurance system is an opportunity for policy because it makes it possible to economize on spending by replacing our current system with one providing universal access. I have estimated that in Massachusetts, a state with a relatively efficient health-insurance system, it would be possible to lower the cost of providing health care by nearly 16% even after providing coverage to everyone in the state currently without insurance (see Table 1). This could be done largely by reducing the cost of administering the private insurance system, with most of the savings coming within providers' offices by reducing the costs of billing and processing insurance claims. This is a conservative estimate made for a state with a relatively efficient health-insurance system. In a report prepared for the state of Vermont, William Hsiao of the Harvard School of Public Health and MIT economist Jonathan Gruber estimate that shifting to a single-payer system could lead to savings of around 25% through reduced administrative cost and improved delivery of care. (They have also noted that administrative savings would be even larger if the entire country shifted to a single-payer system because this would save the cost of billing people with private, out-of-state insurance plans.) In Massachusetts, my conservative estimates suggests that as much as $10 billion a year could be saved by shifting to a single-payer system.

Single-Payer Systems Control Costs by Providing Better Care

Adoption of a single-payer health-insurance program with universal coverage could also save money and improve care by allowing better coordination of care among different providers and by providing a continuity of care that is not possible with competing insurance plans. A comparison of health care in the United States with health care in other countries shows how large these cost savings might be. When Canada first adopted its current health-care financing system in 1968, the health-care share of the national gross domestic product in the United States (7.1%) was

TABLE 1: SOURCES OF SAVINGS AND ADDED COSTS FOR A HYPTHETICAL MASSACHUSETTS SINGLE-PAYER HEALTH SYSTEM

Change in health-care expenditures	Size of change as share of total health-care expenditures
Savings from single-payer system	
Administration costs within health-insurance system	-2.0%
Administrative costs within providers' offices	-10.1%
Reduction in provider prices through reducing market leverage for privileged providers	-5.0%
Savings:	-17.1%
Increased costs from single-payer	
Expansion in coverage to the uninsured	+1.35%
Increased utilization because of elimination of copayments, balanced by improvements in preventive care	+/- 0.0%
Total increased costs:	+1.35%
Net change in health-care expenditures:	-15.75%

Source: Calculations by the author from data in OECD Health Data 2010 (oecd.org).

nearly the same as in Canada (6.9%), and only a little higher than in other advanced economies. Since then, however, health care has become dramatically more expensive in the United States. In the United States, per capita health-care spending since 1971 has risen by over $6,900 compared with an increase of less than $3,600 in Canada and barely $3,200 elsewhere (see Table 2). Physician Steffie Woolhandler and others have shown how much of this discrepancy between the experience of the United States and Canada can be associated with the lower administrative costs of Canada's single-payer system; she has found that administrative costs are nearly twice as high in the United States as in Canada—31% of costs versus 17%.

The United States is unique among advanced economies both for its reliance on private health insurance and for rapid inflation in health-care costs. Health-care costs have risen faster in the United States than in any other advanced economy: twice as fast as in Canada, France, Germany, Sweden, or the United Kingdom. We might accept higher and rapidly rising costs had Americans experienced better health outcomes. But using life expectancy at birth as a measure of general health, we have gone from a relatively healthy country to a relatively unhealthy one. Our gain in life expectancy since 1971 (5.4 years for women) is impressive except when put beside other advanced economies (where the average increase is 7.3 years).

The relatively slow increase in life expectancy in the United States highlights the gross inefficiency of our private health-care system. Had the United States increased life expectancy at the same dollar cost as in other countries, we would have saved nearly $4,500 per person. Or, put another way, had we increased life expectancy at the same rate as other countries, our spending increase since 1971 would have bought an extra 15 years of life expectancy, 10 years more than we have. The failure of American

TABLE 2: GREATER INCREASE IN COST FOR
U.S. HEALTH-CARE SYSTEM, 1971-2007

	U.S. vs. Canada		U.S. vs. 5-country average	
	Dollars	Share of GDP	Dollars	Share of GDP
Extra increase 1971-2007	$3,356	5.40%	$3,690	4.72%
Extra adjusted for smaller life expectancy gain	$4,006	5.98%	$4,480	5.73%
	As share of national health expenditures			
Extra increase 1971-2007	45%		49%	
Extra adjusted for smaller life expectancy gain	53%		59%	

Note: The first line shows how much faster health-care spending rose per person and as a share of gross domestic product in the United States compared with Canada and with the average of five countries (Canada, France, Germany, Sweden, and the United Kingdom). The second row adjusts this increase for the slower rate of growth in life expectancy in the United States than in these other countries. The third and fourth rows estimate the degree of waste in our health-care system as the proportion of total expenditures accounted for by the extra increases in health-care expenditures in the United States.

Source: Calculations by the author from data in OECD Health Data 2010 (oecd.org).

life expectancy to rise as fast as life expectancy elsewhere can be directly tied to the inequitable provision of health care through our private, for-profit health-insurance system. Increases in life expectancy since 1990 have been largely restricted to relatively affluent Americans with better health insurance. Since 1990, men in the top 50% of the income distribution have had a six-year increase in life expectancy at age 65 compared with an increase of only one year for men earning below the median.

R ising health-care costs reflect in part the greater costs of caring for an aging population with more chronic conditions. As such, the United States looks especially bad because our population is aging less quickly than that of other countries because of high rates of immigration, relatively higher fertility, and the slower increase in life expectancy in the United States. Countries also buy higher life expectancy by spending on health care; rising health expenditures have funded improvements in treat-

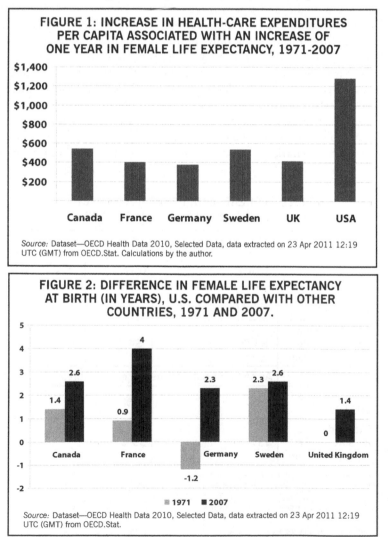

FIGURE 1: INCREASE IN HEALTH-CARE EXPENDITURES PER CAPITA ASSOCIATED WITH AN INCREASE OF ONE YEAR IN FEMALE LIFE EXPECTANCY, 1971-2007

Source: Dataset—OECD Health Data 2010, Selected Data, data extracted on 23 Apr 2011 12:19 UTC (GMT) from OECD.Stat. Calculations by the author.

FIGURE 2: DIFFERENCE IN FEMALE LIFE EXPECTANCY AT BIRTH (IN YEARS), U.S. COMPARED WITH OTHER COUNTRIES, 1971 AND 2007.

Source: Dataset—OECD Health Data 2010, Selected Data, data extracted on 23 Apr 2011 12:19 UTC (GMT) from OECD.Stat.

ment that have contributed to rising life expectancy throughout the world. Female life expectancy at birth has increased by nearly nine years in Germany since 1971, by over eight years in France, by seven years in Canada and the United Kingdom, and by six years in Sweden. By contrast, the United States, where female life expectancy increased by a little over five years, has done relatively poorly despite increasing health-care expenditures that dwarf those of other countries. In other countries, increasing expenditures by about $500 per person is associated with an extra year of life expectancy. With our privatized health-insurance system, we need spending increases over twice as large to gain an extra year of life (see Figure 1, previous page).

The international comparison also provides another perspective on any supposed trade-off between containing costs and expanding coverage. In countries other than the United States, almost all of the increase in health-care spending as a share of national income is due to better quality health care as measured by improvements in life expectancy (see Figure 2, previous page). The problem of rising health-care costs is almost unique to the United States, the only advanced industrialized country without universal coverage and without any effective national health plan.

In short, the question is not whether we can afford a single-payer health-insurance system that would provide adequate health care for all Americans. The real question is: can we afford anything else? ❏

Sources: Cathy Shoen, "How Many Are Underinsured? Trends Among U.S. Adults, 2003 and 2007," Health Affairs, June 10, 2008; "Insured but Poorly Protected: How Many Are Underinsured? U. S. Adults Trends, 2003 to 2007," Commonwealth Fund, June 10, 2008 (commonwealthfund.org); David Cutler and Dan Ly, "The (Paper) Work of Medicine: Understanding International Medical Costs," Journal of Economic Perspectives, Spring 2011; Stephen M. Davidson, Still Broken: Understanding the U.S. Health Care System, Stanford Business Books, 2010; P Franks and C M Clancy, "Health insurance and mortality. Evidence from a national cohort," The Journal of the American Medical Association, August 11, 1993; Allan Garber and Jonathan Skinner, "Is American Health Care Uniquely Inefficient?" Journal of Economic Perspectives, Fall 2008; Jonathan Gruber, "The Role of Consumer Co-payments for Health Care: Lessons from the RAND Health Insurance Experiment and Beyond," Kaiser Family Foundation, October 2006 (kff.org); David Himmelstein and Steffie Woolhandler, "Administrative Waste in the U.S. Health Care System in 2003," International Journal of Health Services, 2004; "The Uninsured: A Primer: Supplemental Data Tables," Kaiser Family Foundation, December 2010; Karen Davis and Cathy Shoen, "Slowing the Growth of U.S. Health Care Expenditures: What are the Options?" Commonwealth Fund, January 2007 (commonwealthfund. org); "Accounting for the Cost of Health Care in the United States," McKinsey Global Institute, January 2007 (mckinsey.com); "Investigation of Health Care Cost Trends and Cost Drivers," Office of Massachusetts Attorney General Martha Coakley, January 29, 2010 (mass.gov); Trends in Mortality Differentials and Life Expectancy for Male Social Security-Covered Workers, by Average Relative Earnings by Hilary Waldron, Social Security Administration, October 2007; Richard G. Wilkinson, The Spirit Level, Bloomsbury Press, 2010; William Hsiao and Steven Kappel, "Act 128: Health System Reform Design. Achieving Affordable Universal Health Care in Vermont," January 21, 2011 (leg.state.vt.us); Steffie Woolhandler and Terry Campbell, "Cost of Health Care Administration in the United States and Canada," New England Journal of Medicine, 2003.

Article 9.3

TRANSFORMING THE FED

BY ROBERT POLLIN
November 1992

The U.S. financial system faces deep structural problems. Households, businesses, and the federal government are burdened by excessive debts. The economy favors short-term speculation over long-term investment. An unrepresentative and unresponsive elite has extensive control over the financial system. Moreover, the federal government is incapable of reversing these patterns through its existing tools, including fiscal, monetary, and financial regulatory policies.

I propose a dramatically different approach: transforming the Federal Reserve System (the "Fed") into a public investment bank. Such a bank would have substantial power to channel credit in ways that counter financial instability and support productive investment by private businesses. The Fed would use its powers to influence how and for what purposes banks, insurance companies, brokers, and other lenders loan money.

The U.S. government has used credit allocation policies, such as low-cost loans, loan guarantees, and home mortgage interest deductions, extensively and with success. Its primary accomplishment has been to create a home mortgage market that, for much of the period since World War II, provided non-wealthy households with unprecedented access to home ownership.

I propose increasing democratic control over the Federal Reserve's activities by decentralizing power to the 12 district Fed banks and instituting popular election of their boards of directors. This would create a mechanism for extending democracy throughout the financial system.

My proposal also offers a vehicle for progressives to address two separate but equally serious questions facing the U.S. economy:

- how to convert our industrial base out of military production and toward the development and adoption of environmentally benign production techniques; and
- how to increase opportunities for high wage, high productivity jobs in the United States. The U.S. needs such jobs to counteract the squeeze on wages from increasingly globalized labor and financial markets.

Transforming the Federal Reserve system into a public investment bank will help define an economic path toward democratic socialism in the United States.

My proposal has several strengths as a transitional program. It offers a mechanism for establishing democratic control over finance and investment—the area where capital's near-dictatorial power is most decisive. The program will also work within the United States' existing legal and institutional framework. We could implement parts of it immediately using existing federal agencies and with minimal demands on the federal budget.

At the same time, if an ascendant progressive movement put most of the program in place, this would represent a dramatic step toward creating a new economic system. Such a system would still give space to market interactions and the pursuit of greed, but would nevertheless strongly promote general well-being over business profits.

How the Fed Fails

At present the Federal Reserve focuses its efforts on managing short-term fluctuations of the economy, primarily by influencing interest rates. When it reduces rates, it seeks to increase borrowing and spending, and thereby stimulate economic growth and job opportunities. When the Fed perceives that wages and prices are rising too fast (a view not necessarily shared by working people), it tries to slow down borrowing and spending by raising interest rates.

This approach has clearly failed to address the structural problems plaguing the financial system. The Fed did nothing, for example, to prevent the collapse of the savings and loan industry. It stood by while highly speculative mergers, buyouts, and takeovers overwhelmed financial markets in the 1980s. It has failed to address the unprecedented levels of indebtedness and credit defaults of private corporations and households.

New Roles for the Fed

Under my proposal, the Federal Reserve would shift its focus from the short to the long term. It would provide more and cheaper credit to banks and other financiers who loan money to create productive assets and infrastructure—which promote high wage, high productivity jobs. The Fed would make credit more expensive for lenders that finance speculative activities such as the mergers, buyouts, and takeovers that dominated the 1980s.

The Fed would also give favorable credit terms to banks that finance decent affordable housing rather than luxury housing and speculative office buildings. It would make low-cost credit available for environmental research and development so the economy can begin the overdue transition to environmentally benign production. Cuts in military spending have idled many workers and productive resources, both of which could be put to work in such transformed industries.

Finally, the Fed would give preferential treatment to loans that finance investment in the United States rather than in foreign countries. This would help counter the trend of U.S. corporations to abandon the domestic economy in search of lower wages and taxes.

The first step in developing the Fed's new role would be for the public to determine which sectors of the economy should get preferential access to credit. One example, suggested above, is industrial conversion from military production to investment in renewable energy and conservation.

Once the public establishes its investment goals, the Fed will have to develop new policy tools and use its existing tools in new ways to accomplish them. I propose that a transformed Federal Reserve use two major methods:

- set variable cash ("asset reserve") requirements for all lenders, based on the social value of the activities the lenders are financing; and
- increase discretionary lending activity by the 12 district Federal Reserve banks.

Varying Banks' Cash Requirements

The Fed currently requires that banks and other financial institutions keep a certain amount of their assets available in cash reserves. Banks, for example, must carry three cents in cash for every dollar they hold in checking accounts. A bank cannot make interest-bearing loans on such "reserves." I propose that the Fed make this percent significantly lower for loans that finance preferred activities than for less desirable investment areas. Let's say the public decides that banks should allocate 10% of all credit to research and development of new environmental technologies, such as non-polluting autos and organic farming. Then financial institutions that have made 10% of their loans in environmental technologies would not have to hold any cash reserves against these loans. But if a bank made no loans in the environmental area, then it would have to hold 10% of its total assets in reserve. The profit motive would force banks to support environmental technologies without any direct expenditure from the federal budget.

All profit-driven firms will naturally want to avoid this reserve requirement. The Fed must therefore apply it uniformly to all businesses that profit through accepting deposits and making loans. These include banks, savings and loans, insurance companies, and investment brokerage houses. If the rules applied only to banks, for example, then banks could circumvent the rules by redefining themselves as another type of lending institution.

Loans to Banks That Do the Right Thing

The Federal Reserve has the authority now to favor some banks over others by making loans to them when they are short on cash. For the most part, however, the Fed has chosen not to exercise such discretionary power. Instead it aids all banks equally, through a complex mechanism known as open market operations, which increases total cash reserves in the banking system. The Fed could increase its discretionary lending to favored banks by changing its operating procedures without the federal government creating any new laws or institutions. Such discretionary lending would have several benefits.

First, to a much greater extent than at present, financial institutions would obtain reserves when they are lending for specific purposes. If a bank's priorities should move away from the established social priorities, the Fed could then either refuse to make more cash available to it, or charge a penalty interest rate, thereby discouraging the bank from making additional loans. The Fed, for example, could impose such obstacles on lenders that are financing mergers, takeovers, and buyouts.

In addition, the Fed could use this procedure to more effectively monitor and regulate financial institutions. Banks, in applying for loans, would have to submit to the Fed's scrutiny on a regular basis. The Fed could more closely link its regulation to banks' choices of which investments to finance.

Implementing this procedure will also increase the authority of the 12 district banks within the Federal Reserve system, since these banks approve the Fed's loans. Each district bank will have more authority to set lending rates and monitor bank compliance with regulations.

The district banks could then more effectively enforce measures such as the Community Reinvestment Act, which currently mandates that banks lend in their home communities. Banks that are committed to their communities and regions, such as the South Shore Bank in Chicago, could gain substantial support under this proposed procedure.

Other Credit Allocation Tools

The Fed can use other tools to shift credit to preferred industries, such as loan guarantees, interest rate subsidies, and government loans. In the past the U.S. government has used these techniques with substantial success. They now primarily support credit for housing, agriculture, and education. Indeed, as of 1991, these programs subsidized roughly one-third of all loans in the United States.

Jesse Jackson's 1988 Presidential platform suggested an innovative way of extending such policies. He proposed that public pension funds channel a portion of their money into a loan guarantee program, with the funds used to finance investments in low cost housing, education, and infrastructure.

There are disadvantages, however, to the government using loan guarantee programs and similar approaches rather than the Fed's employing asset reserve requirements and discretionary lending. Most important is that the former are more expensive and more difficult to administer. Both loan guarantees and direct government loans require the government to pay off the loans when borrowers default. Direct loans also mean substantial administrative costs. Interest subsidies on loans are direct costs to government even when the loans are paid back.

In contrast, with variable asset reserve requirements and discretionary lending policies, the Fed lowers the cost of favored activities, and raises the cost of unfavored ones, without imposing any burden on the government's budget.

Increasing Public Control

The Federal Reserve acts in relative isolation from the political process at present. The U.S. president appoints seven members of the Fed's Board of Governors for 14 year terms, and they are almost always closely tied to banking and big business. The boards of directors of the 12 district banks appoint their presidents, and these boards are also composed of influential bankers and business people within each of the districts.

The changes I propose will mean a major increase in the central bank's role as an economic planning agency for the nation. Unless we dramatically improve democratic control by the public over the Fed, voters will correctly interpret such efforts as an illegitimate grasp for more power by business interests.

Democratization should proceed through redistributing power downward to the 12 district banks. When the Federal Reserve System was formed in 1913, the principle behind creating district banks along with the headquarters in Washington was to disperse the central bank's authority. This remains a valuable idea, but the U.S. government has never seriously attempted it. Right now the district banks are highly undemocratic and have virtually no power.

One way to increase the district banks' power is to create additional seats for them on the Open Market Committee, which influences short-term interest rates by expanding or contracting the money supply.

A second method is to shift authority from the Washington headquarters to the districts. The Board of Governors would then be responsible for setting general guidelines, while the district banks would implement discretionary lending and enforcement of laws such as the Community Reinvestment Act.

The most direct way of democratizing the district banks would be to choose their boards in regular elections along with other local, regional, and state-wide officials. The boards would then choose the top levels of the banks' professional staffs and oversee the banks' activities.

Historical Precedents

Since World War II other capitalist countries have extensively employed the types of credit allocation policies proposed here. Japan, France, and South Korea are the outstanding success stories, though since the early 1980s globalization and deregulation of financial markets have weakened each of their credit policies. When operating at full strength, the Japanese and South Korean programs primarily supported large-scale export industries, such as steel, automobiles, and consumer electronics. France targeted its policies more broadly to coordinate Marshall Plan aid for the development of modern industrial corporations.

We can learn useful lessons from these experiences, not least that credit allocation policies do work when they are implemented well. But substantial differences exist between experiences elsewhere and the need for a public investment bank in the United States.

In these countries a range of other institutions besides the central bank were involved in credit allocation policies. These included their treasury departments and explicit planning agencies, such as the powerful Ministry of International Trade and Industry (MITI) in Japan. In contrast, I propose to centralize the planning effort at the Federal Reserve.

We could create a new planning institution to complement the work of the central bank. But transforming the existing central banking system rather than creating a new institution minimizes both start-up problems and the growth of bureaucracies.

A second and more fundamental difference between my proposal and the experiences in Japan, France, and South Korea is that their public investment institutions were accountable only to a business-oriented elite. This essentially dictatorial approach is antithetical to the goal of increasing democratic control of the financial system.

The challenge, then, is for the United States to implement effective credit allocation policies while broadening, not narrowing, democracy. Our success ultimately will depend on a vigorous political movement that can fuse two equally urgent, but potentially conflicting goals: economic democracy, and equitable and sustainable growth. If we can meet this challenge, it will represent a historic victory toward the construction of a democratic socialist future. ❑

Resources: Robert Pollin, "Transforming the Federal Reserve into a Public Investment Bank: Why it is Necessary; How it Should Be Done," in G. Epstein, G. Dymski and R. Pollin, eds., *Transforming the U.S. Financial System,* M.E. Sharpe, 1993.

Article 9.4

THE RETURN OF CAPITAL CONTROLS

BY ARMAGAN GEZICI
January/February 2013

In the wake of the global financial crisis, low interest rates and slow growth in advanced economies have led to a massive influx of capital into so-called emerging markets, where interest rates and growth have been higher. International investors, seeking higher returns, have moved their funds away from advanced economies into emerging-market securities like stocks, bonds, and mutual funds. The governments of many developing countries, as a result, have become increasingly concerned about the effects of these capital inflows—including stronger currencies, asset-price bubbles, and even inflation. In March 2012, Brazil's president Dilma Rousseff accused developed nations of unleashing a "monetary tsunami," which is undermining the competitiveness of emerging economies like her own. These concerns have motivated many countries to introduce measures to cope with cross-border capital flows.

Starting in late 2009, for example, Brazil began to implement "capital controls"—including a tax on capital inflows and other measures—to keep its currency (the real) from growing stronger against the dollar. Several Asian countries, including South Korea, Taiwan, and Thailand, have also implemented controls of various kinds on capital inflows. Suddenly, it appears, capital controls are back.

What Ever Happened to Capital Controls?

The debate about controls on international capital flows goes back to the World War II era. During the Bretton Woods negotiations (1944) establishing the international monetary order for the postwar period, Britain's chief negotiator, John Maynard Keynes, and his U.S. counterpart, Harry Dexter White, agreed that a distinction should be made between "speculative" capital and "productive" capital. Both believed that speculative (or "hot money") capital flows should be subject to controls. Keynes went further, arguing that "control of capital movements, both inward and outward, should be a permanent feature of the post-war system." For much of the postwar period, controls such as restrictions on the types of assets banks could hold and limits on capital outflows (used even by the United States between 1963 and 1973) were, indeed, implemented by many capitalist countries. Beginning in the 1980s, however, international financial institutions like the International Monetary Fund (IMF), many Western governments, and private high finance began to oppose capital controls. The U. S. government and the IMF became staunch advocates of "capital-account liberalization" (that is, the deregulation of international capital flows) during this period.

The recent crisis resulted in widespread recognition, around the world, that deregulated financial activity can result in major economic disruptions. In most of the world's largest economies, possible measures to re-regulate finance on the national level came back on the political agenda. Cross-border finance, however, was largely left out of the discussion, as if it did not require any regulation. Conventional discussions of this issue have also involved a peculiar twist in terminology: financial regulations are typically called "regulations" when purely domestic, yet when they involve cross-border flows, they carry the more ominous-sounding label of "controls"—as if to emphasize the undesirable nature of these regulations from a free-market perspective.

Why Capital Controls?

The essential problem with international capital flows is that they are "pro-cyclical"—that is, they amplify the patterns of the business cycle. Capital tends to flow in when economies are expanding, promoting "overheating" and inflation, and tends to flow out during downturns, exacerbating the decline in output and rise in unemployment. They also narrow the ability of governments to respond to cyclical economic problems. The economic literature on capital flows cites five fears that drive countries to adopt capital controls:

Fear of appreciation: Massive and rapid capital inflows may cause the country's currency to become stronger (increase in value relative to other currencies), making its exports more expensive and damaging its international competitiveness.

Fear of "hot money": Short-term speculative capital inflows may cause financial instability and increase the fragility of the domestic financial system. The short-term nature of these flows leads to a "maturity mismatch" between domestic financial institutions' assets and liabilities. In effect, they have borrowed short-term while lending long-term. As the sudden reversal of hot money occurs at the whim of international investor sentiments, a domestic banking crisis is likely to follow.

Fear of large inflows that can disrupt the financial system, even if they are not all "hot money": Large inflows of foreign capital may feed asset bubbles, such as unsustainable increases in stock or real-estate prices or unsustainable booms in consumer credit.

Fear of loss of monetary autonomy: It is not possible for a country to achieve (simultaneously) full international capital mobility, monetary-policy autonomy, and exchange-rate stability. (This is known as the "trilemma" of international macroeconomics.) If a country does not control international capital flows, inflows can cause exchange-rate appreciation. The government can counteract this by increasing the money supply, but then its monetary policy is not independent. To avoid exchange-rate appreciation and sustain an independent monetary policy, a country should give up full capital mobility.

Fear of capital flight: In the event of a crisis, "herding" behavior by international investors may expose a country to the risk of sharp reversals in capital flows (with capital leaving just as quickly as it came).

What Happened During the Crisis?

Between 2002 and 2007, there were massive flows of capital into emerging markets with high growth rates and relatively developed financial systems. This surge in capital inflows was interrupted after the collapse of the U.S. investment house Lehman Brothers in September 2008, which led global capital to flee to the "safety" of the U.S. market, wreaking havoc in emerging markets. (See figure.) While there was no comparable financial crisis in these economies, more than half of them experienced negative growth in 2009. Countries with already-large trade deficits were among the hardest hit, as they were highly dependent on capital inflows.

Between 2008 and 2011, however, the governments of the industrialized countries lowered interest rates in an attempt to stimulate production and employment. Capital again began to flow into emerging markets, attracted by higher interest rates and growth. The "carry trade" was a key mechanism that triggered these flows. In the carry trade, investors borrow money in one country at a low interest rate and invest it in another country at a higher rate. This strategy allows investors not only to exploit the differences in interest rates, but also take advantage of exchange-rate movements. If the currency of the country with higher interest rates becomes stronger, over time, relative to the currency of the country with lower interest rates, investors stand to make even larger profits.

By late 2008, government policymakers in emerging economies had become alarmed about the problems these inflows could cause—currency appreciation, asset bubbles, inflation, and the sudden turn toward large outflows. From March 2009 to March 2010, Brazil saw the value of the real go up by 30% against the dollar, due at least in part to the carry trade. Under normal circumstances, the conventional macroeconomic tool to stem asset bubbles or inflation would have been an increase in interest rates. By increasing interest rates, monetary authorities would have curbed the appetite to borrow and reduced the amount of money available for spending in the economy. With less spending, the economy would slow down and inflation would decline. However, because of the carry trade, such a policy could actually fuel further inflows and therefore exacerbate these problems. For example, in 2009, interest rates were around 12% in Brazil and less than 1% in the United States; if Brazil had raised interest rates in an attempt to curb asset bubbles and inflation, it could actually have attracted even higher capital inflows.

The Brazilian government was the most vocal critic of these capital flows at the G-20's 2010 summit in Seoul. The Brazilian finance minister declared the surge in capital flows, the subsequent exchange-rate appreciations, and the various policy responses by emerging countries to be the beginning of a "currency war." In late 2009, the Brazilian government imposed a 2% tax on various forms of capital inflows. In October 2010, it twice increased the tax rate, first to 4% and then to 6%. In January 2011, Brazil introduced new reserve requirements on capital inflows (see sidebar) to curb the appreciation of the real against the dollar.

In 2009, nations across Asia also began to deploy controls, having seen large appreciations of their currencies. Between the end of 2008 and early 2010, South Korea's currency (the won) appreciated by over 30% against the dollar. Starting in July 2010, South Korean banks faced new restrictions on their in-

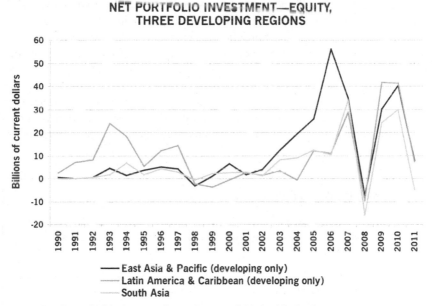

NET PORTFOLIO INVESTMENT—EQUITY, THREE DEVELOPING REGIONS

— East Asia & Pacific (developing only)
— Latin America & Caribbean (developing only)
— South Asia

Source: World Bank, Data, Portfolio equity, net inflows (BoP, current US$), (data.worldbank.org)

ternational currency holdings. The South Korean government also tried to steer investment away from speculation by permitting bank loans in foreign currencies only for the purchase of raw materials, for foreign direct investment, and for repayment of debts. Meanwhile, in November 2009, the government of Taiwan banned foreign investment funds from investing in certificates of deposit with domestic banks, a move aimed at preventing foreign investors from betting on currency appreciation. At the end of 2010, it also placed restrictions on banks' holdings of foreign currencies. In 2010, Thailand introduced a 15% tax on interest income and capital gains earned by foreign investors. Meanwhile, Indonesia placed limits on short-term external borrowing and introduced a one-month minimum holding period for foreign investors purchasing some types of government-issued securities.

It is still too early to draw final conclusions about the effectiveness of these controls. A study by Kevin Gallagher of the Global Development and Environment Institute (GDAE) provides a preliminary assessment for the cases of Brazil, Taiwan, and South Korea. All three were trying to create a space for independent monetary policy and stem the appreciation of their currencies by placing restrictions on capital mobility. Interest rates between the United States and each of these nations have become less correlated. (A strong correlation between interest rates may indicate that, when the U.S. Fed lowers interest rates, causing capital flows to these other countries, the latter are forced to respond with lower interest rates of their own to stem the appreciation of the currency. That is, they lack monetary independence.) So these findings suggest that the controls have, to some extent, allowed a more autonomous monetary policy.

In the cases of Brazil and Taiwan, there is some evidence that controls have been associated with a slower rate of currency appreciation. But in the case of South Korea, currency appreciation has continued and the rate of appreciation has actually increased since controls were initiated. This difference can be explained by the structural differences across these countries, as well as the different types of controls used. South Korea's strong export performance is an important factor putting upward pressure on the value of its currency. (Demand for a country's exports is one factor determining the demand for its currency, since that country's companies usually require payment in the national currency.) Moreover, unlike

---

How to Impose Capital Controls?

The particular form of capital controls that a government imposes depends on its policy goals. If its main goal is to slow down capital inflows, the types of regulations that it can choose from include:

Unremunerated reserve requirements: A certain percentage of new capital inflows must be kept on reserve in the country's central bank. "Unremunerated" in this context refers to the fact that no interest would be earned on these funds.

Taxes on new inflows.

Limits or taxes on how much domestic banks and other financial institutions can owe in foreign currencies.

Restrictions on currency mismatches: Borrowing and lending activities of domestic banks or firms should be denominated in the same currency. For example, only firms with foreign-exchange revenues from exports can borrow in foreign currencies.

Limitations on borrowing abroad: For example, such borrowing may be allowed only for foreign investment and trade activities, or only for firms with positive net revenues in a foreign currency (as from exports).

Mandatory government approvals for some or all international capital transactions.

Minimum stay requirements: Foreign investors might be required to stay in the domestic economy for at least a certain length of time.

On the other hand, different measures are available to a country that wants to focus on preventing or slowing down outflows of capital, including:

Mandatory government approval for domestic residents to invest abroad or hold bank accounts in a foreign currency.

Requirements for domestic residents to report on foreign investments and transactions done with foreign bank accounts.

Limits on sectors in which foreign individuals and companies can invest.

Restrictions on amounts of principal or capital income that foreign investors can send abroad.

Limits on how much non-residents can borrow in the domestic market.

Taxes on capital outflows.

In addition to the distinction between controls imposed on outflows or inflows, measures are usually categorized as "price-based" or "quantity-based," depending on the mechanism through which they impact capital flows. Minimum stay requirements, for example, are one kind of quantity-based control. Taxes on inflows or on outflows are one kind of price-based control.

Brazil and Taiwan, South Korean authorities did not use any of the "price-based controls" (see sidebar) that would have automatically placed additional costs on international investors seeking to enter Korean markets. These differences in effectiveness can shed some light on what kinds of capital controls might work in different countries, given their unique conditions.

The IMF and Capital Controls

Not long after developing-country governments began implementing capital controls, official views about controls began to shift. Since 2010, the IMF has produced a series of official papers on capital-account liberalization, on capital inflows and outflows, and on the multilateral aspects of regulating international capital flows. In November 2012, it released a comprehensive "institutional view" on when and how nations should deploy capital-account regulations. The same institution that pushed for the global deregulation of cross-border finance in the 1990s now says that capital-account liberalization is more of a long-run goal, and is not for every country at all times. The IMF now accepts that capital controls—which it has renamed "capital-flow management measures"—are permissible for inflows, on a temporary basis, en route to liberalization; regulations on capital outflows, meanwhile, are permissible only during or just after financial crises.

While more flexible than its previous stances, the new IMF position still insists on the eventual deregulation of global financial flows and emphasizes that controls should only be temporary. Behind this insistence lies the institution's ideological commitment to free markets, as well as the influence of finance capital and Wall Street interests on the institution's decision making. As the experience of developing economies in the recent crisis bears out, rather than being treated as temporary measures, capital controls should be adopted as permanent tools that can be used counter-cyclically—to smooth out economic booms and busts. As described earlier, international capital flows are strongly pro-cyclical. By regulating inflows during a boom, a government can manage booms better, while avoiding exchange-rate problems or additional inflationary pressures. By restricting outflows during a downturn, it can mitigate capital flight, which has the potential of triggering financial crisis, and create some room for expansionary monetary policy.

The IMF guidelines, in addition, give scant attention to policy-design issues related to capital controls. A great deal of international experience shows that controls can lose their effectiveness over time, as foreign investors learn to evade regulation through the use of financial derivatives and other securities. Nations such as Brazil and South Korea have increasingly "fine-tuned" their regulations in an attempt to keep ahead of investors' ability to circumvent them.

The IMF also fails to acknowledge that capital flows should be regulated at "both ends." The industrialized nations are usually the source of international capital flows, but generally ignore the negative spillover effects on other countries. So far, the entire burden of regulation has fallen on the recipients of inflows, mostly developing countries.

Where to Now?

As industrialized nations aim to recover from the crisis, they hope that credit and capital will stay "at home." Meanwhile, the developing world has little interest in having to receive capital inflows. This creates an obvious alignment of interests. Industrialized nations could adjust their tax codes and deploy other types of regulation to keep capital in their countries, as emerging markets deploy capital controls to reduce the level and change the composition of capital flows that may destabilize their economies.

One important obstacle to such coordination is the prohibition, in many trade and investment treaties, on regulation of cross-border finance. For example, in Asia, where capital controls are most prevalent, the Association of South East Asian Nations (ASEAN) requires member countries to eliminate most controls by 2015, with relatively narrow exceptions. Trade and investment agreements with the United States, such as the North American Free Trade Agreement (NAFTA) and the Dominican Republic-Central America Free Trade Agreement (CAFTA-DR), provide the least flexibility. Since the 2003 U.S.-Chile Free Trade Agreement, every U.S. trade or investment agreement has required the free flow of capital (in both directions) between the United States and its trading partners, without exception.

In January 2011, some 250 economists from across the globe called on the United States to recognize that the consensus on capital controls has shifted and to permit nations the flexibility to deploy controls to prevent and mitigate crises. The appeal was rebuffed by prominent U.S. business associations and the U.S. government. Treasury Secretary Timothy Geithner declared that U.S. policy would remain unchanged: "In general, we believe that those risks are best managed through a mix of fiscal and monetary policy measures, exchange rate adjustment, and carefully designed non-discriminatory prudential measures, such as bank reserve or capital requirements and limitations on exposure to exchange rate risk." In other words, he suggested the use of mainly conventional domestic macroeconomic policies and some domestic financial regulation, but excluded controls on international flows.

With the exception of speculators who profit from volatility in the markets, all nations and actors within them would benefit from the financial stability that an international system of financial regulation could help provide. After the opening of capital markets in developing economies, in varying degrees, we have seen extreme volatility of international capital flows. This volatility has been exacerbated by the monetary policies of advanced economies: over the past 30 years expansionary monetary policy in advanced economies has led to capital flows to emerging-market economies, while contractionary policies have produced the reversal of capital flows and, in turn, helped set off the crises of the 1980s and 1990s. The stability provided by an international system of capital controls would not only allow emerging economies to preserve their own growth and stability but also improve the effectiveness of policies in advanced economies.

Some financial interests, however, would have to bear the costs. Capital controls would either make financial transactions more costly, reducing profit margins, or not allow financial companies to take advantage of certain investment opportunities, again reducing potential profits to investors. These "losers" from a capital-controls regime are highly concentrated and very powerful politically. The "winners," in terms of the general public, are comparatively scattered and weaker politically. Despite the optimism that briefly emerged, especially in policy circles, about a future with more effective regulation of international capital flows, these political realities may be the biggest obstacles for 21st-century capital controls. ❏

Sources: Kevin Gallagher, "Regaining Control? Capital Controls and the Global Financial Crisis," Political Economy Research Institute, Working Paper 250, 2011; Stephany Griffith-Jones and Kevin P. Gallagher, "Curbing Hot Money Flows to Protect the Real Economy," Economic and Political Weekly, January 15, 2011, Vol. XLVI, No 3; Ilene Grabel, "Not Your Grandfather's IMF: Global Crisis, Productive Incoherence, and Developmental Policy Space," Political Economy Research Institute, Working Paper 214, 2010; International Monetary Fund, The Liberalization And Management Of Capital Flows: An Institutional View, Washington, D.C., 2011.

Article 9.5

GREECE AND THE CRISIS OF EUROPE: WHICH WAY OUT?

BY MARJOLEIN van der VEEN

The Greek economy has crashed, and now lies broken on the ground. The causes of the crisis are pretty well understood, but there hasn't been enough attention to the different possible ways out. Our flight crew has shown us only one emergency exit—one that is broken and just making things worse. But there is more than one way out of the crisis, not just the austerity being pushed by the so-called "Troika" (International Monetary Fund (IMF), European Commission, and European Central Bank (ECB)). We need to look around a bit more, since—as they say on every flight—the nearest exit may not be right in front of us. Can an alternative catch hold? And, if so, will it be Keynesian or socialist?

The origins of the crisis are manifold: trade imbalances between Germany and Greece, the previous Greek government's secret debts (hidden with the connivance of Wall Street banks), the 2007 global economic crisis, and the flawed construction of the eurozone (see sidebar). As Greece's economic crisis has continued to deepen, it has created a social disaster: Drastic declines in public health, a rise in suicides, surging child hunger, a massive exodus of young adults, an intensification of exploitation (longer work hours and more work days per week), and the rise of the far right and its attacks on immigrants and the LGBT community. Each new austerity package brokered between the Greek government and the Troika stipulates still more government spending cuts, tax increases, or "economic reforms"—privatization, increases in the retirement age, layoffs of public-sector workers, and wage cuts for those who remain.

While there are numerous possible paths out of the crisis, the neoliberal orthodoxy has maintained that Greece had no choice but to accept austerity. The country was broke, argued the Troika officials, economists, and commentators, and this tough medicine would ultimately help the Greek economy to grow again. As Mark Weisbrot of the Center for Economic and Policy Research (CEPR) put it, "[T]he EU authorities have opted to punish Greece—for various reasons, including the creditors' own interests in punishment, their ideology, imaginary fears of inflation, and to prevent other countries from also demanding a 'growth option.'" By focusing on neoliberal solutions, the mainstream press controls the contours of the debate. Keynesian remedies that break with the punishment paradigm are rarely discussed, let alone socialist proposals. These may well gain more attention, however, as the crisis drags on without end.

Neoliberal Solutions

Despite the fact that 30 years of neoliberalism resulted in the worst economic crisis since the Great Depression, neoliberals are undaunted and have remained intent on dishing out more of the same medicine. What they offered Greece were bailouts and haircuts (write-downs of the debt). While the country—really, the country's banks—got bailouts, the money flowed right back to repay lenders in Germany,

> ### Causes of Greece's Deepening Crisis
>
> *Trade imbalances.* Germany's wage restraint policies and high productivity made German exports more competitive (cheaper), resulting in trade surpluses for Germany and deficits for Greece. Germany then used its surplus funds to invest in Greece and other southern European countries. As German banks shoveled out loans, Greek real estate boomed, inflation rose, their exports became less competitive, and the wealthy siphoned money abroad.
>
> *Hidden debt.* To enter the eurozone in 2001, Greece's budget deficit was supposed to be below the threshold (3% of GDP) set by the Maastricht Treaty. In 2009 the newly elected Panhellenic Socialist Movement (PASOK) government discovered that the outgoing government had been hiding its deficits from the European authorities, with the help of credit default swaps sold to it by Goldman Sachs during 2002-06. The country was actually facing a deficit of 12% of GDP, thanks to extravagant military spending and tax cuts for (and tax evasion by) the rich.
>
> *Global crisis.* When the 2007 global economic crisis struck, Greece was perhaps the hardest-hit country. Investments soured, banks collapsed, and loans could not be repaid. Debt-financed household consumption could no longer be sustained. Firms cut back on investment spending, closed factories, and laid off workers. Output has fallen 20% since 2007, the unemployment rate is now above 25%, (for youth, 58%), household incomes have fallen by more than a third in the last three years, and government debt has surpassed 175% of GDP.
>
> *The eurozone trap.* Greece's government could do little on its own to rescue its economy. With eurozone countries all using the same currency, individual countries could no longer use monetary policy to stimulate their economies (e.g., by devaluing the currency to boost exports or stimulating moderate inflation to reduce the real debt burden). Fiscal policy was also weakened by the Maastricht limits on deficits and debt, resulting in tight constraints on fiscal stimulus.

France, and other countries. Very little actually went to Greek workers who fell into severe poverty. The bailouts invariably came with conditions in the form of austerity, privatization (e.g., water systems, ports, etc.), mass public-sector layoffs, labor-market "flexibilization" (making it easier to fire workers), cutbacks in unemployment insurance, and tax reforms (lowering corporate taxes and raising personal income and sales taxes). In sum, the neoliberal structural adjustment program for Greece shifted the pain onto ordinary people, rather than those most responsible for causing the crisis in the first place.

Austerity and internal devaluation

With steep cuts in government spending, neoliberal policy has been contracting the economy just when it needed to be expanded. Pro-austerity policy makers, however, professed their faith in "expansionary austerity." Harvard economists Alberto Alesina and Silvia Ardagna claimed that austerity (especially spending cuts) could lead to the expectation of increased profits and so stimulate investment. The neoliberals also hoped to boost exports through "internal devaluation" (wage cuts, resulting in lower costs and therefore cheaper exports). An economist with Capital Economics in London claimed that Greece needed a 30–40% decline in real wages to restore competitiveness. A fall in real wages, along with the out-migration

> ### The Role of Goldman Sachs
>
> Greece was able to "hide" its deficits thanks to Goldman Sachs, which had sold financial derivatives called credit-default swaps to Greece between 2002 and 2006. The credit-default swaps operated a bit like subprime loans, enabling Greece to lower its debts on its balance sheets, but at very high borrowing rates. Goldman Sachs had sales teams selling these complicated financial instruments not just to Greece, but to many gullible municipalities and institutions throughout Europe (and the United States), who were told that these deals could lower their borrowing costs. For Greece, the loans blew up in 2008-2009, when interest rates rose and stock markets collapsed. Among those involved in these deals included Mario Draghi (now President of the ECB), who was working at the Greece desk at Goldman Sachs at the time. While these sales generated huge profits for Goldman Sachs, the costs are now being borne by ordinary Greek people in the form of punishing austerity programs. (For more on Goldman Sachs's role, see part four of the PBS documentary "Money, Power, Wall Street.")

of workers, the neoliberals suggested, would allow labor markets to "clear" at a new equilibrium. Of course, they neglected to say how long this would take and how many workers would fall into poverty, get sick, or die in the process.

Meanwhile, international financial capitalists (hedge funds and private equity firms) have been using the crisis as an opportunity to buy up state assets. The European Commission initially expected to raise €50 billion by 2015 from the privatization of state assets (now being revised downward to just over €25 billion through 2020). The magnitude of the fire sale in Greece is still five to ten times larger than that expected for Spain, Portugal, and Ireland. Domestic private companies on the brink of bankruptcy are also vulnerable. As the crisis drags on, private-equity and hedge-fund "vulture capitalists" are swooping in for cheap deals. The other neoliberal reforms—labor and pension reforms, dismantling of the welfare state, and tax reforms—will also boost private profits at the expense of workers.

Default and exit from the euro

Another possible solution was for Greece to default on its debt, and some individuals and companies actively prepared for such a scenario. A default would lift the onerous burden of debt repayment, and would relieve Greece of complying with all the conditions placed on it by the Troika. However, it would likely make future borrowing by both the public and private sectors more difficult and expensive, and so force the government to engage in some sort of austerity of its own.

Some economists on the left have been supportive of a default, and the exit from the euro and return to the drachma that would likely follow. One such advocate is Mark Weisbrot, who has argued that "a threat by Greece to jettison the euro is long overdue, and it should be prepared to carry it out." He acknowledges there would be costs in the short term, but argues they would be less onerous "than many years of recession, stagnation, and high unemployment that the European authorities are offering." A return to the drachma could restore one of the tools to boost export competitiveness: allowing Greece to use currency depreciation to lower the prices of its exports. In this sense, this scenario remains a neoliberal one. (Many IMF "shock therapy" have included currency devaluations as part of the strategy for countries to export their way out of debt.)

The process of exit, however, could be quite painful, with capital flight, bank runs, black markets, significant inflation as the cost of imports rises, and the destruction of savings. There had already been some capital flight—an estimated €72 billion left Greek banks between 2009 and 2012. Furthermore, the threat of a Greek exit created fear of contagion, with the possibility of more countries leaving the euro and even the collapse of the eurozone altogether.

Keynesian Solutions

By late 2012, Keynesian proposals were finally being heard and having some impact on policymakers. Contrary to the neoliberal austerity doctrine, Keynesian solutions typically emphasize running countercyclical policies—especially expansionary fiscal policy (or fiscal "stimulus"), with deficit-spending to counter the collapse in private demand. However, the Greek government is already strapped with high deficits and the interest rates demanded by international creditors have spiked to extremely high levels. Additional deficit spending would require that the ECB (or the newly established European Stability Mechanism (ESM)) intervene by directly buying Greek government bonds to bring down rates. (The ECB has been lending to private banks at low rates, to enable the banks to buy public bonds.) In any case, a Keynesian approach ideally would waive the EU's deficit and debt limits to allow the Greek government more scope for rescuing the economy.

Alternatively, the EU could come forward with more grants and loans, in order to create employment, fund social-welfare spending, and boost demand. This kind of bailout would not go to the banks, but to the people who are suffering from unemployment, cuts in wages and pensions, and poverty. Nor would it come with all the other conditions the neoliberals have demanded (privatization, layoffs, labor-market reforms, etc). The European Investment Bank could also help stimulate new industries, such as alternative energy, and help revive old ones, such as tourism, shipping, and agriculture. In a European Union based on solidarity, the richer regions of Europe would help out poorer ones in a crisis (much as richer states in the United States make transfers to poorer ones, mostly without controversy).

Even some IMF officials finally recognized that austerity was not working. An October 2012 IMF report admitted that the organization had underestimated the fiscal policy multiplier—a measure of how much changes in government spending and taxes will affect economic growth—and therefore the negative impact of austerity policies. By April 2013, economists at UMass-Amherst found serious mistakes in research by Harvard economists Carmen Reinhart and Kenneth Rogoff, alleging that debt-to-GDP ratios of 90% or more seriously undermine future economic growth. Reinhart and Rogoff's claims had been widely cited by supporters of austerity for highly indebted countries. So yet another crack emerged in the pillar supporting austerity policies.

Keynesians have argued, contrary to the "internal devaluation" advocates, that the reduction in real wages just depressed aggregate demand, and made the recession deeper. Economists such as Nobel laureate Paul Krugman proposed that, instead, wages and prices be allowed to rise in the trade-surplus countries of northern Europe (Germany and the Netherlands). This would presumably make these countries' exports less competitive, at some expense to producers of internationally traded goods, though possibly boosting domestic demand thanks to increased wages. Meanwhile, it would help level the playing field for exporters in the southern countries in crisis, and would be done without the punishing reductions in real wages demanded by the Troika. The Keynesian solution thus emphasized stimulating domestic demand through fiscal expansion in both the northern and southern European countries, as well as allowing wages and prices to rise in the northern countries.

Signs pointing in this direction began to emerge in spring 2013, when some Dutch and German trade unions won significant wage increases. In addition, the Dutch government agreed to scrap its demands for wage restraint in some sectors (such as the public sector and education) and to hold off (at least until August) on its demands for more austerity. (Another €4.5 billion cuts had been scheduled for 2014, after the government spent €3.7 billion in January to rescue (through nationalization) one of the country's largest banks.)

Socialist Solutions

For most of the socialist parties in Greece and elsewhere in Europe, the neoliberal solution was clearly wrong-headed, as it worsened the recession to the detriment of workers while industrial and finance capitalists made out like bandits. Greece's Panhellenic Socialist Movement (PASOK) was an exception, going along with austerity, structural reforms, and privatization. (Its acceptance of austerity lost it significant support in the 2012 elections.) Other socialists supported anything that alleviated the recession, including Keynesian prescriptions for more deficit spending, higher wages, and other policies to boost aggregate demand and improve the position of workers. Greece's SYRIZA (a coalition of 16 left-wing parties and whose support surged in the 2012 elections) called for stopping austerity, renegotiating loan agreements, halting wage and pension cuts, restoring the minimum wage, and implementing a type of Marshall Plan-like investment drive. In many ways, these proposale resemble standard Keynesian policies—which have historically served to rescue the capitalist system, without challenging its inherent exploitative structure or vulnerability to recurrent crisis.

While Keynesian deficit-spending could alleviate the crisis in the short-term, who would ultimately bear the costs—ordinary taxpayers? Workers could end up paying for the corruption of the Greek capitalist class, who pushed through tax cuts, spent government funds in ways that mainly benefited themselves, and hid money abroad. Many socialists argued that the Greek capitalists should pay for the crisis, through increased taxes on wealth, corporate profits, and financial transactions, and the abolition of tax loopholes and havens. As SYRIZA leader Alexis Tsipras put it, "It is common knowledge among progressive politicians and activists, but also among the Troika and the Greek government, that the burden of the crisis has been carried exclusively by public and private sector workers and pensioners. This has to stop. It is time for the rich to contribute their share... ."

Slowly, the right-wing government began making gestures in this direction. In 2010, French finance minister Christine Lagarde had given a list of more than 2,000 Greeks with money in Swiss bank accounts to her Greek counterpart George

Papaconstantinou, of the PASOK government, but Papaconstantiou sat on it and did nothing. But in the fall of 2012 the so-called "Lagarde list" was published by the magazine Hot Doc, leading to fury among ordinary Greeks against establishment political leaders (including the PASOK "socialists") who had failed to go after the tax dodgers. Another list of about 400 Greeks who had bought and sold property in London since 2009 was compiled by British financial authorities at the request of the current Greek government. In total, the economist Friedrich Schneider has estimated that about €120 billion of Greek assets (about 65% of GDP) were outside the country, mostly in Switzerland and Britain, but also in the United States, Singapore, and the Cayman Islands. The government also started a clamp down on corruption in past government expenditures. In the Spring of 2013, two politicians (a former defense minister and a former mayor of Thessaloniki, the country's second-largest city) were convicted on corruption charges.

Socialists have also opposed dismantling the public sector, selling off state assets, and selling Greek firms to international private equity firms. Instead of bailouts, many socialists have called for nationalization of the banking sector. "The banking system we envision," SYRIZA leader Alexis Tsipras announced, "will support environmentally viable public investment and cooperative initiatives.... What we need is a banking system devoted to the public interest—not one bowing to capitalist profit. A banking system at the service of society, a banking system that serves as a pillar for growth." While SYRIZA called for renegotiating the Greece's public debt, it favored staying in the euro.

Other socialist parties have put forth their own programs that go beyond Keynesian fiscal expansion, a more equitable tax system, and even beyond nationalizing the banks. For instance, the Alliance of the Anti-Capitalist Left (ANTARSYA) called for nationalizing banks and corporations, worker takeovers of closed factories, and canceling the debt and exiting the euro. The Communist Party of Greece (KKE) proposed a fairly traditional Marxist-Leninist program, with socialization of all the means of production and central planning for the satisfaction of social needs, but also called for disengagement from the EU and abandoning the euro. The Trotskyist Xekinima party called for nationalizing not just the largest banks, but also the largest corporations, and putting them under democratic worker control.

Those within the Marxist and libertarian left, meanwhile, have focused on turning firms, especially those facing bankruptcy, into cooperatives or worker self-directed enterprises. Firms whose boards of directors are composed of worker-representatives and whose workers participate in democratic decision-making would be less likely to distribute surpluses to overpaid CEOs or corrupt politicians and lobbyists, or to pick up and relocate to other places with lower labor costs. While worker self-directed enterprises could decide to forego wage increases or to boost productivity, in order to promote exports, such decisions would be made democratically by the workers themselves, not by capitalist employers or their representatives in government. And it would be the workers themselves who would democratically decide what to do with any increased profits that might arise from those decisions.

Cooperatives Around the World

Efforts at transforming capitalist firms into cooperatives or worker-directed enterprises can draw upon successes in the Basque Country (Spain), Argentina, Venezuela, and elsewhere. The Mondragón Cooperative Corporation, centered in the Basque country, has grown since its founding, in the 1950s, to 85,000 members working in over 300 enterprises. In Venezuela, the Chávez government promoted the development of cooperatives. The total number surged more than 100-fold, to over 100,000, between 1998 and 2006, the last year for which data are available. In Argentina after 2001, failing enterprises were taken over (or "recovered") by workers and turned into cooperatives. The recovered enterprises boasted a survival rate of about 93%. By 2010, 205 of these cooperatives employed a total of almost 10,000 workers.

One Greek company that is trying to survive as a transformed worker cooperative is Vio.Me, a building materials factory in Thessaloniki. In May 2011 when the owners could no longer pay their bills and walked away, the workers decided to occupy the factory. By February 2013, after raising enough funds and community support, the workers started democratically running the company on their own. (They do not intend to buy out the owners, since the company owed the workers a significant amount of money when it abandoned the factory.) They established a worker-board, controlled by workers' general assemblies and subject to recall, to manage the factory. They also changed the business model, shifting to different suppliers, improving environmental practices, and finding new markets. Greek law currently does not allow factory occupations, so the workers are seeking the creation of a legal framework for the recuperated factory, which may enable more such efforts in the future. Vio.Me has received support from SYRIZA and the Greek Green party, from workers at recuperated factories in Argentina (see sidebar), as well as from academics and political activists worldwide.

Whither Europe and the Euro?

As Europe faces this ongoing crisis, it is also grappling with its identity. On the right are the neoliberal attempts to dismantle the welfare state and create a Europe that works for corporations and the wealthy—a capitalist Europe more like the United States. In the center are Keynesian calls to keep the EU intact, with stronger Europe-wide governance and institutions. These involve greater fiscal integration, with a European Treasury, eurobonds (rather than separate bonds for each country), European-wide banking regulations, etc. Keynesians also call for softening the austerity policies on Greece and other countries.

Proposals for European consolidation have inspired criticism and apprehension on both the far right and far left. Some on the far right are calling for exiting the euro, trumpeting nationalism and a return to the nation state. The left, meanwhile, voices concern about the emerging power of the European parliament in Brussels, with its highly paid politicians, bureaucrats, lobbyists, etc. who are able to pass legislation favoring corporations at the expense of workers. Unlike the far right however, the left has proposed a vision for another possible united Europe—one based on social cohesion and inclusion, cooperation and solidarity, rather than on competition and corporate dominance. In particular, socialists call for replacing the capitalist structure of Europe with one that is democratic, participatory, and embodies a socialist economy, with worker protections and participation at all levels of economic and political decision-making. This may very well be the best hope for Europe to escape its current death spiral, which has it living in terror of what the next stage may bring. ❑

Sources: Amitabh Pal, "Austerity is Killing Europe," Common Dreams, April 27, 2012 (commondreams.org); Niki Kitsantonis, "Greece Resumes Talks With Creditors," *New York Times*, April 4, 2013 (nytimes.com); Mark Weisbrot, "Where I Part from Paul Krugman on Greece and the Euro," *The Guardian*, May 13, 2011 (guardian.co.uk); Alberto F. Alesina and Silvia Ardagna, "Large Changes in Fiscal Policy: Taxes Versus Spending," National Bureau of Economic Research (NBER), October 2009 (nber.org); Geert Reuten, "From a false to a 'genuine' EMU," Globalinfo, Oct. 22, 2012 (globalinfo.nl); David Jolly, "Greek Economy Shrank 6.2% in Second Quarter," *New York Times*, Aug. 13, 2012; Joseph Zacune, "Privatizing Europe: Using the Crisis to Entrench Neoliberalism," Transnational Institute, March 2013 (tni.org); Mark Weisbrot, "Why Greece Should Reject the Euro," *New York Times*, May 9, 2011; Ronald Jannsen, "Blame It on the Multiplier," *Social Europe Journal*, Oct. 16, 2012 (social-europe.eu); Landon Thomas, Jr., and David Jolly, "Despite Push for Austerity, European Debt Has Soared," *New York Times*, Oct. 22, 2012; "German Public sector workers win above-inflation pay rise," Reuters, March 9, 2013 (reuters.nl); Liz Alderman, "Greek Businesses Fear Possible Return to Drachma," *New York Times*, May 22, 2012; Landon Thomas, Jr., "In Greece, Taking Aim at Wealthy Tax Dodgers," *New York Times*, Nov. 11, 2012; Rachel Donadio and Liz Alderman, "List of Swiss Accounts Turns Up the Heat in Greece," *New York Times*, Oct. 27, 2012; Landon Thomas, Jr., "Greece Seeks Taxes From Wealthy With Cash Havens in London," *New York Times*, Sept. 27, 2012; Niki Kitsantonis, "Ex-Mayor in Greece Gets Life in Prison for Embezzlement," *New York Times*, Feb. 27, 2013; Sam Bollier, "A guide to Greece's political parties," Al Jazeera, May 1, 2012 (aljazeera.com); Alexis Tsipras, "Syriza London: Public talk," March 16, 2013 (left.gr); Amalia Loizidou, "What way out for Greece and the working class in Europe," Committee for a Workers' International (CWI), March 19, 2013 (socialistworld.net); Richard Wolff, "Yes, there is an alternative to capitalism: Mondragón shows the way," *The Guardian*, June 24, 2012 (guardian.co.uk); Peter Ranis, "Occupy Wall Street: An Opening to Worker-Occupation of Factories and Enterprises in the U.S.," MRzine, Sept. 11, 2011 (mrzine.monthlyreview.org); viome.org.

Article 9.6

BATTLING THE GLOBAL GOLIATHS

Governments and Activists Fight the Corporate "Right" to Sue Governments

BY ROBIN BROAD

February 2014

Over the past several decades, multinational corporate Goliaths have helped to write and rewrite hundreds of rules skewing tax, trade, investment and other policies in their favor. The extraordinary damage these policies have caused has become increasingly apparent to the communities and governments most directly affected by them. This, in turn, has strengthened the potential of a movement that's emerging to try to reverse the momentum. But just like David with his slingshot, the local, environmental and government leaders seeking to revise rules to favor communities and the planet must pick their battles carefully.

We have come to believe strongly that one of the most promising of these battles takes aim at an egregious set of agreements that allow corporations to sue national governments. Until three decades ago, governments could pass laws to protect consumers, workers, health, the environment and domestic firms with little threat of outside legal challenge from corporations. All that changed when corporations started acquiring the "right" to sue governments over actions—including public-interest regulations—that reduce the value of their investments. These rights first appeared in little-known bilateral investment treaties. Twenty years ago, corporate lawyers embedded them in the North American Free Trade Agreement (NAFTA). Today, more than 3,000 trade and investment agreements and even some national investment laws grant foreign investors these powers.

The Obama administration is attempting to insert similar anti-democratic investor protections in new trade and investment agreements with countries that border the Pacific and with the European Union. Hoping to expedite the so-called Trans-Pacific Partnership (TPP) and the Transatlantic Trade and Investment Partnership (TTIP), in early 2014, U.S. congressional leaders introduced fast-track trade promotion legislation that would severely limit Congress's ability to amend such agreements. The widely anticipated move set off a storm of protest from unions, environmentalists, liberal members of Congress and others, and will likely remain a high-profile fight in the United States in the coming months.

The forces aligned against these proposed agreements in the United States are not alone. In *The Nation*, John Cavanagh and I have written about activists across the globe who are developing creative and increasingly effective strategies to push back against investor assaults on their communities, environment and national sovereignty. An important front has opened up in El Salvador, where the Canadian/Australian firm Pacific Rim/OceanaGold is using investor powers to sue the government over the "right" to mine gold. This case represents an extreme assault on democracy: local communities, the majority of the Salvadoran public, and the Salvadoran government all oppose gold mining. But what's happening in El Salvador is not an anomaly. There are crucial battles brewing in several other Latin American countries—including Argentina, Venezuela, Bolivia and Ecuador—as well as in other parts of the developing world.

As the strategies for asserting investor rights proliferate across the globe, new alternatives are sprouting up as communities, activists, and governments confront the challenge with increasing urgency.

In the 1990s, a conservative Bolivian government privatized the water system of its fourth-largest city by granting the concession to the U.S. corporation Bechtel. When Bechtel hiked the rates for consumers, tens of thousands rose up in what became known as the "water war." After Bechtel abandoned the contract as a result of the opposition, it sued Bolivia under a bilateral investment agreement. Following a creative global campaign that included protests outside the company's San Francisco headquarters and a shaming strategy, Bechtel finally caved, settling the case for a mere $1.

In the case of El Salvador, groups as diverse as the Council of Canadians, MiningWatch Canada, U.S. and Australian unions, Oxfam, and the Institute for Policy Studies have come together to do with Pacific Rim what those activists did with Bechtel. They've started a petition drive to pressure Pacific Rim and its parent company OceanaGold to "drop the suit," and they've organized several hundred labor and other citizen groups to push the World Bank to sever its ties with the International Centre for the Settlement of Investment Disputes (ICSID) tribunal.

Several Latin American governments are also challenging corporations' rights to sue them in international tribunals. Brazil has never accepted such rights in any international agreement. Bolivia, Venezuela, and Ecuador have withdrawn from the ICSID tribunal and are rethinking their bilateral and multilateral investment deals. In an important development, Ecuador hosted these governments and several others last April to discuss an alternative to such agreements. Twelve governments are now on record supporting the creation of a regional mechanism "to ensure fair and balanced rules when settling disputes between corporations and States," while laying out a framework for continuing the negotiations and bringing in other governments.

South Africa is terminating its bilateral investment agreements and establishing a new investment law that allows foreign corporations to bring such claims only to domestic courts rather than international tribunals. India is conducting a review of its treaties in the face of several corporate lawsuits. Australia refused to include these corporate rights in the 2005 Australia-U.S. Free Trade Agreement, and so far it has not agreed to subject itself to them in the secretive negotiations surrounding the Trans-Pacific Partnership agreement. Recently leaked documents suggest that several of these governments are attempting to at least scale back investors' rights in the TPP trade deal.

The diverse set of groups that fought NAFTA two decades ago have remained united through the Citizens Trade Campaign, which is trying to stop the fast-track legislation for the TPP and the TTIP. Opponents have gained significant traction by raising questions about the corporate interests behind the proposed agreements.

These fights are critical. If the momentum of corporate investment rules can be slowed or halted, the power of global corporations would be significantly curtailed.

Rules protecting investors' rights are a key strategic front where progress against corporate rule is possible. A victory in the David versus Goliath battle between El Salvador and Pacific Rim/OceanaGold would be huge—both symbolically and substantively—in the fight to shift the momentum back toward the rights of people and the environment they inhabit. ❑

Article 9.7

LEISURE OR UNEMPLOYMENT: IT'S A POLITICAL QUESTION

BY DEAN BAKER
September 2013, Al Jazeera English

As most workers in the United States get a paid day off from work this Labor Day, it is a good time to think about holidays and leisure time in general. Workers in the United States tend to get much too little in the way of paid time off.

We stand apart from other countries in this respect. The United States is the only wealthy country in the world where workers are not guaranteed some amount of paid leave.

In most European countries workers have at least five weeks each year of paid holidays or vacation. In Germany, which is being touted as a great success story, workers have a legal right to almost seven weeks a year of paid time off. Even in Canada, which has a culture and economy very similar to United States, workers can count on almost four weeks of paid holidays or vacation every year.

While most workers in the United States do get some paid time off, few get anywhere near as much as their counterparts in other countries. And a substantial number get nothing at all. Twenty-three percent of all workers report getting neither paid vacation nor paid days off on holidays.

Paid time off is important for people to be able to spend time with their families, to get some rest, or just to enjoy life. But it also can have an important economic benefit in a context where the economy is well below its full employment level of output.

People look to the high rate of unemployment and the large number of people who would like full-time jobs but can only get part-time work and think that times are tough; that this is a period of scarcity. In fact the story is just the opposite.

Most people are being fed, housed, and clothed even though employment is down by almost 9 million workers from its trend level. This is an indication of our wealth. We can meet these needs even while so many people are not working.

Imagine if the 140 million people who are working put in 6 percent fewer hours every year, taking this time as vacation, family leave, or just shorter workweeks. In principle, this would increase the demand for workers by roughly 6 percent, creating more than 8 million new jobs. This would absorb most of the country's unemployed.

Of course in the real world we could not just snap our fingers and shorten everyone's work-time and fill the gap with unemployed workers. Many workers would be difficult to replace since the unemployed may not have the necessary skills. It also is difficult for firms to rearrange schedules.

There also is the essential question of whether workers would get the same pay, even as they work fewer hours. That might be desirable from the standpoint of helping workers and sustaining demand in the economy, since workers will spend a much larger share of their wages than corporations will spend from their profits. However, there is no way easy way of forcing companies to pay higher hourly wages in this story.

There is an issue of market power forcing up wages. In Germany, where the unemployment rate is just 5.4 percent, the average hourly wage, adjusted for inflation, has risen by more than 4.0 percent since 2010. By contrast, in the United States real wages have barely moved for more than a decade. The main difference is that workers have no bargaining power in the United States because of high unemployment.

Many people look to Germany's low unemployment and attribute it to a booming economy. In fact Germany's economy has grown no more rapidly than the U.S. economy since the start of the downturn. Remarkably, Germany's unemployment rate fell by 2 percentage points since 2007, while the unemployment rate rose by almost 3 percentage points in the United States.

The reason for this difference is that Germany has an institutional structure that encourages employers to keep workers on the job but working fewer hours rather than laying them off. This is a good short-term policy to deal with a temporary shortfall in demand. It is also a good long-term policy since it has workers taking part of the benefits of productivity growth in the form of more leisure time.

The average worker in Germany today puts in less than 1,400 hours a year according to the Organization for Economic Cooperation and Development. By comparison, an average worker in the United States works 1,790 hours a year.

If German workers suddenly had to work the same number of hours as workers in the United States, and their pay did not change, then employment would fall by 22 percent. Again, this sort of switch would never actually happen in the world, but it is an interesting thought exercise.

The point is that workers in the United States need not be tied to the current length of the work year. Workers in every country have been enjoying the benefits of more leisure time over the last 3 decades. There is no reason that workers in the United States should not be able to do so also.

Such a reduction in hours will not only have direct benefits for workers enjoying more time off, it will also help to reduce unemployment and increase workers' bargaining power. This will make it more likely that they will be able to share in the benefits of productivity growth in the future. That's certainly a much better picture than high and rising unemployment. ❏

CONTRIBUTORS

Randy Albelda, a *Dollars & Sense* Associate, teaches economics at the University of Massachusetts-Boston.

Sylvia Allegretto is an economist at the Institute for Research on Labor and Employment at the University of California-Berkeley.

Philip Arestis is director of research at the Cambridge Centre for Economic and Public Policy, Department of Land Economy, University of Cambridge, UK.

Dean Baker is co-director of the Center for Economic and Policy Research.

Heather Boushey is a senior economist at the Center for American Progress.

Robin Broad is a profesor of International Development at the School of International Service, American University.

Roger Bybee is a Milwaukee-based writer on labor issues.

John Cavanagh is director of the Institute for Policy Studies in Washington, D.C.

Gerald Friedman is a professor of economics at the University of Massachusetts-Amherst.

Kevin Gallagher is an associate professor in the Department of International Relations at Boston University.

Armagan Gezici is an assistant professor of economics at Keene State College.

Lena Graber is a former *Dollars & Sense* intern.

Paul Krugman, 2008 Nobel laureate in economics, is a professor at Princeton University and a columnist for the *New York Times*.

Arthur MacEwan, a *Dollars & Sense* Associate, is professor emeritus of economics at the University of Massachusetts-Boston.

Gretchen McClain, a former *Dollars & Sense* collective member, is an economic consultant.

John Miller (co-editor of this book) is a *Dollars & Sense* collective member and a professor of economics at Wheaton College.

Fred Moseley is a professor of economics at Mt. Holyoke College.

Doug Orr teaches economics at the City College of San Francisco.

Steven Pitts is a labor policy specialist at the University of California-Berkeley Center for Labor Research and Education.

Robert Pollin teaches economics and is co-director of the Political Economy Research Institute at the University of Massachusetts-Amherst. He is also a *Dollars & Sense* Associate.

Alejandro Reuss is co-editor of *Dollars & Sense* and an instructor at the Labor Relations and Research Center at UMass-Amherst.

Jonathan Rowe was a fellow at the Tomales Bay Institute and a former contributing editor at the *Washington Monthly*. He died in March 2011.

Malcolm Sawyer is a professor of economic at University of Leeds, UK, and managing editor of *International Review of Applied Economics*.

Zoe Sherman (co-editor of this book) is an assistant professor of economics at Merrimack College.

Bryan Snyder (co-editor of this book) is a senior lecturer in economics at Bentley University.

Chris Sturr (co-editor of this book) is co-editor of *Dollars & Sense*.

Bob Sutcliffe is an economist at the University of the Basque Country in Bilbao, Spain.

Jeffrey Thompson is an assistant research professor at the Political Economy Research Institute at the University of Massachusetts-Amherst.

Chris Tilly, a *Dollars & Sense* Associate, is director of the Institute for Research on Labor and Employment and professor of urban planning, both at UCLA.

Marjolein van der Veen is an economist who has taught economics in Massachusetts, the Seattle area, and the Netherlands.

Ramaa Vasudevan is assistant professor of economics at Colorado State University and a former *Dollars & Sense* collective member.

Jeannette Wicks-Lim is an assistant research professor at the Political Economy Research Institute at the University of Massachusetts-Amherst.

Timothy A. Wise is director of the Research and Policy Program at the Global Development and Environment Institute (GDAE), Tufts University.

Marty Wolfson teaches economics at the University of Notre Dame and is a former economist with the Federal Reserve Board in Washington, D.C.

CPSIA information can be obtained at www.ICGtesting.com
Printed in the USA
BVOW08s0924040814

361283BV00001B/1/P